D1065191

Catholicism, Political Culture,
and the Countryside

Social History, Popular Culture, and Politics in Germany
Geoff Eley, Series Editor

Catholicism, Political Culture, and the Countryside

A Social History of the Nazi Party in South Germany

ODED HEILBRONNER

Ann Arbor
THE UNIVERSITY OF MICHIGAN PRESS

2001   2000   1999   1998   4   3   2   1

A CIP catalog record for this book is available from the British Library.

Library of Congress Cataloging-in-Publication Data

Heilbronner, Oded.
    ['Aliyat ha-miflagah ha-Natsit la-shilton. English]
    Catholicism, political culture, and the countryside : a social
history of the Nazi Party in south Germany / Oded Heilbronner.
       p.   cm. — (Social history, popular culture, and politics in
Germany)
    Includes bibliographical references and index.
    ISBN 0-472-10910-3 (alk. paper)
    1. National socialism—Germany—Black Forest Region.   2.
Nationalsozialistische Deutsche Arbeiter-Partei.   3.
Catholics—Germany—Black Forest Region—Political activity.   I.
Title.   II. Series.
DD801.B64   H3813   1998
324.243'038'09434609042—dc21   98-8996
                                                                    CIP

Originally published in Hebrew as *The Nazi Party Seizure of Power: The Black
Forest Region as a Case Study,* by Oded Heilbronner. Jerusalem: Magnes Press,
The Hebrew University Press, 1993.

122198-4796HL

To my sons
Omry and Eyal

Contents

Tables

Acknowledgments

In the course of writing this study, I have incurred many debts that I am now pleased to acknowledge. The book began as a Hebrew University of Jerusalem dissertation. I would like to acknowledge a profound intellectual and personal debt to my doctoral supervisor, teacher, and friend Moshe Zimmermann. He stimulated my original interest in modern German history and gently but uncompromisingly pushed me to take the first plunge into the German Archives in 1987. For his encouragement and his longtime support, I am very grateful.

In Israel I profited from the advice of many teachers, colleagues, and friends. Steven Aschheim, Shlomo Ahronson, and Otto Dov Kulka, from the Hebrew University, and Shulamit Volkov and Dan Dinner, from Tel-Aviv University, took time to sponsor my various research activities as a doctoral and postdoctoral fellow and consistently provided thoughtful comments on my work. The researchers at the Center of German History at the Hebrew University, Jacob Borut, Doron Niederland, Zeev Rosenkranz, Claudia Prestel, and Mathias Schmidt, offered many useful suggestions on ways to refine my hypotheses.

In Germany, I profited from the advice of many researchers and teachers. For their comments on my work and other assistance I am grateful to Jürgen Falter, Irmtraud Götz von Olenhusen, Jürgen Kocka, Wilfried Loth, Hans Mommsen, Josef Mooser, Karl Rohe, Wolfgang Schieder, and Hans Ulrich Wehler. I spent some wonderful summers as a postdoctoral fellow at the Max-Planck-Institut in Göttingen, and I want to thank the director, Hertmut Lehmann, for his hospitality, interest, and comments on my work, and especially Alf Lüdtke who influenced my whole thinking on the connection between Alltagsgeschichte and political history.

In Britain, I benefited from the advice of many colleagues. I would like to thank Richard Bessel, Richard Evans, Conan Fischer, Michael John, Ian Kershaw, Anthony Nicholls, Avner Offer, and Hartmut Pogge von Strandmann. All helped me during one stage or another of my study.

I especially want to thank Detlev Mühlberger for his hospitality and extended discussions in our Lokal during my year in Oxford. In the United States, Geoff Eley, Rudy Koshar, George Mosse, and James Retallack commented on different parts of my work.

South Baden and the Black Forest are the center of my study. I am happy to have the opportunity to thank many researchers who helped to find my way through the trees of the Black Forest: Werner Hamm, Detlev Herbner, Wolfgang Hug, Volkhard Huth, Hans-Jürgen Kremer, Hugo Ott, and Thomas Schnabel (who was the first one to suggest investigating the peculiarities of the Schwarzwald). I also want to thank the many local researchers, priests, mayors, and others who were not afraid to help an Israeli conducting such research. They all opened their houses (and small archives located sometimes in an attic or a basement) to me.

The research for this study is based on work in a number of archives and libraries throughout Germany and especially in the state of Baden-Württemberg. For their helpfulness and patience, I should especially thank Frau L. Krieg from Staatsarchiv Freiburg, which served as my "home archives" for many years, and Dr. F. Hündsnurscher from the Erzbischöfliches Archiv in Freiburg. I also wish to thank the staff of the Bundesarchiv in Koblenz, the Bundesarchiv/Militärarchiv in Freiburg, the Generallandesarchiv and the Landesbibliothek in Karlsruhe, the Hauptstaatsarchiv in Stuttgart, the Kreisarchiv Schwarzwald-Baar, Stadtarchiv Freiburg, and many unknown archivists in the community archives that are listed at the end of the book.

The research for this book would not have been possible without the generous financial support of a number of scholarly institutions and foundations. I am indebted to the Center of German History at the Hebrew University of Jerusalem, the Friedrich-Ebert Foundation, the German Academic Exchange Program (DAAD), the Minerva Foundation, the Rothschild Foundation, the joint program for Foreign Researchers of the Freiburg University and the Hebrew University, and the Max-Planck-Institut in Göttingen.

For preparing the original manuscript for publication in English language I am indebted to Ann Brenner and David Meisel. For the German footnotes correction I am indebted to Mathias Schmidt. At the University of Michigan Press, two anonymous readers reviewed the book with care and critical suggestions. Jan Brill and Kevin Rennells did a wonderful job with the copyediting. My editor Susan Whitlock helped me during the long process of publication. And finally I want to thank Geoff Eley for his kind advice and discussion (mainly, but not only, in a Turkish restaurant in Göttingen and in the Dead Sea), and his determination to include my book in his series on social history, popular culture, and politics in Germany.

It is a pleasure finally to thank those friends in Germany whose hospitality has made the work of research more pleasant. This book could never have been written without the inspired insights and emotional support given me over the years by my aunt Ilo Prinz. In addition I particularly want to thank Winfried Parr from Buchheim, Detlef and Sabine Herbner from Neustadt/ Schw., Volkhard Huth from Freiburg, and Angela and Martin Lampeter from Lahr/Schw.

Grateful acknowledgment is made to Berghan Books Ltd. for permission to reprint "The Disintegration of Social-Religious Life among the Workers," in Conan Fischer, ed., *The Rise of National Socialism and the Working Classes in Weimar Germany* (Oxford: Berghan, 1996), 217–36. I gratefully acknowledge Routledge Ltd. for permission to reprint tables and parts in chapter 11, which originally appeared in "Catholic Plight in a Rural Area of Germany and the Rise of the Nazi Party," *Social History* 20, no. 2 (1995): 219–34.

My final and largest debt of gratitude goes to my family: my parents for their great influence on me and finally to my children, Omry and Eyal, who with their mother, Hani, followed me to the mountains of the Black Forest in the rain and the snow, feeding the ducks in the lakes of the Schwarzwald while waiting for me to finish my work in the local archives. As a necessarily inadequate acknowledgment of their support, this book is dedicated to them.

Abbreviations

Archives and Archives Collections

BAK	Bundesarchiv Koblenz
BDC	Berlin Document Center
BZ	Bezirksamt
ErzAF	Erzbischöfliches Archiv Freiburg
GLAK	Generallandesarchiv Karlsruhe
GmdA	Gemeidearchiv
Kv	Kirchenvisitation
LKK	Landeskommissär Konstanz
PfA	Pfarrarchiv
StaaF	Staatsarchiv Freiburg
StA	Stadtarchiv

Publications

AvK	*Anzeiger vom Kinzigtal*
BSL	*Badisches Statistisches Landesamt*
CEH	*Central European History*
DT	*Donaueschinger Tagblatt*
EvH	*Echo vom Hochfirst*
FDA	*Freiburger Diözesan Archiv*
FZ	*Freiburger Zeitung*
Hoch Schw	*Hochwächter auf dem Schwarzwald*
Hschw	*Hochschwarzwald*
JCH	*Journal of Contemporary History*
JMH	*Journal of Modern History*
KN	*Kinzigtäler Nachrichten*
Schw B	*Schwarzwälder Bote*
Schw T	*Schwarzwälder Tagblatt*
TB	*Triberger Bote*

VJfZ   *Vierteljahreshefte für Zeitgeschichte*
VOBL   *Verordnungsblatt der Reichsleitung der NSDAP*

Associations and Parties

BLB   Badischer Landbund
DDP   Deutsche Demokratische Partei
DNVP   Deutschnationale Volkspartei
DVP   Deutsche Volkspartei
KAV   Katholische Arbeitervereine
KPD   Kommunistische Partei Deutschlands
KuMV   Krieger- und Militärverein
MGV   Männergesangsverein
NSDAP   Nationalsozialistische Deutsche Arbeiterpartei
SPD   Sozialdemokratische Partei Deutschlands
Vv   Der Volksverein für das katholische Deutschland
Z   Zentrum

Introduction

What enabled the Nazi Party to rise to power in Germany? This question continues to trouble scholars to this day, not only in the field of history but also in political science, social science, and economics. With the passage of time, the events of the Third Reich have only heightened interest in the character of the Nazi regime and in the circumstances that brought it into being.

Already the first electoral victories of the Nazi Party in 1929–30 saw the creation of a research literature that sought to comprehend the success of this relatively new party,[1] and the more successful the party grew, the greater was the tide of publications. The years of Nazi rule, the war, and the extermination of the Jews brought about such a proliferation that the Nazi Party and state have become one of the most popular subjects of historical research today.

The historiography of this subject has undergone quite a number of changes. The real turning point came in the 1960s when certain gifted young scholars began turning to innovative new methods of research, mostly from the field of social history, and applying them to the study of the Nazi Party and state, and to the history of modern Germany. The opening of formerly classified archival material contributed substantially to the increase in both the number and quality of the scholarly publications. The famous debate that raged between the so-called Functionalists and Intentionalists was largely nourished by these developments.[2] As we approach the fifth decade since the Nazi rise to power, an enhanced interest in regional studies and the history of daily life (*Alltagsgeschichte*) has produced many critical, even groundbreaking studies, shedding a completely new light on the period before and after 1933.[3]

These studies tend to take a highly critical look at the relationship between the Nazi Party and local German society, both before and after 1933. To what extent did the local population lean toward the Nazi ideology? Did the party really reap success with its policy of "coordination" (*Gleichschaltung*) launched in 1933? Is there any truth to the traditional claim that it was primarily the middle class that provided the social basis of the Nazi Party? How did the party penetrate the local infrastructure? To what extent did the local population come into conflict with the party and the Nazi regime, and to what extent did it collaborate?[4] These and similar questions cropped up again and again in the new studies, and the answers often cast doubt on the conventionally accepted opinions.

This study seeks to examine the Catholic population during the period of the Weimar Republic and its attitude toward the Nazi Party. It is generally believed among scholars that the Catholic population, and especially the agrarian sector, consistently withheld their support from the Nazi Party until 1933. Numerous studies have been written about the negative attitude of the Catholic leaders and institutions to National Socialism, and about the hostility of the Catholic population toward the local Nazi chapters (*Ortsgruppe*). It could be said that this is the assumption held by the majority of scholars today, both those who deal with the Weimar Republic in general and with the history of the Nazi Party and the Catholic Church in particular.[5]

The present study offers something of a challenge to this approach. I suggest that contemporary research of the period is still unduly influenced by certain events that took place in the Weimar Republic, such as the opposition of the Catholic bishops to the Nazi Party, and the partial resistance to the Nazi regime during the Third Reich. It is also strongly influenced by historiographical traditions that are rooted in the Weimar period and that continue in the Federal German Republic to this day. These traditions were dictated and transmitted almost entirely by the West German Catholic establishment, with the help of Catholic publishing houses and research institutes.[6] It is my contention, however, that a shift in research method and approach would lead to conclusions that would undermine the "orthodox" thesis of historiography that finds the Catholics "immune" to National Socialism during the Weimar period. On the contrary, we maintain that in a number of Catholic regions in Germany the Catholic vote for the Nazi Party was higher than average even before 1933, and in a number of cases as early as 1930.

The purpose of the present study is not only to produce evidence to substantiate this thesis but also—or even primarily—to try to explore a number of innovative theses concerning the behavioral patterns and sociopolitical organization of the Catholic population in the Weimar period and the activities of the Nazi Party in this context. We maintain that in a number of regions throughout Germany, the Catholic population not only gave the Nazi Party wide support but did so for a reason that has been relegated until now to the margins of modern research. The Nazi success is commonly ascribed to the innovative and dynamic methods of the Nazi Party in propaganda, organization, and leadership. The majority of scholars, including the most recent, claim that the Great Economic Crisis of 1929 through 1932 provided a fertile testing ground for this innovative ability.[7] We argue, however, that in a number of regions the Nazi Party failed to demonstrate an unusual presence or to show exceptional organizational or propagandist abilities and that it nonetheless met with considerable success. The explanation for this seeming contradiction (whose facts we hope to clarify) is to be found in the organizational modes of the local society, in this case Catholic society, and especially in the organizational mode of the local social life. I would like to argue that from the beginning of the 1920s the disintegration of the local organizational structures was highly evident. This process received prominent expression in the *Vereine,* the social clubs that constituted the most important of the local social institutions in Germany. The organizational vacuum created by the breakdown of the *Vereine* had social and political ramifications of the most far-reaching kind. Intertwined with this process was the worsening economic crisis that began in the late 1920s. In our opinion, it was for these reasons that the Nazi Party was able to penetrate the organizational vacuum without any special effort or techniques, and to win over large sections of the local Catholic society.

Methodology

The sweeping generalization about the opposition of the Catholic population to the Nazi Party derives from a lack of familiarity with the sources and conditions at the local level. At the national level, the results of the Reichstag elections during the years of the Weimar Republic show that Catholic voting districts gave considerable support to the Catholic Party, the *Zentrum.* For many scholars these results constitute evidence of the Nazi failure in Catholic regions. In order to substantiate my own claims, however, I draw attention to the regional division of Germany. A reexamination of Catholic voting patterns in the different villages, towns, and districts in the final years of the Weimar Republic shows that the traditional claims concerning Catholics fail to stand the test at the microlevel. Why did the *Zentrum* gain strong support in certain Catholic districts when, in others, the vote for the Nazi Party exceeded the national average? In this case, a method of research is needed that will allow us to examine the differences in the voting patterns of German Catholics. Moreover, we need a method that will permit us to take a detailed look at the manner in which the Nazi Party made its appeal to the Catholic population.

The regional study provides a valuable tool for examining the general phenomena I have just referred to. It is a methodology commonly used in contemporary historical research for analyzing cultural, social, political, and economic behavioral patterns from the perspective of a separate territorial unit. An understanding of local events, however, also permits us to reach general conclusions concerning institutions and ideologies at the national level and at the level intermediate between the national and local level. A regional study can help us to examine the validity of basic historiographical assumptions dealing in a general way with a similar topic. The geographical atomization so important to Germany's economic, social, and political development in the nineteenth and twentieth centuries makes it necessary to pay special attention to the individual regions. The socioeconomic and political-national fragmentation of Germany in the nineteenth century, and the effects that lingered until the 1930s, transform the "region," or more specifically (following the famous article of the German sociologist R. Lepsius)[8] the "milieu," into the most important characteristic of modern German history, which must therefore be central to any study dealing with cultural patterns of behavior. Local events make up the national map of Germany and are reflected through it. Local problems were a consideration for the "players" at the national level, who tried to integrate the local processes within the broader political system, itself plagued with similar problems.[9]

When seeking to analyze the "regional" aspect of a party or campaign we must realize that the strength of the parties varied from region to region and that in essence they represented regional interests. One of the most important scholars of German history, James Sheehan, argues that in Germany there was a wide gap between the orders given in the center and the implementation of these orders at the periphery.[10] This is a difference that cannot be discerned when focusing attention on the files of the central government. This does not mean that local affairs were more "real" than national concerns, but they were different, and this difference has to be recognized.

We are dealing with *Geschichte von Unten,* "history from below": the social history of politics that aims to reconstruct with the help of cultural patterns of behavior (beliefs, customs, mentality) the socioeconomic structure and cultural behavior of a given region, and to link them with patterns of political behavior. Similarly, it seeks to resolve the contradictions between *theory, model,* and *structure* in this context, and *occurrence* and *event.* As stated, analysis at the microlevel not only permits us to examine the essence of this contradiction more closely, but also to try to resolve it.[11]

For these reasons, and in response to the questions raised at the beginning of this book, I decided to write a regional study with a comparative dimension. My intention was to choose a region homogeneous enough to permit analysis of the observable general trends: a region small enough to permit a single researcher to deal with a copious amount of archival material, and yet one of sufficient magnitude to create a basis for comparison with other regions in which the same event or process took place, although not with the same results. For this reason I chose not to conduct a local study dealing with a specific village, town, or city, since this would make comparison difficult. Here, "region" comes as a compromise between microstudies, which illuminate the density of local relationships, and national studies that reveal broad trends. The regional (rather than local) method of research permits us to diagnose in particular cases the manner in which the orders emanating from the various centers (in this case the Nazi Party and the Catholic Church) were implemented by the local population and institutions, and to examine the ways in which they were obeyed, changed, or sabotaged. In the case of the social history of religious changes (see chap. 11), regional study is, as the British sociologist Robin Gill has argued, "the most accurate means of understanding the subtle dynamics of institutional churches."[12] The size of the Black Forest area did indeed permit us to make comparisons with other areas that had witnessed similar events or processes.

As noted above, the comparative motif is important to our study. Since we are challenging some of the most basic assumptions of historiography, we have preceded the analysis of each problem with a broad historiographical survey whose purpose is to situate our own position within the context of contemporary historiography. Moreover, at the end of each section we have compared our findings with those of other local and regional studies dealing with the same problems in regions with a similar socioeconomic structure (e.g., Catholic rural areas). The comparative element serves to bring the uniqueness of the present study into sharper focus.

My interest in the regional aspects of the rise of the Nazi Party led me to examine the party's activities in the state of Baden. There the party met with electoral success even before the major breakthrough of September 1930. In the course of examining the election results of various campaigns in 1929, I encountered surprising results from south Baden (the Black Forest and the Baar regions). The results were all the more startling in view of the neglect of the region in the secondary literature, and in view of the advice that local historians offered me during my stay in the state archives. I was told, for example, that "nothing ever happens in the Black Forest," or "if you want to examine Nazi successes in Baden, it's best to examine the northern Protestant regions." But none of these comments explained why it was that in a Catholic region, relatively isolated, seemingly conservative, and socially and economically backward, the party met with surprising success, in some areas as early as 1928!

The Sources

In order to carry out a study of the scope and with the goals outlined above, we fell back on sources not generally used by researchers, and whose accessibility presents a special challenge to one not born and bred in

The Black Forest and the Baar regions. (Reproduced from *Statistisches Jahrbuch für das Land Baden*, Badischen Statistischen Landesamt, Karlsruhre, 1930.)

the region under investigation. The very subject and period of the intended study only served to complicate the problem. Without a doubt, the exposition of cases of collaboration with the Nazi Party, or of nonresistance, continues to be a sensitive issue in some parts of Germany, especially when the investigator comes from Israel. The initial sources I required included local newspapers, village archives (*Gemeindearchive*), episcopal archives (*Pfarrarchive*), and personal material in the possession of local families, as well as material found in the state archives. The preliminary work for this study was begun in archives at the state and national level: the Bundesarchiv Koblenz, the Generallandesarchiv Karlsruhe, the Staatsarchiv Freiburg, and the Erzbischöfliche Archiv Freiburg. I soon discovered that much evidence of crucial importance for my hypotheses was lacking. Substantial portions of the material relating to the south Baden had been destroyed in the air raids on Freiburg in 1944. So, for example, all the *Landeskommissär* files pertaining to the southern parts of the Black Forest districts were destroyed. The remaining material while important in itself constituted what might be called a bird's-eye view of the region and was written mostly by officials from Baden, administrative councils, Church inspectors, and others who visited the area and made a written report of their visit. Despite the importance of such documents, they would not allow me to reconstruct the period under investigation, or to see it through the eyes of the people who lived it. The method of oral history, in addition to its significant methodological restrictions, was irrelevant to my work for several reasons. For one, few activists of the Nazi Party agreed to meet me (there were some who rejected my efforts), and their memory of events, to the extent that it existed, was highly selective. The village priests had died or disappeared back in the 1930s, and the once-dominant figures of local social life had passed away long before I began my research.

I consequently looked in the archives (or, more precisely, the storerooms) of the local councils and the attics of priests' homes, where I found the "treasures" that contributed to the breakthrough in my research. Alongside copies of the local press of every shade of the political spectrum I came across reports, memoirs, and descriptions written in the period under investigation by local residents, priests, voluntary associations (*Vereine*) leaders, and local notables. In one case I found the complete archives of the Nazi Party chapter in the town of Schonach. The material had been filed away in the archives of the local priest in the attic of his home. Throughout my work I was greatly assisted by the local inhabitants, whose knowledge of my personal origins and the subject of my research did not prevent them from handing over the necessary information. I added comparative elements mainly in part 2 of the study. By comparisons with secondary literature dealing with rural Catholic regions in Bavaria and the Rheinland, I sought to place my findings from south Baden within a larger context.

Together with the copious amount of archival material from the national and local archives, I found the data published by the *Badisches Statistisches Landesamt* to be extremely helpful, especially in part 1, where the social, economic, and political history of the region was concerned.

The use of such varied sources doubtless helped us to view the Nazi success from an angle little studied until now. They allowed us to see the Nazi Party in the Black Forest and the Baar regions as an integral part of the local society and not as a group that infiltrated into the region from outside, tempting and seducing the local inhabitants. Shifting the emphasis from the Nazi Party to the society in which it operated is a central aspect of the present work, and with the help of this principle we hope to have gained better understanding of how the "worm," as it were, was able to penetrate the long-rotten core of German Catholic society.

Part 1

"The People of the Forest"

*The Economic, Social, and Political History of the
Black Forest from the End of the Nineteenth Century
to the Beginning of the 1930s*

The great charm about the Black Forest house is its sociability. The cows
are in the next room, the horses are upstairs, the geese and ducks are in the
kitchen, while the pigs, the children, and the chickens live all over the
place. You are dressing, when you hear a grunt behind you. . . .

　　　　J. K. Jerome, Three Men on the Bummel *(London, 1900)*

The people of the Black Forest live isolated and remote from the world,
deep in the dark mountains. The harsh nature of the region makes them
silent and withdrawn, but inside they are churning with thoughts about the
problems which occupy the world outside. Their meditative nature makes
them distance themselves from the burden of contemporary technological
problems.

　　　　G. Möller, Die Wirtschaft des Schwarzwaldes *(Oberndorf, 1930)*

CHAPTER 1

Geography, Authority, and Administration

The Black Forest is a mountainous region with special geological characteristics, deeply crossed by valleys and gorges and straddling the mountain ridges from north to south in the state of Baden. Part of the region (the smaller part) is located in the western part of the state of Württemberg. To the west of the mountain ridges the Rhine valley curves along the Upper Rhine River as far as the border of France. To the south, the mountain ridges in the regions of Hotzenwald and Wiesental cascade down to the Rhine River and the border of Switzerland. To the east of the Black Forest (the part that lies in Baden) is the state of Württemberg, and in its southeastern part is the region of the Baar, "the granary of the State of Baden."[1] To the west and north of the area, there are the major cities of Baden, such as Pforzheim and Karlsruhe.

The borders of the Black Forest are indicated variously in different studies. Without a doubt, the geographical definition is of the greatest importance, given the fact that the region under discussion is characterized by unique geographical traits (mountain ridges, a harsh climate, special geological formations). Together with this factor, differences in topography, economics, and social structure, to name only a few, further contribute to the great diversity in the research literature concerning the territorial borders of the region.[2]

The study deals with those regions known as the south and central Black Forest, and with the western part of the Baar bordering on the Black Forest, today known as the administrative unit of the Schwarzwald-Baar (as it will be called throughout the study). Both areas were predominantly Catholic, with the population characteristically dispersed in small towns and villages. This geographical delimitation also influenced the manner in which the majority of the residents earned their livelihood: the greater part of them engaged in agriculture, home industries (*Hausindustrie*), craftsmanship, and, in a few towns, in manufacturing (the clock industry) and the tourist industry, which we will discuss further.

The name "Black Forest" (*Schwarzwald*) is explained in different ways. The most common explanation is that when the Roman legions penetrated the area that today comprises the southern part of the state of Baden, they came up to a mountain ridge whose forest-covered slopes made the whole area look black from a distance, and that even the streams appeared black: in short, it was a veritably "black" forest.[3] However, the harshness of its climate contributed not only to the name of the region but also, and above all, to the conditions in which people lived and the manner in which they settled the land. In a number of regions of the Black Forest, and especially in the more elevated regions around Mt. Feldberg, the highest peak in the area (1,493 meters above sea level), the land was very sparsely populated. As a rule, the Black Forest was characterized by a population living in harsh conditions dictated by the peculiar topography and climate. This fact greatly encumbered the development of a well-ordered and modern economy and agriculture.

Since Baden was a borderland (*Grenzland*) adjoining a number of states, its social and economic features provided it with greater opportunities to make contact with foreigners and to absorb new ideas. In this respect Baden differed from the state of Württemberg, its neighbor to the east. Despite its receptivity and progressiveness, however, its residents did not have a feeling of belonging to the Grand Duchy (*Großherzogtum*) of Baden until the middle of the nineteenth century. The Duchy was characterized by profound regional differences, including vast differences in mentality and the clash of separate interests. Already in the mid–nineteenth century Baden's authorities pursued a policy of centralization aimed at overcoming the regional differences and the desire for separatism that existed in some regions of the Duchy. This centralizing process was largely successful, and most of the regions in Baden were integrated administratively, economically, and socially into the Grand Duchy. The southern Catholic regions proved to be the exception to this rule, for feelings of separatism and uniqueness continued to smolder there long after the process of centralization had been completed in the rest of Baden.[4]

The Black Forest and the Baar regions, in the south of the Duchy, were among the regions that tried to retain their uniqueness and independence. If geographical factors (together with other unique characteristics of south Baden, such as religion, economics, and society) caused the inhabitants of the region to try to preserve their traditional isolation, they also bolstered the tendency in Baden to view the region as some kind of "alien growth," an anomaly in the state's socioeconomic landscape. The remoteness of the region had a decisive influence on the local socioeconomic infrastructure, and also on the patterns of political behavior.

In the course of the centralization process undertaken by the authorities in Baden in the nineteenth century, Baden was divided (in 1863) into four administrative units (*Landeskommissarbezirke*): Mannheim, Karlsruhe, Freiberg (in which most of the Black Forest was located), and Constance (in which the Baar was located). Local administration was organized in accordance with a further breakdown of the units into counties (*Kreise*) and districts (*Bezirke*) (see table 1). This twofold division was of great importance. The districts were placed under state administration and they formed part of Baden's Interior Office. The state was represented in the districts through the district council (*Bezirksrat*). Parallel with this, Baden was divided into counties, which were the areas of self-administration of the inhabitants themselves. The county council (*Kreisrat*) and county assembly (*Kreisverordnete*) represented the internal affairs of the local inhabitants before the authorities. They were also responsible for the internal self-administration of the country.[5]

Some districts were entirely located in the Black Forest, such as Neustadt, Oberkirch, Wolfach, and Schopfheim, while others, such as Donaueschingen, Waldshut, Waldkirch, Freiburg, Lahr, and Offenburg, were only partially contained within the Black Forest region. In addition to the four districts located in the heart of the Black Forest, I have chosen (on the basis of the same criteria noted above) to focus on the Baar districts of Donaueschingen and Villingen, though only their western part. The map at the beginning of the book shows an imaginary line cutting

TABLE 1.   The Black Forest Districts, 1910–33

District	Population		
	1910	1925	1933
Bonndorf[a]	15,514		
Donaueschingen	24,143	39,705	39,014
Neustadt	17,344	27,241	27,862
Oberkirch	19,851	20,485	20,543
Schönau[a]	16,503		
Schopfhein	22,883	42,824	42,742
St. Blasien[a]	9,951		
Triberg[a]	24,842		
Villingen	32,744	48,477	48,938
Wolfach	26,174	31,448	31,990

Source: Statistische Mitteilungen über das Grossherzogtum Baden, NFIII, 1910; *Badische Gemeindestatistik,* Badisches Statistisches Landesamt (BSL) 1927; *Die endgültigen Ergebnisse der Volkszählung vom 16. Juni 1993 in Baden,* BSL, 1933.
[a]In 1924 the district was canceled.

across these districts, and all the place-names west of this line fall within the scope of this study. The fact that there are so few counties in the state of Baden only increases the difficulty in making the administrative units coincide even roughly with the geographical features of the Black Forest. For this reason, my analysis in this study will be based on the district and individual town or village.[6]

CHAPTER 2

Religion

The Black Forest region is predominantly Catholic, and during the period under discussion, over eighty percent of its inhabitants professed the Catholic faith. With the abolition of the various principalities in 1806, following the Napoleonic conquest of the region and the founding of the Grand Duchy of Baden, south Baden was carved into territorial-administrative units whose boundaries did not necessarily correspond to their previous ones. The principalities of Triberg and Wolfach retained their names, but the areas under their domain (today a district or country), together with their rulers, underwent change. The principality of Fürstenberg was transformed into the district of Donaueschingen, and its area was considerably extended. Yet while the names and the boundaries were subject to change, the inhabitants and their religion remained as they were. Thus the Catholics still constituted the majority in south Baden, and continued to dwell side by side with the Protestant enclaves (in Schopfheim or Lahr for example).

In the course of the nineteenth century, the Catholic majority dwindled in the Black Forest. This was partly the result of relocation elsewhere in Germany, but one can also point to examples of Catholics who adopted the Protestant faith. Some people turned to the "Old Catholics" (*Alt Katholiken*), a group that had rebelled against the Catholic Church in 1870–71, objecting to the obligatory framework demanded by the Papal consilia (Konzil) of 1869. The majority were bourgeois professionals who undoubtedly felt that the Church was hindering their patterns of social and economic behavior. This group founded the "Old Catholic Church," and in the Black Forest its members were primarily concentrated in the region of Donaueschingen. In the town of Furtwangen, for example, they constituted 7.1 percent of the inhabitants, in Guetenbach 18.9 percent, with a similar distribution in many other villages. As stated, many members of the group belonged to the local bourgeoisie and were thus an economic force to be reckoned with. Some of them put up a steady and

15

unyielding opposition, one that at times posed a threat to the local Catholic Church and population.[1]

Few Jews lived within the borders of the Black Forest and in the Baar. Some Jews, to be sure, did settle in various towns of the region following the promulgation of the laws of Emancipation in the 1860s. Thus in 1875 we find five Jews in Furtwangen and six in Hufingen, twenty-four Jews in Löffingen and a small number in the larger villages of the region. The Jews concentrated mostly in the region of Schwarzwald-Baar, which was largely in the district of Donaueschingen. In this district the cattle trade provided the most common means of earning a livelihood, and the Jews were the largest traders. Most of them, however, lived in towns and cities outside of the region, and when they came to the Black Forest it was only in order to make the rounds of the towns' marketplaces for reasons of business.[2] Their number declined toward the turn of the century, and by 1925 only a small Jewish population remained in the region. Due to the insignificance of their numbers and of their role in the region's economy, and also in the political culture of the Black Forest (to be described in detail below), anti-Semitism gained little foothold in the region.

The Catholic parishes (*Pfarrei*) in the Black Forest and the Baar belonged to the Archbishopric of Freiburg (*Erzbistum Freiburg*), which was established in 1830. This bishopric had jurisdiction over all the Catholic communities in the Duchy and subsequently in the state of Baden, and also over the Catholic communities in Sigmaringen, in the south of the state of Württemberg, a region that belonged to the state of Prussia. Anticlerical tendencies were common among Catholics in south Baden. We have already seen one example of this, the group of "Old Catholics." Most of the opposition came from the southeastern regions of the Black Forest, in the regions of the Wutach and the Schwarzwald-Baar. In these backward areas anti-Catholic tendencies were in evidence as early as the mid–nineteenth century, and they grew even stronger at the beginning of the twentieth.[3]

CHAPTER 3

The Main Branches of the Economy in the Black Forest at the Time of the Great Economic Crisis, 1930–32

The geographical isolation of the Black Forest and the harshness of its climate and living conditions gave rise to certain occupations in the region. The immediate image that the Black Forest calls to mind is of a region covered with trees, and indeed, the forest and lumber industry played a considerable role in the local economic life during the nineteenth and twentieth centuries. Agriculture was also a popular occupation in the region, which was dotted with middle-sized and large farms. Water and mountains are also plentiful in the Black Forest, and their impact on the region's industry was well evident (energy and mining). The Black Forest region, due to its mountainous terrain and great quantity of snow, served as a popular vacation spot both in summer and winter, not only for Germans, but also for numerous visitors from abroad.

The industry of the Black Forest was quite unique. It was known not only for its clock-making industry, the famous cuckoo clocks above all, but also for its allied industries: precision mechanics, glassware, and various facets of the wood and textile industries. All of these branches formed part of the Black Forest economy, and together they characterized the industrial development of the region in the nineteenth and twentieth centuries.

In this chapter, I shall examine the major characteristics of the Black Forest economy, tracing the geographical distribution of the various industrial groups as well as the changes that overtook local industry as it made the transition to the twentieth century. Finally, we shall try to examine the state of industry during the years of the Weimar Republic. The following is an overview of the major groups active in the region's economy.

Agriculture

Farming and cattle-breeding were chiefly characteristic of the smaller villages in the Black Forest. One can discern two kinds of villages in the region: those where this was the occupation most commonly pursued by the inhabitants, and those where the local population also engaged in crafts, tourism, or industry, either within the village itself or in a nearby town. This latter category was more characteristic of the poorer and more backward villages of the region, in the south of the Black Forest and in the Schwarzwald-Baar region. In addition to the farmers who lived and worked on their land, we also find peasants who lived in large towns and owned plots of land and farms outside the town's boundaries.[1]

Most of the farms had fallen into debt since the nineteenth century. In the northern village of Oberwolfach (in the district of Wolfach), the farms owed the state 377,369 Reichsmarks in 1928. Of all the debts owed by the villages to the state of Baden, this village's obligation was the highest, and it was primarily carried over from the previous century. Many farms took out large mortgages at this time, and their debt spiraled astronomically during the years of inflation. This was the case, for example, in the village of Unadingen, and also in the Wutach. Many farmers had been permitted to take out mortgages in order to make certain changes in the farms, or to undertake urgent repairs.[2]

Together with crafts, agriculture was the primary occupation of the region's inhabitants at the end of the nineteenth century. Those who engaged in crafts and home industries (see later discussion) did so, among other reasons, because of their inability to eke out a living through agriculture alone, and because of the special law of inheritance typical to the Black Forest (see further discussion later). The agrarian economy remained in its backward state up to the third decade of the twentieth century. Even though the agricultural bodies and cooperatives (e.g., the *Zuchtgenossenschaft*) tried to woo the peasants, the latter remained apathetic. The First World War did very little to change the agrarian economic structure of the region. Approximately one-third of the inhabitants dealt in agriculture, and two-thirds in industry and crafts. Nevertheless, industry can be seen to have penetrated a number of villages (e.g., Wolterdingen), and the number of those engaged in industry (alongside crafts) was also on the rise, either in the same locality or in one nearby (table 2). Due to the mounting economic pressure on the farms and the Great Economic Crisis (from the end of the 1920s), more and more inhabitants tended to go back to farming. Among these were some who returned to their home village after seeking their fortune in the city, only to find themselves reduced to working once again on the family farm.[3]

The general reluctance to join the agricultural cooperatives or to mechanize the farms testifies, among other things, to the socioeconomic backwardness of the region. We shall discuss this characteristic of the Black Forest villages at greater length, but for now, let us note that in a number of localities, and especially in the central Black Forest and more mountainous north, the topography made it difficult to use mechanized farming equipment. In the south, however, throughout the regions of the Wutach and Schwarzwald-Baar, the topography was more favorable to the use of mechanized farming, and the objection that arose there was rooted (as we shall see) in the local socioeconomic backwardness. Combines and threshing machines were a rare sight in the region, both before the onset of the Great Economic Crisis and during the crisis itself.[4]

Home Industries

This term refers to all the traditional preindustrial crafts that were performed by the inhabitants of the region within their own town or village, and usually within the home of a master craftsman or next to a small factory. These crafts were typical of the region, and they ranged from the clock-making industry, for which the region was known, to the production of loam. This economic characteristic of the region originated in the unique conditions prevailing there since the eighteenth century. The local home industries flourished over the course of the nineteenth century. We find, for example a high concentration of expert cuckoo clock makers in Oberbränd, manufacturers of tubs and basins in Bernau, watchmakers in Furtwangen and Triberg, glassblowers in Wolfach, straw-makers (*Strohindustrie*) in the villages of Feldberg region and wood carvers in Eisenbach, to name only a few of the crafts that were cultivated.[5]

TABLE 2.   The Social Structure of the Black Forest and the Baar Villages, 1925

Village	Population	Farmer % (1932)	Merchants	Master Craftsman	Workers (working outside the village)
Bachheim	358	78.5	1	1	8 (8)
Ibach	703	65.3	5	—	27 (17)
Oberbränd	221	59.2	—	1	32 (32)
Rohrbach	427	69.3	1	8	35 (35)
Schollach	384	71.8	1	3	11 (11)
Seppenhofen	358	67.6	—	1	18 (18)
Wolterdingen	803	45.1	5	15	71 (16)

Source: Badische Gemeindestatistik, BSL 1927; *Ergebnisse der Volkszählung vom 16. Juni 1933 in Baden,* BSL, 1933.

At the beginning of the twentieth century, industrialization gained momentum in the region and many people turned to factory work, mostly in connection with the clock-making industry. Craftsmen who had formerly worked within the framework of the home industries became employees in factories or large workshops. During the twenties, with the deterioration of the economic situation, the workers and craftsmen in home industries received the final blow. The crisis in agriculture forced the peasants to dismiss the craftsmen in their employ, not only the blacksmith and the wagoner, but also the straw weaver and the potter. The peasant was no longer able to pay the craftsmen, and once he dispensed with their services they were reduced to being agricultural prolateriats engaged only at harvest time. Most of them registered in the district unemployment offices.[6]

The Forest Industry

One of the region's most important sources of income lay in the numerous forests so characteristic of the region. We shall take a closer look at the forest workers (*Waldarbeiter*) and their way of life, but for the time being we shall simply note that the forests constituted an importance source of income both for the local councils and for the peasants and craftsmen in the Black Forest. In the course of the nineteenth century the state sold vast tracts of forest to the councils of the different localities. The lumber industry that developed in the region of the Black Forest was based on the sawing, planing, and sale of the logs.

A number of villages consisted largely of forested areas, and hence the local council was able to depend heavily on this source of raw materials in order to finance its economic activity. However, dependence on this source of income was advantageous only in those periods when the lumber sold for a high price. At the end of the twenties, when the price of lumber suffered a general decline the world over, many towns in the Black Forest fell into a deep economic crisis, intensified by the loss of the markets in Alsace-Lorraine. The worst case was that of Vöhrenbach, which collapsed due to the crisis in the lumber industry.[7]

Crafts

Alongside farming, crafts provided the most important source of income even prior to the nineteenth century. The economic development of the crafts was characterized by two major trends: (1) craftsmen who were also peasants or who worked on a farm in the employ of peasants; and (2) craftsmen who worked at home and who later expanded their workshop into a small manufacturing plant or even a factory. The most popular and well-known craft in the region was clock-making. It originated with merchants from Bohemia and Switzerland who dealt in glassware and clocks, and who reached the area in the sixteenth and seventeenth centuries. The demand for this product stimulated local entrepreneurs to produce their own wooden clocks, and by the eighteenth century many of them were earning their livelihood in this new profession.[8]

Clock-making became extremely popular in the area, and from the beginning of the nineteenth century many turned to this and other crafts, such as blacksmithing, wagoneering, carpentry, baking, and glassblowing. The percentage of craftsmen in the Black Forest was higher than the national average at least until the beginning of the century. They were concentrated in towns such as Triberg, Lenzkirch, Neustadt, Furtwangen, Wolfach, and Eisenbach (centers of clock-making), and Schönau, among others. The clock-making industry was subject to seasonal fluctuations. Thus, toward Christmas time the clock-making establishments worked in full force, while in the summer, there was a perceptible decline in output and employment.

Craftsmen who worked in the employ of local farmers were also a common phenomenon in the region. Some of them lived on the grounds of the farm itself, while others lived in nearby towns.[9] Alongside the clockmaker we also find the more traditional types of craftsmen, such as carpenters, blacksmiths, bakers, and millers. A typical village would have a master craftsman who employed two workers, a master blacksmith and his apprentice, a factory worker of precision mechanics, a number of clockmaking establishments that employed skilled workers (sometimes dozens of them), a shoemaker, and other assorted craftsmen.

Toward the beginning of the twentieth century, the workshops and craftsmen of the region (and not only there, as is often noted in works dealing with the industrialization of Germany) met a crisis. The rapid expansion of the clock-making establishments led to a decrease in the number of independent craftsmen in the clock-making industry.[10] World War I with its demand for textile, steel, iron, and coal products contributed to the expansion of factories to answer the needs of the army, but it dealt a blow to the small workshops and craftsmen, who were forced to turn to the production of explosives, uniforms, and optical equipment. Many of them were forced to work in conjunction with large plants and factories producing clocks and precision mechanics. These, while accommodating their production to the needs of the army, absorbed many of the master craftsmen and workers.

The amalgamation of the factories, the process of mechanization, the galloping inflation, and, finally, the Great Economic Crisis dealt a fatal blow to the local craft-making establishments. We shall discuss the crisis that hit industry in 1926–27 at greater length further on. Side by side with this crisis came the crisis in agriculture, which not only hurt the peasants but also, and even primarily, the occupational groups dependent on the farms for their livelihood. Thus the first to be hurt were the craftsmen and craft-making establishments employed in the service of the local peasants.

The Tourist Industry

Even more important than the clock-making industry was the tourist industry, which was geared to winter sports, health spas, vacationing, and summer outings. An entire way of life evolved around the development of the local tourist industry. The most important centers of tourism were in Hochschwarzwald, in the district of Neustadt, and in the districts formerly known (until 1924) as Schönau and St. Blasien. There were also tourist sites, popular to this day, in Schonach and Triberg in the district of Villingen, and Kniebis in the district of Wolfach. In Hochschwarzwald, in the towns of Hinterzarten and Titisee, this industry developed into the primary source of income for the local inhabitants. Noisy, provocative, and violent activities are scarcely conducive to the success of a tourist industry, and hence it was not only the "quiet and meditative nature" of the people in the Black Forest, to quote G. Moller, that contributed to the tranquil atmosphere of the region, but also the knowledge that rowdy behavior would scare away the tourists and undermine the region's economic basis.[11]

The development and expansion of the tourist industry created a bourgeois social stratum of considerable local importance that included innkeepers (*Gastwirt*). More than one of the region's typical vacation towns can afford us a glimpse of two entirely different kinds of life-style. The first of these revolved around the life of the town and its daily needs, the needs of its inhabitants and the local social and religious activities. The second centered around the local health-resort and vacation spots, almost totally unconnected to the everyday life of the town and catering to the needs of the vacationers. In Hinterzarten, for example, we find that the town was neglected, with garbage piled up in the streets and freely running sewage, beggars, and other concrete evidence of poor administration and backwardness. This stood in flagrant contrast to the areas surrounding the local vacation spots, which were kept scrupulously clean and in good running order. They boasted facilities for golf, cricket, and tennis, and there one could find foreign newspapers and even physicians especially engaged to care for the tourists.[12]

Tourism proved to be a boon to the economy of the Black Forest towns during the years of the great crisis. The collapse of local sources of income during the mid-1920s induced some parts of the local population to turn to a new form of livelihood, tourism. In Lenzkirch, some local inhabitants began dealing in tourist-related commerce and crafts in 1929, and the town leaders urged them to rent their homes out to tourists.

The tourist industry was recognized as important not only to the economy of the region, but to the state of Baden as a whole. For this reason the local press, the local authorities, the state supervisors, the local notables, and, needless to say, innkeepers all urged the proper authorities to further develop the infrastructure of the region, so that it might attract as many tourists as possible. Thus, for example, they insisted that sports fields and golf courses be enlarged, that foreign newspapers be brought into the region, and that there should be publicity campaigns placing advertisements in the pages of the foreign press for the local tourist spots, even for places such as Eisenbach that had turned to tourism only in the wake of the economic crisis. The tax imposed on beer in 1931 in order to help finance the current budget was rescinded in a number of places because it hurt the innkeepers, even though many of these had long become accustomed to serving water instead of beer.[13]

Industry

The industry of the Black Forest was characterized from the end of the nineteenth century by an increasing number of large manufacturing plants and factories, which had begun as large workshops for clock-making, precision mechanics, and wood. Most of the factories in the region dealt in the production and export of these products. Starting in the 1880s and 1890s we are witness to processes of expansion and amalgamation of large workshops into a single large factory, and even to the establishment of factories that were branches of larger concerns based outside the region, and even outside of Baden.[14]

The region's large factories of wood and clock-making were located in Triberg, St. George, Neustadt, Eisenbach, Haslach, Furtwangen, Todtnau, Hausach (which even boasted a steel factory), Lenzkirch, and, needless to say, large Protestant towns such as Gutach, Schiltach, and Hornberg. The Protestant towns were pioneers in the establishment of large mechanized factories, and—what was most important—these factories were privately owned by local people. In contrast, the rest of the factories in the Catholic towns mostly belonged to large concerns. This characteristic of industry in the Black Forest left the factories vulnerable to economic fluctuations and to decisions made by distant centralized owners far from the Black Forest and Baden, without the advice or even the knowledge of the local managers. In addition to this drawback, the loss of the important markets in Alsace-Lorraine, the increased taxes on land and property, and the introduction of mechanization, which led to the dismissal of workers and administrative staff, all combined to create a severe crisis in the factories of the Black Forest after the years of inflation. This crisis commonly overtook the factories in Baden that dealt in clock-making, precision mechanics, and wood and was part of the general crisis in the factories of Germany in those years, prior to the outbreak of the Great Economic Crisis. In Germany the crisis was precipitated by the introduction of mechanization and the processes of modernization, which contributed to the closure of unprofitable factories, the dismissal of workers, and cutbacks of all kinds. The crisis was also engendered by the removal of tax restrictions, thus exposing the German market to foreign competition, and by the imposition of too heavy a burden on the owners of profitable factories, in the forms of taxes for public health and welfare, and of increases in workers' salaries. This was in consequence of a desire to ensure that Weimar possessed the character of a welfare state.[15]

Against this background, local industry suffered a drawn-out crisis that began in 1925–26 (see table 3), prior to the onset of the Great Economic Crisis. This was especially true of the factories that dealt in clock-making and wood in the districts of Neustadt, Villingen, and Donaueschingen. The result of the crisis was the closure of factories, the dismissal of workers, strikes, a cutback of work hours, and bristling tension, not only between the workers and factory owners, but also between the workers and peasants.

The crisis that hit the clock-making factories of the Black Forest began in 1926. The clocks had been destined for sale in the markets of Soviet Russia and England. Soviet Russia, however, was unable and unwilling to purchase these products, partly because it was going through a crisis of its own. England, on the other hand, like Alsace-Lorraine and Switzerland, no longer constituted a profitable market, due to newly imposed protective tariffs and the fact that it had begun to set up clock-making factories of its own. A similar fate overtook the wood factories due to the decline in the price of wood the world over. Moreover, a num-

TABLE 3.   **The Black Forest's Industry Crisis, 1926–29**

	Factories (with more than 20 workers)		Workers	
District	1925	1929	1925	1929
Donaueschingen	29	23	3,464	2,147
Neustadt	18	19	2,100	1,965
Oberkirch	18	18	1,093	1,206
Schopfheim	52	39	7,067	6,061
Villingen	69	59	6,477	6,056
Wolfach	41	45	3,139	3,194

Source: *Statistisches Jahrbuch fur das Land Baden*, BSL, 1930, 119; *Badische Gemeindestatistik*, BSL, 1927.

ber of factories still had not recovered from the war following the demobilization of the soldiers, and the requisition and confiscation of industrial machinery for the war effort. The debts of the factories were partly discharged through the sale of tracts of forests to the banks, the sale of property, and also the receipt of money from a fund designated for areas that had been hurt due to their borderland status (*Grenzlandstarif*). Even so, the debts remained large due to the high costs of welfare, worker salaries, and deductions for health insurance and sickness benefits.[16]

In 1930 through 1932, the entire Black Forest industrial economy collapsed. The Great Economic Crisis accelerated the processes set into motion by the earlier crisis and affected wide sectors of society, such as craftsmen and peasants. Personal distress ran high: many workers returned to work in the factories from which they had been fired in 1927–28 only to be fired once more in a new wave of dismissals in 1931. From 1929 onward, the price of logs fell some 50 percent, and once again it was the factories that dealt in the production of clocks and wood that were the first to be hurt. The scale of the unemployment resembled that from several years earlier. Thus, for example, in Furtwangen during the summer of 1932, we find 558 unemployed and 400 temporary workers. The majority of factories were open for production only three to five days a week. There were claims of heavy losses due to the numerous deductions that were funneled into social welfare. Industrial towns like Vohrenbach and Gutenbach ran into administrative difficulties in following economic sanctions and mass dismissals. In Gutenbach the town's single factory and main important employer collapsed, and hunger was rife. The local industrialist, Schatz, moved to England, selling his factory and dismissing all its workers. In Vöhrenbach the local council was unable to discharge its debts and was eventually declared bankrupt.[17]

CHAPTER 4

The Black Forest Society

The Problem of Socioeconomic Backwardness

We have on more than one occasion noted the backwardness of various areas and population groups in the region. It is common knowledge that Germany's agricultural regions contained whole populations whose lifestyle, mentality, and socioeconomic behavior could be termed preindustrial. The German Catholics were regarded as backward until the beginning of the century, and the literature surrounding its socioeconomic retardation is vast and diversified.[1]

At the beginning of part 1 we quoted the words of Gerhard Möller about the people of the Black Forest who live "isolated and remote from the world." Inspectors who visited the region not infrequently stressed the backwardness of some of the villages, which found expression in the large number of sick and mentally retarded, the high birth rate, the unsanitary living conditions, and the reluctance of farmers to join the cooperatives that represented their economic interests. Even in the 1920s we find villages without a water pump, electricity, paved roads, or other amenities of modern life. In a number of villages the inhabitants were accustomed to dwelling under the same roof with their livestock, and the poor sanitary conditions led to the outbreak of cancer that struck the region in the 1920s. In the region of Reiselfingen there was a high incidence of meningitis, and in Neustadt, the housewives were introduced to ironing only in 1932. More than once, agronomists from outside the region warned that the local agriculture suffered from severe structural problems due to the reluctance of local farmers to learn new ways of planting, harvesting, and working their fields.[2]

We have mentioned the lack of mechanized farming in the villages of the region. This was especially prominent in the southern Black Forest, in the regions of Wutach, Hotzenwald, and the Schwarzwald-Baar. The entire Baar region was characterized by an economy that lagged dozens of years behind the rest of the country. The regional inspectors made their reports (*Ortsbereisung*) every few years, and these unfailingly stressed the backwardness of the villages, both before and during the Weimar era. Among the problems noted were the absence of a sewage system, the garbage that littered the streets, the reluctance of the farmers to join such cooperatives as the *Zuchtgenossenschaft,* the teeming presence of beggars and tramps, the shortage of medical care, and the lack of new construction and *Vereine.*[3] The peasants were still unfamiliar as late as 1930 with the use of a grain silo for protecting the bales of hay in the rain, and it was only in these years that the region received its first fire extinguishers. The *Ortsbereisung* report of Dittishausen in 1927 mentions that the village was backward, the burgomeister a drunk and the treasurer a larcenist. There were signs, moreover, of heavy drinking in the village, the firemen were ill-trained, the town infested with rats, and the water supply inadequate. In chapter 11 we will present the reports made by the local priests concerning the moral-religious aspect of life in these villages. For now, however, it will suffice to mention only that their conclusions were not very different from those of the civilian inspectors, and that, in general, the picture that emerges from these reports goes far in explaining the political patterns of behavior in the region.

The distress was aggravated by the inheritance law (*Geschlossene Hofgüterrecht*) existing in a number of the villages whereby the family farm was handed down intact to the youngest son alone, so that the rest of the family was forced to either leave the farm or to remain on as wage-earning workers. This law was based on the principle of inequality, and it did much to perpetuate the backwardness of the region and the bitterness that tore many families apart. Due to their plight, many people refrained from marrying and taking out mortgages. Even so, the birthrate was high, many infants were born deformed, and some were even born out of wedlock.[4] Frequent childbearing is, of course, one of the most prominent characteristics of a backward society and one that is frequently mentioned in the literature. In the villages of Seppenhofen and Reiselfingen, and in the hamlet of Löffingen, the birth rate was two to three times higher than the average in the state of Baden. The high birthrate was not restricted, however, to the backward villages of the southern Black Forest, for it was found among many other villages and small towns as well, mostly among the peasants. Among the working class, this characteristic was less conspicuous.

And finally, some districts of the Black Forest and the Baar had an inordinately large number of mentally ill, blind, deaf and dumb mutes, and cripples. In the districts of Neustadt and Wolfach the phenomenon was particularly striking. Most of the handicapped were Catholic males employed in some branch of industry or crafts. Among the factors that led to their condition were genetic causes (blindness), childhood diseases such as measles and chicken pox (resulting in deafness and dumbness), alcoholism, and syphilis (resulting in mental illness and retardation). These afflictions were transmitted congenitally, often because of family inbreeding.[5]

Further on, we shall see that it was precisely in the regions of the southeastern Black Forest, mainly in the Wutach and the Barr, that anti-clericalism ran high, and there was a strong feeling of disaffection and social deprivation. These feelings were translated into political patterns of behavior characterized by electoral support for the local protest groups.

The Major Social Groups during the Great Economic Crisis

Agricultural and Forest Workers

Agricultural workers were considered to occupy the lowest rung in the social hierarchy of occupational groups. They had the lowest status in the working class, with the forest workers at the very bottom of the ladder. The forest and agricultural workers in the region did not feel the impact of industrialization, and only those who lived in towns or near them possessed a proleterian consciousness. Some of them were the sons of farmers, forced by the regional law of "undivided inheritance" to hire themselves out as agricultural workers. They were an easygoing, un-radical lot, and the majority did not consider themselves proletariat (even though they were perceived as such by the local inhabitants). Following the revolution of 1918, however, the behavioral patterns of the farmhands demonstrated an increasing radicalism. The shortage of food and its high cost also contributed to the change in their behavior. The influence of the factory workers can increasingly be detected in the agricultural workers who lived far from towns on remotely situated farms. During the years of the economic crisis, many of the unemployed took such work as could be found in the farms and forests of the region. The slump in the price of wood led to a steep rise in the number of unemployed forest workers, while the crisis in agriculture and the deterioration of the farms caused the peasants to have less and less need for agricultural workers, except in harvest time. Many of them joined the swelling ranks of the unemployed.[6]

The Peasants

In the period of the Great Economic Crisis the structural problems that traditionally beset the farms of the region and the agriculture of the Black Forest also affected the condition of the peasants. However, together with the traditional reasons for dissatisfaction, such as the law of "undivided inheritance," the social backwardness, the economic distress, and the dominance of the priest in the village, there were new factors connected with the Weimar welfare state. These included the deductions for the health insurance of shepherds and agricultural workers, and the economic policy of the Weimar government, which was less sympathetic to the interests of the peasants than that of the Second Reich. There were also factors of international commerce behind the economic distress, such as the decline in the price of wood, a phenomenon that affected the livelihood of the peasants, and the decline in the price of cattle and dairy products, which reduced the income the peasant had formerly derived from his livestock. Finally, the "Milk Law," which went into effect in 1931, dealt a blow to peasant private enterprise.[7]

The result of all this, in the words of the *Freiburger Zeitung,* was that "more and more peasants in the region of the Feldberg are reduced, as during the war, to gathering *Wildfrüchte* from the forests for their sustenance."[8] From 1931 on, hunger struck many villages in the region, affecting not only the peasants but also those who provided the farms with various services. The peasant now became his own craftsman and even began baking his own bread so as not to have need, as in the past, of the services of a baker, or of purchasing bread. Many of the farms were sunk heavily in debt, and since the farmers were unable to repay these obligations, confiscations were a frequent occurrence. Many peasants turned to raising rabbits in order to sustain their families and to create another source of income. Their preindustrial and backward way of thinking came under the criticism of the press, the local notables, and the regional inspectors. It was precisely when the economic crisis had already struck that they urged the peasant to become more efficient, to mechanize his farm, as a way to improve his situation.[9]

In addition to the economic problems that characterized those years, a latent social problem arose in the villages. This was the general hostility toward workers who lived in the village, but who worked elsewhere, either in a neighboring town or village or on one of the local farms. Workers were now to be found in the village councils, and the leftist parties, even the extreme left, gained a foothold in village life. An open showdown did not occur, since the inhabitants feared that this might threaten the village's very existence. However, peasants who owned large plots of land, the leaders of the council, and the petty bourgeoisie began to fear the loss of their cultural hegemony. The growing radicalism in the atmosphere of the industrial towns now penetrated the village as well, due to the return of many workers, laid off from their jobs, to the farms of their parents or to temporary employment during the harvest. None of this amounted to an all-out class war or a struggle to redistribute the wealth of the village, but it did threaten the status quo, at least in the eyes of the peasants. This served to undermine their self-confidence and their ability to remain in control of the village. Psychologically, it also undermined their confidence in the continuation of the existing economic order, itself already damaged by the Great Economic Crisis.[10]

Craftsmen and Workers

The combined discussion here of these social strata during the years of the Great Economic Crisis is testimony to the grim economic state, or, more precisely, to the grim socioeconomic state of the craftsmen whose position declined to the level of the working class at the turn of the century. (We are speaking here primarily of master craftsmen, not craftsmen who were considered factory workers.) This process intensified during the years of the Weimar Republic, beginning with the local crisis in industry, which dealt a severe blow to the craftsmen and small workshops connected to local industry, especially the clock-making industry, and ending in the years of the Great Economic Crisis, which saw the final collapse of those industries to which the craftsmen had been connected (iron, steel, clocks, wood, precision mechanics, textiles). The crisis in agriculture also led to the dismissal of local master craftsmen and workers from the service of peasants, and these were forced to eke out their existence as farmhands or to register as unemployed.[11]

From our investigation of the collapse of industry in the Black Forest it emerges that the workers in industry and crafts were seriously hurt. There was a drastic decline in the number of workers employed in local industry, a decline that at times reached sixty to seventy percent of the industrial work force. The majority lost their jobs, and the salaries of the workers were eroded. Even though it is necessary to distinguish between the various categories of workers, between skilled and unskilled workers, assistants, and male and female employees, the average industrial wage in the Black Forest during the 1920s came to sixty-four pfenning an hour (with female workers earning some 30 percent less). In 1930 the worker earned a wage of some sixty pfenning an hour, either because of the shorter workweek introduced by many workshops and factories, or because many of them simply reduced the wages of their employees.

The harsh situation of the craftsmen was demonstrated by the fact that many were reduced to various kinds of "dirty work." In their own words, 1931 was "the worst since World War I, and this year signals our end."[12] Two years before this, in 1929, the craftsmen had sought to defend themselves against the large capitalistic concerns, the commercial trusts, the department stores, and the consumer cooperatives, and to oppose the proletarianization of the middle classes and the policy of taxation, which were disadvantageous to the middle classes. About one year later, the craftsmen demanded that their representatives be merged with those of the steel factory workers. The very fact that the craftsmen viewed their interests to be on a par with those of the workers was expressive not only of their worsening economic state, but also of the way they came to grips, in a relatively short time, with the gravity of their situation. In the end, the craftsmen were indeed reduced to the proleteriat, even while the region's newspapers wrote that "this important class is on the verge of extinction."[13] Their traditional importance and centrality to local economic life and society caused their distress to figure prominently in the reports of the local press during those years. This was despite of the fact that the industrial workers were suffering no less than the craftsmen, however, the workers' political orientation and goals caused them to meet with less sympathy than the craftsmen.

The tragic fate of the craftsmen was also expressed in the social frameworks in which they were active. Internal conflicts, factionalism, and weakness were characteristic of the unions.[14] In part 3, I will examine the fate of the *Vereine* to which many of the craftsmen belonged. While the workers were able to console themselves with the wide-ranging social activity of the workers' *Vereine* and professional unions, craftsmen who were unwilling to join the workers' unions found themselves at a double disadvantage. Their class consciousness, again in contrast to that of the workers, was badly injured. The desire to preserve it was evident in the inability of the craftsmen to adapt themselves to a simpler life-style, and in their refusal to hire their children out to the peasants, both from a sense of pride and because of their rankling hostility toward the peasants, who had dispensed with their services once the crisis began to affect agriculture.

To sum up, the most dominant social groups of the Black Forest and the Baar regions were plunged in economic and social crisis during the period of the Weimar Republic. Quite apart from the negative repercussions this had in terms of economics, the traditional equilibrium between the peasants and craftsmen was thrown entirely off balance. The mortal blow dealt both these classes greatly tarnished the self-image and class pride of their members, causing the status quo of Black Forest society to deteriorate even further.

Side by side, and over the years, the different social strata in the Black Forest developed social and economic frameworks that answered their own particular needs. The geography of the region also contributed to the creation of social groups who lived in close physical proximity to each other, but who differed in their behavior, economic activity, and social organization. This ranged from the socioeconomically backward peasants in the Schwarzwald-Baar, who shut themselves up in their homes without any desire to establish social organizations or social life, to the bustling, eminently bourgeois economic and cultural activity of the local innkeepers, hoteliers, and industrialists (see chap. 10). The economic fate of the various population groups was not monolithic. In the southern Black Forest the peasants were steeped in poverty for years, and the crisis in agriculture only intensified their plight. The peasants of the central and northern part of the region, hurt by the decline in the prices of cattle and wood, sank into economic crisis from the beginning of the 1920s. The workers of the Black Forest knew economic distress from the middle of the twenties, and once the brief respite of 1927–28 had passed, they were hit by crisis all over again, even though its impact was no worse than it had been a few years before. And, finally, the craftsmen in the region were in a state of economic and social crisis already at the beginning of the century.

As we shall see below, the patterns of political and social behavior of each social group were greatly determined by such variables as place of residence, social milieu, and the period in which they were struck by crisis. Just as we are witness to the existence of various social groups that differed in terms of economic, social, and geographical infrastructure, so we will see that their response to crisis and their patterns of political behavior differed from case to case. This variation, moreover, will be clearly evident in the following chapters as we examine the response of the different social groups to the Nazi Party, and the collapse of their social organizations.

CHAPTER 5

Patterns of Political Behavior in the Black Forest and the Baar

I shall now examine the patterns of political behavior of South Baden Catholic society from the end of the nineteenth century to the end of the 1920s. Here too, as we shall see, the geographical isolation left its mark on the region. During the period before World War I, the political struggle was played out between a limited number of parties, or, to be more precise, between the *Zentrum* and the National-Liberal Party. The dizzying rise of the German Social Democratic Party (*Sozialdemokratische Partei—SPD*) was not reflected in the region, and there were few districts in which the party managed until 1912 to gain more than ten percent of the Catholic vote. This was not the case after 1918, when the political map of the region began to show greater diversity. Though the major political blocs still existed, some under new names, there now arose a bloc of parties that addressed itself to specific social classes, which was something new on the local political scene. This bloc gave rise to a local peasant party (*Badischer Landbund—BLB*). Together with this, the leftist bloc gained strength in relation to the pre-1914 years. Our discussion of the local political scene will end in 1928, the year in which the Nazi Party first won the vote of numerous inhabitants of the region.

Political Behavior in the Black Forest from the End of the Nineteenth Century until 1918

Until the end of the 1880s, the National-Liberal Party was dominant in most parts of the Black Forest and south Baden. This was due to the anticlerical nature of the region; to the marginal impact of *Kulturkampf* in the Black Forest, especially in its southern part, the Wutach and the Schwarzwald-Baar; and to the economic structure of the region, which favored individualism and a free-market economy. In these regions the *Zentrum* did not manage to consolidate its political hold until the beginning of the present century, and in a number of places, not even until the end of World War I (see table 4). Anticlerical trends had been smoldering in the region even at the time of the 1848 revolution, originating in the fact that most parts of the region belonged until the 1830s to the liberal Bishopric of Constance and exacerbated by the region's unique economic infrastructure (see chap. 3). The conservative and dogmatic Catholic Ultramontanism, which the Church tried to impose on Baden after 1848, encountered fierce opposition in the Black Forest, especially from the factory owners, peasants, large farmers, and numerous craftsmen who leaned in the direction of economic and political liberalism. In chapter 10 I shall take a closer look at this bourgeois stratum of Black Forest society.[1]

The relative weakness of the *Zentrum* in Baden and the isolation of the Black Forest and the Baar region made it difficult for political Catholicism to consolidate its position there. From the 1880s, with the end of *Kulturkampf* throughout Germany, and mainly after the resignation of Bismarck, the *Zentrum* not only gave many German Catholics political representation but also provided them with a social, cultural, economic, religious, and, needless to say, political framework, within a Catholic "subculture" and "milieu."[2] In many predominantly Catholic regions except Baden, the *Zentrum* managed to serve as a stabilizer in German political life and to transform the Catholic public into a highly viable force, capable of influencing affairs at the national level. The *"Zentrum* polemic" (*Zentrumsstreit*), which took place on the eve of World War I, centered on the question of whether, or to what extent, the party should continue to steer a course of openness, of venturing "outside of the tower" (*Heraus aus dem Turm*), and to relegate matters of dogma to the margins of its activity, or whether the *Zentrum* should bring its policy into line with that of the Catholic Church, which preferred to insulate Catholic society from its surroundings.

No trace of this important polemic penetrated the fastness of the Black Forest. The weakness of the local Catholic press, which had existed in the region only since the end of the last century, and the weakness of the Catholic *Vereine* impeded the consolidation of the Catholic milieu in the Black Forest and contributed to the weakness of the *Zentrum* especially in the south of the region (see chap. 11). Nor was the *Zentrum* all that interested in recruiting inhabitants of such a remote region. Once again, the isolation of the region was reflected in the list of members to the *Zentrumverein* in Baden, the party's most important political body. Only one of the council's sixty-four members came from the southern part of the Black Forest, Düfner of Furtwangen.[3]

The National-Liberal Party, whose goals were openly anticlerical, was dominant in the central and southern Black Forest (and in the whole of the southern part of Baden) until 1905, and it was the party that profited most from the inactivity of the *Zentrum* in the region. At both the local and state levels, the party was characterized as a "party of notables" (*Honoratiorenpartei*). This trait found expression in the absence of a mass political-organizational infrastructure functioning on a daily basis. Instead, a number of people, usually local notables, busied themselves with political activity just before the election, and once the election was over, returned to their daily affairs.

From the beginning of the century the main conflict between the *Zentrum* and the National-Liberal Party was over educational and cultural issues. The ghost of *Kulturkampf,* in which the National-Liberal Party had played a central and extremely hostile role vis-à-vis the *Zentrum,* reemerged frequently in the various election campaigns in Baden, serving the *Zentrum* as its central rallying point in its battle against the liberal party. But in southeastern Baden, due to the anticlerical traditions and claims that the Catholic Church was responsible for the region's backwardness, much of the population joined forces with the National-Liberal Party. Thus in the district of Donaueschingen and in a number of localities in the Black Forest, the party thus managed to maintain a prominent lead over the *Zentrum,* at least until 1912. Once again, we are talking primarily about villages and small towns in the southeastern Black Forest, in the most backward areas and towns, such as Bonndorf, St. Blasien, Lenzkirch, or Schluchsee. The support that the local inhabitants gave the liberal party was due to the party's anticlerical struggle, its economic manifesto, and its *Volkspartei* image. The liberal party found an important supporter in the region's well respected bourgeois newspapers, whose quality and frequency of publication even outdid that of the Catholic newspaper, and in its allied and extensive network of cultural and economic *Vereine,* whose leaders numbered among the activists of the National-Liberal Party. At the beginning of the century, then, the local social infrastructure largely supported the National-Liberal Party.

The 1905 election campaign to the Reichstag in Baden constituted a turning point in the *Zentrum*'s ability to recruit voters in south Baden. The focus on economic and social issues contributed to the party's growth in a large number of villages, even in the Black Forest. Concurrent with this, the strength of the liberal party went into decline, despite the fact that it now appeared (as of 1912) as a liberal bloc in conjunction with liberal bourgeois parties such as the *Fortschrittliche Volkspartei* and the *Deutsche Volkspartei.* In this campaign we are witness to the growing strength of the SPD, particularly in industrial towns such as Triberg, Neustadt, and Furtwangen.

TABLE 4. Reichstag Election in Black Forest Districts, 1903–28

	Bonndorf (1924)	E.V	Donaueschingen	E.V	Neustadt	Oberkirch	St. Blasien (1924)	E.V	Schönau (1924)	Triberg (1924)	E.V	Villingen	E.V	Wolfach	E.V
1903															
Turnout	83.1		86.9		73.1	73	72.5		81.1	79.6		84		79	
SPD	3		4.9		8.9	6.2	7.6		8.4	22.3		13.8		14.4	
National-Liberal	61.6		44.3		31.1	17.2	43.8	52.3	18.1	28.4		40.2		23	
Z	35.4		50.7		59.9	76.4	48.6	47.6	73	49.2		45.1		62.5	
1907															
Turnout	91.4		93.9		86.4	85.6	81		90.6	89.7		91.2		88.6	
SPD	3.9		2.6		12.7	5.1	4.6		9.3	18.7		14.9		12.7	
National-Liberal	46.7	50.1	51.5		28.6	21.3	37.6		18.2	29		40		21.1 (Deutsche Volksp.)	
Z	49.3	49.7	45.9		58.6	73.5	57.8		72.5	52.3		45		61.8	
1912															
Turnout	84.4		90		84.7	86.1	83.8		88.3	88.5		88.5		87.8	
SPD	12		9.4		15	11.1	8.9		11.7	22.4		24.7		16.7	
National-Liberal	38.5	49	44.3	51.7	26.1	19.4	38.8		15	28	47.7	32.8	54.1	21.1 (Fortschrit volkspartei)	
Z	49.5	51	46.2	48.3	58.7	69.4	52.3		73.2	49.6	52.3	42.4	45.9	62	
1919															
Turnout	83.5		83.5		86.1	85.2	79.5		86.8	87.8		86.8		87.9	
Left	22.7		27		25.6	31.8	17		25.3	30.2		30.9		20.7	
Z	57.3		50		60.4	65.5	57.9		62.7	51.3		39.9		57.8	
Bourg-Consv.	18.4		22.9		13.7	12.9	20.5		11.8	22.8		27.6		21.3	
1920															
Turnout	66.5		73.9		77.3	64.4	67.3		77.3	75.8		73.7		74.3	
Left	13.5		18.9		22.4	14.4	20.8		21.1	25.2		29		22.7	

Z 62.9	53.9	59.6	70.6	55.2	67	55	42.4	57.1
Bourg-Consv. 23.4	27.1	17.9	14.8	23.5	11.8	21.8	27.8	19.7
1924 (I)								
Turnout	68.4	68.9	55.8				66.3	65.3
Left	15.8	17.9	11.5				22.7	20.1
Z	51	54.6	61.8				46.1	51.9
Bourg-Consv.	14.8	17.4	14.1				25.7	21.6
NSDAP	1.9	5	0.8				2.2	3.4
Peasant Bund	15.6	5.7	8.7				2.5	1.5
1924 (II) Turnout	70.6	69.5	64.1				70.4	72.8
Left	15.8	17.8	10.2				22.8	21.9
Z	51.9	52.4	68.6				46.8	52.2
Bourg-Consv.	16.7	21.9	16.5				26.4	21.6
NSDAP	1.3	1.3	0.4				0.9	0.5
Peasant Bund	14.2	4.1	3.2				1.7	2.2
1928 Turnout	59.7	60.5	53.7				61	61.7
Left	17.2	18.6	14.5				23.6	25
Z	52.7	50.1	64.4				45.6	49.3
Bourg-Consv.	20.1	21.5	17.5				27.7	18.6
NSDAP	1	2.8	0.6				3.4	0.7
Peasant Bund	8.5	3.4	2.5				—	0.4

Source: BSL(ed), Karlsruhe, *Statistische Mitteilungen über das Grosherzogtum Baden. XX (1903), XXXII (1905), XXIV (1907), Neue Folge Band V (1912), Neue Folge Band VII (1914); Die Wahlen in Baden zur verfassunggebenden badischen und deutschen Nationalsversammlung 1919; Wahlen zum Reichstag am. 6.6.1920, 4.5.1924. 7.12.1924, 20.5.1928.*

Note: (1924) - The year the district was dismantled and was annexed to the nearest district

E.V: Stichwahl

Left: SPD, USPD (1919–1920), KPD (from 1920)

Bourgeois-conservative: DNVP, DVP, DDP, Wirtschaftspartei

NSDAP: in 1924 - (1924 I) - *Deutsche Völkische Freiheitsbewegung,* (1924 II) - *Nationalsozialistische Freiheitsbewegung*

Peasant Bund - 1924 - *Badische Landbund.* 1928- *Deutsche Bauernbund / Christliche Nationale Bauernpartei*

Patterns of Political Behavior in the Black Forest, 1919–28

Although World War I and the revolution that came in its wake undoubtedly left their mark on the local economic infrastructure, the local patterns
of voting did not drastically change. Up until 1920 the leftist bloc (now the
Independent Social-Democratic Party of Germany—*USPD*) waxed
stronger, the *Zentrum* remained stable, and the liberal-bourgeois block
showed continuing signs of erosion. This latter bloc included such parties
as the German Democratic Party (*DDP*), the German People's Party
(*DVP*), the German Nationalist People's Party (*DNVP*), and, from 1924
on, parties of other interest groups as well. The strongholds of the bloc
were still in the towns of the southeastern Black Forest.

The *Zentrum* now formed part of the government coalition in Baden,
together with the bourgeois bloc and the *SPD,* but this did nothing to
make it more popular. Indeed, the opposite is the case, for from 1924
onward we are witness to a slow erosion in its popularity, which lasted
until 1928 (and not only in the Black Forest). Its participation in a government responsible for the implementation of the Versailles Treaty, the
administration of the postwar German economy, and the tribulations of
modernization that characterized Weimar German society all contributed
to the erosion of its strength.

Despite its central role in the Baden government, the *Zentrum* was
unable to make any real gains for the Church and wide sectors of the
Catholic public in the field of education and culture. The "School Crisis" that erupted in Baden in 1926–27 (and that also spread to the rest of
Germany) over the *Zentrum*'s demand to strengthen the religious content of the curriculum in mixed schools (*Simultanschulen*) ended in
defeat. The agreement (*Konkordat*) between Baden and the Church was
signed only in 1932, following a great deal of effort and the opposition
of its partners in the coalition, and long after similar agreements had
been reached in Prussia and Bavaria in the 1920s.[4] By the end of the
decade, the *Zentrum* propaganda leaned increasingly to the right. In the
elections to the Baden Landtag in 1929 the *Zentrum* called for "a strong
and free Baden in a strong and free Reich," a battle against bureaucracy
and poor administration, the cultivation of the German past over slav-
ish imitation of the modern American model, and most of all, battle
aginst the socialist state, the *SPD* and the "socialist catastrophe" (none
of which prevented the *Zentrum,* needless to say, from continuing its
coalition with the *SPD*). The Zentrum accompanied its propaganda
with slogans of a "folk community" (*Volksgemeinschaft*) and represented itself as a "people's party" (*Volkspartei*), a party that cut across
differences of class and special interests and offered the vision of a
united Germany, in contrast to the socialist option. Already at this

period *Zentrum* sympathizers were shouting "Germany, Awake!" in the manner of the region's fledgling Nazi Party.[5]

Two phenomena must be noticed if we are to understand the patterns of political behavior in the Black Forest and the Baar. First, from 1920 onward there was a considerable weakening of the *SPD,* following unusual gains in the previous years under the impact of the German defeat, the "revolution," and the desire for change. This attenuation was not due to any polarization toward the left: in the the villages of south Baden very few voters went over to the radical left. Where, then, did these hundreds of voters go? The answer lies in the patterns of election participation. Here, we are witness to a decline in voter turnout that continued until 1928, and that characterized the Weimar voting patterns even at the national level. These voting patterns can be attibuted to the apathy of the voters and to their sense of alienation from the democratic political system. In villages and towns in the southern Black Forest and the Baar, for example, the strength of the *SPD* completely disappeared in the first half of the 1920s, and many people ceased to vote altogether. Considering the relative stability of the *Zentrum*'s strength until 1928 and the stability of the bourgeois-liberal bloc, we can assume that the majority of those dropping out of the Weimar elections between the years 1920 to 1928–29 were voters of the former leftist bloc.[6] This assumption is strengthened by the fact that while the coalition's major parties did, to be sure, experience setbacks at the polls, these losses were balanced by the growing strength of the bourgeois-interest parties in the coalition or by the growing strength of the *DNVP.* In chapter 7 we will come across these "dropouts" of the Weimar electoral process once again, but this time in an entirely different political camp.

Another striking phenomenon in the Black Forest was the rise of a local protest party among the peasants of the southern Black Forest and the Baar. The region of the Wutach and Schwarzwald-Baar gave birth to the *Badischer Landbund* movement (*BLB*),[7] whose power bases lay in the region of Donaueschingen and in the south of the Neustadt district. The movement was part of a larger peasants' movement active across Baden, one that worked to strengthen the agricultural lobby. Yet even so, the backward and anticlerical character of the southern Black Forest helped create a peasants' movement different in character from the one in northern Baden. In using the term *peasants' movement* we seek to indicate the collective response of the peasants to their inferior social status. The response of the peasants in the Wutach and the Schwarzwald-Baar (whose social status was especially low) was highly radical, and the sweeping goals that it espoused went beyond the political arena into that of culture, society, and religion. Anticlericalism was highly conspicuous in the movement, perpetuating a trend that went back to the middle of the last century. The movement demanded "positive Christianity," the separation of

Church and politics, and respect for private property, and it stressed the role of the youth in Germany's future. It also rejected urban life and socialism. It is no surprise that the *Zentrum* regarded the movement as the heir of the National-Liberal Party, which had been so successful in the region prior to 1914, and that it sought, among its other goals, to revive the spirit of the *Kulturkampf*. Indeed, many members of the National-Liberal Party found their way to the new movement.

The movement's major propagandist in the region was Franz Merk, a peasant and former member of the National-Liberal Party who owned a tavern in Grafenhausen and who used demagogic means to incite the local peasants and craftsmen against the Church. For this purpose he made ample use of local legends and traditions, such as the rumor that the monastery of St. Blasien was a source of local slave labor. He lectured on the peasant revolt of 1525 and published stories and novels (*Heimatroman*) for peasants as a means of propaganda against the Church. Through this activity Merk earned the title of "Catholic enemy number one" in the Black Forest.[8] Working alongside him we find a local poet—a peasant by the name of Josef Albicker—a peasant tavern owner named Frank from Hüfingen, and a farm owner named Toberer from Glöttertal. By the beginning of the century they were National-Liberal supporters, and by 1928 they had found their way over to the Nazi Party!

In 1925 there came a rupture between the *BLB* chapters in the south and its center in north Baden. The rupture was precipitated by the desire of the northern leaders to ally themselves with the *DNVP* and to give the movement a more political nature. The leaders of the south, on the other hand, were more interested in socioeconomic aims. The movement fell apart and its leaders turned to parties such as the *Wirtschafts-Partei* (*WP*) and the *DNVP*, while others joined a new movement, the *Badische Bauern Partei* (*BBP*). Financial problems, desertion to the *Zentrum* camp, and illness among its leaders led to the decline of the new movement, and its leaders began searching for an alternative party willing to accept them. As stated, many of them were to find their way into the Nazi Party.

Summary

By the end of the twenties, there was a growing vacuum in the life of a number of social strata in the region. Workers and craftsmen had long refrained from supporting the parties of the left, and the drift to the right in the *Zentrum* and the hostility of the Church toward the workers prevented them from supporting that party either.[9] The new right-wing orientation of the *SPD*, which made a comeback in the Weimar coalition in 1928 and attempted to salvage the shreds of its prestige, even at the expense of the workers, increased disappointment with this alternative.

The fear of the communist left, which increased against the background of the harsh news filtering in from Soviet Russia of the situation resulting from the inauguration of the Five-Year Plan and collectivization, effectively ruled out the communist alternative.[10] The lower middle class, chiefly the peasants and craftmen employed on the farms in the southern part of the region, were dismayed by the lack of unity in the ranks of the *BLB.* Their anticlerical positions prevented them from supporting the *Zentrum,* and after their first disappointing brush with the *SPD* in 1919 they were no longer willing to gamble on this party. The total inactivity of the parties of the bourgeois bloc in the southern Black Forest and the Baar made them forgo this alternative as well. When the representatives of the bourgeois bloc appeared elsewhere in the region, it was an apathetic audience that they met.[11]

Toward the end of the 1920s, the political, economic, and social infrastructure of the Black Forest and the Baar collapsed. Together with long-standing causes, such as the region's isolation and the socioeconomic backwardness and anticlerical tendencies in the south, came factors that had their origin in the aftershocks of World War I (the region's borderland position): the collapse of local industry, the crisis in agriculture, the crisis in the local councils, and, finally, the political vacuum that set in during the middle of the twenties. The shaky socioeconomic infrastructure and the traditional inability of the Catholic Church to offer the region an attractive alternative also worked to the detriment of its inhabitants. The gloomy atmosphere of the region was deepened by events that made it even more difficult to maintain an ordered existence: a wave of terror on the roads and a series of suicides in the towns and villages. Road accidents—a long-standing problem in the region—increased owing to the poor repair of the roads, and another bane of local life, fire (due to the wooden buildings) struck frequently due to human frailty no less than the financial inability to maintain fire-fighting equipment. In Bonndorf there was a rash of begging, and the same region suffered from a higher incidence of cancer than it had ever known previously. A flu epidemic prevented numerous schools from opening and in the village of Bad-Petersal sixteen children died from compound whooping cough, measles, and scarlet fever.[12] On top of all this came the daily scare of the regional press, which warned of the threat menacing Germany in general, and the Catholic population in particular: the encroachment of the Bolshevik danger.

Part 2

"The Heralds of a New Age?"

A Social History of the Nazi Party in the
Black Forest

Part 2 of this book will discuss various social aspects of Nazi Party activity in the Black Forest region during the years 1928 through 1932. We shall not be concerned here with detailing the various stages in the growth of the Nazi Party during these years, nor shall we attempt to describe its development in terms of period. These aspects have been sufficiently explored in regional studies dealing with the rise of the Nazi Party. What we shall attempt to do, however, is to understand the startling success of the Nazi Party in a solidly Catholic region, and to describe the social basis of the party and the methods of organization of its supporters and local chapters. We shall also examine the propaganda that the party sought to disseminate throughout the region and the tactical strategies that it employed. Our analysis will take the following form: a brief historiographic survey of the issue (social profile, organization, propaganda); a discussion of the issue in relation to our findings vis-à-vis the Black Forest; and, finally, a regional comparison with areas characterized by similar socioreligious traits.

Behind this chapter lies one basic question: Will an analysis of the social basis, organization, and propaganda of the party help us to understand Nazi success in the region of the Black Forest?

The few studies that do discuss the Nazi Party in Baden almost completely ignore the rise of local party chapters (*Ortsgruppen*) and their activities in the Black Forest. Since the dizzying success of the party occurred in the central and northern part of the state, this was naturally the region most studied by the few scholars who did examine the subject, such as Johnpeter Grill and Ernst Bräunche.[1] These scholars are the only ones as yet to have investigated all phases of party development in Baden. They discuss the *völkisch* origins of the Nazi Party and its relations with different *völkisch* groups until 1924, as well as the background of major leaders and agitators such as the *Gauleiter* Robert Wagner, Walter Köhler, Albert Roth, and Karl Lenz. Similarly, they deal with the party's reorganization in 1925 and the manner in which it took over various *völkisch* groups. Other subjects that have come under their investigation are aspects of internal factionalism, organization and propaganda, the social profile of Nazi supporters, the groundwork for different election campaigns, and the results up to 1933, all from a historical-organizational perspective. It will not be our goal to describe this activity and we shall refer to it only when observing the relations between the organizational center of the Nazi Party in Baden (*Gauleitung*) and the local chapters in the Black Forest, or between the decisions of the center and their implementation at the periphery.

While the Nazis achieved conspicuous success in north and central Baden, this is not the only reason for scholarly focus on party activities in that area. This direction of research has also been dictated by the primary sources themselves. The sources mainly come from government ministers, mainly the Ministry of Interior and the political police. The sources naturally include material produced by the Nazi Party itself and incorporated in its archives in Baden, some of which we shall be revealing for the first time. These and other Nazi offices were located in the north Baden city of Karlsruhe, and the material that they produced and assembled constitutes the primary historiographical source for the Nazi Party in Baden. Most of this material relates more to the regions in which the party succeeded than those where it met with defeat.[2] The government ministers generally regarded the Catholic enclaves in Baden as undeveloped areas with only a marginal influence on Baden's internal politics. Moreover, it was only natural for the Ministry of the Interior and the police to focus their attention on regions whose political activity required special surveillance and supervision, and the Protestant regions in central and north Baden undoubtedly fell into this category more than the Catholic regions to the south.[3] Political activities, both before and after 1914, were centered in Karlsruhe, the seat of the local parliament (*Landtag*), and of course in cities of Baden such as Mannheim, Pforzheim, and Heidelberg, where the centers of the large political parties were located. Scholars who have dealt with the sociopolitical activity in Baden in general, and the Nazi Party in particular, have not only chosen to regard these areas as the major theaters of decision making and initiative, but they have also (and perhaps in consequence) fallen under the spell of the chief archives. These archives, as stated, contained material dealing largely with northen and central Baden.[4]

These studies are based on two primary sources: the reports of the Baden political police in 1926 through 1930 and the Nazi Party's chief newspaper, *Der Führer*. The reports of the state police (*Landespolizei*), which covered the activities of the extreme left and right, localized the activities in the north of the state. These reports provide an in-depth survey of Nazi Party activities and constitute an important archival source for post-1945 studies about the party. The image of the Nazi Party that emerges from these reports is that of a decidedly north-central Baden political body. To the extent that the southern part of the state received any mention, the focus was on the cities of Lörrach, Konstanz, and Freiburg.[5] Even *Der Führer* (Karlsruhe) reported primarily on party operations and chapters in the nearby areas. Financial considerations were probably uppermost in this; dispatching journalists and creating a communications network can of course be expensive. The fact that many scholars regard *Der Führer* as a major source of information is an important reason for the inability to pursue the party's development in south Baden. This is all the more true in view of the newspaper's dubious reliability.

CHAPTER 6

The Beginning of Nazi Party Activity in the Black Forest, 1928–29

A decade after the resurrection of the Nazi Party in Baden, its major organ, *Der Führer,* published a special issue surveying the history of the party in various regions of Baden. It had this to say about the Black Forest:

> Just before the Party's rise to power, the Black Forest was a problematic area. People of the region are conservative and difficult to persuade. But once won over they can be counted on without reservation. The work of publicizing National-Socialism there began recently. A small number of Party members toiled for years there but without success; the suspicious people of the Black Forest sent even regional speakers packing. In the Reichstag elections of 1928 we received only 82 votes; 36 alone came from the village of Schwanbach in which a Party member, the teacher Schuppel, operated. In addition, Comrade (*Parteigenosse;* hereafter Pg.) Merk from Grafenhausen also set out to win over the people of the Black Forest. The first meeting was held (as stated by Pg. Schuppel) in Gutach. The first Ortsgruppe was established in Triberg . . . Later on, *Ortsgruppen* in Schiltach and Wolfach were established . . . but when a stand is taken in the Black Forest it doesn't, after all, go to waste. Step by step we advanced. There were no defeats. In the end, the Black Forest came over to National Socialism.

Another article in that issue provides a retrospective view of earlier party activities in the town of Triberg:

> . . . there was already an *Ortsgruppe* by 1924. Its leader, Häringer, established the district of Wolfach-Villingen in the summer of 1928.

49

Activities increased. A first mass rally [was held] in April 1929. The first members . . . were also the organizers and founders of Ortsgruppen in the neighbouring towns . . . towards the end of the year 1929, there were 30 members in the local *Ortsgruppe* . . .[1]

Even if one disregards these figures and takes into account the propagandist intention of these words, both articles in effect describe widespread Nazi operations in the region by 1928 and not, as the first writer claims, just shortly before the party's rise to power.

Scattered evidence about Nazi Party activities in the region reveals that it existed even before 1925. Distinguishing between Nazi activity and those of other *völkisch* groups is not always easy during this period. For one thing, the Nazis often joined forces with different *völkisch* groups.[2] For another, the reports of police agents, journalists, and local officials did not always differentiate between the activities of the Nazis group and those of other *völkisch* groups. Both were termed National Socialist activities.[3] In addition to the brisk activities in north Baden there were also traces of Nazi activity in the town of St. Georgen in 1923 and in neighboring towns at the foothills of the Black Forest. During the 1924 inaugural meeting of the *Deutsche Partei* in Freiburg, members of the Nazi Party from the towns of Schopfheim, Lahr, and Zell.a.Rhein were also present. There is evidence that a number of residents from towns in the Black Forest enrolled in the Munich party chapter, though without becoming active. The evidence can be conflicting at times. A list published by *Der Führer* in 1933 names dozens of activists and party members from the pre-1925 period, but not one of them came from the Black Forest. Conversely, the list of those joining the Nazi Party in September through November 1923 includes a number of card-holding residents from towns such as St. Blasien, Villingen, and Neustadt. They belonged to the Munich chapter as their area did not have a sufficient number of party members to form an independent chapter of its own.[4]

There was also a thriving center of Nazi activity in the southern Black Forest, where the leading agitators in the region of Wiesental were Albert Schoni and Dr. Winter. These men held political meetings, led marches through the hills, and even got into brawls with communist groups. After the outlawing of the Nazi Party in Baden early in the summer of 1922, members of this group adopted such names as *Deutscher Manner* or *Leseverein*. We have no information concerning the establishment of Nazi chapters or operational cells in this region. At that period the activity was confined to single individuals and small groups.[5]

The establishment of the *Völkisch Bloc* in cooperation with the Nazis under the name of *Deutsche Partei* early in 1924 galvanized *völkisch* activity in the region. A large chapter took form in Freiburg;

another chapter probably existed in Neustadt as well.[6] The bloc disintegrated during the summer of that year and some of its members joined the National Socialist Freedom Party (*NSFP*), which stood for election to the Reichstag in December 1924. Despite the small number of votes that it carried in the Black Forest, the new Nazi Party was stronger than any other volkisch group. In a number of places it was even stronger than the *DNVP* (St. Blasien, 3.2 percent; Todtmoos, 3.7 percent; Menzenschwand, 14.83 percent).[7]

Der Führer claimed that a chapter of the Nazi Party was flourishing in the town of Triberg by 1924. This presumably, was a reference to the local *NSFP* chapter. However, this chapter disintegrated along with the few other chapters that may have existed in the region, and we have no evidence of Nazi Party activity in the Black Forest region until 1928. In the Landtag elections of October 1925 the Nazi Party—this time under its original name of *Nationalsozialistische Deutsche Arbeiter Partei* (*NSDAP*)—received the smallest number of votes in the districts of the Black Forest. Even in the few villages where the *NSFP* was relatively strong, the fledgling Nazi Party lost the little support that it had formerly held. Presidential elections were conducted that same year. The candidate of the *Völkisch Bloc* (to which the Nazi Party belonged), Erich Ludendorff, made little headway in Baden and the Black Forest. In the second round of elections the party transferred its support to Hindenburg, who made a respectable showing in the Catholic villages and towns of the Black Forest.[8] According to the reports of the Nazi Party center in Munich (*Reichsleitung*), local chapters of the Nazi Party were not yet active in the Black Forest region.[9] It is important to note that in those years a local chapter was established only when there was a minimum of fifteen party members. Six members were sufficient for creating a *Stützpunkt*.[10] Unfamiliarity with party regulations and propaganda caused the police to make indiscriminate use of the term *chapter,* mistakenly creating the impression of a Nazi Party with thriving activity and a booming membership.

Toward the end of 1927 a number of local agitators began to break ground for the idea of National Socialism in the Black Forest. Their operations centered around two geographical points. The first was in the central part of the region, in the district of Wolfach. The initiative came from party activists and chapters on the outskirts of the Black Forest, in the towns of Lahr and Offenburg.[11] It was here that Pg. Löffler became acquainted with Pg. Emmerich, a worker from Offenburg and a member of the Nazi Party. Under Emmerich's influence Löffler joined the party, thereby becoming the second member in the region of Kinzigtal. (The claim that Pg. Emmerich founded the chapter in Hausach must be treated with caution. During the Reichstag elections of May 1928, after the founding of the chapter, only eleven voters supported the party. Assuming that all eleven voters were party members, where had the other four disappeared to?) Pg. Löffler, for his part, was active in Haslach:

> There were many disappointments. The first activists met with social ostracism and isolation, but the belief in Hitler gave us the strength to persevere. The first meetings were in Fischerbach and Haslach. In the latter place, an Ortsgruppe was founded only in the summer of 1930. There were fifteen Party members in that town. By publicizing on posters, pamphlets and flyers, and also by word of mouth from one comrade to another, more and more members joined the Party but there were also deserters. A few members chose to leave the Party.[12]

This detailed portrayal of party activity in the region—one that is eminently paradigmatic—reveals local initiative without any intervention from Karlsruhe. By 1928 party chapters were founded in a few of the region's Protestant towns, partly by coalition with local völkisch groups.[13] But in the second focus of local Nazi activity, the peasant villages of Wutach and Schwarzwald-Baar in the southeastern Black Forest, the center in Karlsruhe can be seen to have taken the initiative. These areas constituted the power base of the *Badischer Landbund (BLB)*. For reasons that we have already noted in chapter 5, this organization disintegrated in the mid-1920s, and its activists in the Black Forest region began searching for a similar sociopolitical alternative. Few of them joined the Nazi Party in the early stages. Although Dr. Vogel, for example, who came from the village of Grafenhausen, joined the party in 1926,[14] Nazi activity for all intents and purposes existed in the region only from only 1928, with the arrival of the Nazi agitators Roth and Lenz. Leaders of the *BLB,* such as Leo Gut, Franz Merk, and Toberer then joined the Nazi Party. Party operations were centered around the towns of Bonndorf and Löffingen and until 1930 escaped the attention of the *Landespolizei,* whose reports make no mention of intensive Nazi activity in the region.[15]

The first chapter was established in April 1928 in Löffingen, following a meeting initiated by Albert Roth of Karlsruhe. The number of people in attendance varies between 250 and 400, depending on the source that is cited. Nazi leaflets were distributed to the crowd, and the speaker lashed out against the foreign policy of Gustav Stresemann. The initiative for establishing two additional chapters came from Leo Gut. And, indeed, shortly after the meeting in Löffingen meetings were held in Seppenhofen and Unadingen. According to *Der Führer,* local chapters were established there as well.[16] A well-attended meeting took place in Bonndorf on the eve of the Reichstag elections. Once again, the speaker came from outside the region, and his speech was largely devoted to an anti-Semitic tirade.[17] The few meetings held in the region took place a number of weeks before the

Reichstag elections. Even without too strenuous an effort the Nazi Party made considerable headway in the local peasant villages. These achievements went unnoticed by the party center in Karlsruhe and even by the historians of the Nazi Party in Baden[18] (see table 6 and our detailed discussion of the party electorate in the next chapter).

The question at this point concerns the intensive presence that the Nazi Party maintained in the region, just a few weeks before the elections. Did this presence account for the party's success? Operations of similar magnitude took place in the region of Kinzigtal-Wolfach and even in local Protestant towns and villages, but the results in these places were conspicuously poor. Moreover, towns visited by inflammatory leaders from Karlsruhe sometimes showed only modest gains in comparison to villages that had not seen such visitors. By contrast, the party was successful in villages where local agitators such as Leo Gut organized meetings. Interestingly enough, the Nazi Party achieved impressive results in the many villages that did not hold meetings at all (cf. Seppenhofen in table 6, chap. 7). The party's success, therefore, may very well have been related to something other than intensive Nazi activity. We should remember the socioeconomic conditions in the region of Wutach and Schwarzwald-Baar, which we examined in chapters 3 and 4. If we add this factor to the local *BLB*-connected activity or, more precisely, to the vacuum created by the dissolution of the *BLB,* there is reason to think that Nazi success was due more to the local conditions of a given location than to the intensivity, organization, and propaganda of the Nazi leaders. It is this point, together with the connection between local Nazi activity and the initiative of the party center in Karlsruhe, that will be at the center of our discussion. This problem preoccupies many scholars of Nazi activities, and it emerges in discussions about the nature of the liason between the center and the periphery, as well as in studies that attempt to examine the relative weight of pro-Nazi factors at the local level vis-à-vis factors at the national level, such as activities and instructions initiated by the party center in Munich, the Ministry of Propaganda, or key figures such as Hitler, Goebbels, and Strasser.[19]

Following the Reichstag elections in 1928, Nazi activities shifted into low gear throughout the region. Party speakers who visited the region of Wutach and Schwarzwald-Baar promised the peasants to return every three months, a lengthy absence indeed when compared with the frequency of the meetings attended by party activists in north and central Baden.[20] A turning point for Nazi activity in this part of the Black Forest occurred toward the end of 1928, when Franz Merk announced his membership of the Nazi Party. Merk was a member of the village council of Grafenhausen and one of the leaders of the *BLB;* his personal character we have already seen. His anti-Catholic, populistic leanings were streaked with socialist and anticapitalist traits. Merk, Gut, Toberer, and Albicker abandoned the *BLB,* charging it with internal corruption, factionalism, and a shifting political orientation toward the *DNVP.* The overtly anti-Catholic stand of the Nazi Party and its activities among the peasants served as a magnet for disenchanted members of the *BLB,* people who had drifted in and out of many other parties—such as the *Wirtschaftspartei* (*WP*), the *DNVP,* and even the *SPD*—before stopping at this political way station. Merk outlined his political manifesto at this time, demanding changes in the constitution and in the parliamentary system. He also attacked Stresemann and government policy toward the peasants, arguing that this should stand at the forefront of the government socioeconomic policy.[21]

Once Merk and other activists joined the region's Nazi propaganda machine, party-initiated meetings became more frequent. Most of the meetings featured speakers from outside the Black Forest region. In October 1928 *Gauleiter* Wagner appeared in Löffingen. Due to the small number of local sympathizers most of the participants at the meeting were brought in from distant Freiburg. It is interesting to compare the subject matter chosen by local speakers such as Merk and Albicker with that of professional party speakers such as Wagner, Roth, and Lenz. The latter figures made virulent anti-Semitic speeches (for which they were fined and even jailed), prompted to a great extent by their conception of volkisch ideology. Their speeches were filled with talk of Hitler (the policeman reporting the meeting jotted down "Hiller"), and with complaints about the corruption of the political system. Local speakers, on the other hand, emphasized the plight of the peasants and their importance to the National Socialistic state.[22] The frequent meetings in the region contributed to the establishment of a chapter in the town of Bonndorf. The thirty-nine members of this chapter included inhabitants of neighboring villages; some were agricultural laborers, others were peasants. The *Ortsgruppeleiter* (chapter leader) was Franz Steinhoff, a shoemaker who was branded in the town as a simpleton and ousted from the chapter in 1931.[23]

On the eve of the *Landtag* elections in October 1929, there was an increasing number of meetings in the region of Schwarzwald-Baar after a lapse of a year. Local agitators increasingly edged out speakers from outside.[24] Yet the number of people who attended the meetings was steadily dwindling. At a major meeting in Löffingen where both Merk and Toberer were present, only thirty-two people were in attendance, and a meeting in Merk's village of Grafenhausen attracted even fewer. The bulk of the party's effort was directed toward the northern regions of Baden. Popular party speakers, including Himmler and Gregor Strasser, appeared mainly in these regions. The party center in Munich dictated the meeting's central theme—the Young Plan—but the instructions from Munich and

Karlsruhe apparently failed to reach the districts of the Black Forest. There the party speakers were still feuding with the *Zentrum,* demanding a dictatorial state, and describing the work in store for the Nazi Party in the *Landtag.* Other topics were the evil effects of inflation, the culpability of the rich and the hardships of the peasants.

The Nazi success in these elections made them the fourth-largest party in Baden, with seven representatives in the *Landtag,* one of whom was Franz Merk. Yet despite this success, the Nazi propaganda machine— in both the local chapters and the party center—was found to be inefficient. It became evident that disorganization and financial chaos was rampant at all levels of the party. Most serious of all was the lack of coordination. There were crossed invitations for speakers from Munich and, most importantly, a failure to intensify the vituperations against the Young Plan as instructed by Munich. This was largely due to local factors; local speakers, for example, were more interested in tackling the immediate interests of the local public. Most important of all was the gap between the instructions from the center and their implementation by the chapters in the periphery.[25]

Let us, for example, take a closer look at a typical preelection Nazi meeting, one that took place in Bräunlingen, a small town in the region of Schwarzwald-Baar. On October 17, 1929, forty-five people, mainly adults, gathered to listen to Merk on the subject of "the plight of the German people: Who shall deliver them?" His words focused on the financial crisis, blaming the large industrialists and financial entrepreneurs for the runaway inflation. The verdict of the Nazi Party was that the *"Volksgenosse"* could only be of German blood; Jews could not qualify as citizens or officiate in public office. Merk also censured the *Zentrum* for urging religious freedom. Due to the apathy of the onlookers the meeting ended without a debate.[26]

A populist, anticapitalistic tone characterized many of the local party agitators who slowly edged out the activists from Karlsruhe in the organization of local meetings, although we shall see that this was only a temporary phenomenon. Merk, Gut, Albicker, and Vogel denounced the *Zentrum* and the Catholic Church in tones familiar since the days of the pre-1914 National-Liberal Party propaganda and the *BLB* activity in the early 1920s. Tirades against big business were generally interspersed with anti-Semitic slurs. The note most frequently sounded was an agrarian populism that centered on the problems of the local peasants, who were suffering from the galloping inflation like their fellow peasants throughout Germany. The economic crisis in agriculture only aggravated their plight.[27]

Unlike the Reichstag elections of May 1928, the frequency of Nazi meetings in the region did not significantly contribute to a rise in the electoral strength of the Nazi Party.[28] This was mainly due to the renewed activity of the Peasant Movement, the *BLB,* now under the name of the *Badische Bauernpartei.* Despite the frequency of meetings in Braunlingen the Nazi Party succeeded in winning only eleven new voters. Sharp declines were noted in the same villages that witnessed a revival of the chapters of the Peasant Movement in Reiselfingen, Seppenhofen, and Unadingen. Even in Löffingen, a former hub of Nazi activity, the Nazi Party suffered a sharp setback. This, however, was unrelated to the activities of the Peasant Movement, for here the local priest Andris was vigorously at work, luring new voters and even Nazi sympathizers back to the *Zentrum.* In the places where the Peasant Movement (*BBP*) was unsuccessful in revitalizing its chapters, the Nazis reaped victory. Their presence was particularly strong in the town of Grafenhausen, where their strength increased twenty percent at the cost of the *BBP.* Although the *BBP* had won as much as thirty percent of the vote in May 1928, it was now dwindling fast due to the efforts of native villagers Merk and Dr. Vogel.[29]

Additional focal points of Nazi activity in 1929 were the region of Wiesental and the industrial towns of the Black Forest. There in the Wiesental area of the southern Black Forest lay the grave of Albert Leo Schlageter, a Free Corps fighter executed by the French in the Ruhr district in 1923. Whether Schlageter was also a member of the party is not altogether clear. Born and buried in Schönau, in the center of Wiesental, Schlageter's grave became a rallying point for meetings of local nationalist groups, among them members of the Nazi Party. The different nationalist groups merged with the Nazi Party in the course of 1928. While the grave-centered activities served as a focus for Nazi Party operations at least up until 1930, they had no impact whatsoever on Schönau itself, where the party made very little headway. This was partly due to the local opposition against any extremist political activity that might hurt the thriving tourist industry, the town's economic basis. Not very far from Schonau, Nazi activity was flourishing in the town of Todtmoos. An active Nazi "chapter" in this town numbered eight members and supervised the local actions of the party. Todtmoos was also a resort town, but the vociferous opposition of local residents was unable to prevent Nazi activity. Nor could it prevent the electoral success of the *Völkisch* (in 1924) or that of the Nazis (from 1928 onward).[30]

Finally, the Nazi Party began to increase its strength among the workers in the region. Party chapters were set up in the industrial towns of Furtwangen and Triberg, and their propaganda campaign "left all rivals in the shade."[31] Here, too, the local activists developed propaganda tinged with anticapitalism together with propaganda of a strongly anti-Socialist-Bolshevist nature. There was nothing unusual about this combination in these towns. The Zentrum also conducted its campaign against the socialists with strong nationalist overtones. On the eve of the *Landtag* elections, the *Zentrum* called for a strong and free Baden in a strong and free Reich: ". . . out of love of the Reich, including German Austria, we want to send the Socialist-Liberal state straight to Hell . . ." The self-proclaimed goal of the *Zentrum* was to prevent socialist manipulation. In contrast to the socialists, the *Zentrum* represented itself as a Volkspartei that envisioned Germany as a "folk community" (*Volksgemeinschaft*) of the Germans.[32] Similar ideas could also be heard from local Nazi activists. The concept of a "folk community," however, was heard far more in the Catholic camp than in that of the Nazis. Yet anticapitalist populism had more appeal for the workers and craftsmen who were not organized in trade unions or *Vereine* in the region. Moreover, the *Zentrum* was part and parcel of the Weimar regime and also a political ally of the *SPD*. The populist, anticap-italistic propaganda of the Nazi Party earned it the epithet of "right-wing Bolshevism."[33] Competition now settled between the Nazi Party and the *Zentrum*. Public apathy toward the meetings of the rival parties was highly evident in towns such as Triberg and Furtwangen, especially among the bourgeois.[34]

Neither the government authorities in Karlsruhe nor the historians of the Nazi Party took any note of Nazi Party successes in these places. They were also impervious to the fact that Nazi success in small Catholic towns and villages was greater than in Protestant towns (cf. table 6, chap. 7). The Nazi Party in Schiltach won 6.3 percent of the votes in the elections to the Landtag; in Lehengericht, 1.6 percent; and in Gutach, 4.5 percent. These were all Protestant-majority towns in the region of Wolfach.[35]

The public referendum against the Young Plan, in which the Nazi Party was also involved, did not much affect the party chapters in the Black Forest. A number of meetings held in the villages of the Wutach revealed that residents were perceptibly weary of the Nazi Party. The policeman who reported Merk's speech in the local tavern of Münchingen mentioned that Merk looked tired and that the apathetic villagers came to drink rather than to hear a political speech. Perhaps another reason for the meeting's failure was the charge for the pamphlets issued by the chapter in Bonndorf. From here Merk moved on to a neighboring village, where his speech was greeted by resounding applause. He spoke in favor of mili-tarism and dictatorship, and he criticised parliamentism. He also outlined the work facing the Nazi Party in the Landtag. Once again he attacked the financial entrepreneurs and Jews, the representatives of international finance.[36]

Let us summarize our findings up to this point.

1. Intensity of party activity and party success were not necessarily related. Electoral success was more likely to derive from local

protest and discontent than from any sympathy for party activists or goals.

2. The operations of the Nazi Party were not yet characterized by organization, order, and originality in conveying the party's message.

3. Local activists increasingly edged out extraregional speakers in party meetings. The acquaintance with local aims and traditions contributed to the party's future success.

4. With the crystallization of a socialist, anticapitalistic propaganda, the populistic overtones at times clashed with points stressed by the party leadership.

5. There was still a gap between instructions from the centers of party propaganda in Munich and Karlsruhe and their implementation at the local level.

6. Apart from the *Zentrum* and the Nazi Party, there was no unusual political activity in the region to speak of.

CHAPTER 7

The Social Profile of the Nazi Party in the Black Forest

The Members

During the 1970s, studies dealing with the social basis of the Nazi Party were published with increasing frequency. Yet even before 1933 attempts were made to identify the socioeconomic class of party members.[1] These endeavors received a fresh impetus after 1945, reaching their peak with the increased use of social science methodology and computer technology in the study of history. Moreover, scholars were now being admitted to previously inaccessible archives of the relevant material.[2]

Sociological research has long been involved in examining the link between society and politics and the correlation between the different segments of the population and political parties; we need only mention Karl Marx and Max Weber as pioneering figures in this field. Scholars such as Raymond Aron (of France); Seymore Lipset, Reinhard Bendix, and, more recently, Richard Hamilton (all from the United States); and Karl Rohe and Jurgen Falter (of Germany) have dealt with the social foundation of politics, at times with a specific focus on Weimar Germany.[3] The scholar most closely identified with the examination of these subjects in the context of Nazism, however, is Michael Kater. Already in the early 1970s Kater dealt with the question of the social basis of Nazi Party members.[4] While his method of examining this question was accepted by many scholars, recent decades have seen it come increasingly under fire. Kater and other scholars employ the formulas of "social class" and "occupation," and the problematics in defining these concepts provides a ready-made weapon in the hands of their critics. Moreover, they claim enormous problems in correlating occupational groups to social class (especially the lower middle class) and in using the sources that provide the basis for making a social breakdown of the Nazi Party, namely, the dossiers of party center members for documentation in Berlin. Yet another problem derives from

59

the inability to correlate the data from population polls of 1925 and 1933 with the data transmitted by party members or found in the reports of Nazi Party activities. By virtue of these data, occupational categories other than those provided by the population census have to be considered. There is often a discrepancy between a party member's social self-image and his actual social class in reality. The lack of data vital for determining social status—family background, income, workplace, education—makes it harder to compile the social profile of the Nazi Party.[5]

Scholars dealing with the social profile of Nazi Party members ignore yet another important fact. The use of the term *party member* can be misleading, and its misapplication can considerably affect the assessments of research. Not every member of a Nazi Party chapter or person listed as such with the party and the local police force was in fact a bona fide member. Nor was every activist, speaker, or councilman who canvased for support on behalf of the party necessarily a member. Party membership was at times marked by a certain fluidity. Like many other parties, the Nazi Party was characterized by members and voters drifting in and out of its ranks, particularly in those regions where its support was not anchored in the local political culture. There were many cases in which party members left the local chapter or were expelled, even though they remained on the membership list of the Party Center in Munich and of the police and local authorities.[6] Hence, conclusions about the social basis of a specific Nazi chapter are valid only for a certain time span, and they relate to activists and sympathizers as well as to members (though obviously not to voters, about whom we shall soon have more to say). Due to these limitations, studies about the social basis of the Nazi Party must proceed warily, and the data provided in this chapter, accordingly, provide more of a cautious turn of the compass than any definitive conclusion.

Table 5 compares the social profile of 300 Nazi Party members in the Black Forest with the profile of Nazi members in Baden (compiled by the Nazi Bureau of Statistics) and with that of the members in rural areas throughout Germany (compiled by M. Kater).[7] An important fact emerges from these statistics. Workers and craftsmen constituted the predominant occupational group in the region's Nazi Party members and activists. Self-employed professionals (*Selbstständige,* which includes the *Handwerksmeister*) made up the party's second-largest group. Next came the peasants, merchants (mostly *Kaufmänner*), *Beamten* (civil servants, including teachers), and *Angestellten* (the lower ranks of the civil service).[8]

Thus we find that workers and craftsmen constituted the most significant bloc. The hardships endured by many members of this group drove them to seek out a sociopolitical party that would represent their economic interests. The image of the Nazi Party as a new socialist-populist party—at least until 1931—convinced many of these people that they stood to gain more from the Nazis than from any other party.[9] The switching of former *SPD* members and voters to the Nazi camp was a common phenomenon. Former *SPD* members Blasius Müssle and Karl Spiegelhalder accounted for their defection by noting their disillusionment with socialism. In their eyes, the policies of the *SPD* amounted to a betrayal of the workers. As Müssle announced, "Today I am struggling for Hitler, since the *SPD* can be seen to have abandoned the workers." In the town of Zell a.H. the local *Gewerbeverein* leaders left the *SPD* and crossed over to the other side of the body politic—the Nazis—as this, they claimed, would improve the conditions of workers and craftsmen. Some of the workers joined the party in their quest for a political address suited to their goals. For such people the Nazi Party was but another stop along the way. In the town of Schönwald, some of the *SPD* and *KPD* activists who were unconnected with the socialist trade unions defected to the Nazi Party. In the Baar region it was agricultural laborers who transferred their allegiance to the party, and in urban industrial areas it was, let us stress once again, craftsmen and skilled workers who constituted the dominant bloc in the composition of the local Nazi chapters.[10]

Together with the workers and craftsmen there was a relatively large presence of self-employed professionals and civil servants. This phenomenon was linked to an erosion in the position of the local Catholic bourgeoisie following the elections of September 1930 (see chap. 10), among other factors. In the November 1930 elections for the regional and district councils (*Kreis* and *Bezirksräte*) there was a highly visible presence of "sen-

TABLE 5.   **The Social Profile of the Nazi Party in the Black Forest (in comparison to other rural areas of Germany)**

Members	Unskilled Workers	Skilled Workers/ Craftsmen	Master Craftsmen, Self-employed, Academic- Nonacademic Professionals	Merchants	Lower and Intermediate Civil Servants	Peasants	Other
In the Black Forest[a] (N = 300)	11.6	40.2	17.8	7	8.7	13.2	
In Baden[b] (N = ?)		31		19	30	11.4	8.3
In Germany[c] (N = 1,125)	18.2	21.6	21.2	7.8	4.8	20.4	5.1 (Elite)

Source:
[a]See note 7.
[b]*Partei Statistik,* Bd. 1, (ed.) Der Reichsorganisationsleiter der NSDAP, München 1935, 246–48.
[c]Kater, *The Nazi Party,* 250 (Country Joiners).

sible bourgeois" (*Vernunftige Bürger*) in the Nazi Party lists of candidates to the *Bezirksräte*. Some of these candidates were not even party members.[11] In these prestigious lists the party nominated master craftsmen, peasants, government clerks, innkeepers, and small-scale manufacturers. Workers were hardly represented at all.[12] Many of these candidates were active on the local scene: *Vereine* leaders, small-scale businessmen and manufacturers, treasurers and secretaries of local councils. Some of them were former members of local right-wing bourgeois parties who moved over to the Nazi list of candidates. Some of them remained on the lists of bourgeois-interest parties (*WP*) until shortly after the election, when they abandoned them for the Nazi Party.[13] Among them we find members of the local Nazi leadership: heads of propaganda bureaus, treasurers, district leaders (*Kreis leiter*), and important chapter officials.

What was the social profile of a cross section of the local Nazi leadership? *Ortsgruppenleiter* were responsible for the deployment and activity of party members organized within the chapter. This was a small unit, albeit the one most active and important on the local level, at least until 1932 (see chap. 8 for a discussion of chapter activity). In contrast to the situation shown in table 5, self-employed professionals and master craftsmen made up the largest occupational group in the *Ortsgruppenleiter* of the region. This category included physicians, the owners of factories and businesses, and, as was said, the master-craftsmen. There were fewer workers here than among party members. Yet the group consisting of peasants maintains its relative size in both: the thirty *Ortsgruppenleiter* examined for this survey included three doctors (including two pharmacists) and one Protestant pastor from the town of Todtmoos.

Apart from the characteristic features of social class in the Black Forest, consideration should also be given to the age of party members, activists, and *Ortsgruppenleiter*. The year of birth of 300 party members and 12 *Ortsgruppenleiter* in the Black Forest usually falls between 1893 and 1899. If we take 1930 as the starting point for joining the party or engaging in activities on its behalf (especially after the elections of September 1930), most of the newcomers were in their thirties, some well into their late thirties. Their age was undoubtly higher than was required by the image that the party sought to project, of a youth movement answering to the expectations of the "lost generation" of the postwar years.[14] Even Nazi Party organizations with a relatively youthful social profile, such as the *SA* (*Sturmabteilung*), were characterized in the Black Forest by members of a relatively advanced age. (Groups of "Hitler Youth" did not operate in the region until 1932.) Until 1931, and especially in industrial towns, isolated *SA* units were manned by party members and activists largely past the age of thirty. Only from the year 1932 on, with an expanding circle of *SA* recruits from towns sunk in unemployment, did jobless Catholic youths find their way into the organization.[15] But the youthful image that the party was so eager to project and that undoubtedly contributed much to its success in various regions of Germany did not find expression in the Black Forest, at least not until 1932.[16] Most of the new recruits were male. Only in isolated cases did women join the Nazi Party, for the most part in 1932.[17]

The social profile of the Nazi Party in the Black Forest raises a number of questions. First, did the social representation of the party correspond to the support that it received? As we shall see, already by 1928 many peasant owners of small or middle-sized farms in the region of Neustadt and Donaueschingen voted for the Nazi Party. Their induction into the party ranks, however, did not proceed at a comparable rate. Yet this is nothing unusual. Pridham's study of Catholic Bavaria finds that although the peasants voted en masse for the Nazi Party, they were not yet prepared to become members, preferring agriculture to politics. Zofka mentions that although the peasants from the district of Günzburg in Bavarian Swabia joined the party, their allegiance was not absolute. Broszat notes that activists of the *Deutschnationaler Handlungsgehilfenverband* voted for the party but did not become members. Undoubtedly, many supporters avoided joining the Nazi ranks—especially during the economic depression—on account of the heavy demands of the Nazi Party, which required near-total devotion and financial sacrifice from its members. Kater also gives as an additional cause a fear of economic boycott, defamation suits, and court fines.[18] Many craftsmen and workers in the Black Forest region who were unable to engage any longer in their trade felt that they had "nothing to lose" and that Nazi Party activities would not be detrimental to their already grim economic condition. Since many of them were totally disconnected from the Catholic milieu, the threat of boycott and social ostracism could not provide an effective deterrent.[19]

Another question concerned the phenomenon of activists who openly supported the party but nevertheless refrained from becoming members. In a number of places agitators and sympathizers appeared on the rosters of the Nazi Party as candidates to the local council but their names were absent from the membership rolls of the local chapter. Needless to say, this had important implications for the local chapter and its relations with the regional and state party center, as well as the extent to which the center exercised control over the activists (see chap. 8). Furthermore, many activists seem to have regarded their support for a movement antithetical to political Catholicism as a legitimate step in the time-honored tradition of supporting the *BLB*. In other words, protest on account of a specific issue did not necessarily imply identification with the broader aims of a movement and its leaders.[20] In certain towns the phenomenon of non-party member sympathizers and activists was much in evidence. Only one of the eighteen party candidates attending the local meeting in Löffingen was actually a party member at the time of the local elections. Four people joined the party after the elections, four others after January 1933, and the remainder never joined the party at all. In the town of Haslach only five of the seventeen candidates to the local council were party members at election time. The rest joined after 1931.[21]

Another fact that had bearing on the social stratification of the Nazi Party was the ephemeral nature of party membership. Some of those joining the party left after a certain interval; others left only to rejoin at a later time. Of forty-eight chapter members in the town of Schonach in early 1932, ten were no longer members by the following year. Many peasants in the Schwarzwald-Baar region joined the party by 1929, only to abandon it in early 1932. One important recruiting ground for party members was located in the vicinity of Schluchsee, among the concentration of dam workers temporarily located there. Many of these workers came from outside the region, and not all of them returned after going back home for the long winter months. This had an impact on the local Nazi chapter. Upon completion of the dam in 1932 the workers left town altogether, and those who had become members in the party presumably left it as well. Some of these joined another party as one more stop along the road in search of a suitable political base. Thus, for example, the Nazi *Schwärzwalder Tagblatt* reports about fifteen Nazi activists who defected to the Communist Party. Some were unable to maintain the costly membership dues demanded by the Nazi Party, and some were even expelled, mainly for financial reasons.[22] Hence the discrepancy between the official party statistics of chapter members (amassed at the time of paying the first membership dues) and the reports of the local police and authorities (table 5). This discrepancy stems partly from the fact that not every party activist was also a member.

We find, therefore, that the social profile of Nazi Party members and activists in the Black Forest region contradicts the summation of official party statistics. It also runs counter to Grill's conclusions concerning the social basis of the party in Baden and those of Kater concerning the social basis throughout the entire Reich. Their results tend to emphasize the dominance of the lower middle class among members of the Nazi Party in Baden and the Reich as a whole.[23] However, our own conclusions should not be seen as wholly anomalous. Klaus Tenfelde claims that Catholic workers determined their political affiliation on the basis of economic and professional factors rather than religion. Scholars such as W. Brustein, Max Kele, and Detlev Mühlberger have been claiming for years that attention should be focused on the large number of workers in the ranks of the Nazi Party. Catholic areas in Germany also had a striking preponderance of workers among the local chapter members. Fröhlich and Broszat note this phenomenon in the region of Memmingen, as does Pridham in Bavarian Swabia. Gerhard Paul's study of the Saar region confirms this for the Catholic towns and villages where many Nazi Party members were workers and craftsmen, as does Franz Heyen's study of police reports from the region of Koblenz. On the other hand, in Catholic small towns such as Ettlingen in north Baden, most workers refused to join the party.[24] Of course it was the economic crisis that descended on these regions that is generally singled out as the major reason for poeple joining the Nazi Party. We shall be exploring other aspects of this problem:

1. Were those same workers and craftsmen part of the local Catholic milieu or did they perhaps view themselves as being outside of the organized Catholic infrastructure?[25]
2. Why did the solution of National Socialism appeal to so many of them? Why not the Catholic solution or that of the Socialists, both of which were disseminated by a sprawling network of social clubs and associations indigenous to the local milieu?
3. Why were the Catholic and Socialist social infrastructures powerless in preventing potential supporters from thronging to the Nazi Party?

Despite the methodological limitations outlined at the beginning of this chapter, we must stress that the results of our analysis are beyond doubt. Skilled workers and craftsmen clearly made up the dominant group in the region's Nazi Party chapters.

The Voters

Identifying the social basis of the voters is of the utmost importance, since, in the final account, it was they who gave the Nazi Party its ascendancy in the years 1930–32 and created the basis for Hitler's appointment to the chancellorship in January 1933. Since we are dealing with social groups, their pre-1933 political behavior may help us to understand the nature of the German political system and the affinity between social class and voting patterns. It may even, as many scholars contend, provide a better understanding of the pre-1914 sociopolitical system. The identification of the major social groups supporting the Nazi Party did in fact give a fresh impetus to studies that examined the different social classes before and after 1871, with the aim of spotting the factors that would demonstrate continuity in the political conduct of German voters until 1933.[26] The teleological approach was adopted by most scholars who dealt with this area of study (some for political reasons), and only in the last decade, after this approach came under stormy criticism, were attempts first made to defend the political and socioeconomic conduct of the social groups that supported the Nazis after 1929.[27]

One fundamental difficulty in studying the voters for the Nazi Party is the lack of the most essential personal data, given the absence of public opinion polls and interviews. Because of this, scholars have had recourse only to the election results published by the Reich Central Office of Statistics (*Statistik des Deutschen Reiches*) and, more relevant to our own purposes, by the *Badisches Statistisches Landesamt* in Baden. Along with local newspapers and publications, these will provide the main sources for our own study of the question.[28] We have also had access to information concerning the socioeconomic and religious nature of these regions, as well as to printed material published by different social groups on the issue of the National Socialist Party. These publications, however, are less than authoritative in their attitude toward the Nazi Party and can tell us very little about actual political conduct on election day itself.[29]

Until the early 1980s it was the lower middle class that was branded with the stigma of mass support for National Socialism, that was said to bear major responsibility for the Nazi success of 1928 through 1933. This school of thought, which reached large proportions in the 1960s, had its origins in the work of both German and non-German historians of the early 1930s and even of the years after 1945. Many of these scholars left Germany after 1933 and bequeathed their "lower middle class" theory to an entire generation of Anglo-American (mostly American) and German scholars. These scholars, for their part, laid the blame on the lower middle class with the help of research methods derived from social science, enlisting, as we said, the pre-1914 political conduct of this class to prove its post-1919 guilt. A veritable scholarly cult developed around the lower middle class (partly from a desire to "divert the flames" from the other classes). And all this was in order to discover why, in the final analysis, this was the social class to give such massive support to the Nazi Party.[30]

The "lower middle class" theory has increasingly come under fire in studies published during the past decade. New research methods together with revamped empirical research methods have enabled scholars such as T. Childers, J. Falter, and K. Rohe to refute the claims of traditional scholarship and to demonstrate, with a great measure of success, that the social basis of support for the Nazi Party during its years of success was far broader than was previously recognized. Hamilton emphasizes the support of the urban upper middle class for the Nazi Party. Childers focused attention on the *Rentnermittelstand,* the pensioners, and employed the phrase "Catchall Party" and even *"Volkspartei."* Like many other scholars, these researchers aim to depict the Nazi Party as the first "people's party" in the history of modern Germany, a party that to some extent drew its strength from all strata of society. Falter drew attention to the workers who supported the Nazi Party, mainly from 1932 (approximately forty percent of them); Rohe described nationalist elements among the Socialist and Catholic camps that supported the Nazi Party from 1930.[31]

The debate is not limited to the exchange between the advocates of the "lower middle class" theory and those who argue for a wider social basis. Other subjects of controversy center on the political origins of the Nazi supporters. Were the Nazi supporters disenchanted members of other parties, or were they people newly exercising the right to vote? This question raises other questions. Which parties supplied the "human ammunition" for the Nazi Party? Just who were the new voters: young voters freshly given the vote, or apathetic citizens who had participated only desultorily, if at all, in the elections of the Weimar republic?[32] There are questions of age and gender. What is the truth about the youthful image projected by the Nazi Party? Did German women, especially Protestant, throng to the party's support? What about the claim of Catholic historiography—and not just Catholic historiography—that the Catholic population remained steadfast against the Nazi Party prior to March 1933? All of these issues are the subject of historiographical debate.[33]

The results from the Reichstag and Landtag elections of 1929 through 1933 answer these questions only in part. The geographical and regional distribution of the voters did receive accurate expression in the election results, allowing us to determine the place of residence of most of them and, more generally, even their religious persuasion. Some local newspapers published election results precinct by precinct. Allowing for certain limitations, the social class or socioeconomic group dominating a given quarter can thus be linked to a specific candidate.[34] However, even with the help of these data it is difficult to construct a reliable picture of the social groups that supported the Nazi Party.

Most scholars base their studies on results related to official election returns (from the *Statistik des Deutschen Reiches*) giving data on election results of units with a population of 2,000 or more. (Baden and the state of Hessen are exceptional in this respect as their official statistical departments have published the election results of every community.) This is a major problem generally ignored by historians to date. It means we know little about the complexity of electoral configurations at the less-than-2,000 level (lumped inevitably together as "*Restbezirke*" returns in the *Statistik* and hence by most studies), where still in 1925, 35.6 percent of the population lived. We therefore know very little that is specific about the electoral behavior of approximately one-third of the electorate. Can we correct these misconceptions concealed in macro-level studies? A close examination of the *Restbezirke* election results brings us to conclusions

unlike those obtained when viewing the administrative district and localities with a population of more than 2,000. The election results of an electoral district were often largely determined by the vote from the urban
area closest by, in which a high percentage of the district inhabitants were
concentrated. But the urban vote tally did not always accord with that of
the surrounding rural settlements.

Accordingly, the overall results of an electoral or administrative district do not always reflect the real orientation of public opinion in all its
communities. We must further bear in mind that election results were
based on a socioeconomic and religious infrastructure that could vary
from one group of villages to another, and from town to town. The factors
determining the election results of a certain district must be analyzed and
compared with those in all its component communities. For our purposes,
penetration to the micro-level (2,000-inhabitant communities and less) is
essential, because the state of Baden was characterized by an intermingling
of Catholic and Protestant areas. Hence the viable unit for examining the
Catholic vote is that of the individual locality, and not the electoral or
administrative district. Obviously, however, comparative analysis depends
on the access to sufficient socioeconomic, cultural, and political data concerning these localities. This will also be our method in examining Catholic
support for the Nazi Party in the Black Forest.

Let us first survey the historiographical trends concerning the
Catholic vote for the Nazi Party. While the studies of Catholic voting patterns during the Weimar period stress the popularity of the *Zentrum,* they
also emphasize that it was not only the *Zentrum* or its sister party, the
Bavarian People Party (*BVP*), which won Catholic support. Already in the
1920s, Johannes Schauff indicated the trend that has been accepted by
contemporary scholarship at both the macro- and the micro-levels.[35]
Approximately half of the Catholic population voted for all shades of the
political spectrum during the Weimar period. Scholarly consensus with
regard to the electoral basis of the Nazi Party in Catholic areas is as follows: until March 1933, the percentage of those taking part in the Reichstag elections was smaller in Catholic than in Protestant regions. This fact
was more detrimental to the Nazi Party than to other parties in the
Catholic regions.[36] The larger the community the greater was the support
for the Nazis, and vice versa. A public of organized workers weakened the
party's chances to gain wide support, and this was the primary reason
behind its inability to win support in areas inhabited by Catholic workers,
especially in the Ruhr area. In agricultural regions, on the other hand,
which had a high concentration of workers and lower middle class citizens
such as craftsmen and petty merchants, the Nazi Party was able to win
wider support.[37] In the summer of 1930, the majority of party voters in
Catholic regions were new voters, and only a small proportion of them

were former voters for the *Zentrum* and the right-wing parties. However, from 1930 onward, workers who were disillusioned with the *Zentrum* also turned to the Nazi Party. As a rule, in those places where the Catholic milieu was sufficiently strong and historically rooted, the Nazi Party did not succeed in gaining local support. In places where the Catholic milieu had experienced difficulty in tightening its grip even back in the Second Reich,[38] the Nazi Party stood a better chance. As we have already seen in chapter 5, the Black Forest and the eastern Baar regions were areas in which the Catholic milieu had trouble consolidating its hold. Further on, we shall attempt to see if this can provide the explanation for the Nazi success at the polls.

The research of the state of Baden tends to overlook the electoral behavior in the Catholic regions of this state. The clear ascendancy of the Nazi Party in Baden's Protestant regions has served to overshadow its success in the Catholic regions, and scholars continue to abide by the thesis that Catholic Baden was almost unanimous in its opposition to the Nazi Party, at least until March 1933.[39] Our own study seeks to challenge this view, and by penetrating into the heart of the administrative district—into the towns and villages of which it was composed—we hope to show that Catholic support for the Nazi Party was substantially greater than previously thought.

Figure 1 and table 6 show the electoral source of the Nazi success in the localities of the Black Forest and the eastern Baar at the beginning of the 1930s and the sharp rise in the number of new voters. Figure 1 illustrates this clearly. In table 6 we see the increasing strength of the Nazi Party in eleven various localities, chiefly because of the increase in new voters. The *KPD* also grew in strength, while in most areas the *SPD* suffered a setback. There was also a setback in the bourgeois bloc, though it was moderate in most locations. In addition to the new voters in these districts, the voters for the bourgeois bloc and the former left also strayed into the Nazi Party, the second-largest party in these areas no less than in most towns of the region.

Let us recall our view, with regard to pre-1928 electoral patterns in the Black Forest, that many of the region's inhabitants refrained from voting at all from 1924 onward (see chap. 5). By linking this assumption to our conclusions from the tables shown above, it would seem that many voters for the Nazi Party in 1930 were citizens participating in elections after years of political dormancy, and not just young people newly given the right to vote. Thus, for example, in the region of Donaueschingen only 1,539 citizens received the right to vote between the years 1928 and 1930, while the number of new voters increased to 7,058 between May 1928 and the summer of 1930. In the region of Oberkirch only 207 citizens received the right to vote for the first time, whereas the number of voters increased

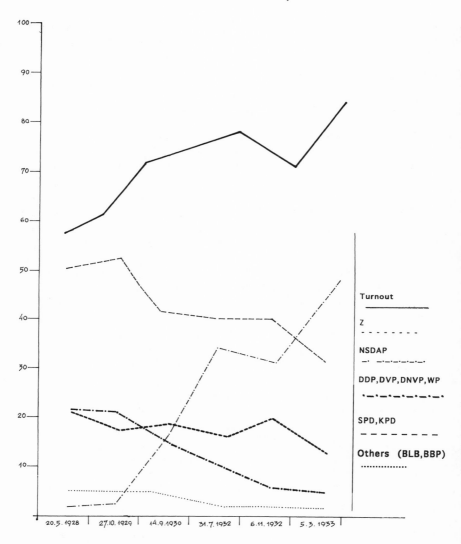

Fig. 1.   Reichstag and Landtag voting in Black Forest, 1928–33

by 2,973. In the former place the Nazi Party won some 3,000 votes in the summer of 1930, and 2,080 votes in the latter.

Moreover, there are reasons to suggest that many voters of the Nazi Party were former voters of the *SPD,* which they abandoned in 1920 or, at the very latest, in 1924 (see chap. 5). An important though not critical role was played by the tourists and holiday-makers lingering on in the region after the summer season, people of means despite the economic depression. These people were able to vote by means of special ballot slips (*Stimmschein*). The famous resort towns were in the Hochschwarzwald, most of which was situated in the region of Neustadt. Many of the vacationers cast their votes for the Nazi Party or, alternatively, for the bourgeois bloc (cf. table 6, the town of Hinterzarten).

The key to the Nazi success in the districts of the Black Forest in 1932 lies in a significant decrease in the strength of the bourgeois parties and in an additional rise in the number of new voters, though not to the extent of 1928–30. In 1932 four election rounds were held: two for the presidency and two for the Reichstag. During the spring months of the presidential campaign, the canvasing for new votes reached its culmination throughout the region. In the summer of 1932, at the time of the Reichstag elections, hundreds of new voters who had refrained from voting in the second round of presidential elections now cast their vote. The Nazi Party more than doubled its strength in the summer of 1932, largely with the help of voters from the bourgeois camp. Yet this was not the landslide of September 1930, in which the Nazis emerged as a key political entity. The election campaigns of 1932 consolidated the position of the Nazi Party but the giant breakthrough of two years before was not reenacted.

At the same time that the Nazi Party was gathering strength, the *KPD* also succeeded in significantly consolidating its position. Yet all this was overshadowed by the collapse of the bourgeois parties and those of the special interest groups, a process that apparently began as early as 1931 (see chap. 10). This collapse was the primary reason for the Nazi success.

The Nazi Party increased its strength from one campaign to the next. More votes were captured by the Nazis in the summer of 1932 than in the presidential elections of March and April. This may be highly significant. Did the term *National Socialism* have more appeal for new voters and the bourgeois bloc than the name of Hitler?

In November 1932 the final elections of the year were held for the Reichstag. Apart from the *KPD,* all of the parties suffered a setback, mostly because of a sharp decline in the number of voters. The percentage of voter participation fell even below the level of September 1930. The strength of the Nazi Party also declined somewhat, due to the apathy of their supporters as well as through desertion to the ranks of the *DNVP* and the *KPD.*

A detailed examination of electoral patterns in the towns and villages of the Black Forest brings to light additional factors in the success of the Nazi Party. In most localities, as we have already said, this success was due to the increased number of new voters (cf. table 6, Schonach, Triberg). Yet in a number of places a redrawing of the political map—especially in connection with the movement of former *Zentrum* voters (Oberbränd) and the

TABLE 6. Examples of Voting Patterns for the Nazi Party in the Black Forest, 1929–32 (in percentages)

The Community	Turnout	SPD/KPD		Bourgeois-Conservative		Z		NSDAP	
Bräunlingen									
L-27.10.1929	56.2	75	10.3	122	17.6	409	56.6	21	2.9
R-14.9.1930	74.9	145	15	82	8.4	433	44.9	262	27.1
G-15.11.1930	67.1	197	23.2	112	13.3	365	42.8	176	20.7
R-31.7.1923	83.2	129	11.3	43	3.6	511	45.3	434	38.4
Eisenbach									
L-27.10.1929	69.8	63	23.2	50	18.5	157	57.9	—	
R-14.9.193	87.9	57	16.8	44	13	141	41.9	88	26.1
R-31.7.1932	74.5	63	20.8	22	7.1	115	38	104	34.7
Furtwangen									
L-27.10.1929	73.2	639	25.8	524	21.2	1100	44.5	172	6.9
R-14.9.1930	85	572	20.9	373	13.5	1046	38.3	698	25.5
R-31.7.1932	74.5	618	21.2	106	3.4	1177	40.6	968	33.3
Hinterzarten									
L-27.10.1929	37.3	36	12.7	52	18.2	172	60.4	20	7
R-14.9.1930	71.5	65	8.4	213	27.7	205	26.4	244	31.8
G-15.11.1930	42.2	27	8.9	35	11.7	53	17.7	77	25.7
R-31.7.1932	81.9	163	12.8	277	21.8	313	24.7	491	38.8
Hüfingen									
L-27.10.1929	63.6	93	12.5	120	16.6	430	57.6	16	2.1
R-14.9.1930	77.7	162	17.4	119	11.1	422	45.5	172	18.5
G-15.11.1930	67	121	15.5	69	8.7	420	54	163	20.9
R-31.7.1932	76.4	124	12.7	42	4.2	446	46	342	35.3
Oberbränd									
L-27.10.1929	80.5	4	3.7	29	26.8	74	68.5	1	0.9
R-14.9.1930	85.6	4	3.7	18	15.8	64	56.6	26	23
G-15.11.1930	66.6	2	2.2	20	21.1	47	52.2	23	25.5
R-31.7.1932	75.6	2	2.7	5	4.5	51	46.7	47	43.1
Reiselfingen									
R-20.5.1928	64.4	—		4	2	100	52.6	49	25.7
L-27.10.1929	60.9	5	2.7	2	1	93	53.1	15	8.5
R-14.9.1930	66.2	—		—		99	51.5	63	32.8
R-31.7.1932	85.2	—		—		137	53.7	114	44.7
Schönwald									
L-27.10.1929	50.9	31	6.2	61	13.2	374	78.4	11	2.3
R-14.9.1930	88.1	53	4.3	76	9	452	54.1	226	27
G-15.11.1930	56.9	24	3.8	28	5.2	353	65.9	113	21.1
R-31.7.1932	72.4	52	5.2	133	13.4	426	43.6	336	36.4
Schonach									
L-27.10.1929	66.8	91	7.7	275	14.2	876	75.9	18	1.5
R-14.9.1930	84.4	105	6.9	131	8.5	991	64.9	277	18.3
G-15.11.1930	63.5	75	6.4	67	5.7	653	56.5	201	17.4
R-31.7.1932	86.9	98	5.6	99	4.9	894	52.7	589	34.7
Seppenhofen									
R-20.5.1928	33.3	3	4.4	5	7	18	26.4	37	54.4
L-27.10.1929	50.5	4	4	6	6	73	74.4	4	4
R-14.9.1930	58.2	5	4.1	11	9.1	60	50.8	39	32.5

TABLE 6.—*Continued*

The Community	Turnout	SPD/KPD		Bourgeois-Conservative		Z		NSDAP	
G-15.11.1930	54.2	5	4.2	39	33.5	47	40.5	23	19.8
R-31.7.1932	88.9	13	6.9	4	2.1	64	34.5	104	56.2
Triberg									
L-27.10.1929	72.7	542	26.2	464	22.5	844	40.9	211	10.2
R-14.9.1930	89.9	685	27	429	16.9	875	34.5	546	21.5
G-15.11.1930	70	487	24.5	406	20.5	635	32	451	22.7
R-31.7.1932	85	611	21.9	276	9.9	805	28.9	1087	39.1

Source: BSL (ed) - *Die Wahlen zum badischen Landtag am* 27.10.1929: *Die Wahlen zum Reichstag am* 14.9.1930, 31.7.1930; *Donaueschinger Tagblatt* 17.11.1930; *Echo vom Hochfirst* 17.11.1930; *Kinzigtäler Nachrichten* 18.11.1930; *Triberger Bote* 17.11.1930.

Note: L - Lantagswahlen, R - Reichstagswahlen, G - Gemeindewahlen, Bourgeois-Conservative—see table 4.

Dates are in day.month.year form.

bourgeois bloc (Wolfach) over to the Nazi Party—also contributed to Nazi consolidation. Together with these factors, let us recall that in villages in the southeastern Black Forest the Nazi Party made great strides as early as 1928, primarily because of the disintegration of the *BLB* (e.g., Seppenhofen, Reiselfingen). Furthermore, we have already mentioned the tendency of many tourists to support the Nazi Party in September 1930, a tendency that was even stronger in April and July 1932, months that constituted the peak of the local tourist season (e.g., Hinterzarten).

Conclusions

We shall sum up this discussion by comparing our results for the Black Forest with other regions in Baden and Germany. Voting patterns in the Black Forest differed from those in the state of Baden, where 58 percent of the population was Catholic. The average turnout in the Black Forest was slightly below the national average, except in the presidential runoff elections. The leftist bloc in the Black Forest districts was weak in relation to the national average and remained so throughout the period. The bourgeois bloc, and the *Zentrum* in particular, proved to be stronger than average in the region under consideration. When compared with Baden, the Nazi Party was perceptibly weak in the Black Forest until 1930, particularly in comparison with its gains in northern areas of Baden (in the Landtag election 7.0 percent compared to 2.7 percent). By 1930, however, the gap was steadily narrowing, and by March 1933 the region's support for the Nazi Party topped that of the national level (47.5 percent compared to

43.9 percent). In southern Baden, particularly in the area of Lake Constance, the Nazi Party made a poor showing in this campaign as well.

The Black Forest demonstrated voting patterns different from other Catholic areas in the state of Baden. By examining a number of the Catholic districts and cities in the states and provinces noted in table 7, we find that the phenomenon of Catholic support for the Nazi Party (above national average) was not restricted to the districts of the Black Forest, not in 1930 nor in July 1932.

Table 7 gives examples of places showing broad Catholic support for the Nazi Party as early as 1930. Particularly surprising is the party's success that year in the Catholic district of Koblenz and the cities of Weiden and Neumarkt. In the government districts (*Regierungsbezirk*) as a whole where these areas were situated, the Nazi Party made little headway. The district of Koblenz and the cities of Weiden and Neumarkt thus represent examples of a Nazi achievement that was not repeated. The success of the Nazi Party in the cities of Forchheim and Bamberg and the district of Staffelstein in the government district of upper Franconia is not surprising. These were Catholic enclaves in Protestant districts known for their enthusiastic support of the Nazi Party already in 1928. Presumably, the strong propaganda of the party in these districts did not fail to affect the Catholic localities. Some of these places—for social reasons of their own—avidly supported the Nazi Party in contrast to other, similar Catholic localities which still tended to favor the Catholic option of the Bavarian People's Party (*BVP*). In the city of Bamberg (unlike Forchheim) the Nazis still maintained their success in 1932. In contrast to the pockets of

TABLE 7.   Catholic Voting Patterns in Selected Catholic (more than 80 percent) Districts and Towns, 1930–32

District/town	Reg. Bez	1930	1932 (July)
Bamberg (town)	Upper Franconia	27.1	40.2
Conz	Trier	27.4	?
Forchheim (town)	Upper Franconia	21.9	27.2
Frankenstein (district)	Breslau	19.6	33.4
Füssen (district)	Swabia	21.8	33
Habelschwerdt (district)	Breslau	24.7	40
Koblenz (district)	Koblenz	18.5	23.5
Lindau (district)	Swabia	24.6	37.4
Markt Oberdorf (district)	Swabia	13.3	38.5
Neumarkt (district)	Oberpfalz	23.3	26.7
Sonthofen (district)	Swabia	21.2	41.4
Staffelstein (district)	Upper Franconia	18.6	36.1
Weiden (town)	Upper Pfalz	24	23.6

Source: Statistik des Deutschen Reiches, vol. 382, Die Wahlen zum Reichstag am 14.9.1930; vol. 434, Die Wahlen zum Reichstag am 31.7.1932, 6.11.1932, 5.3.1933.

Catholic support in upper Franconia, the support for the Nazis in the districts of Füssen, Lindau, Markt Oberdorf, Sonthofen, Frankenstein, and Habelschwerdt was not limited to these places alone but also extended to the government district in its entirety, waxing even stronger in 1932. In Bavarian Swabia the party succeeded in winning the support of the conservative peasants and the bourgeoisie of the Allgäu, a peripheral mountain region in southwestern Bavaria whose sociopolitical tradition and economic structure resembled those of the Black Forest and the Baar. (Both were border areas with anticlerical movements and were strongholds of the National Liberal Party before 1914.) The peripheral mountain regions of Lower Silesia (once the main stronghold of the *Zentrum*) likewise gave enthusiastic support to the Nazi Party, quite possibly against the background of political troubles that had been plaguing the area since the end of the war.[40]

Other Catholic areas in which the Nazis won above-average support were in the Rheingaukreis and Kreis Limburg (*Regierungsbezirk. Wiesbaden*), in many small towns and villages in the districts of Aachen, Bonn, Euskirchen, Koblenz, and Sank Goar in the Rhineland, in some villages in the district of Konstanz (Baden), in the districts of Ebermannstadt and Hammelburg in Upper Franconia, in *Regierungsbezirk* Oppeln (Upper Silesia), and in some localities in the government district of lower Bavaria. There, however, the support came mostly (although not exclusively) from the vacationers and tourists who streamed to the Bavarian Alpine regions in September 1930 and during the summer vacation of 1932. It was they who brought about the sweeping success of the Nazi Party in these Catholic areas.[41]

According to our findings, therefore, Catholic support for the Nazi Party ran broader and deeper than the scholarly consensus maintains. As we are unable to extend the geographical boundaries of our study to include other Catholic areas as well, we shall simply state the conclusion reached so far: namely, that even judging from our admittedly limited examples, voting patterns for the Nazi Party are strikingly unique in the Black Forest, at least until the end of the summer of 1932. Let us turn our attention to the organization of the Nazi chapters in the region and to patterns of Nazi activity, in the hope of gaining a better understanding for the reasons behind Nazi Party success.

CHAPTER 8

Organization

An election campaign "such as the world has never seen . . ."
—*J. Goebbels (1932)*

Many scholars believe that the organization of the Nazi Party contributed greatly to the success of its election campaigns in the years 1929 through 1933. According to this view, the building and organization of a party propaganda machine—dynamic, original, hard-hitting—was one of the chief preconditions for the creation of a fascist public sphere and for the success of the Nazi party. Through its help the Nazis managed to win over millions of citizens, to take control of influential social organizations, and to thus gain a crucial advantage over their rivals on the eve of their rise to power. This argument is accepted by many scholars who are concerned with the rise of the Nazi Party in general, and by those who focus more specifically on the party's sophisticated system of organization.[1]

This historiographical approach, which might be described as the "New Orthodoxy" school in the study of National Socialism[2] (the "Old Orthodoxy" school being that which pinned the Nazi success primarily on Hitler) has gained great popularity, and apart from a few dissenting voices, mostly from a regional perspective,[3] its findings have yet to be challenged by the rise of any new historiographic school.

We propose to examine these basic assumptions in the study of Nazi Party organization from a regional perspective. Our question is: Does the key to the tremendous success of the Nazi Party in the Black Forest region lie in its manner of local organization? Let us extend our question even further: What were the characteristics of party organization in general, and of its Black Forest chapters in particular? To what extent were these two levels coordinated? Was the organization of the party in the periphery indicative of the national level? Were the instructions of the party centers in Munich and Karlsruhe carried out to the letter in the chapters of the Black Forest?

First of all, how were the Nazi chapters in Germany organized? The local chapter constituted the heart of party activity. It was in the local chapter that members were registered, and from there that they went into action. The proof of membership of the Nazi Party was being a dues-paying member of one of its local chapters. Leaving the party or being expelled from its ranks meant leaving the local chapter. It was through the local chapter that the party disseminated its propaganda and reinforced the National Socialistic ideology of its members. Along with these functions, the chapter also served as a conduit for fund-raising and as a springboard for mobility within the party.[4] What was its place in the organizational hierarchy of the Nazi Party? The party's organizational system underwent a number of reforms. The first that was relevant to our own study was undertaken in 1928; the second during the summer of 1932. The moving force behind both of these reforms was Gregor Strasser. After learning of the election results of May 1928, it was decided to initiate broad changes in the organization of party propaganda. The most striking change, one that has been much studied in recent years, was the abandonment of an urban socialism line in favor of a right-wing nationalist form of propaganda. This new line of propaganda received particular expression in socioeconomic issues and in a focus on rural areas, precisely those regions where the party gained such sweeping victories. These victories occurred even in places that had not been visited by party propagandists (we witnessed a similar phenomenon in the regions of Wutach and Schwarzwald-Baar). It was due to these and other reasons that Strasser decided to revamp the party's organizational structure. From 1929 onward, the party hierarchy was organized on three levels: (1) the national leadership (*Reichsleitung*); (2) the region (*Gau*); (3) the chapter (*Ortsgruppe*). The chapter was placed under the regional authority, which in turn was subordinate to the National Leadership. Party strategy, instructions, and initiatives went out from the national leadership, first to the *Gau* and from there to the local chapter. The chapter lost a measure of its former autonomy. The treasurers of the chapters and regions were given a special responsibility and were answerable to the regional leader (*Gauleiter*) and also to the national leadership (*Reichsleitung*). Decision-making policy was conducted as follows: the national leadership was responsible for the administrative decisions, and the *Gauleiter,* who was answerable to Hitler, forwarded these decisions to the regions under his command. The chapters were left to carry out the instructions of the center and the *Gauleiter.*

Despite the reform of 1928, the chapter continued up until 1931 to be relatively independent of the *Gauleiter.* Members of the local chapter were not always involved in party activities, and at times the chapter leader made political decisions of his own. The admission of a new member gave the chapter leader an opportunity for asserting his authority, as he could single-handedly blackball any candidate. But from 1931 onward the decision lay solely in the hands of the *Gauleitung*. The supervision of the chapters was accomplished through the creation of an administrative body known as the district, which mediated between the chapter and the region, as well as through new party orders with instructions for the chapters and outposts (*Stützpunkte*).

So by 1931 all traces of chapter autonomy had disappeared. From then on, the *Gauleiter* was responsible for appointment of chapter leaders. The leader of a local chapter was subordinated directly to the district leader (*Bezirksleiter*).[5]

As long as Strasser stood at the head of the party's organization bureau, supervising even Himmler (the chief of the propaganda bureau), propaganda and organization were combined in Nazi activities. Once Goebbels became chief of the propaganda bureau (*Reichspropagandaleitung*), and, from 1930 on, responsible directly to Hitler, this aspect of Nazi activity was reinforced and the organizational aspect pushed to the side. Though organizational changes were being made at the level of the *Gau* and the local chapters, the chief organization bureau (*Reichsleitung*) was shunted aside. It was Goebbels's propaganda strategy that now set the tone. However, in the summer of 1932, following Goebbels's failures in the presidential campaigns, Strasser regained prominence and announced a broad reform of the organization of the party. As this went into effect only toward the end of the year, it has no bearing on our own interests. It is enough to note that Strasser tightened the supervision over the organization of the party, which had slackened considerably since the spring of 1932. His goals were both political and organizational. The organization of the party was planned so that it could participate in the government coalition without being concerned about its identity and image. Strasser's aim was to turn the party into a microcosm of the German state and society, so that gaining control of the nation would be all the easier when the time came. Changes in personnel and organization were made, culminating in the creation of departments (*Reichsinspektion, Landesinspektion*) to mediate between the regional level and the top leadership and in a stepped-up supervision over the various party organizations.[6] This broad reform undoubtedly testifies to the fact that not everything was running smoothly in the Nazi Party machine, and that the electoral successes of 1932 were accompanied by a certain grinding of the wheels even at the lowest levels.

The necessity for a centralized party organization, streamlined and efficient, was recognized by contemporaries.[7] The "New Orthodox" school, which dealt with the Nazi rise to power, also recognized its importance. The general attack on the "New Orthodox" treatment of the Second Reich[8] did not ignore its treatment of the Third Reich either. The criticism leveled against this school, where the organization of the Nazi Party was concerned, was primarily based on regional studies that questioned the centrist approach and focused instead on the limited ability of the leadership to enforce its instructions on the regions and chapters. William Sheridan Allen took up this position back in the 1960s.[9] Richard Hamilton made the idea of the autonomy of the chapters a central thesis of his writings. Mühlberger claimed that this autonomy existed only until 1930, while Zofka asserted that the chapter enjoyed a great measure of autonomy almost throughout its entire existence.[10] Richard Bessel stretches this thesis to its extreme, claiming that alongside the party's propaganda failure (which we will examine in the next chapter), the primary function of the local chapter was to raise money, and that its activity sprang more from a desire to preserve its existence than from any desire to spread Nazi propaganda.[11]

The studies of these and other scholars tend to be critical of traditional approaches to such matters as the manner in which party activity was funded, the activity of the Nazi press, the administration of the local chapters, and the activities of ancillary Nazi organizations. Most of these studies focus on the area of their immediate interest, and they tend not to extend their analysis to the Nazi chapters elsewhere in Germany. This can have a major effect on their conclusions about regional and chapter autonomy, a point to which we shall return. New historiographical approaches that differ from those of the previously mentioned scholars often fall back on the old theory about the supremacy of the national leadership and propaganda bureau, only with the help of new methods and the use of new sources. Thomas Childers and Ian Kershaw are the leading exponents of this school.[12]

In conclusion let us mention a historiographical approach that has won increasing support in recent decades. According to this approach, the region and society in which the Nazi Party operated was of greater importance than anything the party did by way of activity and organization. The disintegration of the local infrastructure and regional factors and traditions were crucial to the organization and activity of the Nazi Party; and, among other factors that must be considered, the way that the party managed to gain control of the local infrastructure must also be taken into account. This approach combines a study of daily life (*Alltagsgeschichte*) with the major trends in German historiography[13] and takes the regionalist method of Nazi research out of its ghetto once and for all.

Our own approach at this stage corresponds to that of the regionalist school, which opposes the "New Orthodox" school in the research of Nazi organization and activity. Our analysis will focus on the following elements in local chapter activities:

1. Establishment, activity, and leadership
2. The question of centralism—the liaison with the *Reichsleitung* and the *Gauleitung*
3. The financing of chapter activity
4. The chapter's relations with the leadership of the local notables (*Honorationen*)
5. The local Nazi press
6. The *SA*

The Establishment, Activity, and Leadership

How was a chapter of the Nazi Party established? We have already noted a number of examples when describing party activities in the region previous to 1929. In the case of Löffingen, Albert Roth of Karlsruhe arrived in the town, recruited a number of people into the party, and appointed Pg. Ernest Fritsche to serve as the "chapter" leader. This is an example of outside initiative in founding a chapter of the Nazi Party. At that period, the establishment of a chapter required a minimum of fifteen people,[14] a condition that could not be met in Löffingen due to the small number of those joining the party. In nearby Bonndorf, once again through outside initiative, a chapter in the full sense of the word was founded, this time with thirty-nine members. The establishment of this chapter came in the wake of intensive activity by Nazi speakers visiting the region. The large number of meetings sparked interest in the party and resulted in a willingness to join it. The ground for Nazi activities in the region had already been prepared by the activity of the *BLB* and its activists, some of whom joined the ranks of the Nazi Party. Once a chapter was established it was expected to organize meetings that would in turn generate new chapters in the region of the "parent chapter." The Bonndorf chapter, for example, initiated numerous meetings in the peasant villages, thereby laying the groundwork for additional chapters, its primary task. The most common sign of chapter activity in the Black Forest was a propaganda meeting, and it centered primarily around the organization and attendance of other such meetings, whose aim was to extend the party's activity beyond the "parent chapter" and to recruit new members.[15]

A Nazi chapter could also be established in the manner adopted by Pg. Löffler, Emmerich, and their associates in the region of Fischerbach-Haslach. This pattern took the form of independent activity throughout the villages of the region, the conveyance of information by word of mouth, the distribution of propaganda pamphlets, and persuasion of the local residents. The organizational factor was negligible here. Improvisation and spontaneity were the keynotes of this form of chapter building, which explains the inability of the party center at Karlsruhe to supervise the activity of those who identified themselves with the Nazi Party. In Schonach, for example, a group of activists interested in joining the party took the initiative of contacting the center in Karlsruhe (*Gauleitung*).[16] The groundwork had been laid without the center's knowledge, and once the group was ready to formalize its activities it turned to the proper organizational authorities, whose first step was to demand money. As we shall presently see in greater detail, it was the financial obligation that supplied the center with its main weapon for enforcing its authority on such independent initiatives from below.

We must point out that our use of the term *chapter* differs from the formal definition of the party regulations. The local policeman who reported on party activity was totally unaware that party regulations stipulated a minimum of fifteen members in order to establish a chapter.[17] At times party activists reported the establishment of a chapter for propaganda reasons and from a desire to create an aura of success. Moreover, there was a discrepancy between the formal Nazi announcements (especially in the party press) regarding the founding of local chapters and what actually took place in reality. Such was the case in Hüfingen. There the chapter was founded a year after being officially announced in the pages of *Der Führer,* while the chapter founded in Hinterzarten was closed down only a few months after opening.[18] This last example was characteristic of chapters throughout the region. A chapter established with great fanfare might indeed launch its activities, only to have it gradually dwindle owing to a lack of interest, funding, or guidance. Sometimes the chapter was closed down by the center in Karlsruhe, mainly for the failure to meet its financial commitments.[19] While this point will be examined in greater detail, our immediate conclusion is that Nazi Party chapters sometimes had a temporary character and that ascribing the party's success to them does not always correspond to the reality.

The purpose of the chapter, according to the official sources in the Nazi Party, was to disseminate party propaganda and to recruit sympathizers and new members.[20] However, as we have already seen, it was precisely in those places without local chapters that the party had most success. The work of a local chapter did not have much impact on the extent of the party's success in a given location. We have already noted that in the region of Wutach and Schwarzwald-Baar the electoral successes of the Nazi Party were not directly proportionate to the number of chapters or to the intensity of party activities in the area.[21] While the party met with great success in Eisenbach and Hüfingen, a chapter was established there only in 1931.[22] We find the opposite phenomenon in Donaueschingen. There a chapter was founded as early as March 1930, but its local progress was exceptionally poor up until 1931. In Neustadt the party tried to establish a chapter by holding a series of meetings over the course of 1931. This, however, was to no avail, and only in December of that year did the party manage to recruit fifteen of the local residents into its ranks. In the district of Oberkirch the party's first chapter was established only a few weeks prior to its landslide in the Reichstag elections of September 1930.[23] On the other hand, there were long-established and successful chapters in the towns of Bonndorf, Triberg, and Furtwangen.

The question is, to what extent did a chapter's work contribute to the party's success in the various election campaigns? In Triberg the local press noted as early as 1929 that the local Nazi activity greatly overshadowed the activity of the other parties. This was also the case in Furtwangen, where the local chapter was extremely active, especially during the summer season, in organizing meetings and group outings.[24] But the picture would be less than complete were we to ignore the fact that *Gauleiter* Wagner closed down the chapter in Löffingen due to mismanagement just a few months prior to the party's success there in the Reichstag elections of 1930. In Löffingen we even find a large number of party sympathizers who were unwilling to become party members.[25] In Bonndorf the chapter ran into administrative difficulties following the mismanagement of chapter leader Steinhoff, who was ultimately forced to resign. None of this, however, did anything to hurt the party's electoral success there from 1928 onward. In Seppenhofen and Hinterzarten the party was unable to obtain a tavern for its meetings and was forced to hold them out of town.[26] The financial troubles of the Seppenhofen chapter almost totally paralyzed its activities, and the *Deutscher Abend* (German evening) thought up by its organizers was not for the sake of attracting sympathizers and circulating propaganda, but for raising money and extricating itself from the financial morass. We even find the chapter leader requesting a speaker "who wouldn't demand much money,"[27] without being excessively concerned about the speaker's oratorical talents. The intensive activity of the Nazi Party in the Black Forest did not contribute to the establishment of many chapters in the region. Until August 1932 the party succeeded in founding only twelve chapters in the forty-two localities of the Neustadt district. Even so, the party made a respectable showing in most of these places in the Reichstag elections of July 1932.[28]

Chapter activity was largely confined to the organization of propaganda meetings. The marches, outings, and paramilitary drills that typified the propaganda activity of the party elsewhere in Germany did not characterize the activity in the Black Forest. Nor were open-air gatherings held, if only because of the weather conditions, thus making it difficult to hold large-scale rallies. Confrontations with political opponents were also a rare occurence in the region. This was partly due to the absence of violent political opposition (there were few Communist Party chapters in the region), but mostly because of the tacit agreement between the parties concerned that political disturbances would scare away tourists and make economic conditions even worse.[29] The only thing the local chapters could do was to concentrate on the organization of meetings in local taverns (*Lokal, Gastwirtschaft*). The method of organizing and conducting the meetings was dictated by Wagner himself: "First of all, the speaker must be invited in writing . . . the meeting hall must be rented through a written contract . . . the advertisement for the meeting must be posted on the bulletin board . . . There must be announcement in newspapers and propaganda trucks . . ." In the villages an announcement in the local paper and leaflets would suffice. Every meeting was to be geared to a specific topic and the meeting hall decked out with the emblems of National Socialism. Before the meeting, Nazi literature, journals, and pictures were to be on sale. The meeting was to begin with *"Heil Hitler"* and the intermissions used for selling party literature and recruiting new members. Following the intermission there should be a discussion with a speaker from each party, so as to prevent any kind of Marxist demonstration of force. Opponents of the party were not to be allowed to express their views. The meeting was to be brought to an end by singing *"Horst Wessel Lied"* and another *"Heil Hitler."*[30]

Just how far the *Gauleiter*'s instructions were carried out in the Black Forest we will examine at a later point. For the time being, let us focus on the actual ability of the local chapters to put these instructions into effect. The main problem facing the chapter leaders involved the renting of a tavern, due to the reluctance of many tavern keepers to rent their premises to the party. The chapters were advised by the center to join forces with various social *Vereine* in order to gain the use of a tavern[31] (see chap. 10). In reality, however, even in those towns where the party was strong at the polls, the local chapters faced problems in obtaining a meeting place for their gatherings.[32] Generally speaking, the party would come to an agreement with a tavern keeper for an extended length of time. The tavern keeper was usually not a member of the party and, at times, not even a sympathizer. The relationship was purely financial: the speakers received a place to make their speeches, and the listeners purchased beer. In some places the Nazi Party, like other parties, became identified with one specific tavern and vice versa. In Lenzkirch and in Grafenhausen the party used taverns owned by Erwin Weishaar and Franz Merk.[33] The more successful the party grew, the easier it became to rent taverns.

In contrast to the stereotyped view of Nazi activity, the meetings in the Black Forest took place primarily during the preelection season. This was due to several factors. First of all, the region was neglected by the center in Karlsruhe. In the eyes of key party activists and the more desirable speakers (and, as we have seen, even in the eyes of the historians of the

Nazi Party in Baden), the Black Forest was a region of little importance. It was one, moreover, in which the *Zentrum* reigned supreme. The sheer difficulties of transportation due to the difficult terrain contributed to the inability to send speakers and activists there with any regularity.[34] For these and other reasons, supervision of the party chapters in the Black Forest remained lax, at least until 1932. Propaganda campaigns of the type undertaken by the party throughout Germany, in which activists and speakers swept over a given area and made several speeches a day (*Propaganda Konzentration*) during a period of one to two weeks, were held only infrequently in the Black Forest.[35] Even famous speakers stayed away from the region.[36] Misorganization of the party chapters also made it difficult to invite speakers and, most importantly, to finance their appearances. Hence a heavy burden was shouldered by the few local activists and speakers. Their lack of experience and poor liaison with the regional center found expression in the organization of propaganda meetings. Thus, for example, in Hinterzarten and Schönwald the Nazis held propaganda meetings across from the local church, timing them to begin just as the worshippers were leaving the Sunday morning service.[37] While the chapter leaders may have hoped to reach a larger audience in this fashion, the choice of setting was patently misguided. After sitting through a religious sermon it is not clear how eager the people would be to lend an ear to a speech liable to rouse local passions, especially on Sunday, the day of rest. Would not the party activists have been better advised to hold their meeting in the local tavern, where they could generally count on finding the men who preferred their beer to the priest's sermon?

In the very period that the scholars portray as the height of the Nazi propaganda campaign—the election campaigns during the spring and summer of 1932—the party recorded failures in the organization of meetings in a number of places throughout the Black Forest, despite the expansion of its organization and its electoral successes. In Holzlebruck the meeting of the party proved a failure. Only sixty people attended, and of these, a good half of them made a quick exit. The rest were more intent on drinking and playing cards. People wandered in and out during the speech itself. The speaker stumbled over his words in his hurry to catch the last train to Freiburg, and at the end of his speech got up and left. "The Nazi Party left a bad impression there."[38] In Lenzkirch the speaker found himself "preaching to the converted," the members of the Stalhelm, and in Neustadt the speaker had to show patience for a considerable period of time while waiting for thirty-six people to gather, through whose means the meeting could be convened. A few weeks later, the meeting hall in Neustadt remained empty once again, filling up only an hour later with the arrival of fifty people after the close of the nearby Communist Party meeting. In Schonach the chapter leader complained about the boring speakers who were being sent out just before the elections.[39] Delayed beginnings, lack of coordination, and duplicated announcements were characteristic of many of these meetings. Even the weather seemed to be opposed to the Nazi Party, and many meetings were canceled because of snowstorms.[40] However, there were also successful meetings. In Kappel the party did not succeed in mustering up a sufficient number of people to begin a meeting in 1931, but a year later the tavern was full to bursting with the sound of *"Horst Wessel Lied."* This was also the case in Schönau, St. Blasien, and other places where the party had been unable to hold meetings until 1932.[41]

In 1932, a growing number of chapters were established throughout the villages and small towns. The initiative was usually taken by a well-established chapter, which also supervised the activity of the fledgling chapter over a certain period of time.[42] The opening ceremony did not differ much from the ceremony of four years earlier, apart from the now-popular greeting of *"Heil Hitler."* The members would assemble in the local tavern, and the chairman of the new chapter made a speech, as did the Gauleiter and, at times, even an activist from Karlsruhe. In addition, an SA unit would be stationed next to the chapter. The ceremony was brought to a close by singing the *"Horst Wessel Lied."* Such meetings were not without an element of the grotesque. In Gutach the speaker suffered a heart attack while making his speech, while the popular Nazi speaker, Dreher, was unable to reach a meeting in the region due to a nervous breakdown.[43] What was seen as a dignified ceremony in the eyes of the party members became the butt of jokes for the local residents, a source of ridicule over beer and cards. We should mention, by the way, that the drinking of beer was standard procedure during political meetings, and this could work both ways for (or against) the meeting's success. After the meeting the party representatives would join the onlookers in a round of beer, thereby breaking down the political barriers.[44] In effect, the activity of the local Nazi chapter could be described to a great extent as *Verein* activity. We shall take a closer look at this resemblance in chapter 10.

To what extent did the personality of the chapter leader contribute to the chapter's efficiency? Despite the picture generally given by scholars,[45] the chapter leaders in the Black Forest region were usually not well-known local figures. Indeed the local notables (as we shall see) seldom became members of the party at all. We have already reviewed the occupations of the chapter leaders in the beginning of this chapter. Of the chapter leaders who practiced a liberal profession, few enjoyed local prestige or the ability to canvas support for the party. Erwin Weishaar of Lenzkirch served as a member of the local council and was the owner of a tavern, yet the party made little headway there until 1932. Before that he had been unable to attract more than fifteen members to the party ranks. Dr. Rohde of

Vöhrenbach was the town pharmacist, but he left toward the end of 1930. The priest Altenstein was a popular figure in the small Protestant congregation of Todtmoos, but it was from the Catholic circles and tourists of this town that the party drew its considerable support.[46] All these figures were also chapter leaders of respected local standing, but this did not help the Nazi Party to entrench itself any more firmly. A slightly different example is that of Benedict Kuner of Schonach, the leader of the local chapter and a popular figure in the town. It was only toward the close of 1931, however, following the pressure of his fellow party members, that he was appointed chapter leader. Until 1929 he represented the *Zentrum* in the local council, and in that year announced his transfer to the Nazi camp, a step that surely did nothing to increase his popularity among broader circles in town.[47] While a number of chapter leaders moved over to the Nazi Party from the ranks of another party, it is difficult to estimate the effect this had in popularizing the Nazi Party in the towns of the Black Forest. Müssle of Neustadt left the *SPD* for the Nazi Party. This defection aroused furious reactions throughout the entire region, though it neither prevented a chapter from being established in December 1931 nor increased Nazi support by the summer of 1932.[48]

Some of the chapter leaders in the region were somewhat shadowy figures, at times even from the dregs of local society, like Franz Steinhoff of Bonndorf. His presence in that position did nothing to increase the prestige of the local chapter, which ousted him only in 1930. The gains that the party made in this town can surely not be chalked up to his credit. In the end, Steinhoff was accused of spying for the French.[49] The leader of the Oberharmersbach chapter was a forest worker, one of the least respected occupations in the region, while the leader of the powerful chapter in Furtwangen was a mechanic.[50] We do not have any information about why these people joined the Nazi Party, or how their appointment to the leadership of the chapters came about. Chapter leaders who sometimes represented themselves as craftsmen joined the party due to economic hardship and an apprehension, which at times materialized, of erosion in the status of workers. Peasants, former members of the *BLB,* regarded the Nazi Party as another political way station on the long road since leaving the *BLB.* Kuner went over to the Nazi Party out of disillusionment with the *Zentrum*'s municipal policy and was appointed, as we have already mentioned, to serve as chapter leader by popular demand.[51] Until 1931 a great deal of power was concentrated in the hands of the chapter leaders. It was they who could blackball a candidate to the party or even expel a current member. The chapter leader frequently served as the treasurer and the chief of the local propaganda unit. To a great degree, the chapter leader was accountable for the successes and failures of the chapter under his responsibility.

Until 1931 the appointment of the chapter leaders was the internal affair of each individual chapter, although the appointment required formal approval from Karlsruhe. The positions generally fell to veteran Nazi activists. Such, for example, was the case with Steinhoff in Bonndorf and Fritsche in Löffingen, towns in which the Nazis made impressive early showings. At first, the inability of most of these figures to cope with the demands of the job created a vacuum, which was filled by the dominant personality in the chapter. Some of these chapter leaders were subsequently removed, and the replacement of chapter leaders became a common phenomenon in the region. Energetic activists breathed down the necks of the "Old Fighters" (*Alte Kämpfer*) and even volunteered their own services for the position.[52] As we mentioned, the chapter leaders enjoyed great power (at least until 1931), but the position was not without risk. Along with the responsibility for inviting speakers, accepting or rejecting members, and maintaining direct contact with the *Gauleiter,* the chapter leader also stored party material in his own home, thus making himself vulnerable to police harassment and social ostracism.[53] During the course of 1931 a number of local chapters underwent a changing of the guard. Some chapter leaders were ousted, such as Steinhoff, Fritsche, and Wherle from St. Blasien, while others, such as Hummel of Bräunlingen or Seitz of Schonach, resigned their positions. Some were transferred to a more prestigious position, as happened to Walter Schmidt of Donaueschingen. The changes did not increase Nazi success at the polls or bring new momentum to the propaganda activity.

The year 1931 saw little change from the aspect of the region's propaganda meetings.[54] In localities where the chapter had replaced its leader the party did not always succeed in increasing its strength, as it had in 1928 through 1930. This was the case in Eisenbach. Though a local chapter was founded in 1931, the party did not repeat the triumphs it had enjoyed there a year earlier, and this was also the case in Bonndorf and Löffingen.[55] From 1931 onward, the chapter leaders found their steps considerable restricted. The creation of a mediating body between the center and the local chapter (*Bezirk-Kreisleiter*) left them with less room for maneuvering, and the financial administration was taken out of their hands. With the overhaul of the Nazi propaganda machine at the national level, party activists were no longer permitted to speak in meetings, unless their words drew directly from their field of expertise.[56] In addition to these restrictions, and quite possibly even because of them, chapter leaders took less interest in the chapter's activity. From 1931 onward, the majority of chapter leaders became members of the town council and of the assemblies of local delegates. While their sphere of activity narrowed as chapter leaders, their activity in the municipal sphere increased.[57] From 1932 onward party activity also picked up in the region due to the pressure of the frequent election campaigns, which gave special importance to the chiefs of the regional propaganda bureaus. The chapter leaders were transformed into "delivery boys" who distributed the material that the center mailed to their address, and into chairmen of the frequent campaign meetings held in the region.

From all the foregoing, it will be seen that the activity of the local Nazi chapter was unable to make a substantial contribution to party success in the Black Forest region in the years 1928 through 1931. We have attempted to show the side of Nazi activity that is less dazzling than the one generally portrayed in the research. In 1932 the Nazi Party picked up momentum throughout Germany, not excluding the Black Forest, due to the frequent election campaigns of that year. As we noted at the outset, the organization of the party chapters took a back seat to the accelerated activity in the field of propaganda. The chapters devoted more of their time to disseminating propaganda and less to matters of internal organization and the problems we have already seen. Local activists shouldered more and more of the speakers' duties, despite their lack of training for the task.[58] Their work was characterized by a lack of professionalism, an inability to meet the demands of the propaganda center, and this perhaps was the key to their success. Most of their meetings, as we shall see, were marked by deviation from the official line of propaganda. In a number of places once considered immune to the spread of Nazism we glimpse the first signs of massive party support, following a wave of propaganda meetings held by the local activists. This was the case in Neustadt, Donaueschingen, Schluchsee, and St. Blasien, to give only a few examples.

Was the activity of Nazi chapters elsewhere in Germany in any way different? Scholars generally present a picture diametrically opposed to our own. As early as the 1960s, Allen claimed that the activity and initiatives of the local chapter in Northeim greatly determined the success of the party there. Noakes made a similar claim for Lower Saxony, noting dynamic activity and militant chapter leaders as the characteristic traits in this locality, along with unflagging activity even between election campaigns and the use of unusual propaganda techniques, rather than mere propaganda meetings. This approach was adopted by numerous regional researchers and even by many of the researchers who dealt with the organization of the Nazi Party on the national level or who compared Nazi activity with that of other parties.[59] Studies dealing with chapter activity in the Catholic regions put forth a similar claim. Some of them attempt to applaud the stand taken by the Catholic population in the face of the Nazi propaganda machine, with an emphasis on the unique activity of the Nazi Party. Others, such as Pridham, ascribe great importance to the activities of the Nazi chapters in Bavaria, as do E. Fröhlich, who examines Nazi activity in the Catholic villages of Franconia, and Schaefer, who studies the district of Hammelsburgs in Lower Franconia. In contrast to these three scholars, Heyen reveals the less successful side to Nazi Party activity in the regions of Koblenz, Trier, and Aachen, by presenting an uncensored selection of local police reports. From these reports we find that beginning with 1931, setbacks to party activity were also in evidence. The local party chapters were unable to develop energetic propaganda activity or even to increase the number of chapters in the Catholic countryside. Braun, who studied the Catholic district of Tauberbischofsheim in North Baden, comes to the conclusion that the protest culture in the region toward the end of the 1920s contributed more to the Nazi Party's success in 1930 than its efficient machinery did, but that in 1932 the party could not repeat its success of 1930.[60]

The utilization of archival sources is vital not only to the progress of the research itself but also to the resultant scholarly conclusions, and it is here, in our opinion, that the numerous regional studies of the subject betray their weakness. Most of them rely on two specific sources, the first of which is party publications dating to the "Period of Struggle" (*Kampfzeit*) or even to the post-1933 years. These consist of various memoirs and *Festschriften* marking the foundation of Nazi chapters. They also include the memoirs of veteran party members and local residents, whose description of the ruthless efficiency demonstrated by the local chapter endows them with the much sought-after *"Persilschein."* After all, in the face of such dynamic activity, how could they, the tranquil townspeople, withstand the Nazi "temptation" that was, in any case, largely forced upon them?[61] The second source commonly used by many researchers is the local police reports. And indeed, Nazi activity is portrayed by these local policemen as being highly unique on the local political map, hence explaining the overwhelming success of the Nazi Party. Due to the emphasis on the "positive" aspects of party activity, both in the scholarship and in the primary sources, the less successful aspects of party functioning are overlooked. Thus the way is cleared of any obstacle liable to impede the description of skyrocketing Nazi success in the years 1929 through 1933.

Only a change in the working methods of the scholar, in his conceptual framework, can lead to a different utilization of the raw material from the period. The few scholars who do not emphasize the "temptation" of the local population by the Nazi Party and the sophisticated activity and propaganda that the party used do indeed emphasize, more than the others, the less smoothly oiled side to the Nazi machinery. These scholars place the emphasis instead on the adaptation of the party to local traditions and structures. They also stress the different stages of chapter activity during the years 1929 through 1932, which went from improvisation and failure to the studied and efficient application of experience. The most outstanding of these scholars is Zdenek Zofka, whose study of the

Catholic district of Güenzburg in Bavarian Swabia reveals the organizational weakness of the party throughout the villages of the region, its difficulties in establishing chapters, the sluggish activity and dubious character of those who headed the few local chapters. Koshar as well, in his study of Protestant Marburg, claims that there should be less focus on party activity and more on the setting. Pyta and Baranowski, who study Protestant villages in eastern and central Germany, claim that we should shift our focus from the party to the religious (Protestant) milieu, where the party gained its massive success in 1930 and 1932. Here, the interrelation between the local priest, the local teacher, and agrarian politics are the main precondition for the Nazi success.[62] The dialectic between these two opposing concept—that which sees the Nazi Party as a social movement and the product of its surroundings, and that which perceives the party as having overwhelmed the German nation through sheer momentum—will remain with us in the following chapters.

The Question of Centralization: Relations between the Local Chapter and the Center of the Nazi Party

In the course of the discussion touched off by Richard Hamilton's study of bourgeois support for the Nazi Party, Hamilton raised some important questions that have been completely overlooked by scholars. The questions are: To what extent did the party center in Munich monitor the activity of its chapters, and to what extent did the individual chapters maintain their autonomy? To what extent did the chapters comply with the instructions from Munich and the regional centers? To what extent did the chapter leaders and district leaders distribute the propaganda material that reached them from the party centers, and how much of an impact did it make?[63] These questions are connected to two of the most important characteristics of Nazi activity: organization and propaganda. Before turning to deal with the latter issue, let us first examine the coordination between the national and local levels of party organization. To what extent did the organizational directives from Munich and Karlsruhe filter down to the smallest chapters, and to what extent were they implemented? To what extent did the chapters in the Black Forest operate autonomously, and at which periods? We have already seen that the organizational reforms of 1928 were designed to reinforce the idea of the *Führer prinzip* in the party, and to tighten the chain of command extending from the party center in Munich (*Reichsleitung*) to the regional centers (*Gauleitung*), and from there to the individual chapters under their control. Moreover, a new wave of reforms was undertaken in 1931 in order to wipe out the last traces of local autonomy. Was the *Führer prinzip* indeed carried out as instructed? The available evidence indicates that the reform did not achieve its goals in the Black Forest region. At least until 1931 the local chapter could initiate contact with Munich and even follow an independent policy. Munich bypassed the regional center more than once in order to intervene in the mundane affairs of a given chapter.[64] This does not, however, necessarily indicate a close and continuing supervision over chapter activity, since the ability of the center to ensure compliance with its orders was limited by sheer physical distance and, from 1929 on, by the multiplication of the chapters. On the other hand, the circumvention of regional authority may also indicate a certain skepticism with regard to the latter's ability to supervise the chapters under its jurisdiction.[65] Our initial assumption would be that the party chapters in the Black Forest were, to a large degree, fairly autonomous with respect to the party center in Munich, at least until 1931, and in some cases even after that.

Already in the Landtag elections of 1929 it became clear that Munich and Karlsruhe did not keep a close enough eye on chapter activity. Speakers were not dispatched as promised, nor was this the only problem. It was during this period that *Gauleiter* Wagner defined the nature of the liaison between the center and chapter, calling it a "relationship dependent on success."[66] That is to say, chapters (or chapter leaders, in the specific case Wagner was discussing: party activity in the region of Lörrach) would be lent every assistance and a ready ear for their problems only to the extent that the Nazi Party achieved electoral success in an area being worked by party cadres of proven organizational ability. Wagner's declaration greatly influenced Nazi Party activity in the Black Forest in the year 1930. Given the energetic Nazi activity in Furtwangen-Triberg prior to the Landtag elections,[67] it should come as no surprise to find *"Propaganda Konzentrations"* being conducted early that year throughout that region, though not in others. The impression of sluggish Nazi activity in the southern regions of the Black Forest and in the region of Kinzigtal, together with the unimpressive sums raised by the local chapters, was duly noted by the regional center. Karlsruhe responded with a lack of support for the chapters and an inattention to their needs, namely, propaganda material and properly trained speakers.[68]

Let us return to the memoirs from the *"Kampfzeit"* published by *Der Führer* in 1935 and take a look at the reports sent by the local chapters to the party archives in 1934, with their descriptions of Nazi activity in the various regions of Baden in 1925 through 1933. Once again we find that, in contrast with other regions, little of interest took place in the Black Forest. This helps us to understand *Der Führer*'s statement that until shortly before 1933 there was no Nazi activity to speak of in the region, as well as Karlsruhe's neglect of the party chapters in the Black Forest.[69] Hence it was not only the geographical isolation of the region that brought about this situation, or a lack of desire on the part of the Nazis

to penetrate the strongholds of the *Zentrum,* but also the image of the relatively sluggish Nazi activity in the regions of Hochschwarzwald (in contrast to north Baden). As stated earlier, the party center was unaware of
the activity in this part of the Black Forest, and hence the desultoriness of
the liaison between them, which was expressed in yet another way. If we
look through the rosters of senior officials in the party center in Karlsruhe, we find that not one of them came from the Black Forest region.
Most if not all the senior officials were from the region of north Baden,
while a few of them came from the larger towns along the Rhine valley.[70]
This was not an unusual phenomenon in Baden's political landscape.
Other parties also accorded the notables of the Black Forest region a
most limited representation in their list of candidates to the *Landtag,* both
as delegates and deputies (*Ersatzmänner*). In the Nazi Party this fact was
compounded by the minimal involvement of its center in the work of its
Black Forest chapters.

Friedrich Sattler notes in his memoirs that the activity of the Nazi
Party in the region of Neustadt was undertaken on his own initiative and
that of Franz Merk, without any cooperation or advice from higher quar-
ters. Party members Emmerich and Löffler made similar claims.[71] The
appointment of chapter leaders was often made on local initiative. Any
intervention by regional heads was regarded as advice rather than a command.[72] The party's success in the village of Menzenschwand was ascribed
to the independent activity of Dr. Vogel. The refusal of the regional propaganda bureau (*Gaupropagandaleitung*) to send out trained propagandists caused the local activists to make their own speeches and even to disregard the customary external trappings of Nazi meetings: the flag, party
literature, armbands, etc. We shall later examine the discrepancy between
center instructions regarding the propaganda subjects to be covered in the
meetings and what actually happened in the chapters, but it should be
pointed out at this stage that the chapters refused more than once to
accept the speakers sent out to them, claiming that they bored their listeners and failed to adapt their speeches to local requirements. Chapter leaders who complained about the uncooperative propaganda bureaus[73] did
this, as we have seen, by bypassing the regional center and putting their
case directly to Munich, which then instructed the chapter how to act with
regard to membership dues, local elections, and the invitation of speakers.[74] The disregard for the regional center during that period found other
expressions as well. Thus, for example, Karl Lenz begged the propaganda
bureau in Munich to send him better speakers and to do more to promote
the interests of the *Gau* Baden.[75] We must consider the possibility that the
party center in Munich favored certain regions more than others, just as
the regional center had its own preferences.

Munich's circumvention of the regional center can be interpreted in yet another way, namely as expressing a desire to goad the region into independent activity in order to prevent its dependence on Munich. Even though this intention contradicts the reform goals of 1928, a review of the extensive correspondence between Munich and Karlsruhe shows the latter being increasingly urged to take its own initiatives and not to turn to Munich for approval on each and every subject. We find a similiar phenomenon in the relations between the *Gau* and the chapter, with the desire to generate independent initiatives and productive activity causing the *Gau* to overlook the needs of the chapters. This is only one of the reasons that we have already seen for the neglect of the Black Forest region. There can be no doubt that in the various Nazi centers of organization and propaganda, different sets of attitudes existed on the subject of relations with the local chapters, the weaker ones in particular.

Let us now review several examples of chapter autonomy and the inability of the regional center to impose its decisions, at least up to 1931, and at times even beyond. The first example is related to the position of Adolf Hitler in Nazi activity. While this problem will be studied in greater depth in chapter 9, let us for now touch upon one admittedly marginal aspect of the issue, namely, the manner of employing the greeting *"Heil Hitler."* Kershaw contends that from 1926 on, party members began making use of the greeting in order to emphasize their allegiance to the party, and to use Hitler as the rallying point for bringing new and veteran members together. But Kershaw does not indicate whether this was an official directive or whether it was a custom that gradually took root in party ranks.[76] From 1929 onward, we sometimes find official Nazi publications concluding with the standard *"Heil Hitler."*[77] Up to 1930, the correspondence between Munich and Karlsruhe customarily concluded its letters with *"Heil"* and *"Mit Deutschem Gruß."* Rank and file members, on the other hand, perhaps in order to emphasize their loyalty and to promote their own interests, were accustomed at this period to employing the *"Heil Hitler."*[78]

In the Black Forest, however, local chapters refrained as late as 1931 from using *"Heil Hitler"* in their dealings with the party institutions, not to mention those with the local authorities.[79] This evidence is open to various interpretations: the inability of the party centers to sufficiently impress the centrality of Hitler in the consciousness of their members, or perhaps a lack of awareness of the question. It may also demonstrate the reluctance of some members and chapter leaders to take part in a personality cult, or the desire to assert their independence of authoritarian rule. It may also quite possibly demonstrate the reluctance of local members and chapters to lose their autonomy and local flavor, and their ability to influence from below. Toward the end of 1931 and more especially at the begining of the presidential campaign in 1932, the consciousness of

Hitler's position in the party increased among the rank and file of Black Forest party members, and the greeting *"Heil Hitler"* now figured in all their official correspondence.

There were some important points of Nazi organization in which Karlsruhe was unable to impose its authority on the chapters in the Black Forest. Let us cite a few examples. Until the summer of 1932, the leadership was unable to compel senior party activists and sympathizers to become members of the party.[80] While the following chapter will examine the role of anti-Semitism in Nazi propaganda, anti-Semitism had its organizational aspect as well. Party announcements inviting the townspeople to propaganda meetings had to bear the slogan "No admission to Jews" (*Juden Haben Keine Zutritt*). And indeed, party bulletins printed in Munich and Karlsruhe did feature these slogans, but many chapters in the Black Forest either smudged them out or erased them altogether, apparently in apprehension of drawing undue attention from the local residents and tourists. Moreover, the party announcements printed by the chapters themselves did not bear the slogans,[81] and at times the chapters even smudged out the words *Führer Verlag* in order not to flaunt their association with the ill-reputed party newspaper.[82]

Due to the misorganization and physical isolation of the party chapters in the Black Forest, their meetings could not be made to conform with the model demanded by *Gauleiter* Wagner. News of the meetings was generally spread by word of mouth and by announcements posted on the windows of shops owned by party members or sent through the mail.[83] Few towns and villages of the region could boast of a *Plakatsäulenanschlag* on which to post the party announcements, as ordered by Wagner. Activities such as decorating the meeting hall with the National Socialist symbols, the singing of the *"Horst Wessel Lied"* and the sale of Nazi books and printed matter were carried out infrequently in the region, due to the irregular supply of propaganda material. While the *Gauleiter* had issued specific instructions concerning the identity of those who took part in Nazi meetings (Communists and the politically unidentified were barred from discussions, and only the chairman and the designated speaker could hold the floor), these instructions also went disregarded in the Black Forest.[84] Nor were the instructions of the regional propaganda bureau carried out to the letter: for example, "Every peasant must join the SA . . . ," "The *Spießbürger* vereine must be infiltrated . . . ," "The *Kleinkaliberverein* and the *Reiterverein* are important to our goal, in order to militarize our people and to gain access to weapons."[85] Other instructions were related to the speakers, whom the party classified in three groups: (1) Reich speakers (*Reichsredner*); (2) regional speakers (*Gauredner*); and (3) district speakers (*Bezirksredner*). One order specified, "The *Bezirksredner* may speak only with the special permission of the *Gauleiter.*" In many cases, the propaganda deviated from the instructions of the propaganda bureau. The peasants of the regions were not inclined to join the *SA,* just as they were not inclined to join the party. Local activists spoke at party meetings without having undergone professional training, for the more senior speakers failed to show up in the region.[86] The orders of the regional center were generally printed in the party newspaper, *Der Führer.* Inasmuch as these orders reflected the successful party activity in north Baden, they lacked relevance for the chapters of the Black Forest. This striking disregard for orders was also the result of one simple fact: many members were unaccustomed to reading *Der Führer,* which was not even circulated in the region on a regular basis.[87]

Together with this patent disregard for center instructions, we find local chapters taking the initiative and proposing to the regional center ways of better adapting activities to the political landscape and traditions of the Black Forest. Thus, for example, Kuner became leader of the Schonach chapter against the center's recommendation, since the center's nominee admitted to being unfamiliar with the town. Party activists in the region advised the center regarding the Kreiz-Bezirk elections, and Kuner warned the center to increase its supervision of party delegates to the local council, as these were not following official policy. And let us recall once again that the Schonach chapter demanded better speakers from the center, since the local population was taking little interest in those being sent out.[88]

From all this, it can be seen that party chapters in the Black Forest preserved a large measure of autonomy. This makes us ask whether the decisions and activity of the regional center were, to some extent, the result of chapter initiatives. While it is difficult to answer this question with any degree of certainty, we can assume that the activity of the Nazi Party constituted a combination of initiatives from below, their absorption by the party center, the processing of the data, and the issuing of instructions and orders based on the chapters' working experience. A similar description can also be given of the relationship between the regional center and the party center in Munich. Munich read each the region's monthly reports (*Stimmungsberichte*) and issued directions based on their impressions of regional activity. Moreover, the organization center in Munich allowed the regions to exercise a certain freedom in interpreting and transmitting the party instructions according to their own individual traditions.[89] This mutual cooperation existed chiefly from 1931, the year in which the autonomy of the chapters was sharply curtailed, though, at least in the Black Forest, not eliminated altogether. As we have seen, signs of the autonomy of local chapters and even of party regions were still visible in 1932. Strasser's reforms in the summer of that year were designed to end this phenomenon once and for all. This trend, as we recall, had its origins in the accelerated propaganda activity of that year and the lack of organizational supervision: a situation that allowed many chapters to take their own initiatives in the field of propaganda.

The research stresses the reciprocity of relations between the center in Munich and the various regional centers. Relations between the periphery and the Nazi Party center have received a considerable amount of scholarly attention in recent years. In our historiographic review at the beginning of this chapter we noted the work of Mühlberger, Allen, Hamilton, Pridham, Behrend, Noakes, and others who stress the autonomous activity of party regions or chapters. Like ourselves, they also recognize the fact that the last traces of regional autonomy were totally liquidated in 1930–31. Relations between the chapter and center, however, have received less attention from scholars. While Allen argues that the chapter was to a great extent autonomous, he does not base his argument on a systematic comparison between the instructions of the regional center in Braunschweig-Hannover and the degree to which they were carried out in the city of Northeim.[90] Chapters' activity in Catholic regions has also been little examined in the context of relations with the regional center. Zofka contends that in the region of Günzburg the party chapters were largely autonomous and that their success was the fruit of local initiative. His conclusions about Nazi Party activity in a Catholic region correspond with our own conclusions concerning the Black Forest. Pridham's study of Nazi activity in Bavaria detected autonomous activity up until 1930, when the process of centralization in the party's Bavarian regions became conspicuous. Since reference was not made to specific local chapters, it is difficult to know whether the reference is to party chapters in Protestant Franconia or in the regions of Catholic Bavaria.[91] But with Zofka's claims in mind, the question arises: Was the phenomenon of chapter autonomy unique to the Catholic regions? Was it just in this region that the party was unable to wholly impose its authority on Nazi activists? Due to the lack of sufficient comparative elements we find it difficult to answer this question. Hence there is little we can do but agree with Hamilton's comment, which we noted at the outset of our discussion, and trust that the subject of center–periphery relations will eventually take its rightful place in the research on Nazi Party activity.

Financing Chapter Activity

One of the rare political brawls involving the Nazi Party in the Black Forest region occurred in the town of Hornberg in 1931. When years later the party members recalled the event, they described it in terms of a fierce battle between the Nazi Party and the Communists, stressing that "what was most important was that the chapter cash-box was not damaged during the battle, and that the money was still there."[92] The fact that this was the detail to remain engraved in the memory of local party members four years later, and that the emphasis was on the preservation of the party funds, is eloquent testimony to a phenomenon of which we have already taken note: the importance of the financial basis of Nazi Party activity.

The question of the manner in which Nazi activity was financed is generally associated with the question of "Who paid Hitler?" Or, to be more precise, it is connected to the theory linking capitalism to the success of fascism. The scholarly debate between those who claim the existence of such a connection and those who reject it is well known.[93] There would seem to be a consensus among many scholars today concerning the financial source of Nazi chapter activities. The party financed most of its activity from its own resources, with only a small part being financed through the contributions of industrialists, bankers, or other groups of elites.[94] The numerous regional studies that examined the financial source of local Nazi activity also confirm this claim. While the inability to consult the files of the party treasury (*Reichsschatzmeister*) makes it difficult to prove this assertion completely, archival remains from various party chapters and treasury archives of the Rhine region substantiate the claim that the party financed the bulk of its own activity.[95]

The few testimonies concerning the activity of Nazi chapters in the Black Forest offer similar evidence. The chapter financed itself by charging membership dues and entrance fees to meetings, and, among other things, by selling Nazi literature and printed matter. However, we do not propose only to describe this organizational characteristic of regional Nazi activity but also to raise some questions that have been neglected by the scholars. Was the propaganda activity geared toward achieving social and political goals or was it aimed (sometimes primarily) at raising money and, if so, to what extent? Was there a chronic shortage of funds that made the collection of money into the chief goal of the chapter, or even of the *Gau*, to the point where it overshadowed the desire to distribute party propaganda and to promote chapter activity? Did the means, so to speak, became the ends, and was the propaganda activity used for drumming up money? As for the internal resources of the Nazi Party, the research notes the charging of membership dues and admission fees to meetings, marches, and political events, the sale of official party publications, business activity (connections with a number of factories, the collection for the *SA* Assistance Fund [*SA Hilfskasse*], party life insurance), loans, collection of contributions by the *SA,* the revenues accruing from the salaries of party members who also served in high public office, and, finally, contributions of sympathizers outside the party.[96]

Of all these sources, only the first three created the financial basis for Nazi chapter activity in the Black Forest, and they were even expressed in the Nazi Party regulations in Baden.[97] Membership fees were beyond a doubt the most important source of all. Every member had a membership card with empty squares corresponding to the months of the year, and for every square a stamped seal testified to the payment of membership dues. The candidate became a member of the party only after the chapter passed his request on to the regional center, which in turn forwarded it to the treasury office in Munich. In this way Munich was kept informed as to the number of dues-payers in each of the party's administrative units and was thus able to supervise the collection of dues throughout the regions. The chapter treasurer collected the revenues and membership dues, which were duly inscribed in the chapter. Forty percent of the revenues (which included the entrance fees to meetings and the proceeds from the sale of Nazi literature and newpapers) was transferred to Munich and 35 percent to the regional treasury, with the rest of the money remaining in the chapter itself.[98] Anyone seeking to join the party had to first pay his membership dues. This was a candidate's first and foremost obligation, outweighing in importance even his potential as a propagandist or his local prestige. A successful chapter leader suspected of graft was suspended from the party or removed altogether. A member who was less than prompt in paying his dues received a number of warnings and, in the end, was expelled from the party. A chapter that lagged behind in its monthly payments faced a similar fate, and the subsequent sanctions left it without propaganda assistance and the visits of professional speakers. It could also mean the closing down of a chapter. Even chapters that could boast of electoral success at times met with this fate.[99]

There was a tight supervision of the chapter treasuries, both at the national and regional level. While a chapter did exercise the right to determine its own admission price to meetings,[100] the national center was responsible for the financial administration and collection of the proceeds. The local treasurer was subordinate not only to the regional treasurer but also to the national treasurer. The importance that the regional treasurer attributed to the financial activity of the chapter can be seen by the frequency with which the regional office carried out inspections.[101] It should be noted that similar inspections were not carried out by the ministries of organization and propaganda.

Collecting membership dues raised severe problems for the chapters in the Black Forest. Most of the candidates for membership and even the members themselves were workers or craftsmen whose financial condition did not permit them to pay the monthly fee, which in 1931 stood at 1.20 mark on a regular basis.[102] For the sake of comparison, let us note that a loaf of black bread cost 0.40 pfennings in the region, and that the price of a hundred grams of butter was 3.40 marks.[103] Despite repeated warnings their debts increased, and despite their promises to pay up, the shadow of suspension or removal from the party hung over their heads. Hence the chapters had no choice but to hold special events and propaganda meetings in order to cover their obligations to the center and to pay their debts to the local suppliers, from whom they purchased office equipments, rented taverns for meetings, and ordered the printing of announcements and the sewing of flags and armbands.[104] Renting a tavern was a difficult task for most of the chapters. We have already seen that in some places the innkeepers refused to rent their premises to the party. Those who were willing to give the party use of their tavern did so for money as for any other group or club.[105] Due to the inability to hold frequent marches and meetings out in the open or to invite famous speakers, the chapters were left without any choice but to hold their meetings in taverns, which hardly improved the financial state of the chapter. For this reason, the chapters also held special events such as "German evenings" or the screening of movies, in the hope that the admission fees would improve their financial situation and encourage new members to join, whose dues would help to relieve the strain even further.[106]

The election campaigns held by the party proved to be a mixed blessing for the chapters. The intensive organization of meetings required money,[107] but they also brought in funds since so great a number of meetings meant the arrival of dozens of speakers, some of whom were celebrated enough to attract an audience and thus increase the proceeds. This being the case, it is hardly surprising to find the chapters complaining to the center about the boring speakers being sent out.[108] Together with its desire to hold interesting events that would attract new members, the chapter was also interested in receiving financial compensation. The relationship between the speaker and the chapter worked two ways. While the chapter would be interested in a speaker able to attract an audience and contribute to the improvement of the chapter's financial state, the speaker, for his part, would be interested in appearing since this provided him with a source of revenue, a consideration of no little importance in a period of economic crisis.[109] But a chapter could not invite a professional speaker when it did not have the means for paying a fee that ranged between ten to twenty-five marks, and a speaker would not be willing to appear in a chapter known for being in financial straits, or to incur the expenses that the geographical isolation of the chapter would cause. Thus, on the one hand, we find an explanation for the dearth of professional propagandists in the party chapters of the Black Forest and, on the other, for the local initiatives of nonprofessional speakers willing to appear free of charge. Indeed, it was the speakers who showed familiarity with the local political culture and traditions who improved the financial standing of the chapter, although this was the case chiefly in 1932.

There can be no ignoring an additional fact that influenced the financial state of the chapters: financial boycotts and sanctions against the shops and business concerns of the party activists and members.[110] Thus it comes as no surprise to find some of these people turning party interests to their own benefit. The tavern owners among them reaped the benefits from meetings held on their premises, so that not only did the chapter prosper by the meeting but the chapter leader—in this case the tavern owner himself—also turned a profit by selling beer to the members and onlookers.

An additional source of revenue for the party chapters came from the sale and distribution of National Socialist printed matter. While we shall be examining the local Nazi press at greater length, the little evidence we have indicates the paucity of the printed material made available to the local chapters and the indifferent success of its sale.[111] In order to make up for this lack of material, many chapters printed their own announcements, cutting corners in ways that did not conform to the guidelines of the party center and the results of which contained little in the way of eye-catching graphics, no doubt to the detriment of their consumer appeal.[112]

The financial side of the activity of the Nazi Party chapters in the Black Forest only reinforces the aspects that we examined previously: their lack of coordination, their autonomy, and their misorganization of activities. Only one scholar to date has drawn attention to the chapters' preference for raising money over the distribution of propaganda, and his assumption came under strong criticism.[113] We are unable to compare systematically our own finding with other Catholic areas since only few scholars have touched upon this issue, and only briefly. Zofka's work does not even mention this point, whereas Heyen's police reports only note that the party chapters in the area of Moseltal had trouble recruiting new members due to the steep membership fees required of candidates. In Aachen one finds the same situation. The local chapter suffered from financial problems that led to poor results in the elections. The chapter's members were unable to upgrade their activities as they lacked sources of finance. In East Bavaria, the local chapters wanted to invite Hitler to speak at their meetings mainly for financial reasons. The chapter leaders knew that the income from Hitler's presence would contribute to their activity, which was true. When Hitler spoke in Schlossberger in April 1932 the local chapter earned 1057 RM. Many other chapters were aided by local entrepreneurs who contributed money to the Nazi Party. Hammelburg's chapter asked for attractive speakers to be sent since only they could improve the financial conditions of the chapter.[114] Other scholars, led by Turner and Matzerath, agree that the Nazi Party financed itself through internal sources, but they argue that this was first and foremost a means for maintaining the party's political and ideological goals.[115] From our findings concerning chapter activity in the Black Forest, however, we believe that party meetings, membership dues, and propaganda operations were intended not only for strengthening the chapter, circulating propaganda, and recruiting new members, but also, at times, for ensuring the survival of the chapter itself.

Local Notables and the Nazi Party Chapter

To what extent did the local notables (*Honoratioren*) of rural Germany contribute to the success of the Nazi Party? Does the fact that a party sympathizer or member occupied an important post in a given locality also indicate his ability to drum up support for the party? Out of all the factors contributing to the massive support for the Nazi Party in rural Germany, how much weight did the local notable carry? These and other questions concerning the role of local notables in the success of the Nazi Party have engaged the attention of many scholars. Most of them agree with the assertion that one of the preconditions for the success of the Nazi Party was its ability to infiltrate the local social structure of a given area and to win over the local notables.[116]

Just who were the notables in the rural areas and small towns? Max Weber characterizes the local notables as "People (1) whose economic position permits them to hold continuous policy-making and administrative positions in an organization without (more than nominal) remuneration; People (2) who enjoy social prestige of whatever derivation in such a manner that they are likely to hold office by virtue of the members' confidence, which at first is freely given and then traditionally accorded."[117]

The German sociological literature dealing with the subject describes the local notable as being a local physician, councilman, factory owner, pharmacist, priest, or, lastly, one of the teachers in the local school. Such people have the social power, responsibility and professional training that constitute the basis for local prestige and the influence that this provides.[118]

The research dealing with nineteenth-century Germany recognizes the importance of the local notables in political life (*Honoratiorenpolitik*) and in the fabric of rural social life. R. Hamilton and W. Pyta see this as the key factor in the success of the Nazi Party with the rural population in the years 1929 through 1932.[119]

To what extent did the local notables contribute to the success of the Nazi Party in the Black Forest region? Before turning to examine the evidence, let us take note of one local notable, whose importance in the social fabric of a Catholic region belies his place at the end of our list: the local priest. We must point out from the start that not a single Catholic priest is known to have supported the Nazi Party explicitly or otherwise in the region of the Black Forest. Quite the opposite. The clergy used its position to wage an uncompromising battle against the growing Nazi influence.[120] On the basis of our observation of the regional voting patterns, however, we have to conclude that even the clergy exercised only a limited influence, for there were many places in which they were unable to hold back the flood of support for the Nazi Party. This conclusion concerning the power of the priests will, in essence, provide the keynote for the discussion below. Like the priests, the local notables had only a limited influence over the political behavior of their fellow townsmen; and their contribution to the success of the Nazi Party, or any party whatsoever, likewise had its limits.

We have already seen that a majority of chapter leaders and senior party officials did not enjoy local respect in the scene of their activity. The party often succeeded in places where the chapter leaders were anonymous or even unpopular figures. Indeed, the party at times failed in those very places where local notables stood at their head (e.g., in the case of Erwin Weishaar of Lenzkirch for instance). Few notables were willing to demonstrate public support for the Nazi Party. In a few cases, police surveillance uncovered the involvement of highly placed local personages in Nazi activity.[121] Such involvement (while highly important for showing the leanings of the local bourgeoisie) could not generate local support for the Nazi Party, although it is possible that the publication of the facts encouraged other people to follow in their footsteps. The few notables who were publicly known as supporters of the Nazi Party were rarely card-carrying members. The fact that a local notable joined the party did not always induce other local residents to do likewise, and cases are known where such a step caused a backlash of anger and resentment against the person in question and even the party.[122]

Due to the conservative nature of the region and the strength of political Catholicism, the risk of social and economic boycott prevented an open display of sympathy for the Nazi Party.[123] Shopkeepers who made their living from tourism feared, at least until 1932, that the many tourists (most of whom came from the Rhineland and Westphalia) would cease to patronize their shops should their sympathy for the party become known. An official publication of the Nazi Party notes that only one of the region's inns was willing to lend its services free of charge to party members. The local Nazi press emphasized the small number of party members among the local innkeepers.[124]

We are faced with a problem of methodology. How are we to identify the sympathy of a local notable for the party? Can the attendance of local notables at party meetings be interpreted as sympathy with its ideas? Does a favorable comment spoken in a public meeting of the party mean that the speaker also took part in party activity or drew other sympathizers after him?[125] We have no evidence to this effect. Local government officials like others were prohibited by law from voicing approval or participating in the activity of extremist groups.[126] Nor were the heads of the social *Vereine*, people with local prestige (whom we shall examine in part 3), inclined to join the party. Few of them were active in its framework. The most striking of these was Kuner of Schonach, a public figure who enjoyed great popularity in town. There is no doubt that this step encouraged others to walk in his footsteps, especially members of the sprawling Kuner family clan. Since families tended to intermarry in the Black Forest, the phenomenon of family clans (*Sippe*) was a pervasive element in local public behavior. A prominent clan member could draw other clan members after him, and this phenomenon was striking not only with respect to voting patterns for the Nazi Party but also with respect to other parties as well.[127]

A few other cases of local notables who can be assumed—although we have no hard evidence—to have used their influence for canvasing Nazi support were the head of the Old Catholics Church (*Altkatholische Kirche*) and a veterinarian, both of Furtwangen; the Protestant priest of Todtmoos; a number of small manufacturers in the region; the postman and mayor of Breitnau; the pharmacist of Vöhrenbach; and, according to the local Nazi paper, a number of dentists from the region of Donaueschingen.[128]

In one case the Catholic priest of Furtwangen admitted that Edward Dorer, a peasant who had experimented with a number of parties before becoming the leader of the local chapter, persuaded the peasants to join the Nazi Party.[129] But an examination of the number of peasants in the town's party chapter (three out of sixty-four members) shows that his influence could not have been all that great. Hence, we see that it is not enough to note that a party activist or member was also a local notable. We must also examine the social consequences of his actions and his specific contribution to the party's local success. We have already noted that Kuner joined the Nazi Party only after its success of 1930, and earlier he belonged to the *Zentrum*. Emil Wehrle, a respected figure from the village of Rohrbach and a Nazi sympathizer, did not manage until 1933 to stir even a fraction of his fellow villagers into voting for the party. Dr. Ruch was the only physician in Eisenbach and he no doubt drummed up support for the Nazi Party, if only by distributing the Nazi paper in his private clinic. Yet up until 1931 he was unable to round up the additional fourteen people required for establishing a local chapter, even though he had become active in town several years earlier. The same can be said about Stengele, the senior teacher in St. Blasien, or about Dr. Gemmecker of Schönau. In both places the party achieved success a number of years prior to the activity of these people. In Furtwangen the party made headway two years before the local veterinarian and editor of the bourgeois *Schwarzwälder Tagblatt* joined party ranks, and the case of Erwin Weishaar, one of the most popular figures in Lenzkirch, has already been mentioned.[130]

One important means of identifying the local notables who supported the Nazi Party is by cross-checking the names from Nazi membership lists

or police reports with the names of the local public officials and leading
Vereine heads.[131] The correlation of these lists usually yields a negative
result, apart from the few cases we have mentioned. On the other hand,
there is an extremely positive correlation with the leaders of the artisans'
associations throughout the region. Many of these joined the party and a
few even served as the leaders of their chapters.[132]

Having reached this point, let us ask a few critical questions. The first
of these concerns the political past of the local notables who supported the
Nazi Party. Many of them were former members of such political groups
as the *WP, SPD, DVP,* and the *DNVP.* In view of the relative weakness of
these parties in the region, why, it may be asked, were local notables
unable to increase the strength of their respective parties on their home
ground?[133] Another question concerns the number of local notables who
supported the Nazi Party. Researchers who argue for the importance of
the local notables in the party's success generally find isolated cases of
notables who joined the party, but not the majority. The question is not
only why a few local notables gave their support to the party, but also why
the majority of them did not. And finally, we ought not only to stress the
support that this or that notable gave the party, but also his subsequent
disillusionment and abandonment of the local Nazi chapter. This may
probably be ascribed to the influence of his admirers or the fear of social
ostracism, a phenomenon characteristic of Catholic regions.[134] It would
seem that many scholars who exaggerate the power of the local notables
tend to create an often artificial link between the strength of the Nazi Party
and that of the local notables, and to either forget or ignore the highly con-
voluted road that often separated the two groups.

However, if we wished to indicate the people whose party membership or Nazi sympathies paved the way for their fellow townsmen, such
people would fall into three groups: (1) The peasant leaders from the *BLB*
who joined the Nazi Party after passing through a number of other parties
on the way, and who influenced numerous peasants to follow in their footsteps. These leaders, however, did not belong to the group of local notables. This was the agrarian leadership, which set itself up in opposition to
the local administration and to political Catholicism. The very provocation that they offered the local establishment was enough to arouse the
enthusiasm of many peasants (together with agricultural workers and a
number of village craftsmen) who, even years after the dissolution of the
BLB, still cherished fond memories of the *BLB* leaders of the "good old
days" and moved over with them to the Nazi Party;[135] (2) Popular local
figures who gained support for the Nazi Party through their daily contact
with their fellow townsmen. Such people maintained an extremely wide
network of personal relationships. These were the people known for holding the floor in the local tavern, the local bards, people with impressive

rhetorical skills, athletic prowess, and a good head for drinking around the *Stammtisch,* even if they were lacking the socioeconomic prestige defined by the aforementioned sociological literature;[136] (3) This group included the notables and important officeholders, sympathizers of the Nazi Party who were not of local stock but who propagandized for the party while vacationing or resting up in the Black Forest.[137]

It does not seem possible to prove that the political leanings of the local notables were one of the central factors in the success of the party in the region. In any event, we must distinguish between two periods in the relations of the local notables with the Nazi Party: (1) Until 1930, very few of the notables joined or supported the party. It was primarily the leaders of the *BLB* (who could hardly be termed notables) who switched to the Nazi Party at this time; (2) From 1931 onward, there was a growing bourgeois vote for the Nazi Party, which also included a large number of local notables. We should not exclude the possibility, difficult though it is to prove, that many of the local notables contributed to the success of the Nazi Party through their private conversations around the local *Stammtisch.* There, in the privacy of family and friends, they could openly voice their sympathy for the party, and the local grapevine would pick up from there.

How do our own conclusions compare with those reached by the researchers dealing with the local notables and their relations with the Nazi Party? Let us turn our attention to Catholic regions. Most scholars mention the opposition to the party of the most important local notable of all: the priest. Magnus Goett of Legau in the Allgäu, however, was an exceptional case, being one the few priests in Catholic Germany to support the Nazi Party against his congregation's will. Here the "notables theory" doesn't hold. Wilhelm Senn from Sickingen in the Rhineland is another example. He was an agitator in the service of the Nazi Party. Few of the researchers mention the Catholic notables who went over to the party ranks. The most conspicious of these was Dr. Liebl, from the town of Ingolstadt in upper Bavaria. Pridham, who devotes an entire chapter to this figure in his study of the Nazi Party in Bavaria, elevates the subject to a conspicuous place in a study that examines the preconditions of party success. According to Pridham, Dr. Liebl "was a classic example of the much-respected local personality who lent his prestige to the Nazi movement."[138] Pridham's conclusion provides the foundation for the work of many scholars who have dealt with the subject, the chief of whom is Richard Hamilton. Hamilton bases his explanation for the rise of the Nazi Party on the theory of the Base Group, which he believes best explains the question of Hitler's rise to power. Fundamental to this theory is the leaning of the local notables in the direction of the Nazi Party, with Dr. Liebl providing the most conspicuous example. But alongside the emphasis of this Catholic worthy, Hamilton observes that the notables of Catholic regions generally held back from the party.[139] We find, therefore, that the theory of the Base Group is founded on Protestant regions.[140] Zofka, on the other hand, claims that in the region of Günzburg, respected figures from the middle class and the peasant leadership transferred their support to the Nazi Party. E. Fröhlich also portrays the pharmacist from the village of Waischenfeld in upper Franconia as having been instrumental to the party's local success in 1932.[141]

Our conclusions from the Black Forest, which minimize the contribution of the local notables and indicate the limited influence of the local priests, may help to reopen the discussion on the phenomenon of the *Honoratioren* and its relationship to the success of the Nazi Party.

The Press

The question we shall consider in this section is the extent to which the local Nazi and non-Nazi press contributed to the success of the Nazi Party. What was the role of the local Nazi press in distributing propaganda? In recruiting voters and members? Who was its reading public: Party members and sympathizers, or local people who were opposed to the Nazi Party? To what extent did the Nazi press circulate? How was it financed, and to what extent did it conform with official Nazi policy?

The little research that does deal with the Nazi press before 1933 is unanimous as to its effectiveness. It sees the press at both the national (*Der Stürmer Völkischer Beobachter*) and regional level (*Gaupresse*) as having been instrumental to the success of the party, leading to the establishment of a cross-country network for party members and an effective channel of communication between Munich and the outlying regions. The Nazi press is represented as a militant press, the sole representative of the national-*völkisch* press which disseminated the Nazi propaganda to every corner of Germany. In matters of propaganda and layout it is seen to have taken a largely unified approach, due to the process of centralization and unification begun in 1931 by Otto Dietrich, the head of the party's press bureau.[142]

Peter Stein's pioneering study of 1987 takes issue with this research consensus. Basing himself on a detailed examination of most of the regional Nazi press, Stein contends that its role was limited to the party itself, and that it was strictly an internal Nazi communication channel, vital for the creation of the fascist public sphere. Moreover, Stein argues that the previously mentioned process of centralization and unification had not yet made an impact. The regional press gave vent to the various factions within the party; to the conflicting opinions and political aspirations of regional leaders. Few of the newspapers addressed a non-Nazi public. Only with difficulty did the Nazi press manage to persuade the readers of the national press and *"Heimatpresse"* of the justness of its cause, and hence it had only a marginal influence on the voting patterns of the German public.[143] That does not mean, however, that the non-Nazi press did not contribute to the party's success. Richard Hamilton argues that the bourgeois-liberal press was largely sympathetic to the goals of the Nazi Party and thus was indirectly instrumental to its success. Hamilton provides convincing examples of various German cities where the party reaped success following the support of the local press.[144]

Baden was the home of *Der Führer,* one of the first Nazi newspapers. This paper, which started out as a weekly, went to being a semiweekly then to a daily paper. We have already noted the tone and the goals of *Der Führer* at the beginning of our discussion, together with the fact that it did not have much coverage of Nazi Party activity in the Black Forest. There were several Nazi newspapers in addition to *Der Führer* in the major cities of Baden, such as Heidelberg, Mannheim, and Pforzheim. These papers enjoyed relative independence until 1930, when the center in Karlsruhe asserted its authority and brought all the Nazi papers into line with *Der Führer,* making them into regional editions of the the paper (*Kopfzeitung*).[145]

Until 1931, no Nazi press appeared in the Black Forest region. Sympathy for the party was expressed for the most part by a number of papers of bourgeois-liberal orientation, particularly the *Schwarzwälder Tagblatt* of Furtwangen. This paper provided the groundwork for the network of local Nazi papers later to circulate throughout the region. Its editor, Hermann Leitz, was a member of the *DVP* and he adopted a sympathetic attitude toward the Nazi Party as early as 1930. On instructions from his superiors, however, he restrained his anticlerical pro-Nazi tone up until the end of 1931. With the change in publishing policy at that time (one that reflected, as we shall see, the general upsurge among all strata of the local bourgeois in the direction of National Socialism), Leitz began publishing local Nazi papers throughout the Black Forest: *Der Romaus* (Villingen), *Ritter St. George* (St. George), and *Wasserfall* (Triberg).[146] In addition to the *Schwarzwälder Tagblatt,* the official Nazi paper for south Baden, *Der Alemanne* began appearing in Freiburg in October 1931, and some of its pages were devoted to coverage of the Black Forest. At this time, the first local Nazi paper in the region of Neustadt began to be published (as yet independently): the *Feldberg Rundschau.* This paper was founded through the initiative of party member Friedrich Sattler of Neustadt. Its circulation was poor, and Sattler himself distributed the paper throughout the region, meeting with harassment and financial difficulties more than once. Its publication was even forbidden on a number of occasions. In 1932 it was incorporated into the *Schwarzwälder Tagblatt*'s network of local papers.[147]

Apart from the *Schwarzwälder Tagblatt,* the local Nazi papers (and even *Der Alemanne*) can be said to have addressed the already converted. The papers were sold to party members and their sympathizers in Merk's tavern in Grafenhausen, which catered to party members and sympathizers, and similar places. The attempts to circulate the *Feldberg Rundschau* among a broader public resulted more than once in violence.[148] The papers were posted on bulletin boards at the entrance to shops and business concerns belonging to party members and were also distributed in Dr. Ruch's clinic in Eisenbach. They were primarily used for conveying information and propaganda messages on behalf of the center leaders in Karlsruhe (at first by *Der Führer* and later by *Der Alemanne*) and of the regional leaders.[149] Meetings for both the general public and for members were announced in their pages, along with party coverage of local events. On the eve of the elections of 1932 the papers even featured special supplements geared to the various social classes.[150] The circle of subscribers was limited,[151] and it was difficult to obtain copies of the national Nazi press in the region. *Der Führer* was not distributed on a regular basis, and the single copy that reached the chapter in Schenkenzell was posted on the bulletin board. The official Nazi newspaper, *Der Völkischer Beobachter,* could only be obtained at the clinic of Dr. Ruch.

The local papers were financed by private sources. Sattler himself financed the publication and distribution of the *Feldberg Rundschau,*[152] as did Leitz for the *Schwarzwälder Tagblatt.* Obviously the paper was used more than once to raise money for the local chapter, in part through the publication of advertisements. There were few advertisements, however, due to the opposition of many local shop owners to the Nazi Party at least until 1932, and also, of course, due to the economic situation. Poor circulation caused many of the local papers to fold by the end of 1932. Among other reasons for this development, we might mention the cheap paper on which most of these papers were printed and the poor quality of their journalism and news items. Distribution of these papers was forbidden more than once, often due to their infringement of national laws. Beginning in the summer of 1932, the *Feldberger Rundschau* began appearing as a one- or two-page supplement of *Der Alemanne.*[153]

How much did the Nazi press contribute to the party's success in the various elections? Since no Nazi press appeared in the region up until 1931, there was obviously no contribution to the Reichstag elections of September 1930 or to the local election campaigns in November of that year. In reality, it was in the very places where the local papers were not published or distributed that the party met with its most sweeping success (as was the case for a number of remote villages in the region of Wutach, and in the regions of Bonndorf, Schonau, and St. Blasien). Yet, in towns such as Wolfach and Haslach, where the blatantly pro-Nazi *Anzeiger von Kinzigtal* appeared, the party was unable to increase its strength after 1930. The same goes for Urach. Despite the popularity of the *Schwarzwälder Tagblatt* in the village, the party was unable to make any noticeable headway there. In the summer of 1932, twenty-seven people gave their vote to the party out of a total of two hundred and ten inhabitants.[154]

The lack of credibility of the Nazi newspapers is the major obstacle that scholars encounter in making use of this source.[155] A comparison between the news items appearing in the local Nazi papers and in police reports or in the local bourgeois press, which was largely sympathetic to the party from 1932 onward, shows the Nazi press to be of dubious accuracy. This is most striking where the attendance at meetings and the number of people joining the party were concerned. The numbers quoted by the Nazi press tend to be far higher than the numbers figuring in the police reports. Obviously, the numbers were inflated for reasons of propaganda and out of a desire to present themselves as a successful party, with activities second to none.[156]

How much did the local Nazi papers conform to the publication policy of the official Nazi press? If we take *Der Führer* as our yardstick, the conformity was less than complete. *Der Führer* was oriented toward the political climate and local Nazi chapters of north Baden, from which it took its cue. The local papers, on the other hand, tried to adapt themselves to the traditions and factors of the local society. For this reason they refrained from the bitter diatribes against the Catholic Church, which were a standard feature of *Der Führer* and *Der Alemanne,* and there was very little anti-Semitic propaganda. Moreover, the *Schwarzwälder Tagblatt* even published advertisements of Jewish shop owners, despite the official injunctions of the Nazi Party.[157] On the other hand, the political invectives appearing in *Der Führer* found their way into the local papers. The Hitler cult that so characterized the Nazi Party prior to the presidential elections in the spring of 1932 also affected the Nazi press in the Black Forest.

Because of all these factors, our conclusions about the Nazi press in the Black Forest agree with those of Stein. This press did not in general succeed in impressing the local population with its goals or the quality of its journalism, and the old reading habits remained unshaken. The party press seems to have been successful chiefly from the aspect of organization, since it provided an additional means for organizing meetings, raising funds, coordinating chapter activity, and conveying messages and information between the center and the outlying chapters.

None of this means, however, that the press was irrelevant to the local Nazi success. The bourgeois-liberal press and, indirectly, the Catholic press, contributed more than the Nazi press to strengthening the Nazi Party in the Black Forest. We have already seen how the *Schwarzwälder*

Tagblatt shed its bourgeois-liberal character and openly supported the Nazi Party, to the point of becoming its main organ. Even before this the bourgeois *Anzeiger von Kinzigtal* in Haslach urged its readers to support the Nazi Party in the elections of September 1930. This was also true of Oberkirch's *Renchtaler,* which gave favorable reports of local party activity as early as 1930. By the summer of 1932, the entire bourgeois-liberal press of the region was leaning in the direction of National Socialism.[158] The question, then, is whether the newspapers adapted themselves to the new political orientation of their readers, or whether (as Hamilton contends) it was the bourgeois press that caused the voting patterns of the local bourgeoisie to change. There is no doubt that in Haslach and Furtwangen the newspapers led the way, for there the local bourgeoisie transferred its support to the Nazi Party only in 1932. In view of this bourgeois support the *Schwarzwälder Zeitung* of Bonndorf presents an unusual phenomenon. This paper was the nationalistic and anti-Catholic organ of the *BLB,* and it maintained its neutrality as late as 1932, long after many of its peasant readers and leaders of the *BLB* had gone over to the Nazis.[159]

Due to the straitened economic circumstances people bought fewer newspapers. No press was harder hit by this than the one associated with political Catholicism, which now found itself in crisis. With fewer subscribers, a lower circulation, and outdated journalism, it was unsuccessful in competing with the bourgeois press. Whereas the latter managed to increase its circulation and its publication advertisements, to raise its prices and transform some of its papers into dailies, the Catholic press, most of whose readers were poor, did not manage to increase its circulation.[160] Even the Catholic press, however, which fiercely opposed the Nazi Party, contributed indirectly to its success. The anti-Communist hysteria whipped up by these papers and the frequent news of atrocities in Russia all played into the hands of the Nazi Party. The anti-Marxist frenzy also found its way into the bourgeois press, thereby making an important, if unwitting, contribution to the projection of the Nazi Party as Germany's sole and most effective defense.[161]

Returning to our original question, we may conclude that it was not the Nazi press that contributed to the success of the party in the Black Forest. Rather, it was the widely circulating bourgeois-liberal press that leaned toward the new political orientation from 1932 onward. Hamilton's hypothesis corresponds with the events in the Black Forest and also responds to the question of bourgeois voting patterns, as presented in the chapter dealing with this subject.

How did the Nazi press work in other Catholic regions? The subject as we said, has been neglected by the regional studies. Heyen and Zofka did not deal with the question, while Grill failed to distinguish between the Protestant and Catholic regions in his short study of the Nazi press in

Baden, which he sees as having made a real contribution to the party's success.[162] Norbert Frei researched the Nazi takeover of the press in upper Franconia, and although he reviewed the pre-1933 period he did not treat the Nazi press in the Catholic pockets of the region. Pridham dealt with the subject at length in connection with the local press in Bavaria. In his view, the Nazi press suffered a setback in the Catholic (and even Protestant) regions. Many newspapers established by local Nazi activists went out of business, as with the *Deutsche Alpenwacht* in Allgäu, which folded after only three months. The most conspicuously successful Nazi newspaper in a purely Catholic region was the *Donaubote,* from the town of Ingolstadt. Like our case, Pridham also recognizes the importance of the bourgeois press that appeared in the Catholic regions and supported the Nazi Party. Once again, we find a good example of this in the Allgäu. There the bourgeois *Allgäuer Tagblatt* supported the Nazi Party from 1930 on, even though it was not until 1933 that it became the party's official mouthpiece in the region. In Ettlingen (North Baden), the bourgeois *Mittelbadischer Kurier* supported the Nazi Party. From 1932 onward, this bourgeois newspaper regarded the party as *Bürgersalonfähig.*[163]

If we examine the emergence of the Nazi press in other Catholic regions where the party achieved electoral success from 1930 onward, we find that the districts of Glatz and Frankenstein in lower Silesia did not have a local Nazi press until late 1932, and this was also the case in Weiden, in upper Pfalz. In other Catholic regions, such as Paderborn, Münster in north Westphalia, or Würzburg in lower Franconia, the party had trouble establishing Nazi newspapers before 1932, but in these places the Nazis met with consistent failure at the polls. By contrast, a well-established and successful network of Nazi newspapers existed in upper and lower Bavaria, influenced by its proximity to the most important Nazi local, the *Völkischer Beobacher.* This paper was published in Munich and nourished by the region's nationalistic and political traditions, and by the early consolidation of its Nazi chapters, which went back to the beginning of the 1920s.[164]

When compared with other Catholic regions in which the Nazi Party also met with success at the polls, the failure of the Nazi press to contribute to the party's success in the Black Forest is seen to be not unusual. It is thus clear that of all the communications media that existed at that period, it was the bourgeois-liberal press that made the most important, however unintentional, contribution to the success of the Nazi Party.

The *Sturmabteilung*

The contribution of the *SA* (*Sturmabteilung*) to the success of the Nazi Party may be described as that of the workhorse of the party. The brawls with the Communists and the Socialists enhanced the Nazi image as the most effective defense against the communist threat, and the use of uniforms, marches, and a military chain of command helped to create an energetic and paramilitary image. The *SA* protected Nazi meetings, disseminated the National Socialist propaganda in street marches, and handed out its written material.[165] It was the *SA* that gave birth to the party martyrs, of whom Horst Wessel was the most famous, who were killed in street-fighting. The *SA* also served as the most effective means of raising money. Its rebellious and revolutionary character has fascinated many researchers, for it was the *SA* that fomented the opposition to the traditional party leadership and ideology in the early years of the party, until its violent suppression in 1934.[166] The social structure of the *SA* has also occupied the scholars and today the accepted verdict is that most *SA* members were young and unemployed, or if not unemployed, then from the working or lower middle classes, and that some even belonged at one stage or another to the Communist Party.[167]

The neglect of the Black Forest by the *Gauleitung,* its parochial, conservative character and harsh climate, together with the weakness of the leftist organizations, all led to the establishment of the *SA* in the region at a relatively late date, and to the fact that the nature of its activity there was not in conformity with what we have just described. The first evidence of intensive *SA* activity in the region dates from 1931. Until that time, local chapters in need of *SA* assistance in organizing marches and meetings had had to deploy units from the towns and cities at the edge of the Black Forest.[168] But in 1931 small units were set up in industrial-based towns in the Black Forest; and in Eisenbach, Triberg, and Furtwangen, *SA* houses (*SA Heim*) and drilling schools (*Gausturmvorschule*) were also established.[169] There were not many members. In the *SA* unit of *Gau* Donaueschingen (*Sturmbann 6*) there were only sixty-five members, half of them from the town of Donaueschingen. Of the sixty-five members of the party chapter in Furtwangen only five were also members of the *SA*. Even in 1932, a year in which the *SA* expanded its activity in the region, few joined the *SA* units in the local industrial towns.[170]

The social structure of the *SA* units in the Black Forest does conform to the conclusions of the research dealing with this aspect of the organization's development. The majority were either unemployed or workers and craftsmen. Their age, however, was higher than is generally believed. Most of them had passed the age of thirty. The *SA* units in the region formed part of the general command structure of the *SA* units in south Baden. The districts of the Black Forest were included in the *SA* command units, which grouped together a number of districts and had commanders who were not from the region. This applied to *Sturmbann* Wolfach, which together with Oberkirch and Lahr made up *Standart 109,* itself under the command of activists from Lahr and its surroundings. This was also the case for the *SA* unit for the district of Neustadt, which was annexed and placed under the command of activists from the districts of Freiburg and Emmendingen (*Sturmbann 1/113*).[171] This command structure goes to show how unimportant the *SA* units were in the Black Forest. The majority of them were engaged in protecting party meetings or in paramilitary drills without uniform, mostly when there was a letup in the rain. Local events initiated by the *SA,* such as "German evenings," generally required reinforcements from the Stahlhelm activists or *SA* units from Freiburg.[172] The weak communist infrastructure in the region contributed to the fact that there was little violent and provocative activity on the part of the *SA*. Serious disturbances are recalled primarily from Hornberg and St. George.[173] It was clear to the inhabitants of the region, party activists included, that disturbances could well threaten the local tourist industry and deal yet another severe blow to the region's economy.[174] The uncomfortable weather characteristic of the region and its tourist nature also contributed to the fact that the *SA* potential for large-scale and violent activity did not find expression in the Black Forest.

The local inhabitants, however, had an image of the *SA* that did not correspond to the reality. In the eyes of the priests, the Catholic press, and even some of the residents, the *SA* loomed as a huge political army on the verge of launching its putsch. In the summer of 1931 the local police swooped down on the homes of *SA* activists, following a panic instigated by the Catholic press in the wake of suspicious motorcycle rides of *SA* members in the region of Furtwangen. The only thing the search managed to turn up was the desultory means at the disposal of the *SA* units, for the cache included nothing more than a few revolvers, some documents, propaganda leaflets, and various Nazi Party paraphernalia. The plot for seizing power in the region, which the newspapers reported as being based in Furtwangen, was revealed as so much hot air, merely showed the poor capability of the *SA* units.[175]

In 1932, with the expansion of the *SA* units in the region, there came a new kind of activity that threatened to upset the religious status quo in the Black Forest region. On numerous occasions uniformed storm troopers infiltrated religious ceremonies, and this provocation caused the Catholic establishment to intensify its vituperations against the Nazi Party, claiming that the *SA* had terrorized the region. The upsurge of political violence in the streets of Germany and the mounting social tension doubtlessly influenced the *Zentrum* activists and clergy in the region, who were fearful of the *SA* provocations. The police for its part increased its surveillance over the homes of *SA* and party members.[176] Yet through all this, the *SA* units continued their provocations along with their more routine activity in the region: paramilitary exercises in the forests, protecting party meetings, and, for the first time, distributing food to the poor.[177] Since the main propaganda activity in the region centered around meetings that were held in taverns or other closed places, the relationship between the *SA* units and the party chapters came to expression mostly in the deployment of units to guard the tavern doors, or to protect the meetings from inside.

The numerous studies dealing with the *SA* tend to devote little space to the difference between Catholic and Protestant regions in terms of *SA* activity. One of the most prominent investigators of the *SA,* Connan Fischer, argues that the Catholics were less represented in the *SA* than the Protestants, though in Bavaria young Catholics of the working class were more inclined to join the *SA* than the Protestant youth of a similar class. The *SA* was slower to develop in Catholic regions than in Protestant ones.[178] Regional studies of Catholic regions also tend to neglect the difference between Catholic and Protestant regions in respect of *SA* development and activity. Pridham briefly notes the provocations committed by the *SA* during the Catholic ceremonies. Heyen cites police reports indicating brisk *SA* activity in the Mosel Valley. On Easter Sunday in 1930 the *SA* marched across the entire region without stopping, greatly contributing to the image of a vigorous Nazi Party.[179] Zofka and Frölich do not mention *SA* activity prior to 1933 in the regions under their investigation. Hence there is little we can do except compare our findings with those of Fischer, who based his conclusions on regional sources of numerous kinds. From his study of *SA* activity in Catholic regions we learn that the desultory *SA* activity in the Black Forest was no unusual phenomenon, and that it derived from the organization of the party in the region and from the geographical conditions. In places with a well developed party organization, such as Bavaria or the Rhine Valley, the picture was quite different.

CHAPTER 9

Propaganda

... the fact is that by clever and persevering use of propaganda even heaven can be represented as hell to the people and, conversely, the most wretched life as Paradise.

Adolf Hitler in Mein Kampf

The contribution of the Nazi ideology and propaganda to the success of the party before 1933 did not find clear and precise expression in academic studies until a few years ago. In political science, propaganda is regarded as an instrument of socialization, with a decisive and important part to play in every political process. Its role is to instill beliefs, to refine and sharpen existing tendencies. The researchers of the history of the Nazi Party have apparently accepted Hitler's assessment of the importance of propaganda. In his *Mein Kampf,* Hitler devoted several chapters to the subject. The same was also true of Goebbels, who in his much-quoted book describing the Nazi rise to power stressed the importance of propaganda (and hence, of course, his own importance) in the success of the Nazi Party.[1]

Until recently, the treatment of propaganda and its contribution to the Nazi rise to power was decidedly less polemical. Only a few studies considered its role in the Nazi success prior to 1933. While numerous studies, most of them originating in the "Old" and "New Orthodox" schools of Nazi research (some of them written by Marxist scholars), emphasized the crucial role that the Nazi propaganda played, they did not examine the manner in which the propaganda was presented by the Nazis, or just how effective it really was. Most studies were more inclined to view the use of propaganda and the mobilization of the masses as forms of manipulation by the Nazi leadership.[2]

Over the past decade, however, there have been a number of new studies questioning the traditional consensus over the presentation of the Nazi propaganda and the manner in which it functioned. Scholars such as

117

Bessel, Mommsen, Zofka, Hamilton, Allen, Paul, and others, whose critical studies of party organization were reviewed in the last chapter, have shifted the focus to the social processes in the lower echelons of the Nazi Party, in an attempt to discover whether the Nazi propaganda indeed played a crucial role in the recruitment of party members and the creation of mass support.[3]

What were the central motifs of the Nazi propaganda? Most agree that the idea of a "folk community" (*Volksgemeinschaft*) was the most important and influential element: a "folk community" not only in the utopian sense of a society without class distinctions, in which harmony between the estates (*Stände*) reigned supreme, but also a call to build a nationalist and mass-based modern society.[4] Other important elements of the Nazi propaganda were opposition to Marxism, the leader principle (*Führerprinzip*), militarism, the rejection of the liberalist democracy ("the Weimar System"), anti-Semitism, anticapitalism, nationalism, and rejection of the Catholic religion. Another motif central to the Nazi propaganda was the appeal to different social classes and occupational groups, a discussion of their problems, and a promise to solve them in the Nazi state of the future. The Nazi propaganda had a negative, unconstructive nature. It was less eager to make promises than to attack, to lash out, to criticize.[5]

According to scholarly consensus, the Nazi Party was different from other parties in the manner of presenting its propaganda and in the style and techniques that it used. It was not content that mattered but the manner in which it was presented, and herein lay the secret of the party's success. It was a question of using different techniques and media: aeroplanes, films, rapid switching from ordinary meetings to marches and evening events, a paramilitary presence, theater shows, lotteries, dances, sports events, acrobatics, and, most importantly, a large number of mass rallies organized with amazing efficiency.[6]

The critical studies dealing with the subject raise questions about how the central motifs of Nazi propaganda contributed to the party's success, questions such as To what extent did the Nazis use anti-Semitic propaganda? To what extent was the message absorbed by the masses, and how did the masses translate their support of a given propaganda motif at the polls?[7] Or, to what extent did the Nazi propagandists make use of the image of Hitler as a personality and leader? To what extent was his image favorably received by the masses, and was this enough to attract their vote for the party?[8]

In contrast, there are several scholars who question the ability of the Nazi propaganda to sway millions of voters in its wake. They argue that the party did not have a clear platform and that the propaganda was of no special significance. In their opinion, the great success of the Nazi Party was due to its representation as an alternative to the other parties. A person who voted for the Nazi Party did so less to promote some goal of party propaganda than out of disaffection with his old party and the existing political order. Moreover, the propaganda had an internal importance as well. It appealed to the already converted, to the Nazi members and sympathizers. It bridged the gulf between the different groups gathered under the roof of the Nazi Party and helped to finance its activity. Even in places where the party did not aggressively use propaganda it succeeded in winning much sympathy.[9] The central motifs of the propaganda were determined by the national propaganda bureau in Munich (*Reichspropagandaleitung—RPL*). However, a number of scholars maintain that its instructions were not always carried out in the periphery, and at times they were subject to different interpretations. And indeed, as we showed in the last chapter, at the time of the 1929 *Landtag* elections in Baden, relations between the propaganda bureau and the chapters were extremely tenuous.

In the discussion that follows, we will attempt to deal with these issues in relationship to the Nazi propaganda in the Black Forest. We shall begin with a brief description of the structure of the national propaganda bureau (*RPL*) and that of the regional bureaus (*Gaupropagandaleitung—GPL*). Following this, we shall examine two examples of Nazi propaganda activity in the Black Forest and the Baar: (1) the important election campaign of the summer of 1930, when the party stood on the threshold of reaching the national consciousness; (2) the presidential elections of the summer of 1932. We shall note how a number of propaganda motifs characterizing the Nazi Party on the national level found expression in the region, and attempt to examine the party propaganda with regard to its attitude toward the different occupational groups in the region. The propaganda of other parties will play a less prominent role in this discussion, since by "other parties" we essentially referring to the Zentrum, the most active party in the region, and we have already studied some of the most basic tenets of its propaganda in chapter 6. Another reason is that a detailed examination of the propaganda of other political groups would cause us to extend the present work beyond its proper scope. The subject, however, undoubtedly requires a more detailed study.

The Structure of the National and Gau Propaganda Bureaus

Despite Hitler's emphasis on the importance of propaganda, the Nazi propaganda bureau received independent status only in 1931. Until that year, the bureau functioned within the framework of the party organization bureau (*Reichsleitung*), and its leaders, Himmler and later Goebbels, reported directly to Gregor Strasser. Before 1930 the emphasis was on organization, the founding of chapters and the tightening of the relationship between the center and the various *Gaue*. Although Himmler launched innovative propaganda techniques for disseminating the party message, Strasser's influence caused priorities to be switched to the building of cadres within the party.[10] The most important change in party propaganda took place after the Reichstag election campaign in May 1928. To the surprise of senior Nazi officials, the party made substantial gains in rural areas in which there had been hardly any party activity. The official line of propaganda in that period could be described as urban-socialist-nationalist, and it was directed primarily at the workers. Among other elements of the organizational reform initiated by Strasser at the end of 1928 was a greater nationalistic, procapitalistic tone in party propaganda. The Nazi Party tried and succeeded in reaching a new target audience—peasants and members of the lower class. This decisive change in the line of propaganda did not come in the wake of an organizational change in the propaganda bureau, nor did it usher one in. Himmler was responsible for the bureau even in 1929 and 1930, and apart from the increased use of professional speakers, the establishment of a school for training party speakers, and the emphasis on the spoken word, there was no significant change in the bureau's activity.[11] Goebbels was appointed chief of the party propaganda bureau in May 1930, but the change that occurred in the dissemination of party propaganda in the summer of 1930, on the eve of the elections to the Reichstag, cannot be attributed to him. As the *Gauleiter* of Berlin, his deep involvement in the Otto Strasser affair and the Stennes revolt (the first of an *SA* group in Berlin) did not leave him with much time for boning up on innovative propaganda techniques. Once again, it was Himmler who was actively responsible for the Nazi propaganda machine, though it was Hitler who dictated the central motif of the campaign: "For or Against the Young Plan." The primary goal of the propaganda bureau was to conduct as coordinated and unified an election campaign as possible. The *RPL* tightened its supervision over the *Gauleiters* and the propaganda bureaus under their authority. For the first time, large quantities of propaganda leaflets, signs, and bulletins with a unified content were distributed throughout Germany.[12]

Yet, despite the efforts of the propaganda bureau to coordinate the campaign as far as possible, the party's instructions were not always implemented as required. This was partly because the propaganda bureau suffered from overlapping authority: both that of Strasser, who emphasized organizational activity as the key to the party's success, and of Hitler, who saw propaganda as vital to the party's success, but did not play an active role on the operative level of things. One of the lessons of the Reichstag election campaign in September 1930 was the establishment of a national propaganda leadership, the *RPL,* responsible directly to Hitler and headed by Goebbels, who was granted wide independent authority. In 1931 the resources at his disposal were increased, as was his authority over the *Gauleiters*. The *RPL* provided the *Gauleiters* with confidential monthly information about political developments, propaganda techniques and strategies for the upcoming period. The *Gauleiters* in turn provided the *RPL* with monthly reports concerning their territory, based partially on the reports dispatched by the individual chapters. The *Gauleiters* rewrote these reports, which gave them an opportunity to inform the *RPL* of the way propaganda was being distributed in their territory. The *Gauleiters'* reports were analyzed in depth by the *RPL* team, and the most important findings were presented every month in a confidential memorandum (*Stimmungsbericht*) distributed throughout the top echelons of the Nazi Party. Hence every level of the Nazi propaganda bureau received cohesive and unified political guidance from the *RPL* on a monthly basis.[13]

The *RPL* also supervised the appointment of speakers, the party press, and, of course, the administration of the election campaigns at both the regional and national levels. The activity of the *RPL* reached its peak in the summer of 1932. At that period the bureau simultaneously ran the presidential campaigns, the campaign for the Prussian Landtag and that for the Reichstag, in July 1932. Despite the numerous propaganda successes, which ultimately made the Nazi Party the largest party in the Reichstag, the Nazi leaders did not achieve their primary aim of forming the government. It was for that purpose that Strasser had received the go-ahead from Hitler to conduct his sweeping organizational reform from the summer of 1932, as we saw in chapter 8. The reform is important in this context, since it caused the propaganda activity to become less important in the Nazi order of priorities. If we add to this the exhaustion of the Nazi activists, the reduced financial support, the frustration of the *SA* units, and the inability to come up with an appropriate propaganda response to von Papen's "Cabinet of Barons," then we can understand the background to the failure of the party in the Reichstag elections of November 1932.[14] This failure, however, only made Goebbels and the *RPL* attempt once again to prove the effectiveness of Nazi propaganda. Once Strasser resigned from the party and Goebbels's power was increased, the latter showed what propaganda could do in a tight election campaign to the Landtag in the tiny state of Lippe. It was not the content of the Nazi propaganda that was decisive in Lippe but the manner of its presentation, which is described with impressive detail by Ciolek-Kümper.[15]

How did the regional propaganda bureaus (*GPL*)—in our case, the Baden propaganda bureaus—function. In Baden the *GPL* was responsible directly to *Gauleiter* Wagner. It was headed by August Krämer, whose first goal was to enforce his authority over the party speakers. The local chapters in his *Gau* received speakers only through Krämer alone, and only from the pool of speakers under his supervision. The speakers were obliged to report to him directly. In order to supervise the implementation of his instructions and the unity of the propaganda motifs, Krämer began issuing monthly circulars (*Rundschreiben*) containing the instructions of the propaganda bureau. In these circulars he updated the *Bezirkleiters* and chapter leaders about events in the *Gau* and in Munich, and also conveyed his own propaganda instructions, or those of the *RPL,* to the activists out in the field.[16]

The centralization of the Nazi apparatus propaganda took place in Baden even before Goebbels centralized it at the national level. Already at the end of 1930 Wagner launched an organizational reform of his *Gau.* The *Gauleitung* was divided into two organizational units. The first of these had the job of running the party, disseminating its ideas, and winning people over to National Socialism. Krämer continued to manage the propaganda bureau, the department of the unit that was given the highest priority. The groups that made up the second organizational unit had duties of an economic and cultural nature, and it was their job to lay the groundwork for the future Nazi state. The goal of the reform was to tighten control of the various groups and departments contained in the regional office, for the more successful the party became, the more these proliferated.[17]

Wagner's concept of propaganda found expression in a pamphlet that he published in 1931, *Propaganda und Organisation im Gau Baden der NSDAP.* In his eyes, the party's most important task was the presentation of Nazi propaganda, especially via the spoken word. And indeed, until 1932 the propaganda bureau concentrated its efforts on supplying properly trained speakers and supervising their work. The distribution of propaganda leaflets and flyers gained momentum only with the presidential election campaign. The bureau had made no attempt prior to this to supply printed kinds of propaganda, and certainly not in large quantities. The establishment of a district propaganda bureau, which was placed under the combined supervision of the *GLP* and the district leaders (*Bezirkspropagandaleiter*), provided yet another means for supervising the dissemination of propaganda throughout Baden.

As noted in chapter 8, the liaison between the party chapters in the Black Forest and the regional center was very weak at least until 1931, and this extended to the *GPL* as well. We have seen more than once that the chapters complained of a lack of propaganda material and an absence of trained speakers. The most sought-after speakers appeared only infrequently in the region, and the local chapters had to fall back on their own resources with increasing frequency. In the following chapters we shall attempt to see if at certain periods the propaganda activity of local activists in the Black Forest made use of motifs that contradicted those disseminated by the *RPL* and the *GPL*.

The Nazi Party Propaganda in the Black Forest: The Reichstag Elections of Summer 1930 and the Presidential Election of Spring 1932

What was the economic situation of the Black Forest region at the time of the Reichstag elections in the summer of 1930? According to the statistics printed in the local newpapers and by Baden's employment office, the economic crisis had abated somewhat. The most important indication of this lay in the number of unemployed. During the months of August through September the number of people seeking employment (*Arbeitsuchende*) dropped to its lowest level that year. The employment office (*Arbeitsamt*) in Villingen registered 2,676 unemployed in the districts of Donaueschingen and Villingen, of whom 1,103 received unemployment benefits (*Arbeitslosenunterstützung*). Eight months before, the number of job-seekers had reached 3,586, and those receiving unemployment benefits 2,326. In the towns of the Donaueschingen district the number of people seeking work decreased by 50 percent. In the smaller towns the number of people receiving unemployment benefits was extremely low: in Schonach 9 and in Schönwald 3. The second indication of a letup in the crisis was that the situation of the craftsmen also showed signs of improvement in a few places, with the renewal of activity in the construction trade. The same was true for the peasants. After a dry and rainless year, the summer of 1930 was blessed with an abundant harvest. The local press reported a successful season. Even the tourist season, which was drawing to its close, had been a good one. Local industry, however, was still feeling the pinch of the economic crisis. Only in the clock-making industry did things pick up for a while, due to the traditional Christmas orders that it received during that season, so that here the crisis was felt only from the end of the year.[18]

Obviously, these statistics indicate only a temporary letup in the crisis. As noted above in chapter 3, the hardships of the local peasants and craftsmen intensified from 1929 on, and once the summer of 1930 had passed the crisis became even worse. This is an important point to keep in mind, since below we will be emphasizing the fact that the Reichstag election campaign in August through September 1930 was conducted in an atmosphere of more economic optimism than the region had known a year earlier.

Brüning's announcement about moving the elections up to July 1930 found the Nazi Party center in the midst of accelerated activity. Though the election campaign to the Saxony *Landtag* had ended a number of weeks before this, the party was still engaged in energetic propaganda activity, even though new elections were not on the horizon. In Baden they were still studying the lessons of the *Landtag* election campaign in October 1928 and beginning to make preparations for the local election campaign that November. In Karlsruhe it had been suggested that the *Landtag* election campaign had brought a number of basic weaknesses to light.[19]

In the Black Forest, things were quiet politically following the local Landtag elections in October 1929. While the Nazis still conducted some propaganda activity in certain places, this did not last for more than a few days. The police reported that the region remained quiet throughout the entire period, including the summer months of 1930. Few chapters were established in that period and relations with the *GPL* were still weak.[20]

The Nazi propaganda campaign got under way relatively late in the region. Only toward the end of August were the first meetings held, and these were targeted at the large villages and towns. The party still did not have sufficient activists to disseminate the propaganda in the smaller villages. The difficulties faced by Nazi activities were also increased by problems within the party itself. Some chapters ceased to function, and a few chapter leaders were ousted. The meetings were held at the peak of the tourist season, and the police warnings against any provocations that might lead to unrest also contributed to the low key of the election campaign.[21] Nazi propaganda was disseminated only in public meetings in local taverns. There was very little distribution of printed propaganda material in the region, but then this was a nationwide phenomenon, since the *RPL* did not yet have the means to distribute it through every region in Germany.[22] Party activity in the region had to do without *SA* marches, nor was there any use of trucks equipped with loudspeakers or special evening events. The emphasis was on the spoken word.

Despite all these drawbacks, however, party meetings drew a large crowd, including vacationers, who proved generally sympathetic.[23] The majority of speakers were unknown to the local inhabitants. The police noted more than once that they spoke quietly and did not attempt to make use of provocative methods.[24] Meetings were announced by the most ordinary looking posters, their slogans reading, "The Parties to the End of the Road" or "An End to the Blacks and the Reds." Were it not for the number "nine" (the party's number in these elections) accompanied by the swastika, it would be difficult to identify them as Nazi posters, so vague was their content. The local press charged that "All the Nazi Party's strength is in propaganda. Not in organization, nor in its program or even in its ideology." It further charged that the party's activities in the region were in no way different from those of any other party.[25] In order to examine the truth of this charge, let us take a look at the central propaganda motifs of the Nazi Party in the Black Forest.

First of all, what were the primary motifs of party propaganda in the Reichstag election campaign? Hackett and Childers both emphasize the centrality of the Young Plan: "The election slogan: 'For or Against Young' ; everywhere in Germany the same placards will be posted, the same leaflets distributed. . . . Flyers, leaflets, etc., should be passed out early Sunday so that the worker, the civil servants and the Spiesser has them in hand before the expected flood of trash sets in."

The party subsequently made use of an additional motto deploring the deterioration of political life and its transformation into an accumulation of special interests.[26] Hackett, in his analysis of the Nazi propaganda leaflets, argues that the Nazis appealed primarily to the workers. The party most attacked was the *SPD*. Issues that directly affected the workers were mentioned frequently, and terms like *The mass, reactionary, high finance,* and *capitalism* were used with abandon. Hackett further maintains that words such as *Germany, German, folk (Volk)*, and *State* also appeared frequently, as did the names of Hitler and Frick. The Young Plan was mentioned in almost every leaflet. On the other hand, anti-Semitic slogans, the Nazi movement, and subjects of concern to the middle class were seldom mentioned. Turner, who also deals with this election campaign, claims, for reasons of his own, that the Nazi propaganda had a socialist, almost Marxist character.[27]

In order to discover words and issues most popular in the speeches of party activists in the Black Forest, we have examined these speeches by means of the linguistic analysis adopted by Hackett (table 8). Through this we learn that, in general, the single most popular issue was the "bad" government in Berlin, a rundown of its mistakes and the acts of corruption linked to its name, as well as the deep discontent of the people with the democratic-parliamentary system responsible for the unsatisfactory economic policies. Another issue popular with the party speakers was Frick's policy in Thuringia and his decision to institute prayers in the schools. The following table was compiled from the words selected by Hackett (who gave no explanation of his methodology), together with words that seem important to us in relation to the picture in our region.

The table shows that words with a nationalistic character, such as *the German people, Germany, State, Homeland* were used 39 times. Words expressive of criticism of the "system," the government ministers and the corruption of the government and the various parties were used 39 times (the word *ministers* occurs 17 times). Economic issues, different social classes, the economic crisis, different branches of the economy, and the plight of the workers are mentioned 28 times (this group includes *taxes* [11], *wages* [5], *unemployment* [4], the *Working Class* [1]). The most frequently mentioned parties were the *SPD* (6) and the *Zentrum* (5). The *KPD* was not mentioned at all, local subjects were not mentioned, and

Baden was mentioned only 3 times. Frick was named 8 times but Hitler only once. The *NSDAP* [9], the Jews [6], and the Young Plan, which scholars claim was the center of the election campaign, were mentioned only 7 times, and the Marxist-Bolshevist danger 7 times. The motif that scholars consider most important—the idea of a "folk community"—was not mentioned at all.

Contrary to the instructions of the propaganda center in Munich, and despite the claim of contemporary scholars concerning the emphasis on local issues in Nazi Party propaganda,[28] there is almost no reference in the Black Forest to local problems. The speakers did not make use of the key

TABLE 8. The Frequency of Words Used in the Speeches of Nazi Party Activists

Word	Frequency	Word	Frequency
Minister	17	Agriculture	3
Taxes	11	Workers	2
Germany	10	Marxism	2
People	10	Dawes Plan	2
NSDAP	9	Reparations ("Tribut")	2
System (Weimar)	8	Capitalist	2
Frick (Thüringen)	8	Bourgeois	2
Marxismus-Bolshevism	7	Slavery	2
State	7	1918	2
Young Plan	7	Versailles	2
German	7	Brüning	2
SPD	6	Department stores	2
Jews	6	Hitler	1
Zentrum/BVP	5	Parties	1
Culture	5	Swindler	1
Salary	5	Catholic	1
Unemployment	4	White-collar workers	1
War Period	4	Peasant	1
France	3	Bourgeoisie	1
High Finance	3	Misery	1
Christians	3	Hunger	1
International	3	Order	1
Bigwig	3	National	1
Living space	3	*Heimat*	1
Mussolini (Italy)	3	The Economic Crisis	1
Baden	3	*KPD,* Constitution, USSR,	
Bismarck (the pre-		Soldier, Socialism, Democrat,	
1914 period)	3	Fulfillment, Community	0

Source: Hackett, *The Nazi Party in the Reichstag Election of 1930,* 285; StaaF, BZ Neustadt, 244/183-24.8.1930 (Neustadt), 24.8.1930 (Hinterzarten) 25.8.1930, (Lenzkirch), 31.8.1930, (Kappel), 25.8.1930, (Löffingen); GLAK - 347,1943, 18-29, 1.9.30 (Furtwangen).

issues touching upon the region itself, such as the loss of Alsace-Lorraine and the impact that this had on local industry, the price of lumber in the wake of competition with the Soviet Union, problems of agriculture and tourism, the paving of local roads, or the construction of the much contested Schluchsee dam. Even the issues that were certain to raise interest in the region, such as the link between political Catholicism and the Church or German politics before 1914, were not mentioned. The fact that the Young Plan was mentioned so seldom demonstrates the speaker's disregard of instructions from the national propaganda bureau in Munich, and perhaps even their ignorance of its policies.

Generally speaking, there was a lot of similarity between the propaganda of the Nazi Party and that of the *Zentrum* (as described in chap. 6).[29] The Nazi propaganda was of a predominantly populistic character, but unlike the *Zentrum,* the Nazi propaganda was fulled with socialist, almost Marxist elements that caused the local press to depict the party as antibourgeois, close to socialism and communism.[30] Naturally, the news about the *SA* revolt in Berlin and of the break between Otto Strasser and Hitler only reinforced this view. But, in addition, the press also played on the fear of Bolshevism that was so rampant in the region. The depiction of the Nazi Party as a party close to socialism and communism, together with the anticapitalistic motifs and vigorous anti-Bolshevist attacks that the speeches often contained, may well have been enough to cause the peasants, skilled workers, and craftsmen to demonstrate mass support for the party in the summer of 1930.

There were a number of factors that helped to create the protest-party image of the Nazi Party: the negative character of Nazi propaganda, the failure to present an alternative program, and even more important, the fact that the party was not a partner in the local or national government. Such being the case, it seems likely that the vote that the previously mentioned social classes gave to the Nazi Party was to a great extent a protest vote of groups harboring feelings of deprivation and disaffection, turning its back on the dominant political culture of the region. We have already seen the substantial representation of workers and craftsmen in the ranks of the Nazi Party, and even suggested that the majority of voters for the party in September 1930 were former SPD supporters who transferred their support to the party after years of abstaining from voting. While there can be no doubt that certain propaganda motifs drew their attention to the Nazi Party, this is not enough to explain why it was precisely the Nazi Party that won their massive support. In 1930, the Nazi Party had not yet become so unique and attractive an alternative to the other parties. Notwithstanding the few advantages that we noted above, the party's organizational and propaganda message was still incomplete. The full answer to the question of why peasants and workers supported the Nazi

Party may well be rooted less in the party to which they turned than in the collective feelings of frustration, alienation, and disaffection. This made it easier for the Nazi Party to penetrate, without any particular effort, the social and organizational vacuum that existed in these social classes during the summer of 1930.[31] In the following chapters we will deal with this issue more in greater depth.

As 1931 was characterized by little propaganda activity, let us turn to the presidential election campaigns of March through April 1932. Later we shall examine in greater detail the extent to which Hitler dominated the party propaganda. For the present, however, let us simply note that in the campaign bearing his name, Hitler did not always play a central role. The election campaign was run by Goebbels, who had been granted the most extensive powers for this campaign, his first as chief of the *RPL*. In 1932 the party's propaganda activity was directed entirely by the *RPL*. The processes launched a year earlier—the centralization and tightened supervision over the individual chapters—reached their peak in July 1932, as the party ran its election campaigns for the presidency, the Prussian *Landtag,* and the Reichstag. Yet together with the centralizing processes, the party also displayed a greater sensitivity to local differences than it had in the summer of 1930. Leaflets, placards, and flyers were drawn up by the *RPL* in dozens of different examples, so that every *Gauleiter* or propaganda chief could select the one most suited to his own region and particular needs. The importance of the *RPL* activity lay in giving a unified character to all of the regional factors and variables that received expression in the party propaganda, and that made the Nazi Party "such an impressive political phenomenon to contemporaries."[32]

Even before Hitler declared his candidacy, *Gauleiter* Wagner advised Baden to mobilize all its resources for the presidential election campaign. The *GPL* directly supervised all the propaganda activity and decided on the allocation of speakers, the distribution of printed material, and the manner of activity on election day itself. Every activist was obliged to make sure that the state would be plastered with leaflets, posters, and propaganda flyers.[33] The election slogan chosen by Goebbels was *"Schluss Jetzt"*: "Everyone's voting for Adolf Hitler." "This slogan must appear on every picture and leaflet . . ." "Every chapter must order its own propaganda material through the order form." The distribution of the propaganda material was meticulously arranged: "In places where the *GPL* is unable to dispatch speakers, the local chapter is to organize a concert or hand out leaflets."[34]

In the Black Forest the chapters stepped up their propaganda activity, and the results were far more successful than they had been in the summer of 1930. In contrast to other regions in Germany, periods without elections saw little Nazi activity in the Black Forest. It was the *KPD,* rather, which was active "in these dry periods," far surpassing the Nazi Party in the number of propaganda meetings that it organized. Once the presidential election campaigns were announced, however, the Nazi Party shifted into high gear. Numerous propaganda meetings were held every day, even in small and remotely situated villages.[35] There were a number of other differences between the campaigns of 1932 and those of the summer of 1930, the most important being the current economic situation, which had worsened considerably and was now affecting a broader and more diversified group of people (see chap. 3). The second important difference can be attributed to the weather. The presidential election campaign came at the end of a particularly harsh winter, causing many propaganda plans in the Black Forest to be shelved. Meetings were canceled due to the heavy snows, and the distribution of printed material was not always carried out with success. Relations with the *GPL* were far better than they had been in the summer of 1930, but due to the elements and the inability to keep tight control of the activists, there was still some slack.[36] One final difference between the two campaigns was that this time, the majority of speakers were local people.[37] Later, we will take a look at the propaganda motifs used by these speakers and try to assess the extent to which they conformed with the instructions of the *RPL* and the *GPL*.

In contradiction to the orders of the *RPL*, numerous propaganda leaflets were printed by local activists. Many of these leaflets did not carry the *"Schluss jetzt"* election slogan. Both the oral and printed propaganda put a greater emphasis on the anticapitalist motifs. Some of the propaganda leaflets had been printed in Berlin and Hamburg, and they were of a socialist, almost Marxist character. The *"Wehrataler"* leaflet, which was printed in the district of Schopfheim, represented National Socialism as:

> . . . the greatest German freedom movement of the last hundred years. The significance of this is absolute solidarity of the entire Volksgenossen . . . Capitalism is revealed as the greatest obstacle on the road to achieving these goals. Our struggle must be understood by the fact that Capitalism is not found in its proper place. It can and must be made to serve the economic needs of the people.[38]

One leaflet declared that "Parliamentary democracy is the most perfect form of developed modern Capitalism . . . ,"[39] and another proclaimed, "The German people is collapsing under the weight of the worldwide Jewish finance capitalism. . . ."[40] In many cases Hindenberg was depicted as the epitome of capitalism, and Hitler as the defender of the poor and starving workers. As we stated, many of the anticapitalist leaflets came from the larger towns of the Black Forest and even from outside the region. Side by side with the intensified use of the anticapitalist motif came a greater emphasis on the plight of the peasants. Some of the new local speakers were themselves peasants, and they focused on issues with which they were highly familiar. The Catholic issue also received greater stress, especially the connection between the Church and the *Zentrum* and the ability of the clergy to make believers support political Catholicism. One new-old motif that surfaced in the Nazi propaganda in the Black Forest— old since it had long been employed by the *Zentrum*—was the idea of a "folk community," even though local Nazi speakers did not make frequent use of the term itself. Instead, they depicted a kind of ideal goal for the party, the creation of a society that overcame socioreligious polarization.[41] Together with some of the older motifs that we noted in the Reichstag election campaign, such as nationalism and the attacks on the "System" and Marxism, we find an intensified use of Hitler's name and political activity. Without doubt, the presence of local speakers made for a range of propaganda motifs that was not only wider but also adapted to local conditions, with a focus on issues that most concerned the local population. Many of the speakers had not undergone professional training in the party's school for speakers, and as a result, their speeches did not always conform to *RPL* standards.

If we compare the election campaign of September 1930 with that of spring 1932, we find that the 1932 campaign had a more diversified tone to its propaganda, and that it was characterized by an adaptation to the needs of the inhabitants, an emphasis on local issues, and the participation of local speakers. The activity was not only more intense but also better planned and coordinated, even if occasional mishaps did occur (see chap. 8). The question is whether the conclusions that we have reached with regard to the presidential election campaign can be linked to the voting patterns for the Nazi Party during this period. The party's electoral strength saw a considerable increase, and we may conjecture that it drew support from other social groups as well as the workers. Through a comparison with the results of the Reichstag election several months later, we learn that many voters abandoned the bourgeois parties as early as spring 1932. The ability of the Nazi Party to attract a wide range of voters seems to have been rooted in a number of factors: the frequent appeal to the peasants, the motif of the "folk community," the anti-Marxist and anticapitalist rhetoric, and last, but not least, the projection of an effective, strong, and well-organized party that relied on local activists. Some of these voters apparently came from the ranks of the local bourgeoisie, a conjecture that we will seek to prove at a later point, when analyzing the social message that the party sought to convey to the bourgeois strata.

Was there any difference between party propaganda in the Black Forest and in other Catholic regions? The Reichstag election campaign in the summer of 1930 was characterized by vigorous propaganda activity in numerous Catholic regions. This was true of Catholic Bavaria and lower Franconia, the region of Koblenz-Mainz-Trier and the Catholic "pockets" in Upper Franconia. Police reports from the region of Koblenz indicate strenuous propaganda activity in the region even before the announcement about moving the elections forward. In the Moselle Valley the propaganda was adapted to the needs of the local workers in the vineyards, and the *SA* and local chapters held strenuous activity even on Easter Sunday, with *SA* marches and participation in religious rites. Hence there was nothing extraordinary about the vigorous propaganda activity held in this area during the campaign period.[42] Bavaria provides a similar example of a region where aggressive propaganda activity in Catholic regions did not preclude "pockets" of sluggish activity elsewhere. In some areas around Munich, the party even used an airplane for distributing its propaganda, and Hitler and Ritter von Epp made frequent appearances. In Swabia, however, the brisk activity in the district of Memmingen did not prevent the activity in Günzburg from being notably poor.[43] In his study of this district, Zofka argues that while the party did increase its activity during the visits of Strasser and Hitler, party events were still not that numerous since the visits caught the peasants in the middle of the busy harvest season. There was an organizational reason as well: the scarcity of chapters and activists. Yet despite all this, the party was successful at the polls. The Nazi propaganda in the district was of a highly general nature. Speeches centered more on foreign policy, economics, and Bolshevism than on the immediate problems of the local peasants. In this region it was the motifs of antisocialism that spoke to the heart of the peasants, and not the fear of communism. None of this activity was accompanied by any significant or tangible solution, and it is possible, as Zofka argues, that it is precisely this which holds the key to understanding the support for the Nazi Party. It was the most generalized but all-embracing antisocialistic motifs that cast their spell on the local society.[44] In the district of Ebermannstadt the intense Nazi propaganda got a boost from gifted orators, such as Hans Schemm, who came in from the nearby Protestant regions. There was almost a paramilitary character to party meetings and activity, and the propaganda made use of religious motifs. The same picture comes from the district of Hammelburgs in Lower Franconia. There the Nazi Party organized ten meetings in the month before the election of 1930. The same *Aufschwung* was evident in Rosenheim. General von Epp's speech attracted many listeners although most of them came because of his personality and not because they were interested in the Nazi Party. Unlike Günzburg, these efforts did not end with good results in the 1930 election. In Hammelburgs the party won 13.2 percent of the votes and in Rosenheim 17 percent.[45]

Propaganda Motifs in Nazi Party Activity

Let us turn now to the motifs that many scholars consider central to the Nazi propaganda. We will attempt to analyze the extent to which the Nazi activists made use of these motifs in the Black Forest and the way they were received by the local population. Finally, we will attempt to discern the motifs most frequently used by the activists in the region.

Hitler: "Der Führer"

One of our original intentions in conducting this research was to examine Adolf Hitler's contribution to the success of the Nazi Party in the Black Forest, and to analyze the way in which his image as man and myth, the leader of a political party and master of organization, received expression at the local level. We thought to examine how his role as *"Der Führer"* contributed to the success of the party at the local level, and how he was perceived in the eyes of local activists and inhabitants. The fact that we have not elevated this subject to a more prominent place essentially speaks for itself. Already at an early stage of the research we reached the conclusion that as far as the Black Forest was concerned, Hitler's actual contribution to Nazi activity was marginal in the extreme, and that it increases only as the level becomes more abstract. Such being the case, the manner in which Hitler was projected in the Black Forest cannot be counted as a major factor in Nazi propaganda.

Our work in this chapter is an attempt to break somewhat new ground. The research literature is characterized by an almost unanimous consent concerning Hitler's importance to the Nazi success prior to 1933, and the recent republication of Ian Kershaw's seminal study about the Hitler myth only reinforced this conception. In his study, Kershaw reconfirms the theory that Hitler was important not only in the practical sense but also, as Broszat puts it, in the sense of a symbol that helped to crystallize and consolidate the party, so that the Hitler image helped prevent the disintegration of the party from within. Kershaw makes his case with the use of new sources.[46] While scholars of the Functionalist school did attempt to question the centrality of Hitler's role in the Third Reich, this investigation was not extended to the earlier period, and to this day no attempt has been made to apply their methodology to an examination of Hitler's status and role prior to 1933.[47] Despite the general state of research, however, a few historians have tried to argue against the centrality of Hitler in Nazi activity prior to 1933. Scholars such as Allen, Hamilton, Koshar, and Farquharson considerably play down his contribution to Nazi activity throughout the various regions of Germany. Farquharson even argues that Hitler was little more than a name to the German peasants.[48] But these arguments are in the manner of brief comments and not an in-depth study of the question.

It was precisely in the Catholic regions that Hitler's name and image could have been put to effective use. More than a few Nazi activists noted that Hitler himself was Catholic, a remark that brought down the indignation of the Church, which declared that the Nazi Party acted contrary to Christian dogma.[49] In the region of the Black Forest we find certain qualifications with respect to the use of Hitler's name. For one thing, Hitler did not visit the region until 1932. To be sure, in 1930 he did make a speech in Offenburg, at the edge of the Black Forest, but few activists from the region came to hear him.[50] There was no direct link between Hitler and the activists, then, until 1932. Of further importance is the fact that it was mostly nonlocal activists who invoked Hitler's name. Finally, at least until 1931, Hitler's name came up only infrequently in propaganda meetings and in the pages of the local Nazi press.

Memoirs written by party activists from the region portray Hitler as a source of hope and inspiration through the darkest periods of despair, and yet his name is not even mentioned in more than one description of the local Nazi victory.[51] In chapter 8 we showed that until 1931, official Nazi correspondence was rarely begun or concluded with a *"Heil Hitler."* We found a similar phenomenon in our analysis of the speeches made by activists in the Nazi propaganda meetings. During the Reichstag election campaign in the summer of 1930, for example, his name came up only once in the propaganda meetings. In the local elections a number of months later, neither his name nor his image were at all called into use. In 1931, when one Nazi activist summed up the party's activity in the Baar region he concluded his report with the words "work, freedom, and bread." A year later he employed the same words in his report of the Nazi activity, only this time he brought his report to a close with a ringing "Heil Hitler!"[52] We find signs of Hitler worship in the region only from 1931 on, when the leader of the party chapter in Dittishausen named his son Adolf Hitler. That this worship had become more extreme by 1932 we learn from the fact that in Neustadt, the leader of the local Nazi chapter named his daughter *Hitlermaid.*[53]

The presidential election campaign saw an important change in the projection of Hitler's image in the region. To begin with, Hitler made a speech in Schwenningen, at the eastern tip of the Black Forest, and the thousands of activists who went to hear him returned full of "mystical" ecstasy from the experience.[54] The local Nazi press also contributed substantially to the glorification of his name, as did, needless to say, the speeches and leaflets that flooded the region. Until 1931 Hitler was commonly recognized as the leader of the Nazi Party, but little more. By 1931, however, he was described with increasing frequency as the savior of Germany. Here too the distinction between local and nonlocal activists becomes important. While the former adopted the veneration of Hitler relatively late, the activists who came from outside the region were more exposed to the Nazi propaganda at the national level, and they adopted expressions of Hitler worship at an earlier period.[55]

How can we measure Hitler's role in the success of the election campaigns? It would seem that in 1930 the party succeeded in the elections to the Reichstag and the local councils without drawing upon Hitler's name and image. There can be no doubt that the "Führer" worship served to intensify the activity with sacrificial overtones among the members beginning with 1932. However, the decline in the Nazi popularity that began in the summer of 1932, just after the elections to the Reichstag, coincided with the intensification of the "Führer worship" and with the use of his name in every form of propaganda activity. It would seem that while the disappointment with Hitler's political activity in Berlin did nothing to lessen the veneration for him, it did slow down the pace of activity.

A less than respectful attitude toward Hitler can be discerned even among card-carrying Nazis. More than one agitator was expelled from the party for showing contempt for the "Führer," and party activists often struck out his name from propaganda leaflets for the presidential election, replacing it with "The National Socialist Party." Interestingly enough, it was just when the Hitler worship reached its peak in the Black Forest, and when local peasant activists were recounting his praises, that many peasants chose to abandon the party.[56] A few activists even objected to Hitler's Catholicism being linked to the propaganda representing the party as the defender of the Church. Hitler's program was mentioned very little once he reached power, and the few promises that were made to the peasants or workers were not made in his name.

If so, what did his name signify to the inhabitants of the region, and did their sympathy for the party spring from a sympathy for Hitler, or was it the other way around? The groups belonging to political Catholicism were relentless in their attack of Hitler. Yet even in this camp moderate strains were to be heard. So, for example, Vicar Riefer of Loffingen claimed that Hitler was an excellent speaker, to be sure, but noted that his artistic temperament made him erratic, and that "Germany needs a north German leader, strong and sturdy as a tree."[57] The priest of Zell a.H. claimed that Hitler was the candidate of the down and out, while in Bräunlingen the local bourgeoisie showed itself indifferent to Hitler's image and message (or so the local Nazi paper claimed), none of which kept it from giving Hitler mass support in the presidential elections. A local housewife asked if Hitler was a native of the region.[58] The bourgeois daily *Lahrer Anzeiger* claimed that Hitler was half Jewish, while the bourgeois regional daily, *Hochwächter,* which was not anti-Nazi, warned that "the Nazi Party has a leader whom nobody knows," and this was just at the start of the presidential election campaign. Six months later this same paper demanded that Hitler be made chancellor.[59]

We do not mean to say that Hitler was an unknown in the region. The authorities had identified Hitler with the party for years. When they published the names of the competing parties, the Nazi Party was called the "Hitler Movement" (*Hitlerbewegung*). The clergy also termed the party sympathizers and voters the "Hitler group."[60] But Hitler's importance was largely restricted to the party itself, and even there in a limited fashion from 1931. The veneration that surrounded him did not prevent internal problems from shaking the party in the autumn of 1932. The limits of Hitler's charisma on local inhabitants can be seen in the second round of the presidential election campaign. The strength of the party increased very little after Hitler's speech in Schwenningen, which was attended by numerous activists and local inhabitants. This was in flagrant contrast to the respectable increase after the first round of presidential elections, which began without any direct contact with the "Fuhrer," and only at the start of the "Fuhrer worship." It is not impossible that it was the worn-out activists, exhausted by the first round of elections, who were most affected by Hitler's speech. Our assumption, then, is that Hitler's popularity was dependent on the popularity of the Nazi Party, and not the other way around.

Hitler appeared frequently in Catholic regions across Germany even before the presidential election campaign. In Bavaria and along the Rhine he already appeared often in the Reichstag election campaign in the summer of 1930. While the success of these appearances has been scrupulously documented by the research, there has been almost no systematic attempt to examine his actual contribution to the Nazi electoral success. The only researcher to have done so is Zofka, and his arguments are similar to our own. To be sure, Hitler did speak in the district of Günzburg on the eve of the Reichstag elections in 1930, but his visit did not cause a sensation or even stimulate party activity. Hitler did not stand at the focus of the Nazi propaganda campaign. Though he was represented more and more as a brilliant politician, a leader, it was not his personality that stood on the agenda. Once again, it would seem that Hitler's popularity resulted from the mediating role of the Nazi Party, and that his reputation rested upon that of the party. In Rosenheim Hitler was compared by the local Nazis to Bismarck, but his performance in April 1932 in the town was described by the local police's report as boring.[61]

Anti-Semitism

How did the Nazis use the idea of anti-Semitism and racism in order to mobilize the masses? In view of the history of anti-Semitism in Europe and in Germany, the Nazi paranoia of Jews, and, of course, the tragedy of the

Holocaust, it is clear why many historians have chosen to focus on Nazi anti-Semitism. To be sure, little attention has been diverted to the period prior to 1933, but it is commonly assumed that party supporters could not but have sensed that anti-Semitism was central to the Nazi platform. Though numerous scholars have recognized the importance of the subject, they have not examined it in depth prior to 1933, perhaps because they assumed that the subject left no room for doubt.[62]

In the regional studies dealing with the Nazi rise to power, there is generally little systematic treatment of anti-Semitic propaganda. This is as true of Catholic as of Protestant regions, and of German and non-German scholars from the schools of both social history and political science. The careful distinction between "Jewish" and "German" subjects and the avoidance of anti-Semitism is also characteristic of German historiography, both regional and general. Nonetheless, we find that there are scholars, of different nationalities and from different schools of thought, who reached the conclusion, somewhere in the margins of their papers, that after 1929 anti-Semitism did not often figure in the Nazi Party propaganda in most regions of Germany.[63] The few studies that deal with the Nazi Party in the state of Baden limit the anti-Semitic Nazi propaganda to one specific region, that of north Baden, and to the city of Heidelberg in particular. In cities at the edge of the Black Forest the party often adopted anti-Semitic propaganda, but—and this is the most important conclusion—anti-Semitic propaganda was not used in the Black Forest.[64]

In chapter 8 we saw that the leaflets inviting people to propaganda meetings in the Black Forest did not carry the anti-Semitic slogans. On the other hand, numerous leaflets that reached the *GPL* from Munich did carry these slogans, as did the leaflets that were printed in Karlsruhe and distributed by the *GPL* throughout Baden. Indeed, in regions along the Rhine the leaflets were distributed as printed, without change or deletion. But the leaflets that reached the towns of the Black Forest were emended so that the "No Entrance to Jews" was blotted out. Moreover, in propaganda leaflets printed in the region, inviting the inhabitants to public meetings, the slogan was missing altogether.[65] We have already noted that the Nazi local daily, the *Schwarzwälder Tagblatt,* published advertisements for Jews side by side with anti-Semitic invectives. The Nazi daily, *Der Alemanne,* viciously attacked the medical practice of Dr. Mayer, the Jewish physician of the Neustadt district, but this did not prevent numerous Nazi activists from thronging his clinic.[66] The anti-Semitic slurs were sounded in the party meetings primarily in the years 1928 through 1930, and mainly by speakers who came from Karlsruhe, Heidelberg, or cities at the edge of the Black Forest. One such speaker was Dr. Rombach of Offenburg, who made a racist speech about blood and the Jewish race. There was also an anonymous speaker from Heidelberg who regarded Jews as a "swelling

abscess, a lice-ridden chancre." *Gauleiter* Wagner did not miss an opportunity to unleash anti-Semitic propaganda before the local inhabitants,
and the same was true of Albert Roth and Walter Köhler, the chief Nazi
propagandists in Baden.[67] However, even the activists who reached the
region after 1930 lowered the anti-Semitic tone of their tirades, to the
point where it caught the attention of the policemen watching over the
party meetings.[68] In the Reichstag election campaign in the summer of
1930, the Jews were mentioned only six times in the speeches of the
activists, all of whom came from outside of the region. The local Nazi
press showed no sign of anti-Semitic propaganda, in stark contrast to the
press at the national level, where papers such as *Der Führer* or *Der Alemanne* were saturated with propaganda of this kind.

How did local party activists regard Jews, and how did the local
inhabitants react to the anti-Semitic Nazi propaganda? The most senior
Nazi leader in the area, Merk, began his career in the Nazi Party without
any kind of negative attitude toward Jews. In the platform of the *BLB,*
which he published at the beginning of the 1920s (together with other
members who afterward joined the Nazi Party along with him), there was
no reference to Jews at all. Nor did he ever mention them when giving his
reasons for having joined the Nazi Party or his analysis of the sociopolitical situation in Germany. However, the more he moved up the local party
hierarchy, the more studded his words were with anti-Jewish motifs,
though without any trace of racism or extremism. He limited his words to
political anti-Semitism, calling for the expulsion of Jews from high public
office.[69] In his memoirs from 1937, Frederich Sattler mentions his business
dealings with Jews in order to explain his own hostility toward them, yet
his speeches from the "Period of Struggle" make no reference to the "Jewish question." Hermann Letiz, the editor of the *Schwarzwälder Tagblatt,*
published articles with anti-Semitic content after he began supporting the
party in 1931, yet not before. It would seem, then, that local Nazi activists
adopted an anti-Semitic approach only after they joined the party, and
that they had no anti-Semitic background or tradition. Dr. Vogel, to be
sure, made use of the speaker's podium more than once in order to deliver
anti-Semitic attacks, but he was not native to the region.[70] And indeed, the
Black Forest did not have a native tradition of anti-Semitism. We have
already noted in chapter 1 that few Jews lived in the region. The little contact that Black Forest inhabitants did have with Jews came mostly
through trade with cattle merchants from the Baar or with vacationers, so
anti-Semitic activity might have jeopardized the region's economic basis.
The geographical isolation also contributed to the traditional lack of anti-
Semitism and thus to the absence of anti-Semitic activity on the part of the
local political Catholicism. Therefore, when Nazi speakers gave vent to
anti-Semitic attacks, one local peasant responded, "To us, the peasants,

the theory about the Jews and the productive German blood is something new," and the local Catholic daily thundered, "shame, shame, shame when such things are spoken in a pure Catholic community." The Catholic propaganda even held up Nazi anti-Semitism as proof of the movement's primitive nature.[71] Local speakers spiced their words with anti-Semitic propaganda after 1930, but rarely made it their main goal. Stresemann or the SPD speakers, when attacking Freemasons, might accompany their words with anti-Semitic slurs; and when attacking the communists, they might make reference to the fact that most of the Marxists in Russia were Jews. But it was not the Jews who were represented as the chief enemy, but the "system" and Bolshevism.

The low key of the anti-Semitic propaganda or its absence altogether can be seen as part of the party's "adaptation" to local traditions. Following the virulent anti-Semitic propaganda of 1928–29 the Nazis realized that this motif would not help them at the polls. They thus lowered the anti-Semitic tone without offering any reason at all and at times even refrained from mentioning the subject altogether.

From a review of the anti-Semitic Nazi activity in other Catholic regions, we may conclude that in Catholic Bavaria anti-Semitic propaganda played a secondary role. This was the case in the districts of Memmingen and Günzburg. In the districts of Lower Bavaria it was activists from Franconia who at times disseminated the anti-Semitic propaganda, but the local activists refrained from dealing with this motif. In contrast, the scholars dealing with Nazi activity along the Rhine comment on the intensity of the anti-Semitic activity, however, as stated, these comments were not made in the framework of an incisive analysis of the Nazi propaganda. In Rosenheim the local Nazis critized the local Jews but did not hurt or insult them. In Ettlingen (North Baden) the only anti-Semitic activity of the local Nazi chapter was against slaughter.[72] Again, the research on both places refrained from systematic analysis of the question of local Nazi anti-Semitism.

It was precisely in the Catholic regions that the religious element could have been used to the greatest effect in anti-Semitic propaganda. However, it seems that due to the instructions of the *RPL* to refrain from using such motifs,[73] the indifference of the local population, and the character of the local activists, anti-Semitic propaganda was shoved to the side in the Catholic regions, including the Black Forest.

Catholicism

The Nazi propaganda in the Black Forest and in many Catholic regions gave special attention to the subject of the Catholic Church and the attitude best adopted toward its members, activists, and the *Zentrum* Party.

The Nazi Party loomed as an anti-Catholic party in the public eye, and this image was reinforced by a number of factors: the demand for a "positive Christianity" in the party platform, Hitler's own words in *Mein Kampf,* the attitude displayed by Rosenberg and Ludendorff, and the fact that a number of senior activists, headed by Arthur Dinter, engaged in vigorous anti-Catholic propaganda. Following the end of the party's *völkisch* period in the mid-1920s, Hitler tried to forestall any confrontation with the Catholic Church. Creating a mass movement while battling with the Church was in the manner of political suicide, and this pragmatism essentially dictated the propaganda that the Nazis directed toward the Catholics. It was not the Church with which the party sought to wrestle but only the *Zentrum* and political Catholicism. Beginning with 1929, Hitler became interested in developing a relationship with the Church. In his view, there was no conflict between the Catholic faith and the idea of National Socialism, and his goal was to reach an agreement similar to the one effected between Mussolini and the Church in Italy.[74] The election campaign to the Reichstag in 1930 caught the propaganda bureau off-balance on the entire issue of religion. The bureau had not yet consolidated its policy toward the Church, and its responses were of a haphazard nature. From 1930 on, however, the *GPL* engineered a policy that actively sought to avoid confrontation with the Church or to engage in any kind of declaration or provocative activity liable to open the party to charges of *Kulturkampf.* The *Zentrum,* however, was fair game, and the *GPL* directed that stress should be placed on the way the *Zentrum* was exploiting the Catholic faith and mixing politics with religion. More than anything, the Nazi propaganda stressed that the *Zentrum* was in league with the *SPD,* thus paving the road to Marxism (*Zentro Bolschewismus*).[75]

The Black Forest affords us precedents for the Nazi use of anticlerical propaganda. In chapter 6 we discussed at length the anti-Catholic propaganda of the *BLB* at the beginning of the 1920s. The fact that starting in 1928 central activists known for their animosity toward the Church joined the Nazi Party only increased the mistrust and suspicion of local Catholic elements toward the party. In the south of the Black Forest, where a sizable part of the *BLB* was drifting in the direction of the Nazi Party, and even in other areas of the region, the local activists (most of them believing Catholics) tried to avoid the religious issue altogether, and certainly to refrain from any attack on the Church and its activists. Until the end of 1930 the party's propaganda speeches and leaflets showed little anti-Catholicism and a less than intensive occupation with the *Zentrum.*

The year 1931 saw the crystallization of a number of points, sometimes contradictory, in the Nazi policy toward Catholicism in the Black Forest:

1. From 1931 on, the party tried to avoid embarrassing issues, such as the anti-Catholic book published by Rosenberg in October 1930; the virulent anti-Catholic rhetoric of Julius Streicher and Karl Holz from Franconia; and the declarations made by the synod of bishops in Mainz, in March 1931. Local activists claimed that Rosenberg's book reflected his opinion alone.[76]
2. The Nazi propaganda sought to make trouble between the Zentrum and the local inhabitants. Toward this goal the party made the utmost effort to prove the ineffectiveness of the Zentrum, and to show that its collaboration with the *SPD* was clearing the way for Bolshevism.[77]
3. "National Socialism bows its head before the Christian cross, the symbol of the Christian faith"—such was the essence of the religious image that the party tried to project in the region. According to this, the party supported the Catholic religion in principle, and the fact that Interior Minister Frick had instituted prayers in the schools of Thuringia was all to the credit of the Nazi Party. Who was more Catholic than Hitler? claimed the Nazi propaganda during the presidential elections in the spring of 1932.[78]
4. Beginning in 1932, however, the local Nazi propaganda removed all restraint, blatantly denouncing the Church and local clergy. It also engaged in openly provocative behavior, mostly by infiltrating uniformed *SA* troops into religious ceremonies. The Nazi press reported on the corruption of the clergy and the misuse of confessional cells for the conveying of political messages, and it denounced what it called "the weak nature" of the priests. In Grafenhausen Dr. Vogel demanded the presence of the local priest at the burial of a Nazi activist, but did not hide his intention to have the swastika and the cross chiseled side by side on the gravestone. The propaganda attack on the Catholic Church was primarily characteristic of the second half of 1932.[79]
5. The most publicized claim of the local activists was that Bolshevism was on the verge of infiltrating Germany, with the active help of the *Zentrum,* and that only the Nazi Party would be able to hold back the tide. Only the party would be able to fight communism. Pitting the Nazi strength against the communist menace and the impotence of the *Zentrum* was the most striking feature of the Nazi propaganda addressed to Catholics in the Black Forest.[80]

As noted above, neither religious nor historically based anti-Semitism played a role in the propaganda aimed at the Catholic inhabitants of the Black Forest. In the absence of hard facts Nazi activists did not try to claim that central Catholic activists or priests from the region went over to the party ranks. The only example that they were able to dredge up—and it was widely disseminated throughout the region—was the sermon of the priest Senn, "Catholicism and National Socialism: An Address to German Catholicism," in which the priest recapped the major points of the Nazi Party propaganda toward the Church and the *Zentrum,* while stressing the Bolshevist danger.[81]

To what extent did the local inhabitants respond to the Nazi propaganda attacks? Here we must distinguish between two sectors of the Catholic population: those who were loyal to political Catholicism and the local Catholic milieu, and whose response to the Nazi Party was generally negative; and those who did not belong to the Catholic milieu (see chap. 11). Despite their differences, both sectors were affected by the anti-Marxist propaganda. Members of the first group took every opportunity to publicly butt heads with the party, especially through the quotation of appropriate passages from Rosenberg's book or examples meant to illustrate the Nazis' paganism, but their internal correspondence betrays their confusion. They did not know how to explain to their flock why the bishops of Mainz decided to withhold sacrament from the party members or the right to participate in religious ceremonies, and at times they even hinted at the justness of the Nazi cause in certain issues.[82] Of greater interest, however, is the second of the groups noted above, the one that did not belong to the local Catholic milieu, and later we will deal with this at greater length. For now, let us only mention that despite the intensification of the anti-Catholic activity in the summer of 1932, the party picked up considerable strength in Catholic areas during the Reichstag elections of July 1932. Later we will seek to identify the circles willing to provide the Nazi Party with electoral support, despite the attacks on the Church.

Did the Catholic issue stand at the center of party propaganda in every Catholic region? Pridham argues that this subject greatly occupied the leaders of the party in Bavaria, as they sought ways to address the Catholic population without making the party appear anticlerical. This goal was hindered by the activity of Nazi leaders in Protestant areas of Franconia: Streicher, Holz, and Schemm. The Nazi propaganda focused on the Church's abuse of power and its interference in political issues. At times, the Catholic-aimed propaganda also focused on anti-Semitic issues, together with mention of Catholic activists who crossed over to the Nazi camp. These last two motifs were absent from the Nazi Party propaganda in the Black Forest. Pridham further claims that the Nazi propaganda succeeded in disguising its anti-Church aspect, creating the impression that different attitudes reigned in the Nazi Party on this issue, and that it was communism that posed the real threat to the Catholic Church.[83]

In contrast to Pridham, studies dealing with various districts in Bavaria contend that the religious issue was not the focus of Nazi propaganda. In Lower Bavaria it was economic issues that took center role. In the district of Günzburg, the Bavarian People's Party (*BVP*) denounced the Nazis as the enemy of Christianity, even though the local Nazi propaganda rarely made use of the religious motif. Both areas made abundant use of anticommunist and antisocialist motifs. In the Catholic district of Ebermannstadt in Upper Franconia and in Hammelburg in Lower Franconia, the anti-Catholic nature of the party was more readily apparent, due to the vigorous activity of Nazi leaders hostile to the Church, such as Hans Schemm, Dr. Hellmuth, and Karl Holz, who frequently visited the area.[84]

Nazi propaganda in western parts of Germany made use of similar motifs. Here, too, the party refrained from attacking the Church, preferring instead to wage war against the *Zentrum,* claiming that politics and religion should be kept apart.[85] In regional studies written by Catholic scholars describing the resistance that the Catholics showed Nazism, there is a greater emphasis on the antireligious character of the Nazi Party and on central propaganda motifs attacking the Catholic Church.[86] This approach dominated the Catholic historiography after the war and was influenced, needless to say, by the policy of the Third Reich toward the Catholic Church.

The Nazi propaganda was characterized by an effort to soften the anti-Catholic impression of the Nazi Party, and to insinuate that it was indeed the *Zentrum* that was undermining Catholic interests in Germany. Toward this goal the party used the motif of the communist danger, which it showed as stalking the Church, and represented the Nazi Party as the defender of the Catholic minority in Germany. On this issue the Nazi propaganda presented a united front in most regions of Catholic Germany, including the Black Forest.

Local Traditions and Problems

To what extent did the party activists exploit the various crises threatening the region for the purposes of propaganda? To what extent did they use local issues, and how popular were these with the local inhabitants? In our survey of the election campaigns in the summer of 1930 and the spring of 1932, we noted that party propaganda did not make use of local issues in the region, even though the *RPL* supported the use of local overtones and traditions in Nazi propaganda. On the other hand, Allen, Hamilton, and other scholars noted that the party's propaganda tactics were indeed characterized by the use of local issues. The use or nonuse of local traditions in the Nazi propaganda may be able, among other things, to testify to the essence of that which led to the rise of the Nazi Party in Germany. Did local traditions color party activity in different regions, so that there can be no talk of a unified Nazi propaganda? Such is to say: Was the Nazi phenomenon a regional one, which sprang up almost without coordination or guidance from above, intersecting at certain points and at given times with the policies of the Nazi centers in Munich and Berlin? The relations between the center and the periphery, so essential to our study, take on a new light when we review the local variations in Nazi propaganda and the manner in which these variations intersected with the central propaganda issues of Nazi activity in the region at the time of the general elections.

The Nazi leaders did not clearly recognize the potential that the exploitation of local government bodies could have for party activity. Until 1933 local politics and government played no strategic role in the Nazi assumption of power. The party's intervention in local government issues was only precipitated by the financial hardships facing the individual communities. The Nazi Party and its factions in the local councils strongly criticized a number of points on the local agenda, the most prominent of them being the salaries drawn by the officials and the head of the council, the high interest rates, the redundancy in the work of some council members, and local corruption. The Nazis tended to blame the crisis in local government on the inflated salaries of the council officials. Until 1933, however, the party had no official policy on the subject of its relations with the bodies of self-administration. The Nazi representatives in the institutions of local government were subordinated entirely to the party policy, a fact that limited their activity and made them, in essence, little more than a rubber stamp, with nothing to do but receive and implement orders on any subject in which there was no official policy. The chapter leaders usually led the party factions in the council. It was no easy task to find people who were identified politically with the Nazi Party and, together with this, capable of local administration. Experienced local notables and politicians were often solicited by the Nazi Party to serve as their candidates for administrative bodies, but usually in vain. The local press indulged in more than a few jokes about the doings of party members in the local government.[87]

The local Nazi specialist on municipal government in the Black Forest was Benedict Kuner, a former representative of the *Zentrum* in the town council of Schonach and an expert on the subject of local administration. Kuner abandoned the *Zentrum* in 1930 after expressing disappointment with its municipal activity and, turning to the Nazi Party, began to concentrate its activity on the subject of local government.[88] Even before Kuner entered the picture, however, the *Gau* organization bureau organized activity on the subject of local government, launching its preparations well ahead of time, at the beginning of 1930, for the local election campaign (*Gemeindewahlen*) scheduled for November. In Baden, the party propaganda bureau turned its attention to local issues as soon as the Reichstag elections were over.[89] The election campaigns to the local governing bodies were characterized by factors of economic self-interest. The parties dropped the issues of more national interest, concentrating instead on local economic and administrative problems. Parties were established especially for this goal under names such as "The Union of Bourgeoisie," "The Free Bourgeoisie," and "The Union List of Peasants," leaving no doubt as to the bourgeois character of the campaign and of the majority of competing parties.[90] The bourgeois and antisocialist nature of this election campaign stood in sharp contrast to the anticapitalist approach taken by the Nazis only a few months before, in the summer elections of 1930. This turnaround caused the party more than a few problems, and later we will see how it managed to overcome them.

In the local elections, the Nazi Party conducted its activity on two different levels: (1) Throughout most towns and villages of the region it joined forces with the bourgeois interests, at times even with the *Zentrum,* and common lists of candidates were submitted. The bourgeois orientation, whose interest was patently economic, testifies to a new direction in the Nazi propaganda and activity, and it was one that was neither imposed nor engineered by the Nazi centers at the higher levels. This is one example of the way that the individual chapters expressed their adaptation to local political traditions and customs.[91] (2) There were some towns in which the party appeared in an independent list, raising propaganda motifs totally unlike the ones from two months before. In Haslach, for example, the Nazi candidates demanded that all financial and economic affairs first be ratified by the council of citizens (*Bürgerausschuss*) before being submitted to the local council. It further demanded that the local institutions patronize only local shops, that employees of the local council not use two different offices, and that council employees refrain from all journeys that were not strictly necessary. Local agriculture was to be promoted and unused food and land handed over to the local peasants. The party demanded a "Productive Folk Community" (*Volksgemeinschaft aller Schaffenden*) and came out against political patronage, against Marxisim, against the *Zentrum,* against bourgeois compromise, but in favor of keeping the town clean.[92] The local press claimed that no one heard any more about the socialism of the Nazi Party, and indeed the press had something to go on. In Schonach the party joined the "Union of Bourgeoisie" in demanding the construction of a local swimming pool, and in Schonwald it linked forces with other bourgeois groups in calling for the repeal of the beer tax, since this hurt the owners of taverns and inns.[93]

While the Nazi propaganda demonstrated its nationalist, at times populist character, it was its concern for local bourgeois interests that took pride of place. We noted in chapter 7 that in contrast to the Reichstag election campaign, people who had formerly voted for the local bourgeois lists tended to shift their allegiance to the new Nazi list. In our analysis of the social basis of party members we noted, moreover, that activists in the bourgeois lists went over to the Nazis even before election day, and that this trend gained momentum thereafter. We may not be wrong in conjecturing that it was through their influence that the party propaganda changed its tone.

In the years 1931 and 1932 we are witness to intensive activity (at times to the point of absurdity) by Nazi delegates in local councils and meetings. Thanks to the coverage of the local press, we are able to view the work of the Nazi representatives in the manner in which it reached public notice. The series of proposals that they introduced may be summed up with the following points: (1) foreign workers were to be forbidden within the community limits; (2) roads were to be paved and factories established, once again with a local work force; (3) the unemployed should not have to travel to a distant employment office in order to receive unemployment. In Bonndorf the Nazi faction demanded that the unemployed be paid there on the spot, noting that this would also help stimulate local business life; (4) the council should be encouraged to raise memorials to the fallen soldiers, despite the economic plight; (5) the number of local officials should be cut back and their salaries reduced; (6) the council leaders had to present their political identification and platform if they wanted to be elected to office; (7) public works projects were needed for the unemployed; (8) taxes detrimental to merchants, craftsmen, and small manufacturers were to be repealed; (9) support for the workers' organizations and professional unions should be prevented, due to the political nature of the action.[94] These proposals, with slight local variations, characterized the party activity in the local councils and, as stated, were brought to public notice via the local press, among other channels.

The Nazi propaganda did feature populistic elements and proposals for the protection of workers, but what is important is that alongside these factors, there were others aimed specifically at the local bourgeois class. The Nazi Party was no different from any other party in its propaganda on local affairs. All of the bourgeois parties and even the *Zentrum* held similar attitudes on local issues. What made the Nazi Party different, however, was that it had never been part of the local government. Following the election of 1930, the local bourgeoisie began to view the Nazi Party as a champion of middle-class interests as well. The election campaigns to the presidency and the Reichstag in the summer of 1932 saw little discussion of local problems, although some local speakers stressed the issues relevant to the region. Throughout all this, the party continued its activity in the local administrative bodies, adding wide strata of the local bourgeois class to the ranks of its traditional voting public (new voters and workers).

The dearth of research literature concerning the propaganda on local issues in other Catholic regions prevents us from making a comparative survey of the topic. Suffice it to mention that in the Günzburg district, as noted by Zofka, the party refrained from dealing with local issues. Holmes, however, argues just the opposite in his discussion of the Nazi propaganda in Lower Bavaria. There, the propaganda of the local activists dealt with the modernization of local agriculture and the needs of the peasants, transforming this into their central propaganda motif. In East Bavaria the local party's chapter invested their efforts in local politics. Although the local chapters could not develop a clear Nazi policy in the local councils, they were aware of the importance of this kind of politics. Pridham does not review the activity of the party at the level of the local government, and the same is true of the police reports from the regions of Koblenz-Mainz-Trier.[95]

The Communist Threat

Of all the propaganda motifs used by the Nazi Party, the issue of anti-Bolshevism emerges as the most prominent in the Black Forest region. The Nazi Party made frequent use of this motif from 1929 until 1933, despite the changes that occurred in the tone of its propaganda and activity, the replacement of local leaders, and the impressive gains at the polls. This statement, of course, is scarcely new to research. Indeed many scholars see this motif as having been central to the propaganda of the Nazi Party,[96] and not theirs alone. Other parties also made heavy use of anti-Marxist propaganda, especially the *Zentrum.* The local press was tireless in its coverage of the situation in Soviet Russia. It painted a vivid picture of the atrocities being committed by the communist regime and of the activity of the Communist Party in Germany, and it warned its readers that a communist putsch would result in civil war.[97]

The Nazi propaganda in the region was not all that different from the propaganda used by the *Zentrum* or the bourgeois-interest parties. It too reported frequently on the "terror in Soviet Russia," using catchphrases such as "Bolshevism is Destruction" and "Victory in Moscow Means the Death of Germany," and ran numerous stories about the horrors of daily life there. The main tenor of all these slogans was that Bolshevism, if not contained within the borders of Soviet Russia, would toll the end of Germany and its Catholic minority. This motif was sometimes interspersed with slogans depicting Hitler as the savior of Bolshevist-threatened Germany, or describing the collaboration between the *Zentrum* and the Socialist Party. Another motif, and one that spoke to the heart of the local wood industry, which found itself on the point of collapse, was the economic competition with the parallel industry in Soviet Russia. Alongside all these were blood-chilling accounts of the Soviet policy against the peasants, the churches, and the Russian bourgeoisie.[98]

The bourgeois-liberal press was also instrumental in disseminating the fear of communism throughout the region. Its reports of the extermination of the Russian peasants brought the danger graphically home to the inhabitants of the Black Forest. There was little communist activity in the region up until 1932, but the little that did exist met with a generally negative response,[99] and delegates of the Communist Party were never partner to the institutions of local government. The local press, to be sure, often referred to the Nazi Party as "right-wing Bolshevism,"[100] due to the anticapitalist motifs interspersed in its propaganda. But the more that members of the middle class joined the party, and the more that patently bourgeois and middle-class motifs were added to its propaganda, the more this image tended to fade. The taint of socialism still clung to the National Socialists, but the fear receded.[101] The question that poses itself, therefore, is What was unique about the anti-Marxist propaganda of the Nazi Party? The answer to this lies not in the use of the motif itself, but rather in the intensity with which it was used, in the proven "recipe" of direct action against radical communist activity in Berlin and elsewhere, and in the fact that police searches of members' homes revealed its active preparations against a communist putsch.[102] Nor was this all. The *Zentrum,* or the *Deutsche Staatspartei,* also conducted fiercely anti-communist-socialist propaganda, but once the elections were over made common cause with the Socialists. Even the local press came to the assistance of the party propaganda, since the anticommunist hysteria that it whipped up played into the hands of the Nazi Party in the region. It was not the fact of using anti-Marxist propaganda that stood the party in good stead in its relations with the local population, but the intensity and panic-raising use of the motif.

The fear of a Bolshevized Germany characterized wide sectors of German society. The Nazis exploited the fear of Bolshevism throughout the whole of Germany, and hence this aspect of the propaganda cannot be seen as unique to the Black Forest. In Lower Bavaria the peasants were steeped in fear, almost to hysteria, of a communist takeover, and the same was true of the Saar and the districts of Aachen, Koblenz, and Trier. Pridham stresses that the combined fear of communism and the threat against the Catholic Church was of great help to the Nazi propaganda. Zofka, on the other hand, makes a distinction between the anti-Bolshevist and anti-socialist propaganda. In the Günzburg district it was antisocialism that characterized the Nazi propaganda, since the Bolshevist danger was irrelevant and essentially unknown to the local peasants. In Rosenheim, Hammelburg, and Ettlingen the same picture rises: the anti-Bolshevic stance of the Nazi Party was the main feature of the Nazi propaganda.[103]

One other point deserves mention. Many historians regard the anti-Bolshevist propaganda as another side to the anti-Semitic propaganda, since it was the Jews (according to the Nazi ideology) who stood behind Marxism and communism. In the view of these historians, then, when the Nazis dealt with Bolshevism it was really the Jews that they had in mind.[104] Yet let us take note of the fact that in the Black Forest, at least, such an association did not exist in the conceptual world of the local activists and inhabitants. The motifs of "Judeo-Marxism" and the "Jewish-Bolshevist conspiracy" did not play a role in the Nazi propaganda in the region, and, as noted above, the anti-Semitic propaganda there was less than intense. Taken together, these two factors lead us to think that, in general, when the local propagandists and press mentioned the communist danger, they were not insinuating the Jews.

Other Propaganda Motifs

In addition to the propaganda motifs noted up to this point, let us mention a number of other motifs common to the Nazi activity. First and foremost were the attacks on the Weimar "System": the government and various heads of government, the parties, the constitution, and other political bodies or events of one kind or another. This motif was not only the most popular in the election campaign in the summer of 1930, but even before this and after. All of the parties active in the Black Forest heaped abuse on the "System" in those years, each from its own starting point. The fact that the Nazi Party had never been partner to the Weimar "System" stood well with the voters.

The Nazi propaganda also took advantage of the economic crisis stalking Germany since 1930. Indeed most of the parties made capital of the crisis in agricultural, the mass unemployment, the collapse of the banks, the emergency economic measures, and the cutback on salaries. The Nazi Party exploited the economic crisis primarily for political gain, contending that the entire political system had to be changed and that it was not just a question of voting in a new administration. Issues of national concern were exploited in the same kind of way: the militarization of Germany, the humiliating clauses in the Versailles Treaty, the defeat of the German people and the need for its revitalization. At times there was also mention of the treaty with England, the expansion of the navy, and the acquisition of colonies. The attacks against the "System" and the political exploitation of the economic crisis were all delivered in a national or nationalist tone whose major thrust was the revitalization of the German people. This was true not only of the Nazi propaganda, for the calls of "Germany Awake" resounded through the *Zentrum* meetings as well, along with their widely disseminated idea of a "folk community." Many scholars note this last motif as having been highly influential in the Nazi propaganda, but in the Black Forest it remained in the background, even after it reemerged in 1932. Nazi propagandists who summoned up the vision of a classless society rarely employed the term "folk community." While there was increased use of the motif in the Reichstag election campaign of summer 1932, it never emerged as a central motif in the region.[105] It seems likely that several elements in Catholic society (as we shall see) were influenced, among other factors, by the Nazi proposal for a society in which distinctions of class, religion, and ideology would disappear—especially among those groups that felt alienated from the Catholic public sphere. However, due to the infrequency with which this motif was used, we are unable to measure the extent of its influence.

Occupational Groups as Targets of Nazi Propaganda

The Weimar parties aimed their propaganda primarily at the different occupational groups, and class-specific issues played a key role in the election politics of all parties concerned, from that of the Nazis to the Communists. This conclusion, first formulated in Thomas Childers's pioneering study, constitutes something of a consensus among scholars today. Indeed, this seminal study remains one of the only attempts to examine the manner in which the Weimar parties courted the various occupational groups.[106] Examination of the party propaganda shows it to be a highly valuable source for analyzing the social focus of the Nazi electoral strategy and also for clarifying the identity of the different social groups that turned to the Nazi Party in 1928–32. Morever, since socioeconomic issues were uppermost in the concern of the German voting public in 1929–32, the Nazi propaganda aimed at social groups can be viewed as a valuable source for recruiting supporters and members, one that held out even more appeal than the motifs that we have seen up till this point.

In contrast to the verdict reached by Childers, however, the Black Forest is testimony to a region in which few propaganda motifs were aimed directly at one specific class or occupational group. The following analysis will explore the target groups of the Nazi propaganda in the Black Forest, through reference to the social categories employed by Childers: (1) the old middle class of peasants, merchants, master craftsmen, and shopkeepers; (2) the new middle class of white-collar workers and civil servants; (3) the working class of blue-collar workers employed in the factories and mines, agricultural laborers, and skilled workers. The second group, that of the *Rentnermittelstand,* was almost numerically insignificant in the region (cf. chap. 5). There is no evidence that this group ever came up as an issue in the Nazi propaganda in the Black Forest and hence we will not deal with it here. Nor will the third group, that of the new middle class, figure prominently in our discussion, due to its numerical insignificance in the region. The first group, however, that of the old middle class, constituted one of the two most predominant social strata in the region, particularly the sector consisting of peasants, craftsmen, and master craftsmen, and we shall relate to them as a target group in the local Nazi propaganda. The working class (the fourth group) constituted the second largest social stratum in the region, though in the Black Forest it consisted mostly of agricultural laborers and skilled workers. Blue-collar workers were but a relatively small group in the Black Forest, due to the undeveloped state of local industry.

The Peasants

We have already seen that, as a group, the peasants lent the Nazi Party some initial support as early as 1928 in the region of Schwarzwald-Baar and the Wutach. In chapter 5 we examined the plight of the peasants in those regions and also noted that only a minority actually joined the Nazi Party. On the basis of information appearing in the contemporary press, we learned that in 1932 there was a tendency among the peasants to leave the Nazi Party and to transfer their support elsewhere.[107] The most senior Nazi activists in the area were characterized by a concern with agriculture: Merk, Leo Gutt, Albicker, Frank, Huber (from the village of Ibach), and the majority of BLB leaders who shifted their allegiance to the Nazi Party at the end of the 1920s.

For this reason, it is surprising to find so few propaganda motifs addressed to the peasants in the region, especially when we recall that peasants became central to its propaganda from 1930 on, after Walter Darre became chief of the Nazi bureau of Agriculture. Darre created an organizational network that encompassed the entire Reich, and although the bureau demanded a strict implementation of official orders from Munich, it also displayed a keen sensitivity to local conditions and traditions. The bureau placed an agronomist alongside every chapter of the party, whether on the level of the village or the *Gau*, in order to advise on matters of agriculture and to supervise the party propaganda and activity in the agricultural sector. The bureau of agriculture (*Agrarpolitischer Apparat—Aa*) was founded in the summer of 1930, shortly before the elections to the Reichstag, and thus had little impact on the electoral gains of the party. After the elections the bureau concentrated on recruiting peasants from every corner of the Reich, in the effort to gain control of the agricultural organizations and lobbies. The Nazi propaganda courted the peasants through use of the catchphrase "Our struggle for blood and soil."

Its struggle to gain mastery of the peasant organizations reaped success in 1931, when a Nazi delegate was elected to serve as one of the four presidents of the "National Rural League" (*Reichslandbund*). The Nazi propaganda demanded agricultural autarky, the revitalization of the agricultural lobby, a lowering of taxes and interest rates, and assistance to farms in financial trouble. "Under a National Socialist state," it declared, "no German farm will be permitted to be auctioned off owing to foreclosure and no peasant will be driven from his hearth." Here too the party propaganda waged war against capitalism and Marxism, and also against the modern technology said to be undermining the peasants' family, faith, morality, and traditions. These motifs were not all that different from the propaganda used by other parties in courting the peasants, particularly the numerous peasant parties that sprang up across Germany. Yet, once again, the fact that the Nazi Party had never been partner to any government policy toward the peasants worked in its favor. And indeed, in the 1930 election campaigns and in the summer of 1932, the party enjoyed mass support from the German peasants.[108]

In north and central Baden, the party received mass support from the Protestant peasants as early as 1928. The *Gau* bureau of agriculture, which was founded at the end of 1930 and placed first under Plesch and then Huber, strove to take over the largest peasant organization, the *BLB,* and indeed succeeded in doing so in 1931. The bureau also took a highly active role in the dissemination of party propaganda and even urged the peasants of Baden to revolt.[109] However, none of this activity had much of an effect on party activists in the Black Forest. Despite the collapse of the *BLB* infrastructure in the region already in 1928–29, the party did not conduct intensive propaganda in the local peasant villages. Nor did the absence of organized peasant opposition spur the party into action in the villages of the Wutach, where it won strong support beginning with 1928. The party propaganda was almost oblivious to the special needs of the Black Forest peasants, who were mostly interested in linking their farms to the region's network of roads, the collapse of the price of milk, the modernization of agriculture, the improvement of living standards and a relaxation of debts, vaccinations against disease, and even the law of inheritance specific to the Black Forest (see chap. 4), a traditional source of discontent in the region.

In the summer of 1930, the activists mentioned the peasant estate only once in their speeches. The party did not run on an independent slate in the local village elections in November 1930, and at times it preferred to work toward forming a coalition with the bourgeois lists, which were embroiled in argument with the local peasant list.[110] The problem confronting the party in its efforts to win over the local peasants can be explained by organizational reasons (the fact that most of the peasants were committed to the Catholic *Bauernverein*), the character of the peasants, and the background of the speakers and propagandists. Until 1932 the majority of speakers came from outside the region and could not claim an agricultural background. Agrarian propaganda demanded a new approach, one that differed from the political propaganda in which the propagandists who visited the region had been trained. The bureau of agriculture made a point of stressing that, in the villages, the propaganda meetings should assume a more personal nature and that the propaganda ought to confront specific issues. Due to the suspicious and conservative nature of the peasants, moreover, a lot of hard and patient groundwork was required. The pride that the peasant took in his achievements and status required motifs of a less negative nature, motifs that would emphasize his achievements of the past and his brighter future under a Nazi regime. The propaganda meeting had to be organized with the greatest of care, and the speaker had to be cognizant of the special problems in each village. It was desirable to extend a personal invitation to each farmer. It was desirable to hold a "German evening" that would serve to attract the peasant and make him want to attend other events. In the meeting the speaker had to address the specific problems of the peasants and to describe how the Nazi Party was battling in the Reichstag to solve them, to stress the Christian nature of the party and hold out promises for the future. It was also advisable to use the anticommunist and antisocialist propaganda that fell so receptively on many peasant ears. The bureau reasoned that through the use of psychological tactics that took the character of the peasant into account, together with the presence of specially trained agronomists and efficient organization, it would be possible to overcome the barrier in reaching the heart of the peasant villages.[111]

However, due to the absence of capable local speakers and Karlsruhe's neglect of the region, the majority of speakers made every mistake imaginable when speaking before peasant audiences. The problems of the peasants were not specifically addressed and the propaganda continued to churn out its typically unconstructive criticism. At times, it was precisely the anticapitalistic side of the Nazi Party that the speakers chose to parade before their peasant audiences. In many cases the activists did not bother to reach the smaller villages and left the farmers to reach the meeting by their own devices.[112] That the majority of speakers had not the slightest knowledge of local problems goes without saying. The specially trained agronomist was indeed active for a while in the region, but after quarreling with the *Bezirkleiter* preferred to resign his position. The only thing left to interest the peasants, both in the meetings and in the party literature geared to them, was the fight against Marxism and socialism.[113] It was not until 1932 that a turning point came in the tactics used for the local peasants. It began with the greater involvement of local speakers, some with an agricultural background. Meetings with headlines such as "Peasants, where are we standing?" or "National Socialism and Agriculture" were held with greater frequency.[114] An additional reason for the turnaround was rooted in the bitter argument in Baden over the reform of the dairy industry, which involved the amalgation of all branches of dairy production and the marketing of its products through middlemen rather than directly by the peasants themselves. The Nazi Party was obliged to take a stand on the issue, and the one it adopted was largely negative. It argued that important nutritional elements would be lost during the process of pasteurization in the central dairies, and that the quality of the product would thus be compromised. The almagation of the dairies would also increase the overhead and make the milk more expensive. Even though the peasants of the Black Forest objected to the reform for different reasons, the party activists in the region pounced on the issue as a way of showing support for the peasants.[115]

Let us now take a look at a typical Nazi propaganda meeting in the region, one that was held in the village of Unterbaldingen. The speaker was Joseph Albicker, a known figure in the region and a former *BLB* activist. In the meeting Albicker surveyed the history of the peasants in Germany from the days of the Second Reich up until the 1930s. He mentioned the protective tariffs that assured the peasants of a noncompetitive status, the end of the Bismarck era, the transformation of Germany into an industrialized nation, the controlled economy (*Zwangwirtschaft*) during the war, the inflation-caused profiteering, the heavy debts shackling the farms, the cancellation of the protective tariffs on agriculture, and a number of similar issues. He summed up his words by describing the Nazi Party as the savior of the peasants. Yet even though the speaker was a peasant, a native of the nearby village, and a popular figure addressing immediate problems, most of the audience remained apathetic and a few people even attacked him vehemently.[116] Here we are witness to the paradox that characterized relations between the local party chapters in the region and the peasant class. The more the Nazi propaganda tried to beat a path to their door, the more the peasants tended to abandon their support of the party. It was precisely in the years when there was little party activity in the villages and when the propaganda was largely oblivious to their problems that the Nazi Party won a great deal of support. But the more the peasants recognized the goals and the nature of the party's activity (with its conspicuously socialist strains), and the more they witnessed the totalitarian and revolutionary nature of its solutions—the powerful commitments demanded of would-be party members—the more hesitant and suspicious they showed themselves, to the point where there is evidence of peasants deserting the Nazi Party in the latter half of 1932 (see chap. 7).

The Nazi propaganda aimed at the peasants of the region failed. The support that they gave the party until 1932 was primarily the result of the organizational vacuum in peasant life following the dissolution of the peasant organizations in the region. When, in 1932, the party tried to fill this vacuum with agrarian content and stepped-up activity, the peasants came to realize the nature of the proposed substitute and most of them rejected it outright. Neither in other Catholic regions was the party able to win the mass support of the peasants, including 1930. In Lower Bavaria the party toned down the ideological motifs dealing with "Blood and Soil" and stressed the economic issues closer to the peasant's heart, such as the modernization of agriculture, the establishment of educational frameworks for their sons, improved agricultural training, autarky, a return to the self-sustenance of the German people through reinforcing the purchasing power of the agricultural population and limiting the import of seed and food. The Nazi propaganda emphasized the totalitarian and unified nature of the solution that it offered the local peasants. The party also tried to take up issues formerly considered the exclusive property of the Bavarian Peasants League (*BBB*) and to present itself as being in a better position to solve them.

Despite the strenuous agrarian propaganda, however, the party was unable to mobilize mass support among the peasants until 1933 in the district of Tauberbischofsheim (north Baden); the party's agriculture message could not penetrate the local peasants' hearts since the party's organization there could not compete with the *Bauernverein* of the *Zentrum*. In the Günzburg district the peasants heard a generalized kind of propaganda that dealt more with foreign affairs, socialism, politics, and economics than anything concerning their immediate problems. The Nazi propaganda did not present significant and clearly outlined solutions. Sweeping slogans such as "the breaking of interest slavery" were translated by the peasants themselves into a totalitarian solution for all their problems, one that would change everything and wash away their taxes and debts. The antisocialist mofits in the party propaganda spoke to the heart of the peasants, and this was one of the reasons why they supported the Nazi Party in 1930, but by the summer of 1932 their support waned. In Catholic Bavaria the party worked vigorously with the peasants, but this did not ensure its success in each and every region. The motifs prominent in their propaganda resembled the ones emphasized by the *Aa* and were designed to tug at the Catholic heartstrings of the peasants. In Lower Bavaria they failed, in the Allgäu they met with considerable success, and the same goes for the district of Ebermannstadt in Upper Franconia. Despite the unified tone of the Nazi activity and propaganda among the peasants of Bavaria and elsewhere, the results differed from region to region, due to the local traditions and changing socioreligious conditions.[117]

Craftsmen, Shopkeepers, Innkeepers, and Hoteliers

Alongside the peasants, these occupational groups constituted the heart of the old middle class. (Innkeepers and hoteliers were not included in Childers's categories, but we have added them here due to their traditional great importance in the Black Forest region.) The crumbling economic state of the old middle class and its mounting fear of the workers and large business concerns originated in several different factors: the laws for stabilizing the economy in 1923–24, the sympathetic policy toward the working class from 1928 on, and the economic crisis beginning in 1930. Even though many small business owners managed to weather the low turnover of merchandise and the cutback in sales, they became increasingly apprehensive of economic collapse and demotion to the ranks of the proletariat.[118] The Nazi propaganda made a concerted effort to reach these social strata, attacking the Marxism and socialism that threatened the middle class, along with the consumer associations, department stores, and large business concerns turning a comfortable profit at the expense of small businessmen. Together with this, the Nazi Party extolled the role of the old middle class in the cooperative society of the future, one that would embrace all ranks of the productive classes and in which "handicrafts and commerce would again find justice and honor."[119]

In the Black Forest region, the old middle class was dominated by craftsmen, shopkeepers, innkeepers, and hoteliers. Of all the groups, it was the craftsmen who had the longest standing in the commercial and industrial life of the region. We have already seen in chapter 5 that it was their skills that formed the basis for the large workshops connected to clockmaking, lumber, and precision mechanics. While some of these workshops were transformed into factories employing hundreds of workers, they did not dispense with the craftsmen altogether, and indeed there were many craftsmen who provided the factories with a wide variety of services. There were also carpenters, wagoneers, painters, sawyers, and blacksmiths who earned their livelihood in the large farms that dotted the region. Many of the independent craftsmen had fallen victim to the processes of industrialization, modernization, and, ultimately, the Great Economic Crisis that overtook the region already in the mid-twenties, and they made their living as skilled workers in factories or as petty craftsmen dependent on one factory or another, and as farmhands. The independent master craftsmen formed a relatively large group in the Nazi Party in the region, as did the innkeepers and hoteliers. However, the relative size of this group stood in inverse proportion to its importance as a target group in the Nazi propaganda. The party did not have a concrete program on the subject of the middle class. Few local craftsmen became speakers for the party, while nonlocal speakers were unaware of the importance of the craftsmen and their problems. The local Dr. Vogel, for example, preferred to speak about Bolshevism and Jews, but Herr Winterhalder, who was not sympathetic to the party, and who was also the owner of a sawmill, "reminded" him during the discussion of the plight of the region's wood industry and of the craftsmen connected to it.[120] To be sure, speakers did, on occasion, mention the party's battle against the Jewish department stores, naturally interspersing anticapitalist motifs into their attacks against the large concerns, banks, and industrial magnates.[121] Yet alongside these motifs, which doubtlessly spoke to the heart of the craftsmen, the speakers also voiced socialist, almost Marxist attitudes, and these were utterly opposed to the worldview of the craftsmen. The insensitivity to the craftsmen's plight was most apparent when the party held propaganda meetings in the villages and towns in which craftsmen comprised the dominant social strata, as in Eisenbach, Triberg, Furtwangen, and Wolfach.[122] In these towns the party also made respectable gains, partly due to the support of the craftsmen, but this fact was also ignored by the Nazi propagandists. On the municipal level, however, the party factions in the local council concentrated more on the problems of local craftsmen, demanding that their taxes be lowered and that the townspeople restrict their purchases to the local shops. We may conjecture that such attitudes at the local level of Nazi propaganda went far in projecting the party as the defender of middle-class interests in general, and of the craftsmen's interests in particular, and helped soften the socialist image of the Nazi Party in the region.[123]

It is particularly interesting to note how oblivious the Nazi propaganda was to the subject of tourism and health resorts, so vital to the socioeconomic life of the region. Nazi propagandists showed no compunction in vigorously denouncing England and France, despite the teeming presence of citizens from both these countries in the region's health spas and resorts.[124] Issues that could have made highly attractive propaganda motifs, such as the taxes imposed on the visitors and the work on the Schluchsee dam, were not employed by the party propaganda. In the local councils the party factions demanded the outlawing of business with foreigners, certainly a potential blow to local tourism. To be sure, the party's demand to repeal the beer tax (*Biersteuer*) was a touch of propaganda that spoke to the heart of the innkeepers and hoteliers. However, we must also bear in mind that many members of this category not only belonged to the party but even held senior positions in its ranks, and it is possible that the opposition to the beer tax sprang from their own personal interests.[125] There is a final and entirely different way in which the activity of the Nazi Party in the region adapted itself to the demands of the local old middle class: namely, the fact that its activity and propaganda were not of a provocative or violent nature, since this might have proved detrimental to local tourism and the economic life of the region, especially for the owners of small businesses.

Vigorous propaganda aimed at the old middle class characterized the Nazi Party activity in many Catholic regions, and here the Black Forest is not an exception. It is interesting that in the district of Günzburg, to be sure, the party did not consolidate any economic program for the middle class. But the distress rising from the competition with the large stores and industry helped swing middle-class support toward the Nazi Party. The tirades against the great department stores and the anti-Marxist-socialist slogans made for a highly potent combination in the propaganda aimed at the old middle class.[126]

The New Middle Class

The Nazi propaganda directed toward civil servants and white-collar workers in the Black Forest stood in total contrast to its propaganda at the national level. The propaganda at the national level sought to win over the civil servants (*Beamten*) and white-collar workers (*Angestellten*), opposing any cutback in their salaries or injury to their status, not to mention the mass dismissals conceived by Bruning's deflationary policy.[127] In the Black Forest, however, the party directed its propaganda against these groups. This opposition was mostly sounded in the local councils, where they were picked up by the local press and brought to the attention of the public. The members of the Nazi factions voiced their opposition to the salaries of the local council officials and demanded supervision over their wages and job placement. They called for the resignation of officials from the Ministry of Finance and painted a graphic picture of the way the officials were hastening the destruction of the peasant class. These motifs were sounded by the party propaganda beginning in 1930, at the opening of the election campaign to the local councils.[128] It was only in the second half of 1932, primarily after the Reichstag elections in July, that the local Nazi propaganda changed its tone, bringing it into line with the propaganda on the national level. It now stated that the party would protect the special privileges of these groups under the Nazi regime, and that it did not intend (unlike the *Zentrum*) to fire civil servants.[129] However, it was not in the local councils that these kind of promises were proclaimed, but in the regional Nazi press.

The Working Class

An examination of party propaganda aimed at the working class stands at the center of the historiographic argument concerning the change in the party's activity and propaganda after 1928. We have already noted that many scholars contend that once the party learned the results of the Reichstag elections in May 1928 it turned to the middle class, formerly only a marginal target group. This move was diametrically opposed to the activity of the party in the cities and to the socialist motifs that had typified its propaganda up till then. A few scholars argue that even after 1928 the Nazi propaganda continued to show strikingly socialist-Marxist traits, and that in some regions, the socialist motifs even retained their centrality.[130]

At the beginning of the 1930s the Nazi propaganda claimed that if the working class was interested in freedom, it had to break the bonds of Marxism and capitalism. The party demanded the creation of public works projects that would engage in the repair and construction of roads, dams, canals, and the renovation of buildings. The government was responsible for providing its citizens with work; hence it had to establish a compulsory work force that would take the unemployed off the streets and make them part of the "folk community." The party propaganda disseminated generalized slogans such as "Work and Bread" and "The Right to Work," but did not concern itself with specific economic problems, such as questions of currency and autarky. "Full employment," the Nazi propaganda claimed, "was the heart of socialism." Socialism was "a moral, not an economic imperative." It demanded justice, the general welfare, and protection against exploitation. Capitalism was defined as "the exclusive control by capital over the opportunity to work; [under capitalism] it is the exclusive right of capital to decide whether or not one works."

In the Nazi people's community, however, "Capital will no longer decide, Labor will." These motifs were interspersed with fierce invectives against Marxism and the *SPD,* the latter being blamed for the end of the eight-hour workday, the mass unemployment, the emergency measures, the reduction in wages, and the blow to social security. These were the principal motifs in the propaganda of the Nazi Party aimed at the working class.[131]

As we have already noted in chapter 5, the working class in the Black Forest region was composed of workers from a number of different branches: forest workers, agricultural laborers, factory workers, skilled workers in workshops, master craftsmen forced by the economic crisis out of their workshops and into the factories and farms, and also the large group of workers constructing the Schluchsee dam. The weakness of the Socialist and Communist parties, the economic crisis that struck at these groups already in the mid-1920s, and, most importantly, the fact that some of them had removed themselves from the Catholic milieu, all conspired to make the working class particularly vulnerable to extremist propaganda and activity on the part of the opposition.

The group of skilled workers and laborers was the largest of the groups making up the Nazi Party (see chap. 7). Many voters of the party came from towns economically based on factories, home industry, and large workshops. We have also discussed the possibility that many of the new voters in 1930 cast their vote for the *SPD* at the beginning of the 1920s, before resigning themselves to political apathy. Some party members in senior positions of the Nazi organization in the region were, during the early 1920s, members of the *SPD*. This was the case with Dr. Vogel, Merk, Müssle, Albicker, and Sattler from Neustadt. Over the course of 1930 the local press labeled the Nazi Party as "right-wing Bolshevism" and played up its resemblance to communism and socialism. The press explained the Nazi success in different towns as the migration of voters from the communist camp into that of the Nazis.[132]

The Nazi Party retained its image as a socialist party at least up until 1931, and to a certain extent even after. Did the Nazi propaganda in the Black Forest actually justify this image? Together with the anti-Marxist motifs, we may conclude that socialist motifs were more characteristic of Nazi propaganda than anything else in the region. Even after 1930, with the penetration of bourgeois strains into its propaganda, the party did not abandon its old motifs. This line of propaganda originated in the local chapters of the region itself, and it did not conform with the party propaganda in Baden. There, as elsewhere in Germany, the Nazi propaganda continued to use socialist, at times Marxist motifs, but did not place these at the center of its propaganda. In the Black Forest, an anticapitalist and prosocialist tone indeed characterized the party propaganda in the Reichstag election campaign of summer 1930. But once this was over the local Nazi press projected the National Socialist Party as a workers' party, battling on the side of the unemployed worker.[133] The slogans were usually of the most general nature, and the propaganda made no attempt to lure any specific element of the working class into its net. So, for example, when Nazi speakers made their pitch in the region of the Schluchsee dam, it was not the problems of the local dam workers that they addressed but rather those of the peasants, and despite this the Nazi Party managed to draw numerous dam workers.[134] To cite another example, the Nazi propaganda did not give fitting expression to the problems facing the clock-making industry even in those towns where the problems were most relevant. Nor did the forest workers, the largest and most ignominious social group in the region, receive any attention from the local speakers. The primary reason for the neglect of specific social groups originated in the fact that most of the speakers were not native to the region. Yet none of this mattered. For the majority of suffering workers and craftsmen, the sweeping socialistic slogans of the Nazi propaganda were enough to make them transfer their allegiance to the Nazi Party and to cast their vote in its favor.[135]

Party activists in the region were aware that social groups connected to the working class were streaming en masse toward the Nazi Party, and despite its new bourgeois orientation after 1930 they continued to cultivate the old motifs, even at the expense of social groups from the middle class now joining its ranks. When the chapter in Schonach ordered the special issue of *Der Führer* at the time of the presidential election campaign, it ordered 400 copies of the issue directed especially at the workers, and only 300 copies of those geared to the peasants and middle class! The local Nazi press quoted verbatim the workers who supported the party, while the party factions in the local councils demanded a compulsory work service and public works projects. They further demanded that the salaries of the civil servants be reduced and placed on a par with those of the workers, asking "why should they [i.e., the workers] be the only ones to suffer starvation wages?"[136] The party distributed leaflets overflowing with anticapitalist and prosocialist motifs: "What is the significance of the Five-Year Program for the German workers?" "The perpetuation of slavery," "National freedom and social equality," and "Our enemies are Marxism, parliamentarianism, and high finance." In a few propaganda pamphlets the party urged the nationalization of the capitalist system, all-out war against the large department stores, and the retransformation of agriculture into the economic basis of the German people.[137]

At times, the socialist strains of the Nazi propaganda utterly contradicted its antisocialist and bourgeois motifs, and this contradiction cost the party some votes. Working groups who recognized this fundamental contradiction abandoned the party ranks,[138] as did some peasants, once the intensification of the propaganda activity made them aware of its socialist, quasi-Marxist content. But the strong anticommunist tones, the attack on the political system, and the emphasis that political change had to come before any economic change provided the cement uniting all social classes in support of the party, the workers included.

The anticapitalist, prosocialist propaganda of the Nazi Party constituted almost the only sign that the local Nazi leadership had made a correct reading of the region's socioeconomic structure and of the groups that supported the Nazi Party. Merk and Dr. Vogel in the southern Black Forest, despite their initial support of the *SPD* at the beginning of the 1920s and the *BLB* after that, recognized the importance of the social protest rankling in the hearts of many agricultural laborers and craftsmen reduced to working on local farms. This was a striking phenomenon in their own village of Grafenhausen, where numerous craftsmen who had formerly plied their trade in the service of peasants were forced by the Great Economic Crisis to hire themselves out as farmhands or workers in the forests and factories.[139] The leaders of the party chapters in Triberg,

Wolfach, and Furtwangen came themselves from the ranks of the skilled workers and craftsmen, and they were familiar with these problems from up close. However, the party did not always manage to penetrate to the heart of the towns in which the dominant stratum belonged to the working class. This was the case in Gutenbach, where the communists got an early start and won considerable support in a village suffering from mass unemployment and hunger, following the closure of its one and only factory.[140] Such was also the case in Villingen, Hausach, and St. George, industrial towns of importance in the region. In a number of industrial towns (e.g., Haslach, Wolfach) the party did not manage in 1932 to repeat its success of 1930, despite the swelling unemployment in the ranks of the workers. We have grounds for believing that many workers and craftsmen abandoned the Nazi Party just as it was hammering out a program directed at the middle class.[141]

Until 1929, whatever socialist propaganda could be heard in the region came primarily from the considerably weakened chapters of the *SPD.* Beginning with 1931, however, the Communist Party became extremely active in the Black Forest and the socialist propaganda intensified along with it. Later, we will try to see why so many voters from the working class preferred the National Socialist solution to that of the communists and the socialists. We will also attempt to discover why, if they were seeking socialist content, they turned to National Socialism rather than the numerous *Vereine* of the Catholic milieu, which also offered socialist content. Later we will seek to examine the reasons for the organizational vacuum in the heart of the working class and to identify its essence and properties in order to understand why it was precisely the Nazi Party that penetrated with such ease, and in so unsophisticated a manner, the different groups of workers in the region.

The socialist propaganda of the Nazi Party in rural Catholic areas of Germany has not been as intensively researched as the propaganda addressed to the peasants and middle class. Pridham notes that in the regions of Bavaria the party did not make any special effort to disseminate socialist propaganda. From the secondary literature on the Oberpfalz, the district of Hammelburg in Lower Franconia, the district of Ebermannstadt in Upper Franconia, the district of Tauberbischofsheim in North Baden, and the Rheinland districts we do not have evidence of Nazi-sozi propaganda. Typical for this situation are the rural areas in Swabia. Zofka has argued that in the Günzburg district, due to the *SPD*'s hold over the working sector, the Nazi Party did not make any attempt to break through. In the Saar region the party was considered to be a workers' party in every respect, but we are unable to compare an industrialized region such as the Saar with rural Catholic regions in Germany.[142] On the basis of the available evidence, therefore, it appears that in comparison with other rural Catholic regions, the phenomenon of socialist-strained Nazi propaganda was unique to the Black Forest.

Summary

Part 2 presents a description of the National-Socialist public sphere[143] at the local level with comparative elements from many Catholic rural regions. It seeks to clarify the extent to which this public sphere constituted an attraction for the residents of the Black Forest, and to what extent the success of the Nazi Party can be attributed to its activity in the region. Over the course of our discussion we attempted to understand the difficulties that the Nazi public sphere had in consolidating its position, and we argued that Nazi activity, organization, and propaganda are unable to provide a convincing explanation for the mass support that it drew. Let us sum up several of the most salient characteristics of Nazi Party activity.

1. The power bases of the party were located in the peasant villages of the southern Black Forest, in the villages and towns based on small-scale industry and in the health resort villages and towns. In terms of socioeconomic groups the party found its power base among the peasants (1928), skilled workers and former independent craftsmen (1930), and independent craftsmen and the self-employed (1932).
2. Most of the voters for the party in 1928 and 1930 were voters who had not taken part in the Weimar elections for a number of years. Many of them voted for the *SPD* and the *BLB* in the early 1920s and did not vote again until 1930. In 1932 they were joined by the former voters of the bourgeois parties. Up until 1932 the vote for the Nazi Party can be termed as "negative participation" in the sense of constituting a protest vote for an antidemocratic group opposing the "Weimar System."[144]
3. Nazi Party activity took place in an isolated and undeveloped region. The liaison between the local Nazi chapters and the centers in Munich and Karlsruhe was weak.
4. Party organization was highly flawed.
5. Factors considered crucial to the success of the Nazi Party played only a marginal role in the Black Forest, among them the Nazi press, local notables, unusual propaganda techniques, and aggressive local leadership. The same is true of propaganda motifs such as "folk community," Hitler as "Der Führer," anti-Semitism, and so forth.

6. The hostility to Marxism and Bolshevism was among the most basic ideological elements in the Nazi Party propaganda, along with populist-socialist motifs that were almost Marxist in themselves. The combination of the two made the party propaganda in the region unique in comparison to the haphazard propaganda of other parties in the Black Forest, and even in comparison to the Nazi propaganda in other Catholic regions.

7. Both in respect of its social basis and the image that it sought to project, the Nazi Party was a "people's party" (*Volkspartei*) standing above the interests of any one specific occupational group. One can, however, discern a socialist nature that made the propaganda unique up until 1930–31, and the presence of particularly large groups of workers and laborers in its ranks.[145]

8. There was little political activity in the Black Forest region, apart from that of the *Zentrum* and the Nazis.

Our comparison with other Catholic regions showed that Nazi activity assumed a different character in different places. It was mainly in the district of Günzburg that we have found similiar elements. Moreover, our examination of the liaison between local Nazi activity and the national level leads us to conclude that the activity differed from region to region at both the micro- and macro-level. At the micro-level the Nazi public sphere dealt with the local public sphere (*Loklae Öffentlichkeit*):[146] the ways in which members and activists behaved within a given set of social parameters, the influence of daily politics on chapter activity, and the manner in which the party functioned at the local level. At the macro-level, on the other hand, we saw the great importance attributed to the masses, to whom the events of a more public character were addressed. Among these events we may include the "Party Day" (*Parteitag*) in Nürnberg, the "Hitler flights" above the skies of Germany, the oiling of the propaganda machine, and the political wheeling and dealing in Berlin.[147]

Part 3

The Loneliness of the *Stammtisch*

*The Disintegration of Social Life in the Black Forest,
1929–32*

In the chapters below, the Catholic milieu will serve as the starting point
for our discussion. The *milieu* has come to be a highly important concept
in the study of German Catholicism over the last decade, one that serves as
a drawing point for many of its critical conclusions. In using the term
Catholic milieu we refer to the patterns of cultural, socioeconomic, and
political behavior often found among the Catholic inhabitants in various
regions of Germany, especially the rural regions. These patterns bore the
authoritative hallmark of the Catholic Church, the *Zentrum,* and the
Catholic unions and *Vereine.*[1] We wish to argue that in overconcentrating
on this one milieu, the study has obscured the existence of a Catholic population living on the margins of the political Catholic milieu, or outside of
it altogether. In point of fact, not only were there many Catholics who had
a highly tenuous relationship with the milieu, but there were others who
were indifferent to it altogether. The Catholic population that we shall
examine below is one that did not recognize the authority of the Catholic
Church in questions of life-style, or that recognized it only in part. It did
little or nothing to support the Catholic Center Party, took no part in the
activities of the Catholic *Vereine,* and expressed moderate to rabid hostility against the organized Catholic Church.

Before we begin our exploration of this social group, let us loosely
define a *milieu* as the system of values, beliefs, mentalities, and life-style
common to a group of people living in one specific area. The milieu
emphasizes the cultural dimension in the behavioral patterns of different
social groups.[2] Needless to say, the examination of different regions
reveals a wide range of behavioral patterns, the differences of which can be
attributed to the cultural variables in the given region. Against this background, we can understand why certain factors so prominent in the daily

life-style of one region, such as class or religion, are less so in another. The cultural variables are the ones that form and mold the infrastructure of local society. Together with the patterns of socioeconomic and political behavior, the *cultural hegemony* (to use the term coined by Gramsci) greatly influences the system of values and mentalities in any given region. In Gramsci's own words, this term incorporates "the spontaneous consent given by the great masses of the population to the general direction imposed on social life by the dominant fundamental group; this consent is 'historically' caused by the prestige (and consequent confidence) which the dominant group enjoys because of its position and function in the world of production."[3]

As a result, this dominant group has the ability to determine the local norms of behavior, values, beliefs, and mentalities, and even to influence local voting patterns. Needless to say, the dominant group may at times find itself struggling with other groups for the local cultural (and hence economic or political) hegemony. So, for example, there were numerous localized conflicts between the liberals and the Church during the 1860s in Baden, and in the Ruhr, the socialist milieu was partially marked by the struggle against political Catholicism and the Church from the 1890s.

The fact that Catholics constituted the majority in a given area does not mean that belief and religion were necessarily correlated. There might be a number of reasons why a Catholic population (as determined by the post-Reformation state and rulers) might have established norms wholly unlike those that scholarly consensus commonly attributes to the Catholic sector. This means that a Catholic area may have created patterns of sociopolitical behavior rooted in cultural variables of local origin, rather than the one that the study traditionally associates with the Catholic milieu dominated by the Church, political Catholicism, the Catholic press, and *Vereine*. Regional variations in the patterns of Catholic life stemmed from the cultural hegemony of a given region, a factor crucial in determining local voting patterns. It was the different cultural hegemonies, and hence the different cultural variables at the regional level, that contributed to the lack of uniformity in voting patterns.

In sum, let us conclude by saying that a number of Catholic milieus existed during the Second Reich and even before then, and that not all of them were characterized by the same features generally portrayed in the relevant literature. The Catholic milieu of Cologne was different from the one in Munster, neither resembled the one in Breslau, and all three differed from those in southwestern Germany, which will stand as the focus of our discussion below. While different social groups may well have a common socioeconomic denominator, there will be noticeable differences in life-style, mentality, and the system of values as one goes from one region to another and from milieu to milieu. In the discussion below we will take a closer look at the Catholic milieu during the Weimar Republic and examine its most outstanding features and limitations. Part 3 of our study will examine a number of different aspects in the disintegration of social life in the Black Forest, in order to try to understand the reasons for the Nazi success in this region. We have already mentioned that in seeking to explain the growing success of the Nazi Party, it may be best to remove the focus from the party itself and put it onto the socioeconomic conditions of the surrounding society.

In the following discussion, we will take a closer look at the social groups most prominent in supporting the Nazi Party: broad segments of the local bourgeoisie (from 1931), the peasants, and the groups of skilled workers and craftsmen. The chapter headings below reflect the sociopolitical analysis undertaken in the preceding chapters. There we saw that a number of large socioeconomic strata existed in the Black Forest one alongside the other: industrial workers employed in factories for clockmaking, precision mechanics, and wood production; craftsmen engaged in the service of farms and industries; independent master craftsmen; peasants; and the owners of hotels and taverns. We will examine the way each of these related to the organizational frameworks of the Catholic milieu, in which allegiance to the Catholic Church and the *Zentrum* was strong. We will identify the social groups that either did not belong to the organizational frameworks of this milieu or that had temporarily abandoned them. The most important of these groups is the Catholic bourgeoisie, yet they were not alone: during the years of the Weimar Republic their ranks were swelled by a very sizable number of workers and peasants.

The main "heroes" in this part are the *Vereine* and the *Stammtisch* (the drinking table that served *Verein* members as the gathering point of their meetings in the tavern). With the help of these two institutions, we will try to understand how local social life functioned during the Weimar Republic, especially during the worst years of the economic crisis. We will attempt to show that the collapse of these institutions, which were second to none in their importance to German social life in towns and rural regions, contributed much to the disintegration of local social life and to the creation of the socio-organizational vacuum stretching through the dominant social strata in the region. It was this, rather than the quality of Nazi activity in the region (which was actually quite desultory), that made broad segments of the Black Forest population perceive the Nazi Party as a viable political alternative, one capable of responding to their plight and meeting their social, economic, and even cultural needs.

The Disintegration of the Bourgeois Infrastructure and the Rise of the Nazi Party

In the chapter below, we intend to examine the connection between the collapse of the bourgeois parties in 1932 and the dizzying rise of the Nazi Party in the July Reichstag elections of that year. This connection has been examined by us up until now strictly in terms of the political arena, in the chapter dealing with local voting patterns (see chap. 7). In this chapter we shall try to tighten the connection between the two phenomena by examining the most salient features of bourgeois society during those years. Were there structural changes in bourgeois organization that hastened the decline of the local bourgeois-liberal parties, thus paving the way for Nazi success?

The weakness of the liberal parties during the Weimar Republic and their gradual disintegration beginning in 1924 were crucial to the fall of the republic and thus to the Nazi rise to power. There can be no doubt that the failing strength of the bourgeois infrastructure from the mid–nineteenth century also played a key role in this process. Wide sectors of the German bourgeoisie began to regard the Nazi alternative as a response to social problems, creating one of the major preconditions of Nazi success. His- torical scholarship has long dealt with this political aspect of the Nazi buildup and has taken note of almost every aspect connected to the decline of the bourgeois camp, such as the stream of bourgeois voters toward the Nazi Party;[1] the defection of local notables (*Honoratioren*) from the bour- geois camp in both urban and rural areas;[2] the tendency of the *Bildungs- bürgertum,* especially of the academic world, to lean toward political and national ideologies;[3] the close ties between certain parts of the German business world and highly placed members of the Nazi Party;[4] and the fact that upper-middle-class interest organizations tended to lean toward the National Socialist solution.[5] These and many other phenomena all testify to the ruptures that had weakened the bourgeois camp and left it deeply divided.

We intend to examine the collapse of the bourgeoisie via a study of the voluntary associations (*Vereine*) so important to Germany's social, economic, and cultural landscape.[6] These *Vereine* may be characterized as the very cornerstone of the local bourgeoisie, and as the most eloquent expression of its rise to prominence from the mid–nineteenth century. In order to better understand their importance to bourgeois society, let us first take a look at the historical and theoretical evolution of the bourgeois *Vereine* during the nineteenth and early twentieth centuries.

The Sociopolitical Significance of the Bourgeois *Vereine* from the Second Half of the Nineteenth Century

The vast literature dealing with various theoretical aspects of the *Verein* is divided in its approach over the definition of this important institution, which is in principle a legal definition. The *Verein* Law of 1908 defines it as a *"Dauernde Verbindung einer grosseren zahl von Personen zur Erreichung eines gemeinsamen Zweckes gewollt und anzusehen ist."*[7] Similar broad definitions have been offered by Thomas Nipperdey, David Blackbourn, and Rudi Koshar in their studies of bourgeois society and the bourgeois *Vereine*.[8] There have been intensive efforts over the past few decades to narrow the definition of the *Verein* and to view it as a less than homogenous entity, by referring to such criteria as size, location, and activity, or the extent to which it served as a springboard to political power and influence. The *Vereine* were also distinguished by their particular aims. Some *Vereine* functioned as a kind of pressure group, a lobby to preserve or change the sociopolitical order, while others were primarily interested in *Verein* activities. There was also the question of membership standards and requirements.[9]

Many scholars distinguish between *Vereine* of a cultural and social nature (*Gesang und Musikvereine Turn und Sportvereine Vereine zur Pflege des geselligen Lebens*) and those whose goals were specifically political or economic (*Politische Vereine, Berufs- und sonstige wirtschaftliche Vereine*). This division has been preserved in the present study. The *Vereine* that we will examine below were active in small communities, founded on a voluntary basis, and willing to accept all members of the community regardless of religion or social class.[10] The goals of these *Vereine* were cultural or social in nature, rather than economic, political, or religious. Thus our discussion will not include the *Vereine* that were connected in one way or another to political Catholicism, the Catholic Church, or the working sector, or those that cultivated interests of an economic and political nature.

The reason for choosing this kind of *Verein* is that the social *Vereine* may well be said to have constituted "the public conscience of the burghers, the defenders of their values and traditions, the initiators and institutional base for a revitalized and restructured political community. In short, the cultural clubs were the Paladins of the *Burgertum.*"[11]

Since this chapter seeks to examine the disintegration of the bourgeois infrastructure in small communities, it seems natural to choose the *Verein,* the cornerstone of local bourgeois life, as the focus for our discussion. The desire to establish *Vereine* became stronger toward the middle of the nine-teenth century. While *Vereine* devoted to a variety of purposes (reading, music, sports, brotherhood) existed already in the late eighteenth century, their development after 1830 turned them into a major pillar of urban bourgeois life. The goals of these *Vereine* now came to embrace all aspects of bourgeois existence. The waning of the corporate powers wielded by the Church, aristocracy, and guilds gave rise to a kind of vacuum, from which a public sphere slowly emerged. This was the sphere between the family and the state, and it was here that the *Vereine* took their place, strengthen-ing the family and reinforcing the social and personal relations within the propertied and educated bourgeoisie. In this sphere it became possible to formulate and express an alternative opinion, and to do so in collective fashion. With the help of the *Vereine,* the bourgeoisie was able to stabilize and perpetuate its position of leadership in society.[12]

Toward the end of the nineteenth century, the goals and functions of the *Vereine* began to change. Alongside the *Vereine* of the old model, new *Vereine* began to emerge with interests of class and economics. If the tra-ditional *Vereine* were for the most part apolitical, the new ones went through a process of politicization and were transformed into interest groups of a highly specific nature. This change was not without impact for the more traditional *Vereine.* The very attempt to defend their control of the community caused them to develop into seats of local power, to lose their apolitical nature and at times even to lean toward a nationalist ideol-ogy. The powerful chasms that divided society during the Second Reich were also expressed in the *Vereine,* as these became geared, among other things, to the perpetuation of social differences. There was no class with-out its *Verein,* and workers who had once belonged to the bourgeois *Vereine* now left them for the *Vereine* that represented the working class or the Catholics. In everything related to activity and goals, the new *Vereine* strove to model themselves along the lines of the bourgeois model. Thus they elected their officials in the same fashion, made the same kind of rules and regulations, met for rehearsals and held meetings in taverns, and used songs, banners, and pennants for creating a sense of brotherhood.[13]

It was approximately during this time that a number of *Vereine* began to spring up in the smaller towns and villages of Germany. Through the initiative of local notables and respected citizens, the model of the urban *Verein* was transferred to the rural regions either in part or in whole. The new kind of *Verein* that thus came into being had a social or cultural message that was different from that of its urban model.[14] These *Vereine* served to indirectly uphold and support the structure of local society; to serve as a means of social control and as a form of expression. They helped to create power bases for people interested in positions of local prestige and also to cultivate the individual by allowing him to acquire various kinds of knowledge in a wide variety of fields, such as music, sports, literature, and cattle-breeding. The *Vereine* served its members as a means of expressing community solidarity and, even more importantly, as an instrument of social mobility. They provided an integrative element that encouraged the democratization of local life. The cultural events, the celebrations, the rehearsals: all these helped to create a real sense of community by allowing people to participate in *Verein* activity regardless of age, family background, and status, and even to move up the ladder of *Verein* leadership.[15] In these small communities the *Vereine* could also be a political and economic power worth reckoning with, since small-town politics and party activity little resembled that of the large urban areas. Yet despite the ability of the *Verein* to influence the processes of political decision making, many *Vereine* prevented their members from actively dealing in political topics.[16] Communities with *Vereine* devoted to economic and class-oriented goals often found them helpful in promoting economic development and growth.[17]

The functions of the bourgeois cultural *Vereine* testify to their tremendous importance in local society. This was especially true of the sports and music *Vereine,* the veritable backbone of the bourgeoisie in agricultural areas and small towns. Not only did these *Vereine* carry the highest prestige, but their leaders also held key positions in the administration and socioeconomic life of their community.[18]

There are few studies dealing with the rise of the bourgeois *Vereine* from the end of the nineteenth century up until the Nazi period, the most notable being Rudi Koshar's study of the *Vereine* in the town of Marburg. These studies mention the changes that overtook the *Vereine* as paralleling the processes of disintegration in German bourgeois society. To be sure, the *Vereine* multiplied after World War I, and their importance to local society increased as well. There are also a number of scholars who emphasize the politicization of the *Vereine* even before the war, in a trend that gradually eroded the democratic element once characteristic of them.[19] However, other scholars argue that the more German society moved in the direction of political extremism, the less inclined the *Vereine* were toward politics. Leaders of the *Vereine* no longer came from the most prestigious ranks of society, as they had in the years before 1918. Though indeed more attuned to questions of national interest than their predecessors, they continued to steer *Verein* activity away from politics. The motif of a "people's community" (*Volksgemeinschaft*) did find its way into the *Vereine,* only without its usual political overtones.[20] Following a temporary period of instability in *Verein* functioning during the worst years of inflation, the stabilizing Weimar period was characterized by a striking growth in leisure and consumer patterns. This meant a surge of *Verein* activity and the vigorous recruitment of new members, largely through the observance of national holidays and commemorative events. In holding events of this nature the *Vereine* not only courted new members but also drummed up support for the local bourgeois parties.[21]

There are few studies of the bourgeois *Vereine* during the Weimar period, and even fewer in the context of the disintegrating bourgeois infrastructure.[22] In none of them has the role of the *Vereine* been examined in relation to the Great Economic Crisis. Koshar's noteworthy study briefly mentions that the *Vereine* successfully weathered the hardships of the period by increasing their activity and expanding their membership.[23] A few studies dealing with the rise of the Nazi Party in various parts of Germany and the response of the local population also came to a similar conclusion: it was precisely in the years 1929 through 1932 that the activity of the bourgeois *Vereine* gained momentum and that its impact on the individual increased. This argument was used by some scholars as a means of dealing with claims made back in the 1950s by Hanna Arendt and Wilhelm Kornhauser, in relation to the atomization of German society at the time of the Great Economic Crisis and the "mass society" theory. These scholars contend that it was precisely during these years of hardship that the individual felt secure and protected, safely enmeshed in a network of stable social and cultural organizations that gave meaning to his existence. Far from going into decline, *Verein* activity actually flourished during this period and became highly important not only to the inhabitants of the local community but to the Nazi Party as well. In its efforts to storm the bastions of bourgeois life and to gain control of its infrastructure, the Nazi Party attempted at times successfully to infiltrate its own members into the ranks of the *Vereine* and to win *Verein* members over to their side.[24]

These and other scholars who recognized the importance of the *Vereine* in the fabric of social bourgeois life, and who took due note of its disintegration, made no effort to connect or even to examine the paradox that stands before us now: the collapse of the bourgeois infrastructure and the stability of that which constituted the very cornerstone of bourgeois existence: the bourgeois *Vereine.*[25]

The Catholic Bourgeoisie and the Bourgeois *Vereine* in the
Black Forest from the Second Half of the Nineteenth Century

In the following discussion, the Catholic bourgeoisie will be at the center of our interest. Although much has been written about the German bourgeoisie over the past twenty years, the research has had little to say about the Catholic bourgeoisie,[26] focusing instead almost exclusively on the bourgeoisie in the Protestant sector. The many studies dealing with the backwardness of the Catholic population and the "ghetto" mentality of German Catholicism generally mention the absence of a Catholic bourgeois stratum, at least until the Weimar period.[27] Yet such a stratum did exist in the Black Forest, and it is this which we wish to explore. As we will see below, the founding and activity of *Vereine,* the "social, cultural and political cornerstone of the *Bildungsbürgertum*"[28] faithful to the model of the Protestant bourgeois *Verein,* will provide us with our most eloquent testimony to the existence of this stratum.

We will examine the functioning of the bourgeois *Vereine* during the Great Economic Crisis in Germany and try to connect it with the success of the Nazi Party. In contrast to the scholarly consensus on the subject, we intend to argue that *Verein* activity was adversely affected by the economic crisis. This in turn damaged the bourgeois infrastructure in villages and small towns, thus hastening the collapse of the bourgeois political parties. Once the *Vereine* lost their economic basis, members and sympathizers abandoned both the *Vereine* and their political representatives and turned to the Nazi alternative. This line of argument raises a number of questions: To what extent did the *Vereine* depend on their economic basis in order to function? What was the relationship between the *Vereine* and the bourgeois parties? What caused the voters of the bourgeois parties to transfer their support to the Nazi Party? What was the nature of the connection between the Nazi Party and the cultural *Vereine?*

These and other questions will guide us in our study of the disintegration of the bourgeois infrastructure in the Black Forest. We have already noted, in chapter 7, how the bourgeois bloc leaned toward the Nazi Party. This study leans heavily on methods taken from the field of political science, and it will thus make extensive use of techniques such as voting pattern and political behavior analysis.

Clearly, the bourgeois *Vereine* were entirely different from the Catholic *Vereine,* although both were of crucial importance in local society. In the agrarian regions of the southeastern Black Forest and the Baar, however, bourgeois *Vereine* were no more common than Catholic ones. The villages of the Wutach and the Baar did not have a bourgeois stratum. As we have already noted, the peasant villages in these regions were socially and economically backward, traditionally reluctant to take cooperative action in any shape or form. The bitterness over the socioeconomic situation in these regions led to the atomization of social life and a surge in anticapitalistic and antibourgeois feelings. One way these traits came to expression was through support for the local peasant party (the *BLB*) initially, and for the Nazi Party thereafter. Toward the end of the 1920s there were few *Vereine* in this backward region.[29]

In contrast to this region, bourgeois *Vereine* flourished in other parts of the Black Forest. The founding of these *Vereine* was closely related to the region's socioeconomic development. Industrialization came relatively late here. Only in the last third of the nineteenth century did the industrially based towns emerge, and it was only then that a propertied middle class anxious to adapt the socioeconomic patterns of the Protestant bourgeoisie came into existence. This is not to say that the region lacked any propertied social class whatsoever prior to the advent of industrialization. At the beginning of the nineteenth century, owners of factories for clock-making, lumber, and precision mechanics had already emerged as a social and economic force in the region, one that found itself constantly struggling with the Catholic Church for the region's "cultural hegemony." The local bourgeoisie aspired to become the dominant social stratum in the region, similar to the Protestant model in Baden and in Reich. The harsh geographical conditions made it difficult for foreign influences to penetrate the Black Forest area, so that the local bourgeoisie found itself relegated to a kind of cultural ghetto. The establishment of rail connections with the large Protestant cities at the edge of the Black Forest, the industrialization, the end of the *Kulturkampf,* and the founding of a newspaper network with a bourgeois national orientation all contributed to a partial exodus of the Catholic bourgeoisie from the isolation in which they were stranded. This came to expression, among other ways, in the establishment of professional and social bourgeois *Vereine* totally unrelated to the life of the local Catholic Church. The men presiding over these *Vereine* were local notables, and though Catholic they were also anticlerical. These men were primarily interested in strengthening the "cultural hegemony" of the local bourgeoisie by extending the local sociocultural life beyond the closed circle of the Catholic Church, and in reaping, moreover, all the extra benefits and personal influence that went with being active in the *Vereine*.[30]

The *Verein* was able to accommodate, rather than displace, the more traditional bonds of community life. Small towns and even peasant villages found it easier to organize *Vereine* of all kinds. This is especially true of Baden, where the liberal Community Ordinance of 1832 granted municipal status to hundreds of tiny hamlets and villages. In those communities there was no clear line of demarcation between "traditional" and *"bürgerlich"* forms of organization, and the latter were merely superimposed on the more traditional forms. Social relations and leisure activities in every aspect of life—the home, the village corner, the church—were remolded in the national and liberal "spirit," with ample use of all the symbols, rituals, and ceremonies common to the bourgeois culture of *Vereinswesen*.[31]

Music and sports *Vereine* were established in the region only toward the end of the nineteenth century. Some communities could boast of *Vereine* as early as the mid–nineteenth century, but most of these were dissolved following the *Reaktionzeit* of the 1850s, and their subsequent reestablishment took place on a different basis. A similar process occurred to the *Vereine* associated with the Catholic Church and the workers (see chap. 11). Many of these were established during the second half of the nineteenth century. The bourgeois *Vereine* were established and supported by local notables and local small industrialists as a means of helping to preserve their sociocultural control.[32] The social composition of the *Vereine* reflected the makeup of the individual communities (see table 9). Towns with a broad industrial infrastructure provided the *Vereine* with members who were also skilled workers, primarily craftsmen. Other members came from the ranks of the merchants, innkeepers, tavern owners, council men, and even *Burgermeister*. In the villages, on the other hand, it was not always possible to find *Vereine* along the model of the urban bourgeoisie. When such *Vereine* did exist they generally owed their establishment to rich local peasants, tavern keepers, or the *Burgermeister*. The dominant members of the village *Vereine* came from the ranks of the peasants, the craftsmen, and the agricultural workers. In tourist-based towns the dominant members were primarily hotel owners, tavern keepers, and government officials. The most respected and prestigious *Vereine* were the *Krieg und Militärverein* (*KuMV*), the *Männergesangvereine* (*MGV*), the *Schützenverein*, and the *Turnverein*, and it is these *Vereine* that will be the focus of the following discussion.

The members of these last-named *Vereine* came from the ranks of the petty bourgeoisie and the groups of skilled workers (see table 9). They were usually headed by a local notable or by prominent members of the local bourgeoisie: owners of factories and hotels, or members of the local council. There were some people who belonged to several different *Vereine* with the same goals, though in the years of the Great Economic Crisis they were forced to limit their activity to one single *Verein*, since they were unable to pay more than one set of membership dues or to devote their time to leisure activity. The fact that workers preferred the bourgeois *Vereine* over those related to the workers' camp may possibly be indicative of their nationalist conservative outlook devoid of any proletariat consciousness and of their desire to become part of the local bourgeoisie. We may also be able to learn something about the nature of the bourgeois *Vereine* themselves, for the open-door policy not only permitted upward

TABLE 9. The Social Profile of the Bourgeois Vereine

The Verein	Unskilled Workers	Skilled Workers/ Craftsmen	Master Craftsmen	Small Employers	Lower Civil Servants (including teachers)	Merchants	Peasants	Entrepreneur, Imkeepers, Town Councilmen	Free Professions, Academics
MGV "Liederkranz" Wolfach, 1929 63 members		35	8	6	6		4	4	
KuMV Eisenbach, 1929 148 members	7	20	17	1	1	1			1
KuMV Neustadt, 1921 90 members	21	21	14	15		7	5	3	4
Fahrradverein "Wanderlust" Dittishausen, 1930 47 members	18	5	5		1		17	1	

Source: Stadt/village archives: Wolfach- 032.Bd 1; Neustadt- 3214; Eisenbach- XII/4; Dittishausen- 51/4.

mobility, but also served to forestall social unrest. In opening their doors, the bourgeois *Vereine* helped integrate social groups that had formerly been outside the bourgeois camp and on the margins of local society.

Activity in the Catholic bourgeois *Vereine* followed a pattern similar to that of the *Vereine* in the Protestant regions: gatherings in the tavern around the *Stammtisch,* nonrepresentation of women, and the use of such items as flags, banners, and placards. Like their Protestant counterparts, the bourgeois Catholic *Vereine* appointed a new chairman and board every year, held monthly meetings in order to schedule activities, participated in interregional tournaments, and used music as the leitmotif of *Verein* activity. Even language came under *Verein* jurisdiction as members cultivated distinctive speech patterns and the vocabulary became studded with popular, almost folklike values connected to the German *Heimat.*

Many of the *Vereine* adopted anticlerical expressions, a tradition that went back to the earliest days of the *Kulturkampf.* Let us recall that we are speaking of Catholics who tried to emulate the ways of the Protestant bourgeoisie, of which the anti-Catholic rhetoric was so much a part. Even after the *Kulturkampf* came to an end in the late 1870s, hostility toward political Catholicism continued to smolder, in some places as late as the 1930s. The perennial struggle between the Catholic *Vereine* and the bourgeois *Vereine* made the latter regard Catholic demands as a threat.[33] Yet, despite the hostility of these relations, it was not the anticlerical, but rather the antisocialist rhetoric that stands out as the most striking characteristic of the bourgeois *Vereine.* Antisocialist feelings indeed ran high among all elements of the bourgeois camp and constituted their single most common denominator. The more the workers increased their *Verein* activity, the more hostile the bourgeois *Vereine* became. The fact that the bourgeois *Vereine* opened their doors to the workers can be seen as a strategy designed, among other things, to erode the strength of the working camp.

These brief comments concerning the attitudes of the bourgeois *Vereine* have been made in order to show that the members of these *Vereine* were not oblivious to the issues of political concern in the Black Forest. The bourgeois *Vereine* in the Second Reich and Weimar Republic were more concerned with the nationalist climate than with the need to make a strong political stand or to express their position on party affairs.

The Struggle to Preserve Sociocultural Hegemony: The Bourgeois *Vereine* in the Weimar Period

The flourishing state of *Verein* activity after World War I left its imprint on the Black Forest. Of the numerous *Vereine* devoted to sports in the region, as everywhere in Germany, approximately one-half were founded between the years 1919 and 1921. The *Sportvereine* brought together the bourgeoisie and strata close to the bourgeoisie. In the town of Lenzkirch, it was only in the mid-1920s that the bourgeois *Sportverein* was refounded again. The climate of mass politics, the *SPD*'s newfound strength just after the war, the impact of national political events even in small, relatively isolated communities, were all perceived as a threat to local bourgeois hegemony. It was not in direct fashion that the bourgeoisie responded to events, but in the organization of its members and in the founding of new *Vereine*. The *Vereine* were made to accommodate those elements of society seen as posing the most threat to the existing social order. We can credit the founding of new *Vereine* and the flourishing state of the old ones to the economic conditions of the period of inflation. During the economic "prosperity" of the mid-1920s, which swept over Germany as a whole and the Black Forest in particular, many *Vereine* took out substantial loans in order to improve and expand their activity.[34]

However, the bubble burst in the Black Forest region as Germany began to face increasing economic difficulties in the "golden" twenties. The economic crisis that struck the Black Forest during the mid-twenties had a perceptible impact on the activity of certain *Vereine,* especially in towns with an industrial basis. Beginning with 1926, more and more *Vereine* turned to local councils or to individual contributors with appeals for assistance.[35] Even at this date there was a perceptible movement of people deserting the *Vereine,* and the numbers increased at the beginning of the 1930s. Many of the *Vereine* were no longer able to meet their heavy debts, and they turned to their creditors with requests for relief. There were cases in which a *Verein* was forced to take leave of its chairman, either because he had his own business obligations to attend to or because the *Verein* was dissatisfied with his performance. Such changes in *Verein* personnel should not be lightly dismissed. The forced replacement of a chairman testifies to a situation in which things were running less than smoothly. The chairman of the *Verein* was generally the owner of a local business, a highly respected figure about town, and if such a person was unable to devote the majority of his time to *Verein* activity, this was very likely a sign of financial trouble. Another important change involved the funds formerly channeled to the *Vereine* by individuals and businesses in the community. This was had been the financial backbone of the *Vereine,* the basis of their existence. These contributions now began to slow down considerably.

The local councils ran into their own financial problems and so cut back their support of the *Vereine.* A number of *Vereine* were forced, much to their dismay, to take part in Church activity in order to supplement their income, while others were forced to transgress the most fundamental of *Verein* laws and charge admission to their performances.[36] Yet another grim aspect to be considered is that of the numerous losses incurred in the war and the impact this had on the younger age brackets in the region.

Even though many of the *Vereine* were founded only after 1918 few young people became members, and not because they found them unappealing. Needless to say, the impact that the war had on this particular cohort greatly depleted the *Vereine*'s pool of potential members, especially the *Vereine* that were devoted to athletics. To be sure, *Sportvereine* were indeed founded at an accelerated pace after the war, yet their programs were not always comprehensive, nor their ranks thronged with members.[37]

Despite these telltale signs of *Verein* misfunctioning, the consequences were largely restricted to the rural, relatively undeveloped regions of the southern Black Forest. The activity of the bourgeois *Vereine* there, never that flourishing to begin with, came to a virtual halt as a result of the severe economic crisis in this part of the Black Forest, while the activity of the bourgeois parties ceased altogether. Taken in conjunction with the weakness of political Catholicism in the region (as we will see in the next chapter), the early mass enthusiasm for the Nazi Party becomes more readily comprehensible.

The lessons of 1926 through 1928 were studied by both the *Vereine* and the organizations that supported them. The *Vereine* tried to rely more and more on private sources of income and to improve their operations via voluntary activity that required little financial help from the local councils.[38] However, the local councils reached the conclusion that there was little to be gained economically from so many *Vereine* in such small communities, even if they did contribute to local pride and prestige. While it was indeed true that the great number of *Vereine* went far in diversifying local society and culture, those who wielded power in the local hegemony felt there were more important considerations at stake. The sheer number of organizations made it effectively impossible for the bourgeoisie to control them, or to turn them into a means of perpetuating the local bourgeois hegemony.[39] The rivalry with the *Vereine* of the workers and Catholics, together with the growing socialist presence in everyday life, deepened the anxiety of the leaders of the bourgeois camp.

On the eve of the Great Economic Crisis, the local bourgeoisie found itself in a dilemma over its policy toward the bourgeois *Vereine*. Though unable to control and support such a vast number of *Vereine*, they also feared their rivals' activity. The dilemma was eventually resolved through a policy that clearly discriminated in favor of the bourgeois *Vereine*, but that also cut back on their financial support. The transfer of funds to the bourgeois *Vereine* continued, though not at the same rate as in former years, while funds to the Catholic and especially the workers' *Vereine*, increasingly viewed as a threat to the bourgeois hegemony, ground to almost a complete halt.

Another way of perpetuating the bourgeois hegemony was in refusing to defray the travel expenses of their rival *Vereine* when they took part in activities outside the community. These journeys were important to the *Vereine,* both as a means of social crystallization and as an additional source of income. The use of motor vehicles, the cost of fuel, food, and lodging: these were all expenses that had once been borne to one extent or another by the local councils. Now, however, it was only in the case of a bourgeois *Verein* that the council continued this policy. Even the mass media—the radio, cinema, and theater—were harnessed to the greater glory of the bourgeois hegemony. Concerts of the *MGV* were broadcast live on the radio (even though radio was still in its swaddling stages in the region), the movies screened at *Vereine* meetings bore a nationalist character, and a few *Vereine* even mounted anti-Bolshevist plays.[40] There was nothing new in the rivalry between the *Vereine.* The fear of socialism had long been gnawing at the bourgeoisie.[41] But the rapidly growing strength of the rival *Vereine* (and their political and economic support), the economic crisis that temporarily harmed the *Vereine,* and the heightened passions of the new mass politics all made the bourgeoisie increasingly fearful over their ability to retain their grip on the community.

Yet even while discriminating and inciting against its rival *Vereine,* the bourgeoisie was also laying the foundations for cooperative action with the very social forces it feared. Opening its doors to the workers and clergy was only one of the steps that the bourgeois *Vereine* took in this direction. In one unusual case, in the town of Furtwangen, the chairman of the *Arbeitergesangverein* was asked to preside over the local *MGV.*[42] Including people from all walks of life in the various memorial services, national ceremonies, and even in the festivities of a specific *Verein* was aimed at preventing social unrest. Yet this step should not be seen for its manipulative aspects alone, since it is also signals the desire to preserve social tranquillity and to make at least an outward show of community solidarity. The fear that the bourgeoisie had of socialism testifies more to its own insecurity than to the actual intentions of its opponents. The fact that the workers established *Vereine* of their own testifies to a desire to create a new identity within the bourgeois framework, and to cultivate bourgeois values and goals. Every *Verein* was anxious to represent its community with dignity. This was no less true of the workers, who tried to end class rivalry in a way that would not threaten the existing socioeconomic order. If social tensions did exist they were held closely in check, for the lower class was highly dependent both socially and economically on the bourgeoisie. Had certain workers' groups wished to pitch battle against the sources of local economic influence, their lack of political organization would have been a real obstacle.[43] Due to the weakness of the workers' union and the *SPD* in the region and the dominance of the Catholic Church over some social groups, the workers confined themselves to sociocultural activities, and not to political activism. There were very few strikes in the region, and disturbances based on socioeconomic back-ground never did take place, even in the tense days following the revolutions of November 1918.

Crisis and Dissolution: The Disintegration of the *Vereine* and the Bourgeois Parties

The years 1932 through 1933, which are usually noted in the academic studies as the end of one chapter in Weimar history and the beginning of a new one, also saw significant changes in the way that the *Vereine* in the Black Forest functioned. Processes set into motion during the 1920s, and which led to the slow disintegration of the *Vereine* even before 1930, were now in full swing. The withdrawal of council support was keenly felt on both the financial and organizational sides of things. Together with this, the rival *Vereine* continued to grow both in scope and in membership, especially those that belonged to the workers' camp. The loss of financial support and the rapidly declining finances of its members did nothing to alter the sense of common cause or the spirit of volunteerism, and there was a perceptible rise in the number of new members, most of them now unemployed. The weakness of the bourgeois camp found expression first and foremost in the disintegration of its political representation. The collapse of the bourgeois parties represents the culmination of the process that led to the disintegration of the bourgeois infrastructure and offers a key to understanding why the Nazi Party succeeded in the region in 1932.

From the elections of 1930, there was no way of knowing what lay ahead. In both the Reichstag elections of September 1930 and in the local elections (*Gemeindewahlen*), the bourgeoisie maintained its strength (see table 6, chap. 7). The local elections of November 1930 were especially important, since they had served the bourgeoisie in the past as a means of retaining its control over local politics and society. Local social issues figured prominently in the elections, and the candidates mostly represented groups of an improvised nature and with clearly economic interests. There was little of the party politics that characterized the elections to the Landtag or the Reichstag.[44] The candidates of the bourgeois parties were local notables with an obvious financial stake in the outcome of things, eager to protect the interests of a specific economic sector in the community. The candidates who identified with the bourgeoisie all came from the upper echelons of the bourgeois *Vereine,* especially the more prestigious ones like the *MGV* and the *Turnverein.* The *Vereine* served them as a kind of launching pad from which to begin their political career and also as a lobby, an economic pressure group, since a *Verein* activist who was also a member of the local council held enough economic power in his hands to use it for his own benefit or for that of his *Verein.* It was one of the ironies of fate that the very men who worked as central activists in the *Vereine* were later to serve in the same councils that cut off the flow of funds to the *Vereine* and thus hastened their end.

As in the past, the results of the local elections permitted the bourgeoisie to control the local councils, together with the *Zentrum*. The only innovation was the appearance of a relatively new and triumphant group, the Nazi Party, that did not pretend to represent any specific social or economic sector. The fact that the Nazis and the workers managed to get more of their representatives into the local councils than in 1926 was the only thing to cast a shadow over the triumph of the bourgeoisie (and that of the *Zentrum*), or to raise any doubt as to its unchallenged position in the Black Forest community.

But it was a Pyrrhic victory. The bourgeois *Vereine* were the very foundations of the bourgeois infrastructure, and the ground underneath them was burning. The policy that the local councils adopted toward the *Vereine* did not respond to the new socioeconomic reality, of which the economic crisis was its most material expression. On the surface, the *Vereine* were able to broaden the scope of their activity at this time and to anchor their position even more firmly. Under the sheltering wing of the *Vereine*, any person who suffered either physical or psychological distress because of the crisis could seek relief in the volunteer services of the *Vereine*, which offered a sense of fellowship and a warm and congenial atmosphere. These services however, were contingent on two things: the ability of the *Verein* to provide them, and the willingness of the *Verein* to take on new members. The more prestigious *Vereine* made strenuous requirements of their members. There were some *Vereine*, such as the *MGV* or the *TurnVerein*, that required certain kinds of physical prowess or a good singing voice, while the *KuMV* demanded military service of its members. It was indeed the *KuMV* that ran into the most trouble during the Great Economic Crisis. One might have expected this *Verein* to absorb many new members at the beginning of the Great Economic Crisis, given its high reputation and the relative ease with which one could join, as well as its nationalistic-bourgeois image. This image did attract many inhabitants who were not connected to the workers' camp, and who were not even particularly sympathetic toward them. Nevertheless, the *KuMV* failed to increase its membership or to keep its promise of supporting the families of fallen soldiers. Its attempt to use nationalistic propaganda for the sake of recruiting new members was rejected by the local population, which was anxious to protect the region's health-resort image at home and abroad and thus prevent financial loss.[45] The plight of the cultural *Vereine* was even more grave. Being accepted into these *Vereine* was always more difficult since they maintained high professional standards and attributed a great deal of importance to family name and background. We have already mentioned that because of the war's impact on the younger age brackets, the reservoir of potential members had been considerably depleted, especially for the sports *Vereine.* We have already seen that in the years prior to the eruption of the Great Economic Crisis, the straitened finances of these *Vereine* left them less able to meet the needs of those hurt by the crisis. The bourgeois *Vereine,* whose stated goals might have led people to assume otherwise, found it hard to carry out their objectives and to support local society, since they themselves had stumbled on hard times.

There were many aspects to the crisis of the bourgeois *Vereine* in 1930 through 1932, but the decline in membership and activity was by far the most striking. The loss of members was due to several factors. For example, not every member or potential member was able to pay the membership dues. This not only led to a drop in new members, but also to the resignation of long-standing members, now largely unemployed. So stringent were the demands of the sports and music *Vereine* that members were obliged to make certain sacrifices of family life and economic interests. In times such as these, few people could permit themselves the luxury of taking part in rehearsals, even though it meant risking their membership in the *Verein* altogether. Cutting back on rehearsals meant compromising the quality of the performance, and this resulted in fewer invitations to appear. The *KuMV* reduced its support of the families of fallen or wounded soldiers, causing some people to give up their membership. The dwindling number of activities made the *Vereine* seem less attractive, and hence much less likely to attract lots of new members.[46] The payment of membership dues—especially to the bourgeois *Vereine*—constituted one of the heaviest burdens of all. Over the course of the years, many *Vereine* did what they could to lighten the burden. But this was the one source of income on which the *Verein* could depend, and the only one not dependent on the good graces of benefactors or the number of invitations to appear. This being the case, it is no surprise that many *Vereine* found it difficult to take the plunge and reduce membership fees. As late as 1930 there were some *Vereine* that refused to give their unemployed members a discount, and it was some time before this policy changed. However, the membership dues were never totally eliminated, and even the lower sums caused members to grumble. Moreover, many *Vereine* were unable to cope with the reduced financial support and thus raised their membership dues, a step that only led to the loss of additional members.

Together with the decline in membership, the slowdown in *Verein* activity was a painful blow to members and community alike. The decline in membership obviously meant less activity as well. However, even in cases where members remained faithful to their *Verein,* and even when there was a stream of new members, the *Vereine* were no longer able to hold their annual Christmas and New Year festivities, to make public appearances, or to take part in a long list of former activities. None of this did the Verein's public image much good, and it certainly did nothing to improve its financial resources. This situation also reflects the plight of the institutions where the *Vereine* had formerly been wont to appear, such as health spas, hotels, local councils, and schools.[47] Blow after blow rained down on the *Vereine,* as councils and contributors reduced their support of the *Vereine* or put an end to it altogether. There were even cases where the local council slapped a tax on the *Verein*'s earnings. The local tavern keeper was no longer willing to turn his tavern over to the *Vereine* for their meetings. Why should he, when the members could no longer pay for the drinks they imbibed or the wood with which they warmed themselves? What was even worse was that they no longer attracted an audience who would come to hear and buy drinks. The tavern keeper became especially adamant when the local council was no longer paying its share in his relationship with the *Verein.* As a result, more and more *Vereine* were forced to rehearse out in open lots or in private homes. Yet another blow was the death of several *Verein* leaders and supporters, and of local notables whose prestige reflected favorably on their *Vereine.* Such things were a common occurrence, to be expected in any period, but in these difficult times they took on an added gravity.

The bourgeois *Vereine* responded to the new situation in a variety of ways. Some of them made a change of administration. Any attempt of the council to intervene on the subject was rejected by the *Verein* members, who felt that if the council was going to cut off its support, it also lost the right to intervene in its affairs. In a number of cases, highly respected members of a *Verein* were no longer willing to serve as chairmen, and in order to prevent total collapse the *Verein* offered the job to the head of the council. However, in many cases the *Vereine* were forced to cease their activities or to disband altogether, a step that meant disaster in terms of the region's cultural activity.[48]

One solution already taken by many of the *Verein* in 1929 was to unite *Vereine* of similar natures in the same geographical region. In the southern Black Forest the *Vereine* devoted to music combined into one single *Verein.* The bourgeois *Vereine* were now willing to perform with members of the workers' *Vereine,* even at political events, in order to make some money. The plight of their fellow townsmen no doubt spurred the *Vereine* into action, seeing that not the least of their goals was to make local life more agreeable. It was for this reason that they held charity functions for the poor and the unemployed, and also mobilized themselves for the sake of special projects that the council devised for the needy. In many *Vereine,* however, members were perceptibly reluctant to take part in such activities when they themselves were in need, so that the initial wave of enthusiasm soon waned and the *Vereine* renounced one of their most cherished goals: personal commitment to the well-being of the community.

In order to change their image in the eyes of the young and to make them eager to join, a few *Vereine* tried to emend their charter and to allow young people to serve as leaders of the *Verein,* to give new members a grace period of three months before paying their dues, to reduce the payment to the *Verein,* and to allow the *Verein's* passive members to forgo their dues altogether. However, not only did young people fail to join the *Vereine* in significant numbers, but the few who did often dropped out after a short period. Those who did remain often brought something of the frenetic political climate into the *Verein,* severely criticizing the present leaders and in a few cases even demanding that they be changed. The performances that the *Vereine* traditionally gave in honor of the Weimarian "Constitution Day" were now rejected by many young people, and some of them left the *Vereine* for political reasons.

Table 10 shows a number of *Vereine* in the towns of Donaueschingen, Triberg, Wolfach, and Neustadt, in which there is a perceptible decline in the number of members and in the amount of activity. These *Vereine* represent the most important ones devoted to goals of culture and sociality. Not all of them show a drastic decline in activity. In the town of Neustadt, the *Vereine* devoted to sociality show increased activity from the end of 1930 to the beginning of 1932. The same goes for the *Vereine* that engaged in music and singing in Triberg during the months of October through December in 1930 and 1931. The sports *Vereine* in Neustadt and Triberg, on the other hand, reduced their activity in significant fashion. The funds required by the *Vereine* for the purpose of maintaining their activity—the leasing of a lot, the purchase of implements, clothing, travel—were no longer available as in former years. A considerable drop in the number of members characterizes the important *Vereine,* such as the *MGV* and *Turnerein*-1864 in the towns of Donaueschingen and Wolfach. In the case of *Turnerein*-1864, there was a perceptible rise in the number of events between the years 1929 (13) and 1932 (21), despite the decline in its membership. However, many of the *Vereine* in that period experienced the crisis in one of two ways: a decline in membership or a decline in activity.[49] This was certainly true of the *KuMV,* for though it increased the frequency of its meetings between the years 1929 and 1932, the drastic decline in membership beginning in 1931 led to its collapse just prior to the Nazi rise to power. In contrast to the disintegrating trends of the bourgeois *Vereine,* the *Vereine* of the Catholics and workers held their own during the years of the crisis and even increased their activity, as we will shortly see.

What can be said of the political behavior of the bourgeois camp, in light of the facts thus far mentioned? Though we have already discussed this question in chapter 7, let us briefly recap our most important findings.

The number of eligible voters rose significantly between the elections to the national Landtag in 1929 and the Reichstag elections in September 1930. This was the source of Nazi strength in the elections of September 1930. Although there can be no denying that the Nazi Party also won the votes of people who had formerly supported other parties (as happened in Wolfach), most of its support came from people who had not voted in 1929. The Catholic and workers' blocs maintained their stability and even enjoyed the support of new voters. In the summer of 1932 the trend was entirely different, and this is important for our own conclusions. In the workers' camp there was a trend of continuing stability with a tendency toward decline (Neustadt), in the Catholic camp there was a rise in sup-

TABLE 10.   The Crisis in the Bourgeois Vereine, 1930–32

Town	Verein	1929	1930	1931	1932
Members					
Wolfach:	*MGV*				
	"Liederkranz"	256	224	187	171
Donaueschingen:	Musikfreunde;	240	193	166	
	KuMV;	520		496	444
	Turnverein - 1864		639		493
Triberg:			Oct.–Dec.	Oct.–Dec.	
No. of	Turn und				
Entertainments	Sportvereine;		25	11	
	Gesang und				
	Musikvereine;		13	15	
	Vereine zur				
	Pflege des				
	geselligen				
	Lebens		10	3	
Neustadt:	Turn und		Sept.–Nov.		Jan.–Mar.
No. of	Sportvereine;		27		12
Entertainments	Gesang und				
	Musikvereine;		22		7
	Vereine zur				
	Pflege des				
	geselligen				
	Lebens		4		7

Source: Stadtarchiv Wolfach - 032.Bd.2 - MGV "Liederkranz"; Stadtarchiv Donaueschingen, Chroniken der Stadtverwaltung. Donaueschingen-Vereine. *TB*- 1930–1932. *EvH, Hschw.*- 1930–1932.

Note: Vereine in Triberg and Neustadt.

Sportvereine: Wintersportverein. Fusballklub-1910. Turnverein-1860. Kleinkaliber-Schützen Gesellschaft, Schützenverein. Reiterverein, Skiklub, Turnverein-Neustadt.

Gesang u. Musikvereine: Streichkonzert. Stadtkapelle. Hauskapelle. Gesangverein "Sängerbund" (Triberg), Männergesangverein "Hochfirst" (Neustadt), Stadtmusik (Neustadt), Hand - Harmonik club.

Gesselligenlebenvereine: Funkverein. Kneippverein. Schwarzwaldverein. Kriegshilfeverein. Krieg u. Militärverein. "Ungemütlichkeit." Badische Heimat. Geflügelzuchtverein. Museumgesellschaft.

port for the Zentrum, the bourgeois camp lost almost half of its strength, and the Nazi Party doubled theirs. Since the number of eligible voters rose very little in these elections when compared with the Reichstag elections of 1930 (the unique character of the local elections does not permit us to compare this election campaign to those to the Landtag and Reichstag), we may surmise that this time, many supporters of the bourgeois parties gave their vote to the Nazis. To be sure, the few new votes were distributed between the Nazi Party, the Zentrum, and the workers' party (which won very little support), and there may possibly have been some shifting of votes between the Zentrum and the bourgeois parties, and even between the Zentrum and the Nazi Party. Nonetheless, one can, in our opinion, explain the doubled strength of the Nazi Party more in terms of the collapsing bourgeois parties than of votes from the Catholic and workers' blocs, or as the result of new voters (see also table 6, chap. 7).

Our assessment of the voting patterns in the bourgeois camp in 1932 is accepted by many scholars who seek to explain the Nazi success in the summer of 1932. However, connecting the Nazi success to the disintegration of the bourgeois *Vereine,* and from there to the disintegration of the bourgeois infrastructure—which caused bourgeois voters to transfer their vote to the Nazi Party—is to some extent a new argument. Contemporary onlookers perceived this process in a clearer fashion. Thus on the eve of the Reichstag elections in summer 1932, the *Donaubote* implored the bourgeois camp to be on its guard against the threatening wave of National Socialism. The fragmentation within the bourgeois camp, the passivity, the disintegration of values, the cessation of *Verein* activity were all quoted by the Donaubote as "laying the grave for the good and ancient traditions of the German Bourgeoisie." The *Freiburger Zeitung* called the inability of the *SportVereine* to function in times of crisis a harsh blow to the bourgeoisie, while the *Süddeutsche Musikverein* beseeched the council in Gutenbach to support the local *Musikverein,* for in their words, "the national importance of folk music in these times is great . . . the efforts of the *Verein* members to make the life of our poor people pleasant must be recognized . . . they are making the bourgeoisie strong against those who rise to destroy it."[50]

The Bourgeois *Vereine,* Bourgeois Society, and the Nazi Party

Why did the bourgeois camp turn to the Nazi Party? Is there a connection between the activity and structure of the cultural-bourgeois *Vereine* and that of the Nazi Party? Did the party seek to win control of this vital source of power, as it had done in other important organizations? Were the members of the *Vereine* also members of the Nazi Party? In order to answer these questions, let us briefly consider some points of methodological interest (see further chap. 8). It is necessary to distinguish between the support for the Nazi Party that received expression at the polls and the kind of support that expressed itself on a daily basis, through membership in the Nazi Party and activity on its behalf. In the Black Forest the party launched intensive activity only at the beginning of 1930, and while many were willing to give it their vote, working for the party or even joining its ranks was quite another thing. The reason for this stems partly from the Catholic-conservative nature of the region, the fear of social and religious ostracism, the activity of the Church and the clergy, and even the fumbling and not always convincing activity of the party itself. Though the party was able to attract the protest vote, it was less successful in signing up actual members. Another point worth mentioning is the transience of the support for the Nazi Party. Not every person who joined the party after September 1930 remained there through 1931, and not every person who supported the party prior to election day continued to do so once the results were in. The membership rosters of the local branches are not always reliable, since they reflect only one specific period of time. Many members left a year after joining the party, and much depends on the person who was compiling the lists. The local policeman, for example, would enter the name of anyone whom he considered to be even remotely identified with the party, whereas the chapter leader only published his dues-paying members, so that the attempt to match the two lists yields unreliable results.

Thus, it is difficult on the basis of the existing data to make any definitive conclusions concerning the composition of the party chapters and their connections with the bourgeois *Vereine.* That some *Vereine* members also belonged to the Nazi Party goes without saying. However, the prohibition against political wheeling and dealing within the *Vereine,* the relatively minor importance of rank-and-file members (many of whom were probably quite passive) in *Verein* decision making, together with the inability to identify the *Vereine* members who belonged to the party or to assess their importance within their *Vereine,* all make the question irrelevant.

On the other hand, it is highly important to locate the Nazi vanguard among the upper echelons of *Verein* leaders and members. Influential *Verein* members who also belonged to or supported the Nazi Party would have been able to influence the path taken by their *Verein* and the attitude it adopted toward the party. However, there is little evidence that leaders of respected *Vereine* were also supporters or members of the Nazi Party. There are known cases of Nazi Party members who played leading roles in different *Vereine* years before joining the Nazi Party and who thus acquired a certain local prestige.[51] A number of party members also helped form new *Vereine,* such as the *Segelfliegerverein* and even the *Jazzverein* (!) in Schonach, but these *Vereine* exerted only a marginal influence in local society. There were indeed some towns in which senior members of the *Vereine* were also members of the Nazi Party or supported it in the local elections. It was precisely in *Vereine* such as the *KuMV,* which had the most potential for drumming up support, that we do not find highly placed members who also belonged to the Nazi Party. None of this proves, however, that party supporters used their *Verein* to disseminate Nazi propaganda, or that they tried to whip up Nazi support among the *Verein* members. Indeed we may assume just the opposite. The *Verein* dislike of politics, the hostility of the local councils toward the Nazi Party, and the need to receive financial support from either the local council or private businesses—most of which were unsympathetic to the party—provide a basis for conjecturing that the few Nazis who also served as leaders in the *Vereine* did not actively try to emphasize their party affiliations. In any case, the fact that we are speaking of such a small number of people makes the entire question something of a moot point.

The Nazi Party, for its part, tried to penetrate the ranks of the *Vereine,* especially the ones devoted to sports, in order to provide its members with military training, political clout, and, in the case of the *Reiterverein* and the *Schützenverein,* access to weapons. Most important of all was to gain a foothold in the local tavern, so that party members would later have a place for their political meetings. Such were the instructions of *Gauleiter* Wagner from 1931,[52] but things proceeded somewhat differently in actual fact. This was especially true of traditional bourgeois *Vereine* where membership, and especially leadership positions, were not just a matter of individual talents but also, and even primarily, a question of family prestige and local sociopolitical status. To sum things up: despite the picture generally portrayed of Verein life in many localities, in the Black Forest relations were extremely weak between the Nazi Party and the bourgeois *Vereine* devoted to culture and fellowship.

If this was the case, what motivated many of the bourgeoisie to support the Nazi Party, and what was the connection between this support and their membership in the *Vereine*? There are solid grounds for thinking that a considerable number of party supporters in 1932 had either left the *Vereine* or were in the process of doing so and thus found themselves beyond the pale of local society. In their search for a refuge, an organization willing to accept them, the Nazi Party appeared to be another *Verein,* as it indeed it appeared even to some of the organized bourgeoisie.[53] It was a *Verein* with a different style, to be sure, more political, but in terms of structure it was organized like a *Verein.* Like the *Verein,* it too had a local chapter, leader, treasurer, secretary, daily agenda, departments for sports and singing. Even more important, Nazi ideology and political idioms were amazingly similar to those of the organized bourgeois establishment.[54] By this we are referring to the anticlerical slogans, the aversion toward political Catholicism, the political populism, the fight against socialism and especially against Bolshevism. Taking part in the events of the cultural *Vereine* was now exchanged for the National Socialist "German Evenings" (*Deutscher Abend*), whose content was similar to that of the *Vereine.* In many cases, the supporters of the party found their fellow *Verein* members playing away for a fee. Bourgeois music *Vereine* were hired by the party "to make the German Evenings pleasant" and the *Vereine* were only too glad to snap up such offers. Their economic state did not permit them to turn down these invitations even when they came from the Socialists or the Church, and certainly not when they came from the Nazis, whose ideology and content was close to their own heart. The fact that a bourgeois *Verein* appeared in the Nazi chapter gave the local party chapter a certain legitimacy. For its part, the Nazi Party projected itself as another *Verein,* something along the lines of the *Sportvereine,* sworn to the traditions of the local bourgeois *Vereine.*[55] Most important of all, however, was the fact that the party's clearly anti-socialist-Bolshevist populist nature (presented side by side with anticapitalist slogans) was well suited to the mood of many members of the bourgeois camp who still belonged to the *Vereine,* but who could feel the ground trembling under their feet following the economic crisis and the growing strength of the communists.

In addition to all the reasons already mentioned, we must also weigh the possibility that for the local Catholic bourgeoisie, the Nazi Party represented a way of escaping its socioeconomic and political isolation. We have already stressed that certain sectors of the local bourgeoisie sought to use *Verein* activity as a means of emulating the Protestant bourgeoisie and of removing themselves from the ghetto-like isolation of their existence. The identification with the Liberal-Bourgeois Party is also characteristic of this trend. Probably the support for the Nazi Party in 1932 was another way of expressing the desire to take part in a social and economic order that challenged the one decreed by the Catholic establishment. If so, in the eyes of some of the local bourgeoisie, the Nazi Party loomed as a modern phenomenon, an alternative that would hasten the path of modernization. If we accept this argument (supported by a substantial literature that views Nazism as a modern revolution, in contrast to the no less popular attitude viewing Nazism as an antimodern revolution or movement), it should come as no surprise to learn that many craftsmen were members of the bourgeois *Vereine* (see table 9). This occupational group, whose economic problems during the Weimar Republic were partly caused by an inability to adapt to the processes of modernization and the rationalization of the German economy (see chap. 3), was panic-stricken at the idea of being "demoted" to the class of skilled laborers. Segments of this anticlerical bourgeois class (or the petite bourgeoisie, as they were called by the upper bourgeoisie) perceived the benefits of leaving the socioeconomic isolation and backwardness so characteristic of the Black Forest, first by emulating the cultural-political model of the Protestant bourgeoisie, and ultimately, by supporting the Nazi Party.[56]

Summary

Our discussion of the Black Forest region has focused on the atomization of bourgeois society (which was partly the result of people dropping out of the *Vereine*), the disintegration of the local social and cultural life, and the fact that many young people existed outside the frameworks of local social life. All these factors made a crucial (though not exclusive) contribution to the success of the Nazi Party in 1932. In certain contrast to the picture generally painted in the studies dealing with the rise of the Nazi Party, and as we noted already in part 2, our explanation does not rest upon the local notables who supported the party and led the way for other members of the community, nor does it rest upon the press and the leaders of the bourgeois *Vereine* who preached the Nazi cause. It was not even the Nazi Party itself—with its image of a dynamic and well-oiled propaganda machine adroitly manipulating the masses, projecting its message via a charismatic leadership and unique ideology—which swept the local bourgeoisie up after it.[57] The core of the apple was rotten already, making it easier for the worms to get in and gnaw away from inside.

Why has treatment of the *Vereine* been pushed aside in the many studies portraying the rise of the Nazi Party? Without doubt, the dizzying success of the party caused many scholars to concentrate more on the party and the party's activity than the society in which it flourished. It further seems that the model that we have presented of the disintegrating activity of the bourgeois *Verein* finds no counterpart elsewhere in Catholic regions in Germany. Let us keep in mind that the bourgeois *Vereine* in the Black Forest had to cope at one and the same time on two hostile fronts— the Catholic and the socialist—and that this was not the case in many other parts of Germany during this time. The severe economic crisis also struck and influenced the region in a way that was unlike anything experienced in many other parts of Germany. But more than anything, the lack until recently of scholarly interest in the bourgeois *Vereine* of the Weimar period stems, in our opinion, from the overall neglect of the subject in the scholarly literature. The current state of research is both a result and expression of the lack of attention given the German bourgeoisie in its ebb tide of the twentieth century. The intensive study of the nineteenth-century German bourgeoisie and bourgeois *Vereine* rose from the desire to study a social group that was on the ascendant; one that exercised the cultural, economic, and, at times, even the political hegemony.[58] A social group on the wane holds less interest for the scholars, and the result is a historiographical "black hole" with which the research will have to contend. We may speculate that intensive studies of the kind given the nineteenth-century German bourgeoisie will lead us to conclusions that reinforce the theories especially prevalent among Marxist historians, in connection with the role of the German bourgeoisie in the Nazi rise to power, only this time from a different starting point, through the use of "history from below."

There can be no ignoring the fact that the disintegration of the bourgeois establishment in the Black Forest and its shift to the Nazi Party found expression in additional fields of life as well—economic, religious, and social—some already examined above. These include the mass unemployment, the particular plight of Black Forest industry, the inability to form a political bloc in the local councils from 1931 on, the strong desire to break the vicious circle of isolation and to leave the "ghetto" behind. Most important of all was the fear of Bolshevism that gripped the local bourgeoisie, fed by the growing strength of the Communist Party. The local press gave a running account of the events taking place in Bolshevist Russia, as though they were an omen of what was in store for the Catholic population (and not only them) in the Black Forest. The frightened hostility against Bolshevism and the inability of the bourgeoisie to take a united stand against the encroaching threat found expression in every aspect of bourgeois existence. On the local level—in the small town and village— where local politics ran its own separate course, the study of these subjects is still in its infancy, especially that dealing with the Catholic regions.[59] The results of World War I, together with the economic crises that followed in its wake, undermined the already shaken self-confidence of the bourgeoisie and ultimately penetrated the very cornerstone of bourgeois existence—the *Vereine*—before the Great Economic Crisis finished it off altogether. Among the people ejected by the *Vereine* were those who voted for the NSDAP in 1932; they still saw themselves as belonging to bourgeois society, but being dismissed from the ranks of the most prestigious bourgeois institution hurt their self-image. Their feeling of threat, unjustified by the actual strength of the socialists, their legitimate fear of communism and sense of distress at the "treachery" of their immediate social surroundings, all conspired to push those standing at the margins of bourgeois society in 1932 into the arms of the Nazi Party. Can one view their support of Nazism as a way of avenging themselves on the rejecting bourgeois institution? Apparently there is some truth in the gloomy prediction of the *Donaubote,* which viewed the presence of *Bürgertum* in the ranks of the Nazi Party as the death of the bourgeoisie.[60] The loneliness of the Stammtisch in the *KuMV* meetings in Titisee led to the crowdedness in another room in the tavern, the one where a Nazi propaganda meeting was taking place,[61] and it made it easier for National Socialism to put the process of *Gleichschaltung* into effect, when, after 1933, the party used this as a means of counteracting the disintegrating infrastructure of the German bourgeoisie.

CHAPTER 11

The Disintegration of Catholic Nonbourgeois Society

The Catholic Milieu in the Second Reich and the Weimar Period

A Catholic milieu (or "milieus") in the previously mentioned sense began to crystallize in Germany during the last decade of the nineteenth century. There were several factors behind the rise of the Catholic milieu: the crystallization of a Catholic public sphere and of political Catholicism during the years of *Kulturkampf,* and also the increasing democratization of German life at the grass roots level, due in no small part to the trauma of *Kulturkampf* on Catholic thought and ideas. Although the formation of these milieus helped create a sense of Catholic solidarity, it also deepened Catholic isolation in German society. The bulwark against outside influences contributed to the inability of the Catholic inhabitants to open themselves to modern socioeconomic influences. The result was a ghetto mentality, social and economic backwardness, and a cultural gap that increasingly separated large sectors of the Catholic population from that of the Protestants. The subject of Catholic backwardness has come under intensive study since the early years of the century, largely through the work of Protestant scholars,[1] and hence there is little need to review the way in which these traits found expression in the Black Forest. Let us merely recall that, as noted, the Black Forest was not the only backward region to exist in Germany. Indeed, one can identify other regions similar to the Black Forest in this respect, such as the Allgäu, the Mosel-Eifel regions in the Rhineland, Lower Franconia, and several parts of Lower Silesia, all agricultural regions. The social life of the local Catholic inhabitants may be summed up in some of these cases as preindustrial, premodern, and precapitalistic. The Catholics generally clustered in communities of less than 5,000 population and engaged in agriculture, mining, and crafts. Very few dealt in trade, industry, management, or tourism. In the larger cities, needless to say, there was a wide stratum of Catholics with considerable property and means. This was mainly true of the cities along the Rhine, though also for such places as Munchen, Regensburg, Passau, and many other cities in south Germany.

The pillars of the Catholic milieus, and the features by which they were most known, were the *Zentrum,* the Catholic press, and the Catholic *Vereine,* especially those of a sociopolitical nature. So omnipresent were these *Vereine* in German Catholic society that, to quote Thomas Nipperdey, "German Catholicism became a Catholicism of *Vereine* and unions."[2] There were many different kinds of *Vereine,* as we will see below:

1. *Vereine* that were closely related to the Church and that dealt in particular aspects of Church life: the *Glaubensvereine*—that dealt in the rites of Sundays and holidays, with the sacrament and missionary work, for example; *Bonifätiusverein*—for German Catholics outside Germany; *Borromäusverein*—for the distribution of popular Catholic books. The *Caritativer Vinzentinerverein* for charity goals, and many other *Vereine* were noted for their strong dependence on the Church.

2. *Vereine* geared to a specific gender and age group: the *Jugend und Jungmännervereine* for young men; the *Katholische Jungfrauenvereinigungen Frauenbund* for young girls; the *Muttervereine* for women. Most of these *Vereine* were under the auspices of the Church.

3. *Vereine* geared to specific classes and occupational groups, generally organized outside of the Church but under its supervision: *Gesellenverein* for the master craftsmen and artisans (founded by Adolf Kolping in the mid–nineteenth century); *Katholische Arbeitervereine* for workers; *Bauernverein* for peasants; and others.

4. *Vereine* that were close to the Church in matters of principle but not under Church jurisdiction. The most prominent of these was the *Volksverein für das katholische Deutschland* (of which we will have more to say later).

In addition to the *Vereine* of these categories there were also many culturally oriented *Vereine,* all of which took their cue from the bourgeois *Vereine.* Of particular importance were the *Augustinusverein* for the press and the *Görres Gesellshaft* for the promotion of Catholic study. There were also *Vereine* for the promotion of political ideals, of which the *Zentrum* was the most important and well-known. It is worth noting once again, however, that *Zentrum* policy and goals went against the Church on more than one occasion, and that on the eve of World War I the party claimed little more than half of the Catholic vote. Most of these voters were members of the lower middle class, many of whom attained senior positions as representatives of various middle-class factions within the party. By the end of the Second Reich the party had lost its sectarian character and turned into one of the most important parties in the Reichstag, a pressure group that represented the interests of the lower middle class and the Catholic peasants.[3]

The most important *Verein* was closely allied to the *Zentrum:* the *Volksverein für das katholische Deutschland* (*Vv*). The *Vv* was founded in 1890 by the *Zentrum*'s then leading figure, Ludwig Windthorst. Its goal was to promote the Christian order in Germany society; to propagate the importance of Christianity in an era when, in the words of Windthorst, it was necessary "to fight against the forces of sin and destruction in Catholic society and to elevate the sociospiritual level of all Catholic occupation groups." The *Vv* oversaw the activities and organization of all class-based *Vereine.* Its most important task revolved around the community meetings held in both urban and rural locations. The discussions in these meetings generally touched upon issues of economics, religion, and politics. At the height of its power, just before the war, the *Vv* boasted a membership of some 800,000 people across Germany. Its goals became increasingly social and socialistic, and during that period the bulk of its activity was concentrated among the ranks of the Catholic workers. The *Vv* constituted the pillar of Catholic society, even though its goals at times conflicted with those of the Catholic Church.[4]

In sum, the Catholic *Vereine* played a complex and at times contradictory role in society. They provided an instrument for strengthening the processes of modernization and emancipation in Catholic society, yet also hindered the process of getting "out of the ghetto," due to their role in creating the Catholic milieu.

What was the fate of the Catholic milieus that rose in the post-1918 years of Wilhelmine Germany? Even before the war, tensions ran high between the exponents of two opposing sides in the Catholic milieus. On the one side were those who sought to encourage modernization, reform, social struggle, and emancipation, led primarily by the *Vv* and the Rhine-based *Zentrum* (i.e., the party leaders from the vicinity of Cologne). On the other side were those who wanted the milieu to retain its closed and sectarian nature, in the spirit of the Roman Catholic Church. The leading figures in this faction were the bishops of Bresslau and Trier, and many of the Church leaders in Bavaria. Those who sided with modernization carried the day, and their attitudes grew increasingly militant in the first years after the war.[5]

The Catholic milieu in the Weimar period was influenced by these struggles, and also by the many processes then sweeping over Weimar Germany in various aspects of social, economic, and political life. In comparison with the preceding period, Weimar society was considerably more open and democratic, and this new trend had a decisive impact on the secularizing processes that had been present in Catholic society since the end of the previous century. Many Catholic groups made their exodus "out of the ghetto" at this time and gained equal rights in a number of different fields, including education and civil service promotion. The rights of the Catholic minority were guaranteed by the constitutions of Weimar Germany and the individual states, and also by the concordats governing the relations between them. The enfranchisement of women strengthened the Church and, needless to say, the *Zentrum* as well.

The growing strength of the *Zentrum* and the Bavarian People's Party (the Bayerische Volkspartei, which seceded from the *Zentrum* in 1919 following a dispute over cooperation with the *SPD*), was not just due to the votes that it received at the polls. Even more important was the role it played as an arbiter of political power in Weimarian political life, a fact that had great impact on the Catholic milieus. Signs of Catholic withdrawal from the surrounding society grew increasingly rare. It was not only a new openness that the growing intimacy with Protestant society indicated, but also the ability of external influences to penetrate the Catholic milieu. Indeed, one of the most striking characteristics of the Catholic milieus under Weimar was the way in which Catholics crossed over the lines to political camps considered until 1918 as enemy territory, such as the extreme right (the *DNVP* until 1929) and left.[6] The forces that splintered the Catholic milieus into sympathizers of the extreme left and right, and the *Zentrum*-supporting majority (though in the Weimar period its support declined to less than fifty percent) also cast a shadow over the activity of the Church, and of the Catholic *Vereine* in particular. The Church remained firmly opposed to the extreme left and at times to the right, and in contrast to its policy before 1914 now showed open hostility to the *Vereine* of socialist leanings. This hostility had its source in one of the most important characteristics of the Catholic Church—and hence of the Catholic milieu as a whole—namely, the ferment of religious activity among individual Catholics and Catholic communities. Through this activity the Church hoped to strengthen the religious consciousness of the individual and to reverse the trend toward secularization. Unlike the nineteenth century, when politics and society were considered the proper spheres for Church activity, the focus now shifted to the domain of Church life. The sociopolitical goals of former years were no longer necessary, having been chiseled into the various constitutions and guaranteed by the strength of the *Zentrum*.

The class-based Catholic *Vereine,* and the *Vv* in particular, sank into crisis from the mid-1920s. The trade unions, the *Katholische Arbeitervereine* (*KAV*), and the *Gesellenvereine* also suffered from instability.

Despite the ambivalence of their attitudes toward democracy, and the left-
and right-wing parties, the class-based *Vereine* did cooperate with the
republic. Their social activity and sociopolitical outlook brought down the
fury of Church leaders. Yet, many groups of workers also took a dim view
of the relations between their own *Vereine* and the *Zentrum* (which leaned
toward the right from the mid-1920s on). Even more significant was the
decline of Church support for these *Vereine,* which made it virtually
impossible for them to carry out their objectives. It was against this background that the *Christlich Soziale Reichspartei* rose in 1927, claiming to
represent the true interests of the Catholic workers. The success of the
party was brief, however, and it was confined to a limited number of
regions. Many of its members were disgruntled workers angered by the
vacillation of the *Zentrum* between their own demands and those of the
peasants and middle class, and who thus abandoned the *Zentrum* and even
the *KAV.* A similar process occurred in the *Gesellenverein,* where the leadership was sharply divided. Both these *Vereine* tried from the end of the
1920s to fill their activity with nationalistic content and to express support
for a more authoritative government, in order to show support for Chancellor Brüning and to conform with the policy of the *Zentrum* and the
Church. Beginning with 1932, these *Vereine* also agreed to contact with the
National Socialists.[7]

The leaning toward the right, anti-Semitism, the growing hostility
toward the left, the weakness of the class-based *Vereine,* the ideas of the
"folk community" and of a society based on family pedigree (rather than
economic status, as is common in class-based societies today), the fear of
Bolshevism: all these represented both the dilemma and the upheavals facing the Catholic milieus under Weimar. These phenomena should not be
seen only as a reaction to World War I and the economic crises that came
in its wake, but also as an expression of the growing Catholic desire to
burst through the stifling "ghetto walls" of the Wilhelmine period. As a
result, we are witness to the growing polarization between those who managed to burst through the ghetto and those who remained inside; between
the trends of release and those of entrenchment; between a desire to take
part in the mainstream of German society (also leaning rightward) and the
fundamental nature of the Catholic bourgeois *Vereine,* the Church, and
the *Zentrum.*

Given the inadequate state of studies on the Catholic milieu during
the Weimar period, it is especially interesting to ask whether the processes
sketched in the historiography of the period, and which are based largely
on material of a Catholic nature (e.g., official Church bulletins, memoirs
of Catholic leaders, the minutes of clerical synods), came to expression at
the local level of the Catholic milieu. Did a social vacuum really set in as a
result of *Vv* inactivity, and did the crisis affect other *Vereine* as well? Was

this vacuum filled by Catholic activity of a religious nature, as the Church indeed demanded? Was there, on the local level, a phenomenon of estrangement between Catholic workers and the Church and *Zentrum*? And what alternative did the Catholic workers have? We will try to answer these question by describing the problems facing the Catholic milieu in the Black Forest. Before turning to this next issue, however, we must briefly review the way in which the Church and Catholic milieu regarded the Nazi Party.

The Catholic Milieu and the Nazi Party

Against the background of processes already described, is it possible to understand the attitude of the Catholic milieu toward the Nazi Party? In chapter 9 we saw how the party viewed religion, Catholic society, and the *Zentrum*. The attitude of the Church, the *Zentrum*, and Catholic society toward the Nazi Party has been meticulously documented by Catholic historians both in Germany and abroad, the most prominent of them being the late German scholar Klaus Scholder. We will not go into detail here about the way the Church and the *Zentrum* viewed National Socialism. We will only mention that despite differences of opinion, the attitude that officially reigned in the Catholic Church was one that rejected National Socialism. We find this in the declaration made by the bishops of Mainz in October 1930, where it was stated that: (1) a Catholic could not be a party member; (2) a party member could not take part in Church ceremonies; (3) a party member could not receive Holy Communion. While such severity did not meet with unanimous acceptance from all of the bishops, they did agree to its major principles in one form or another up until 1933. The *Zentrum* also rejected any dialogue with the National Socialists and it was only in 1932, after the Nazis triumphed in the July elections, that it entered into coalition negotiations with them.[8]

According to the official Catholic historiography, the Catholic milieu was almost united in its objection to the National Socialists. The clergy waged unceasing battle against the Nazi Party and even used their role as confessor to pressure the erring members of their flock. Did the Catholic population behave toward the Nazi Party according to the dictates of its leaders? Let us take a look at a description that has come down to us from a priest in the Catholic village of Schenkenzell, in the middle of the Black Forest:[9]

> In the last elections the Nazis won 150 votes. They held meetings and made all kinds of lies against the *Zentrum*, the bishops, and the priests. Immediately after that they founded a chapter there . . . People can read *Der Führer* and the *Völkischer Beobachter* on the daily

bulletin boards. The declaration of the Mainz Bishopric [from October 1930] posted there drew down criticism. Even simple folk criticize the decision of the Church and the bishops practically every day. Many who were members of the *Zentrum* until now, regular Church-goers who even received Holy Communion, are members of the party. They claim: "We are good Catholics, but in politics we are convinced of Hitler (*"Überzeugte Hitler"*), and so long as the Archbishopric in Freiburg remains undecided we'll stay with Hitler. What other bishops decide is no concern of ours . . ." The authority of the Church and bishops in this quiet place is in decline . . . It is hard for a priest to give people an answer on the subject when there is no clear response from the Kanzel. The church choir, which until now gave support to the priest, has choir members who work for the Hitler movement, among them women singers who will become members in the newly reestablished *Marianische Jungfrauenkongregation,* as of November 30. The time has come for the Bishopric to lead us against this heathen movement and to let everyone know that Catholicism has no place next to Hitler.

In a letter to the head of the local Nazi chapter, Father Bihler has this to say: "Thank you for your invitation to speak to the members of my congregation in your chapter on the subject of National Socialism and its attitude toward the Catholic religion and the Catholic Church . . . It is not possible for me to speak on this subject in a political meeting. When I discuss this question I speak from a Catholic and not political point of view . . . Inasmuch as the entire Catholic Church, the Pope in his Christmas communication, Cardinal Bertram [of Bresslau], the synod of the bishops in Fulda and all the bishops in Bavaria have ruled that National Socialism is an *Irrlehre* [a "doctrine of error"]), it is forbidden to anyone of the Catholic religion anywhere to cooperate . . . Discussing the Catholic worldview and taking a stand on the matter can only be done inside of a church, at a sermon or church meeting held by the Catholic *Vereine.* Outside of it, [only] by the *Vv,* whose task this is, and for which purpose it was founded. . . ."

And in a letter to the Freiburg *Ordinariat:* "The leader of the local party chapter, Karl Haberer, a lieutenant in the war, a merchant thereafter and today head of a work crew in the Junghans Factory, put a question to the priest and asked for a clear answer . . . 'Can I [Haberer], as a member of the Nazi Party, be a member of the Catholic Church . . . The order of the Council of Bishops of the upper Rhine [from March 1931] allows me to raise this question a second time . . . Can I, as a faithful member of the Nazi Party, receive the holy sacrament or not? Easter is next Sunday, and hence I would thank you for a swift reply.' Haberer has four children, and

I have refrained from taking a stand until now for this reason . . . In time, Haberer and his children could find themselves outside the Church for belonging to the party. I am unable to come up with any answer, nor do I find one in the resolution taken by the bishops of Bavaria . . . clear instructions from the [Freiburg] bishopric would be welcome."

This was not the only village in the Black Forest where such things occurred. Pridham reports similar cases in Bavaria, as does Plum in the region of Aachen. Police reports from the area outside of Koblenz mention uniformed SA men infiltrating Church ceremonies, thus deepening the tension between the Catholic Church and the Nazi Party. The letters written by Father Bihler allow us to draw some important conclusions. For one, the Catholic *Vereine* were still instrumental in dealing with problems that arose in the Catholic Weltanschauung. For another, the position of the priest was not what it had been. He was no longer able to prevent members of his church from leaning in the direction of the Nazi Party. His major job was to make sure that the *Zentrum* held onto its strength, and even this he was unable to do in the villages. We are also witness to the rupture between the priest and his superiors in the Freiburg *Ordinariat.* This last is an important point. The fact that Church leaders reached a decision does not mean that it was always carried out to the letter in each and every community. Their decisions were not even always clear, and many important decisions seem to have fallen onto the shoulders of the local priest. Thus much depended on the individual personality of the priest himself. The position that a priest occupied in local society was instrumental in determining the quality of religious life in the community, no less than its attitude toward the Nazi Party.

In Baden, the Freiburg Bishopric made no bones over its dislike of the Nazi Party, whose propaganda was particularly vicious in these parts (as we learn, for example, from *Der Führer*). The Nazi Party made deliberate provocations against the Church and *Zentrum.* The death of Archbishop Karl Fritz and his replacement by Konrad Gröber, who was said to support the German right, sent a wave of rumors about the changes due to occur in the Bishopric's policy toward the Nazi Party. Gröber, however, did not take definite steps in the direction of the Nazi Party until 1933 (in contrast to the ambivalence of his policy thereafter), and the Nazi Party continued to be ostracized.[10]

The Catholic Milieu in the Black Forest during the Weimar Period

The battle against National Socialism constitutes one of the most striking features of the Catholic milieus in 1930 through 1932 (and obviously thereafter), together with the even more fiercely pitched battle against communism. The study generally emphasizes the resistance of these milieus to the encroaching enemy, and in a few rare cases we read how one milieu or another collapsed under the pressure of the Nazi onslaught. We are arguing that not only did the Catholic milieu in the Black Forest fail to resist Nazi activity, but that it also did not collapse as a result of Nazi pressure. The Catholic milieu had begun to crumble long before the Nazi Party first appeared on the scene. It was this inexorable process of deterioration that allowed the Nazi Party to sweep voters along after it, almost without any special effort on its part.

In earlier chapters we saw the deterioration of the bourgeois infrastructure, which was separate from the Catholic milieu in the region. Let us now turn to two major social groups that provided the Nazi Party with its major source of strength: the peasants and workers. In chapter 3 we reviewed the socioeconomic crisis that affected these groups. We will now take a look at the nature of the socioreligious life in the region during the Weimar Period and attempt to show why we have seen fit to call this area the Achilles' heel of German Catholicism. Needless to say, the plight of religious life in the region must be viewed in the context of the region's socioeconomic background, as presented earlier in this study. Once again, the *Vereine* will stand at the focus of our discussion, but this time the Catholic *Vereine,* with an additional look at the role of the priest in the local community. We will also look at the religious ceremonies and their socioeconomic significance in the community, as well as the anticlerical aspirations (*kirchenfeindliche Bestrebungen*) and the moral problems (*sittliche Übelstand*) that the local priests noted in their congregations (*Pfarrei*). Our goal is not only to assess the extent to which the local milieu resisted the secularizing processes at large in Catholic society, but also to examine whether the local communities indeed complied with the demand to increase their religious activity, as contemporary studies tend to submit.

The Disintegration of Social-Religious Life in the Peasant Villages and among the Workers

The Problems in the Peasant Villages

We will open our discussion with an excerpt from a letter addressed to the priest Andris, anonymous yet highly evocative:

> . . . when the train pulled into Löffingen at seven that night, I thought the Communists had infiltrated the town. From the main street came sounds of screaming and shouting and the Catholic hit song (*Schlager*) *"O Dona Klara"* . . . Some of these youngsters are out of work, yet where do they get the money to buy liquor? They get them-

selves drunk every Saturday and Sunday . . . They know only part of
the way to church on Sunday, while others loiter at the church square
smoking cigarettes, or sitting in the pub until church is out . . .

To this state of affairs Andris replied:

> . . . I was not aware of this behavior, but you are right in saying that
> the youngsters must be organized. At present they have no organiza-
> tional framework at all . . . The *Zentrum* here is paralyzed . . . The
> local *Vereine,* which do not belong to the Church, are all fighting
> against it. All of them are secular. They have *BLB* sympathizers who
> either are members of the Nazi Party or unaffiliated now with any
> party whatsoever . . . The secular *Vereine* are the offspring of the lib-
> eral Weltanschauung. They have always been strong in these parts
> and opposed to the Catholic *Vereine,* which have never been well
> organized in our region . . .[11]

This correspondence captures the plight of the rural Catholic areas
from the close of the nineteenth century, and it testifies to the inability of
the Catholic public sphere to consolidate itself. Geographically, the letter
refers to the south and southeastern regions of the Black Forest: Hotzenwald and Wutach. No Catholic milieu ever succeeded in establishing itself
in this region, which was made up of small, very backward villages. The
region was socially, economically, and politically homogeneous. Its
staunch support of the Nazi Party (cf. Reiselfingen, Seppenhofen; table 6,
chap. 7), beginning in the years 1928 through 1930, was preceded by support for the *BLB*. Before the war, the Liberal-National party enjoyed a
great deal of support.

Traces of anticlerical activity lingered in the region long after *Kulturkampf* came to its official end in Baden and Prussia, and even after the
end of World War I. The task of giving anticlericalism its political expression was assumed by the *BLB*. In the social sphere, anticlericalism received
expression in the inability of Catholic *Vereine* to form roots in the area.
The few *Vereine* that did manage to entrench themselves locally faced considerable obstacles. Even though chapters of the *Vv* existed on paper in
almost every village of the Black Forest before World War I, they were virtually inactive for reasons that ranged from the difficulties of terrain and
location to the apathy and indifference of the local youth.[12] The *Bauernverein,* which bore the stamp of the Catholic Church, had only ten major
branches through all the Black Forest region, including two in the south.
The class-based *Vereine* (*KAV, Gesellenverein*) were only established in the
first part of the twentieth century. Prior to the war the *KAV* chapters were
confined to the larger towns; the only chapters in the southern region were

in Lenzkirch, Vöhrenbach, and Donaueschingen. Few places had *Gesellenvereine,* and only after 1918. Youth organizations such as the *Jungmannerverein* were confined to Bonndorf, Lenzkirch, and Vöhrenbach. The activity of these *Vereine* (as far as it went) was mostly concentrated in the larger towns. Though many villagers also worked in these towns, few were able to participate in *Verein* activity since they had to make the journey back home after work. Thus the local *Vereine* became the exclusive domain of the (small) townspeople, while the villagers had to content themselves with such activity as was organized by the local priest, who often objected to the activity of the class-based *Vereine.*[13] Even the Catholic press, which in any case appeared relatively late on the scene, had a poor circulation. Prominent Catholic figures such as leaders of the *Zentrum* rarely visited the region, and there was little evidence of *Zentrum* propaganda. Nonetheless, the *Zentrum* did manage to preserve its existing strength up until 1932 without too great an effort (as did the Nazi Party thereafter). Thus it fell to the priest, through the rites that he led and the *Vereine* that he headed, to provide the mainstay of the Church in the region. Let us then turn to examine the role that the priests played in the Weimar years.

After the war, the clergy constituted a major target for violence in the region of the Schwarzwald-Baar. With the establishment of the *BLB* in 1921–22, the peasants and craftsmen who thronged to the radical peasant movement openly sought to provoke the local Catholic Church and clergy. Yet despite their avowed anticlericalism they continued to see themselves as staunchly Catholic, placing their faith in the traditional saints and beliefs. The phenomenon was not confined to the southern Black Forest. Even north of the area incidents such as these took place, and there is little wonder that the memory of *Kulturkampf* continued to smolder among the supporters of the Church and the *Zentrum* in the region. While there were no doubt other factors as well, it is against this background that we find priests requesting leaves of absence from the *Ordinariat* in Freiburg, citing fatigue and loss of confidence among their reasons.[14]

Given the importance of the priest in local society, his broad network of relations throughout the community, this wave of resignations greatly undermined the stability of the Catholic milieu during the mid-1920s. The Church was not unaware of the problem. The difficulty of assuming a new pastorate could easily erode the religious life of an entire community. The Nazi electoral success is strongly correlated to a rapid turnover of priests in various localities. To cite one example: small towns and villages such as Lenzkirch, Schollach, and Altglashütten experienced a turnover of their priests only in 1932, the same year in which the Nazi Party first gained a local foothold. Conversely, the "problematic" areas of the Black Forest—

those that exhibited massive support for the Nazi Party early on (table 6)—were also the ones to undergo a frequent turnover of priests at an earlier stage. Many of the newly installed priests were unacquainted with the members of their congregation, and their unfamiliarity with the norms of local society left them without the moral and political authority so vital to a Catholic milieu.

Yet it was not only the new priests who confronted these problems. Even so venerable a priest as Vogt of Rohrbach indicated that many members of his congregation had turned their backs on the Church rites. According to Vogt the entire religious order of the village was at stake, and it was "not only the young who prefer the tavern over the Church." In Löffingen the old priest Andris and his assistant met with resistance from the local authorities when they sought to repair their dilapidated church building. A leaking roof, inadequate heating, and poor sanitary conditions were the bane of the priest's existence. It was factors such as these, together with the steadily shrinking salary, that undoubtedly fostered the sense of unease and the problems the priests met in performing their duties.[15]

The strained relations between the priests and the local officials received expression not only in the denial of funds to repair the ailing churches, but also in the incessant wrangling over the construction of mixed swimming pools, a project common to many resort towns and villages in the region from the mid-1920s. The priests were opposed to such projects, but the pools were built despite their opposition. In many places the relations between the priest and local *Bürgermeister* took a turn for the worse, in yet another indication of the decline of the priest's status. Another problem that faced local priests concerned the policy of the *Zentrum* in local administration and government. The fact that local residents had to take themselves off to the district capital in order to receive unemployment benefits or to arrange financial matters was blamed squarely on the local priest, the *Zentrum* incarnate in the eyes of the villagers. In such circumstances, the local priest would then have little choice but to notify the Church that his own authority had thus been compromised, and that in the forthcoming elections he might withdraw his support from the *Zentrum*.[16] At times the priests tried to lure members of their flock with promises of economic benefit in order to strengthen their obedience to the Church, but they were not always able to keep these promises. Thus on the eve of the 1930 Reichstag elections, residents of Eisenbach declared that they would not be voting for the *Zentrum* due to just such unfulfilled promises (this may well give us some insight as to why the Nazi Party won such support in the village). In Gütenbach the local priest failed to make good on his promises to the craftsmen. He withheld work, moreover, from local residents who had

not paid their *Kirchensteur* ("Church tax"). Affairs were further compli-
cated by the refusal of the only factory in town, up until 1931, to employ
workers who belonged to the Church. Quite possibly, the growing
strength of the *KPD* and the Nazi Party can be explained by just such
occurrences as these (*KPD,* July 1932, 21.2 percent).[17]

One of the victims of the Church tax was Dr. Vogel, a major activist
for the Nazi Party in the region. The priest in Grafenhausen threatened to
confiscate Vogel's property for reason of nonpayment. The Church tax
was a painful subject to priest and congregation alike, especially in poorer
areas such as the Wutach or Hotzenwald. In many communities people
were required to increase the tax that they paid to the Church. Church
funds (*Kirchenstiftung*) collapsed following the period of inflation, the
local councils cut back on their support, and the cost of social assistance
rose higher and higher. In certain places where the tax had long gone
uncollected, plans were now made to have it reinstated. This was the case
in Schenkenzell, for example, and there can be little doubt that this only
served to increase the bitterness of the townspeople toward Bihler, the
local priest. If we recall Bihler's description of his relations with the local
Nazis, and further mention that this village had three different priests
between 1930 and 1932, we may well have part of the answer as to why the
Nazi Party was so victorious here. In Lenzkirch, where the party made
very little headway up until 1932, there was no increase in the tax, in contrast to the steepness of the increase in surrounding villages.

The reading of journalism "hostile to the Church" (*Kirchen-feindliche
Presse*) was also widespread in the region. The national Catholic press
rarely penetrated the remote villages of the southern Black Forest, leaving
the *BLB* to distribute its *Schwarzwälder Zeitung* without fear of competition. Church authorities were aware of the sorry state of the Catholic
press, and in meetings of the Dekanat clergymen warned that its inferior
quality left the Church open to contempt. The local Catholic paper (and
the Nazi paper thereafter) was popular with the poorer residents of the
Furtwangen, but only because it was cheaper than the liberal bourgeois
press. However, the biweekly appearance of the paper meant that it made
less of an impact than the *Schwarzwälder Tagblatt,* which appeared daily
beginning in 1931.[18]

In seeking to obtain a better picture of the Catholic milieu prior to the
rise of the Nazi Party, our efforts are greatly assisted by one particularly
rich source of information: the *Kirchenvisitationen* reports. These reports
documented various Catholic communities throughout the Black Forest
and were drawn up by clergymen under the auspices of the Ordinariat in
Freiburg every four or five years. Although these reports contain the
answers to a wide set of questions, the following discussion will address
only one particular aspect of local life: that of religion and morals.

In these reports, the local priest was requested to list the moral flaws and deviations that he observed in his own congregation and to identify the people hostile to the Church (table 11). The prevailing attitude in these places may also be gauged by the number of Catholics not taking part in Easter Communion (*Osterkommunion*). Considering the importance of communion in the Catholic religion, the refusal to receive it may be indicative of a negative attitude toward the local Church and clergy. It does not, however, necessarily imply hostility toward the Church as a whole.

Table 11 shows the dismal state of religion and morals in many peasant villages throughout the Black Forest. Even in places located in the north-central part of the region, such as Oberwolfach, Fischerbach, and Schenkenzell, the situation was visibly in decline. In the Wutach, the village of Bachheim stands out for its favorable report, so that the date of the report (1931) is worth considering. Throughout most of the Weimar period it seems that Bachheim managed to preserve the moral and religious conditions of village life. It had a high standard of living when compared with the backward villages of the region, and the local priest commanded the respect of his community. The village, moreover, was run with a firm hand by its mayor, Hermann Kramer, an authoritative figure who also represented the *Zentrum* in the Baden Landtag. For these reasons the Nazi Party won little support up until 1932, an unusual phenomenon in a region otherwise characterized by broad Nazi support beginning in 1928. In September 1930 the party won 13.3 percent of the votes cast in Bachheim, and it was not until July 1932 that the party was able to break through and capture more than fifty percent of the vote. Since we have no information about religious life in the village after 1931, we can only surmise about the role this played in the party's success. We do know, however, that Kramer died in 1930, and this leads us to connect the death of the local power broker to the success of the Nazi Party (which little frequented the local pub in the summer of 1932).

There can be no doubt that the situation in Bachheim constitutes an unusual phenomenon in the context of the Wutach, a region whose political and economic characteristics we have already seen. Outside the region, one does find other villages where the priest gave the existing moral-religious order a favorable report, as in Todtmoos, Hinterzarten, and even Oberwolfach, which was located in the very heart of the Black Forest. In the first two villages the priest noted that tourists helped fan the winds of anticlericalism, thus corroborating our conclusions about the success of the Nazi Party in tourist towns. As previously noted, tourists and vacationers contributed to the success that the party experienced in these towns up until 1932. In the towns and villages of the Wutach and the Schwarzwald-Baar, signs of a deteriorating moral and religious order were visible already at the beginning of the 1920s. While it is true that church attendance remained stable and at times even rose, it is difficult to see this as an indicator of the extent to which the Church did or did not face opposition, inasmuch as the church was also perceived as a place of social gathering. Local inhabitants were not the only ones to attend church services, for they were also a stopping-off point for travelers, sight-seers, or organized groups of Catholics. Not going to church might be due to more than a dislike of the local priest or a desire to spend one's Sunday drinking, sleeping, or fishing. It could also be embarrassment at not owning a respectable suit of clothes, or possibly a reluctance to see the neighbors with whom one was currently feuding.

In contrast to church attendance, however, the number of people who refrained from receiving Easter Communion (*Osterkommunion*) does provide a reliable indicator of the anticlerical feelings abroad in the community. This is the most solemn ceremony of the Catholic year, one that requires the celebrant to partake of the Host and to be confessed of his sins. Refusing Easter Communion testifies to a negative view of the Church and the priest, though it does not necessarily indicate anti-Catholicism as well. Once again, villages such as Hinterzarten, Todtmoos, and Bachheim were but the exceptions to the rule. In these villages no more than a few dozen people refrained from taking part in the ceremonies. In the rest of the villages, however, opposition to Communion was widespread. A similar trend, though on a lesser scale, can be found in the number of *Heiligekommunionen* distributed. The priest would offer them not only to the worshippers of his congregation but also to such as happened to be in attendance: travelers, tourists, and the large groups of visitors who sometimes reached the villages in the framework of the *Katholische Aktion* or *Mission.* Hence this number was subject to seasonal fluctuations. Yet there are also times when this number can teach us something about the authority of the local priest. In Bonndorf there was a sharp decline in the number of Kommunionen being distributed at mass, though in subsequent years the number increased. The same can be said of Ewattingen, Grafenhausen (where the decline was particularly sharp), Hinterzarten, Löffingen (mostly until 1931), and even Schluchsee. Once again, Bachheim is an exception to the rule, as is Schenkenzell, which we have already seen in previous chapters of our study. The Mission organized in Schenkenzell during the mid-1920s may well have made local inhabitants more willing to take part in religious ceremonies, including *Osterkommunion.*[19]

Important evidence of the extent to which a given priest wielded authority can be found in the village birthrate, and also in the number of infants born out of wedlock. The latter set of data finds conspicuous expression toward the close of the 1920s. In a number of villages surrounding the Schluchsee dam we find a large number of births out of wedlock, a fact that is linked to the numerous dam workers clustered in the

TABLE 11. The Religious and Moral Situation in the Community (Author's summary of *Kirchenvisitationen* from selected villages)

Bonndorf (+2 villages) pop. 2,254	Apathy, 130 to 150 occasional churchgoers. Drunken behavior (1925). Apathy, rowdiness among youth. Insobriety, political dissension, broken families. Abstainers from *Osterkommunion*—1534 (1931). (*NSDAP* vote in Sept. 1930: 19.8 percent)
Ewattingen (including Münchingen) pop. 965	Unsatisfactory. On one holiday only 4 men came to church, in addition to the women worshippers. Loitering on the streets at night. Insobriety, womanizing. Abstainers from *Osterkommunion*—682 (1928). (*NSDAP* vote in Sept. 1930: 23.6 percent)
Bachheim pop. 346	Excellent condition. No apathy or moral deviation. Some drinking in the pub. Abstainers from *Osterkommunion*—6 (1931). (*NSDAP* vote in Sept. 1930: 13.3 percent)
Fischerbach pop. 953	Most residents are believers (1925). Abstainers from *Osterkommunion*—614 (1930). (NSDAP vote in Sept. 1930—20.5 percent)
Grafenhausen (+9 villages) pop. 1,303	Good. No apathy or moral deviations. Some insobriety and reading of liberal press. Presence of local "enemies" of the Church (1927). The situation is good, but apathy runs high among local residents. Insobriety, drunken behavior, unwelcome political trends. Mixed swimming pool. Declining birthrate. Inactive *Vereine*. Abstainers from *Osterkommunion*—48 (1932). (NSDAP vote in Sept. 1930—29.3 percent)
Löffingen (+2 villages) pop. 2,230	Skepticism, apathy, anti-Church incitement. Insobriety, gluttony, womanizing. Lack of personal safety. Sacrilege on the part of women as well. Even so, there are many who do fulfill their duties. Abstainers from *Osterkommunion*—200 (1928). (*NSDAP* vote in Sept. 1930: 21.4 percent)
Hinterzarten pop. 1,309	Good situation; tourists and holiday-makers significantly contributing to the deterioration of morals. Dancing in the pub. No *Verein* life. Abstainers from *Osterkommunion*—20–23 (1928). (*NSDAP* vote in Sept. 1930: 31.8 percent)
Oberwolfach pop. 1,889	Strained relations between the priest and the mayor. Low circulation of Catholic press but community has respect for the priest (1928). (*NSDAP* vote in Sept. 1930: 11.6 percent)
Reiselfingen pop. 472	Not a bad situation but considerable apathy. Climate of licentiousness. Girls lounging around the pub. Parents shirking their responsibilities (1925). (NSDAP vote in Sept. 1930: 32.8 percent)
Schenkenzell pop. 1,653	Widespread apathy and lack of belief, yet regarded as a good Catholic community nonetheless. Propaganda against the Church. Abstainers from *Osterkommunion*—1,000 (1928). (*NSDAP* vote in Sept. 1930: 36.6 percent)
Schluchsee (+8 villages) pop. 845	Intemperance, even during Sunday services (1924). Hooliganism among the youth, even the 6 to 8 year olds. Radical trends among dam workers and the young. National Socialist propaganda. Foreign dam workers living with local families. Corrupt youth (1931). (*NSDAP* vote in July 1932: 39.6 percent)

TABLE 11.—*Continued*

Todtmoos (+4 villages) pop. 3,452	Situation still good, though with some resistance on the part of certain individuals. Tourists exerting negative influence, but most inhabitants loyal to the Church. Abstainers from *Osterkommunion*—20 to 25 (1928). (NSDAP vote in Sept. 1930: 21.9 percent)

Source: Kirchenvisitationen reports in parish archives *(Pfararchiv)* in the above localities. Dates of reports in parentheses.

area, who thus contributed to the decline of morals in village life. We also find a perceptible drop in birthrate during the Weimar period, not only because of the more frequent use of contraceptives and the growing economic plight, but perhaps also because of the waning authority of the local priest. The decline in funds donated to charity (*Klingelbeutelkollekten*) and the upkeep of the Church, and the rising circulation of the liberal-national press, also indicate the shakiness of the priests' status in the villages of the south and central Black Forest.[20]

Before turning to an analysis of local *Verein* activity, let us sum things up by saying that we are witness to a trend of growing instability in the religious and moral life of the region, beginning with the mid-1920s. This trend stands in contrast to the description given at the outset of our words, in which the years under Weimar are depicted as a period of fervent religious awakening. With the upsurge of political activity in the region—the anticlerical activity from the mid-1920s (aided first by the *BLB* and then by the Nazis), the activity of the *Zentrum,* and the increasing frequency of various election rounds—religious activity was pushed to the side and campaigns for the *Katholische Aktion* ceased altogether. There can be no doubt that all this did little to enhance the authority of the priest or to strengthen the religious convictions of local inhabitants, when they had not always been that strong to begin with. One case in point is the festival honoring St. Barbara, patron saint of warriors and arms-bearing men (*Tag der Heilige Barbara*), recently reinstated after a long period of nonobservance in the Black Forest. What caused the people of the Black Forest to bring back these observances just now? The regional press chalked it up to the harsh conditions of local life and the people's desire to forget their worries. Thus we learn that it was not an order from the Bishopric that led to the renewed festivities, but a local initiative born of economic concerns.[21] There may be yet another factor as well, for it is possible that even if people of anticlerical sentiment rejected the Church as an institution, they continued to take their local customs and patron saints seriously.

Let us now turn to the very heart of the Catholic activity, namely, that which was held by the Catholic *Vereine*. Their activity dropped to an unprecedented low in 1930, especially in the region of the Schwarzwald-Baar.[22] Activists for the Catholic *Vereine*—and for the *Vv* in particular—charged that internal dissent was leading to the formation of factions and a consequent decline in activity and membership. Internal dissent, however, should not be seen as the primary factor in their inability to function. We have already seen that the Catholic *Vereine* were few and far between, and that most were virtually inactive. Even if a *Verein* did try to hold activities of one kind or another, it met with hostility from the bourgeois *Vereine* and even more from the local officials. Since we have already reviewed this subject at length, let it suffice to recall how disadvantaged the *Gesellenverein* felt in comparison with the bourgeois *Vereine*. The *Gesellenverein* did not have a meeting place of its own, nor was it linked to a particular tavern or *Stammtisch*. The gravity of its plight was further compounded by the lack of support from its headquarters in Cologne. In Löffingen, the priest Andris charged that the bourgeois *Vereine* were battling tooth and nail against the Catholic *Vereine* and severely undermining their activities. While some Catholic *Vereine* did manage to keep up an active schedule of meetings and events, such meetings rarely bore a religious nature. The priest now had to fight on two different fronts. It was not only the secular foes with whom he had to contend, but also the Catholic *Vereine* who were busy estranging members from their religious values. Many young people regarded membership in the Catholic *Vereine* simply as a means of making money in these difficult times. Quite a few *Vereine* found additional sources of income by staging social and theatrical events, with a portion of the earnings going to those who helped organize and perform in them.[23]

As we see in table 12, there were few Catholic *Vereine* in the villages of the region, and then mostly in the larger ones. We are also witness to the inability of the *Vv* to take root in villages located to the south of the region. While *Vv* chapters did exist in Bonndorf and Grafenhausen, their membership steadily declined over the years. There were, to be sure, registered members in some of the chapters, but these were reluctant to pay their dues or to take part in *Verein*-sponsored activity. The crisis of the *Vv* after 1918 is amply illustrated by the Catholic milieu of the Black Forest. In this part of Germany, no member of the organized Catholic Church evinced any interest in *Vv* activity at least until 1930. In places where chapters of the *Vv* did exist the priests actively obstructed their activity. The galloping inflation further contributed to the declining number of both chapters and members.

The lack of currency following the stabilization of the mark prevented many members from paying their dues, and any attempt to raise dues even higher discouraged new members from joining. The chronic lack of ready money and the subsequent inability to maintain a steady program of appealing activity finds frequent mention in the reports of local *Vv* leaders. While this dilemma was not restricted to the Black Forest,[24] the peculiar geography of the region and the vast distance between chapters made it particularly difficult to hold *Vv* activity, especially when the chapters were established relatively late in the region. In addition to these handicaps, local peasants refrained from joining the *Vv* due to their traditional reluctance to join groups of any kind and their disapproval over the *Vv*'s frequent excursions into politics and its aura of socialism. Against this background, it comes as no surprise to find the "Marxist danger" being transformed into one of the *Vv*'s primary slogans, a phenomenon that, as we have already seen, occurred across Germany. So prevalent was the fear of Bolshevism on the local sociopolitical scene that leaders of the local *Vv* chapters pounced on the slogan as a means of winning new supporters. But even this step proved unsuccessful. In Hinterzarten the priest noted that the *Vv* held one meeting a year—far too little to meet the religious needs of the town—and on this point the priests in other towns fully agreed. They believed that well-organized Church *Vereine* would make an effective defense against anticlerical aspirations.[25]

To sum things up, we find that in many communities throughout the Black Forest, Catholic *Vereine* were either nonexistent or virtually inoperative, thus clearing the stage for activity against the Church. As already

TABLE 12.   Membership in the *Volksverein* in peasant villages

	1914	1926	1930
Bonndorf	260	226	170
Bachheim	—	—	—
Birkendorf	65	—	—
Brunnadern	—	—	—
Ewattingen	—	—	—
Grafenhausen	75	48	25
Löffingen	—	32	no membership dues
Hinterzarten	?	?	50 (no activity)
Fischerbach	—	—	—
Reiselfingen	65	—	—
Schenkenzell	—	120 (1928)	?
Schluchsee	—	—	—
Todtmoos	?	?	defunct

Source: See table 11 above, and Hans J. Kremer, "Der Volksverein für das katolische Deutschland in Baden 1890–1933" *Freiburger Diözesan Archiv,* 104 (1984): 267–73; Pfa Bonndorf-254; ErzAF, B2-55-146, Katholische *Volkverein* Tätigkeitsbericht 1920–32.

Note: (—) no chapter in existence; (?) no data available.

noted, such activity took place first under the banner of the *BLB* and, from 1928 on, under that of the Nazi Party. The disorganization of the *Vereine* was also apparent in villages such as Bachheim and Oberwolfach, where the party met with defeat until 1931. However, as already noted, these places at least maintained reasonable standards of morality and religion during the period. In the Schwarzwald-Baar village of Hufingen the young people were reluctant to join the Catholic *Vereine* and the priest did not press them to do so, when the *Vereine* were class-based. The same was true of Löffingen, in which many young people tended to drop out of the *Gesellenverein*. In Reiselfingen it was difficult to establish the *Jungmannerverein,* since local sympathizers of the Nazi Party prevented young people from reaching the meeting. The village priest found it especially difficult to establish Catholic *Vereine* in town, not least because of the chronic lack of money. It was not only in Reiselfingen that the Nazi threat spurred the local priest into action, but also in other places where Nazi strength was on the rise. One local paper, the Catholic *Echo von Hochfirst,* claimed that National Socialism could be fought only with the help of the *Vereine.* In sessions of the *Dekanat,* priests were suddenly ordered to encourage *Vv* activity in the region in order to stem the tide of Catholic support for National Socialism. In a few villages where the Nazi Party did not make impressive gains, we are witness to renewed and intensive activity on the part of the *Gesellenverein.* Nationalist themes made their way into a number of meetings held by the Catholic *Vereine,* which like the bourgeois *Vereine* conducted their meetings in the local tavern, gathered round the *Stammtisch.* Because the priest recognized the importance of these *Vereine,* he had little choice but to accept the secular nature of their meetings. More than once do we hear of rivalry between Catholic *Vereine* and the local chapter of the Nazi Party as they competed for members in the local community. We have already noted the common perception concerning the *Verein*-like nature of the Nazi Party, and here too we find the party perceived as a *Verein,* jockeying to fill the same secular role as the class-based Catholic *Vereine* (though obviously without their religious nature).[26]

The Disintegration of Social-Religious Life among the Workers

The Black Forest workers who worked in crafts and industry, agricultural labor, or forest work in the state- or locally owned forests made up the other source of Nazi electoral strength, beginning with 1930. The workers were grouped in three separate regions: (1) small towns (pop. 2,000–5,000) with a sprinkling of small factories for clock-making, precision mechanics, and lumber (e.g., Neustadt, Wolfach, Haslach, Furtwangen); (2) small towns and villages with only a few clock-making or lumber manufacturers, or that housed the workers who plied their craft in other towns; (3) the small town of Schluchsee, where construction of a local dam resulted in the concentration of thousands of workers. These workers lived in Schluchsee itself or in nearby small towns and villages (e.g., St. Blasien, Bonndorf, and Grafenhausen), where the quality of religious and moral life had never been high to begin with. In the discussion below, we will first take a look at the third category of workers before turning our attention to the first two groups—towns with an industrial infrastructure.

The Catholic workers constituted a loyal element in the Church and *Zentrum* from the end of the nineteenth century up until the period under Weimar. During the course of the twentieth century, however, their loyalty changed to apathy and hostility. The workers proved to be a big headache for the Church authorities, from the Bishopric in Freiburg down to the priest at the local level, and during the Weimar period even beyond the immediate confines of the Black Forest. In the first part of chapter 11, we took note of the tension that increasingly divided the workers and their parties from the leaders of the *Zentrum* and Church, and of the establishment of the *Christlich-Soziale Reichspartei (CSRP)* in 1927. This new party, which met with some success even in the Black Forest, advocated the separation of politics and religion, claiming that a Catholic worker could vote against the *Zentrum* and still be a loyal Catholic—a claim that reminds us of the one made by a certain other political party two years down the road. In the Black Forest, the *CSRP* drew support from villages located in the district of Offenburg. Activists for the new party waged an unusually intensive campaign in the area around the town of Zell.a.H, unchallenged by rival Catholic groups such as the *BLB,* which kept away from the region. Things were much the same in Schwaibach, Biberach, Ober-Harmersbach, and Unter-Harmersbach (table 13).

As we see from the case of Ober-Harmersbach, some of the workers who supported the party in 1928 returned to the *Zentrum* camp in the Landtag elections of 1929, while others preferred not to vote at all. In 1930 we can assume that many of these went over to the Nazi party.

Beginning in 1928, the discussion in various sessions of the *Dekanat* focused on the problem of workers dropping out of the Church. Both priests and leading Church officials stressed the importance of the Catholic *Vereine* in combatting the socialist consciousness of the workers, who were now abandoning the Church in droves. In the *Dekanat* of Kinzigtal it was argued that "most industrial workers are lost to the Church, and as of today are beyond the orb of Church life."[27] In the area of Villingen, home to many of the workers employed in industrial towns such as Villingen and Schweningen (in the state of Wurttemberg), the Dekanat stressed the gravity of the situation and urged priests to promote *Vv* activity among the workers. The political tendencies of Catholic workers in the Black Forest came under scrutiny in a special report drawn up in 1928, which noted that many workers were turning in the direction of a non-Catholic socialism. Members in class-based *Vereine* such as the *KAV* and even the *Gesellenverein* also belonged to socialist trade unions, and it was feared that the heavy doses of socialist "poison" might cause them to renounce the Church altogether. The Catholic *Vereine,* the author of the report goes on to lament, were particularly weak in the Black Forest area.[28]

Things were much the same among the dam workers in Schluchsee whose influence, to quote the local priests, was "destructive" for the inhabitants of the nearby villages. That there was little Catholic activity among the workers was blamed not only on the workers, who rejected any attempts on the part of the Church, but even on the Church itself, whose failure to keep the *KAV* active in the region left workers with little choice but to prefer the Protestant *Arbeiterheim.* In the words of the priests, "We cannot offer workers the support of the Catholic trade unions, since these have not taken any step in this direction." The clergy further complained that Catholic vacationers were being all but ignored in regions of resort towns and villages, such as Schluchsee and St. Blasien. Catholic workers were being inundated with socialist and communist propaganda, it was charged, while the *KAV* and the Catholic trade unions looked idly on. The priests took their complaints to Freiburg, where they urged Church authorities to increase activity among the workers, and not through meetings alone. They recommended that the workers be provided with entertainment, that Catholic newspapers be circulated with greater frequency, and that the Church seek out workers whose views accorded well with Catholicism, in order to align them with the organized associations of Catholic workers. Drinks were to be provided in the workplace canteen, and the local priest was to devise other ways and means of presenting Catholicism in a more favorable light. Despite all the criticism, however, the priests were all too aware of the problems stalking the region. It was not only the poverty of the villages with which they had to contend, or the vast distances between them, but also the presence of radical factors long disruptive to Catholic activity, such as the *BLB.* Together, all these factors

TABLE 13.   **Voting Patterns for the *CSRP* and *NSDAP* in Ober-Harmersbach, 1928–30**

Elections	Eligible Voters	Leftist Bloc	*Zentrum*	Bourgeois Bloc	NSDAP	CSRP	Miscellaneous
May 20, 1928	684	34	485	50	2	96	17
October 27, 1929	699	40	566	55	17	17	4
September 14, 1930	914	27	475	112	288	12	—

made it especially difficult for the priests and Catholic *Vereine* to be active among the dam workers.[29]

Things were not much better in the towns with industrial workers and craftsmen. There, too, the priest had lost much of his authority, and the trends of secularization were in far higher gear. The towns were not only more diversified than the villages in terms of social stratification, but also richer in civic institutions (e.g., the local council and town meeting, the bourgeois *Vereine,* the police, the post office, the school—though not in every town) and places of entertainment. In a town, the priest was not able to control daily life in the same way that he could in the village. There were also more pockets of resistance to his authority, as illustrated by the failure to prevent local authorities from building mixed swimming pools. The growing hostility toward the priests found expression, first and foremost, in the hostility of the bourgeois *Vereine* toward the Catholic *Vereine,* as we have already seen in chapter 10. Father Andris of Löffingen charged that the non-Catholic *Vereine* were a breeding ground for liberalism, and that they fought the Church and Church-related organizations. We have already seen that during the economic crisis the local councils and town meetings—made up of Catholics, as we recall—refused to transfer funds for Church-related needs and organizations or even for the repair of the church building itself, no matter what the local priest said. In the towns, there was also a persistent phenomenon of priests who abandoned their posts for less troublesome regions. The priest's fast-shrinking salary made it harder for him to make ends meet in town, while in the village his needs were considerably more modest. Towns were also the scene of violence against priests and the Church, as stones were thrown at Church windows and the priests subjected to catcalls and other forms of verbal abuse. In Schonach, four priests left their post in the years just before the rise of the Nazi Party. The year 1930 proved to be particularly critical for the *Dekanat* of Villingen, with a turnover of priests in nearly every community. It was not only the economic plight that the newcomers had to face, but also the growing strength of the Nazi Party.[30]

In most towns in the Black Forest, the working groups actively opposed the priest and the Church in one way or another, though they did not renounce the Catholic faith. In places where the Church was able to organize workers in the framework of class-based Catholic *Vereine (KAV, Gesellenverein, Jungmännerverein)* and the Catholic trade unions, the priest and workers did manage to establish a working relationship. However, as the economic crisis continued with even graver consequences for the factories and workshops, the hostility of the workers increased. We find a striking example of this in the town of Schonach, where several hundred workers, not all of them local, were employed. The workers of Schonach had a long tradition of hostility toward the Church, in contrast to the attitude of the local peasants. The troubles they made for their priests contributed to the frequent turnover of priests in town. Most of the inhabitants were apathetic about the various religious ceremonies. Local workers expressed their disgruntlement with the Church and the *Zentrum* in any number of assemblies and meetings, and church windows were shattered time and again. Signs of secularization became increasingly common as outside visitors began streaming to Schonach in growing numbers, attracted by the town's newly developed ski facilities.[31]

Needless to say, the phenomenon of rebel workers was not confined to Schonach alone. Signs of discontent were expressed in other towns as well, sometimes in even more radical fashion. We have already mentioned that during the Weimar period relations were strained between the workers and the Church. The rise of the *CSRP,* the declining number of workers who belonged to the Catholic *Vereine* or even the Church, the reluctance to take part in religious rites, and the paralysis of the class-based *Vereine,* especially the *Vv,* all eloquently testify to this situation. Let us try and analyze these processes by taking an overview of the *Kv* active in the towns of the Black Forest, while giving special attention to the activity of the class-based Catholic *Vereine.* Once again, our sources come from the Kirchenvisitationen written up by the priests (table 14).

Table 14 presents the religious and moral conditions of life in a number of towns throughout the Black Forest. Not all of them can be termed working-class. Oppenau, Schönwald and St. Blasien were primarily centers of tourism and recreation, despite the recent influx of workers employed in a number of local textile factories. It is also hard to characterize Oberkirch and Todtnau as industrial towns, considering the small number of workers and factories. The rest of the towns were inhabited largely by workers and craftsmen, and also by peasants who tended large plots of land outside town. In industrialized towns such as Furtwangen and Schonach, we learn of anti-Church activity on the part of the workers and, more emphatically, of the deteriorating moral conditions.

One opposition group that frequently crops up in these reports is that of "Jehovah's Witnesses" (*Bibelforscher*). These people were influenced by contemporary theories originating in the United States, which advocated a more scientific approach to the Bible and challenged the traditional interpretations of both the Old and New Testaments. Inasmuch as no organized groups of Bibelforscher lived in the Black Forest area, we can assume that the priests were referring to individual voices of dissent. The vacationers and tourists, as already noted, helped fan the winds of anti-clericalism (e.g., St. Blasien). In contrast to the villages that we have seen up till now, where religious morality was poor throughout the entire decade, the towns in table 14 deteriorated at a steady rate during the 1920s.

The majority of reports indicate a satisfactory moral order during the early 1920s (e.g., Schönau, Haslach, Furtwangen, Schönwald), and a decline in morals at the beginning of the 1930s. Here we find a positive correlation between communities in which the situation was still relatively good at the beginning of the 1930s and the lack of success of the Nazi Party. Similarly, there is a positive correlation between communities in which the fabric of social and moral life had been damaged and the rising strength of the Nazi Party.

The number of people who abstained from receiving Easter Communion provides a clear expression of working-class opposition to the Church and the priest. We have already mentioned the importance of this ceremony and the significance of not taking part in its rites. In the Black Forest we are witness to a sharp separation between working-class towns with a large number of nonparticipants, and tourist towns or towns with greater social diversity, where the number was significantly lower. Thus we are witness to the large number of people who refused Easter Communion in Furtwangen (though the number grew during the following years), in Haslach, where we are witness to the great number of abstainers already at the beginning of the decade, as well as in Schonach and Vöhrenbach. Let us recall that we are speaking of towns with different populations. Furtwangen and Haslach had several thousand inhabitants, Schonach and Vöhrenbach approximately two thousand. In tourist towns such as Oppenau few people refrained from receiving Holy Communion, a fact that reinforces our argument that in some of the towns, the Nazis derived their strength from the votes of the tourists, at least until 1932. And finally, let us mention towns such as St. Blasien (population approximately 2,000), where very few refused to receive Easter Communion, and where the Nazi Party was noticeably weak. The number of people not receiving Easter Communion in Oberkirch partially explains the growing strength of the party in this town, but it also contradicts the priest's report from 1932, in which the community is given good marks. In addition to the workers and craftsmen, let us once again mention the anticlerical sector of the local bourgeoisie, which largely refrained from receiving Easter Communion (as noted in previous chapters).

Towns with concentrated numbers of workers show a declining birthrate throughout the 1920s, which the economic crisis obviously did nothing to halt. In St. Blasien there is a plummeting birthrate from the 1920s, though by the end of the decade we are witness to a sharp rise, apparently because of the large number of dam workers living in town. Incidentally, the high percentage of infants born out of wedlock is found in other towns as well (e.g., Furtwangen—twelve percent in 1932).[32] The towns of the Black Forest also show a perceptible decline in charitable contributions made to the priest, and even in the circulation of the

TABLE 14. The Moral and Religious Conditions in the Community

Furtwangen pop. 4,625	Generally good. Socialist activity and propaganda (1924). Still generally good. Good relations between the priest and local authorities. Attempt at winning over the workers. Some 800 to 900 people not fulfilling their religious duties. Religious-moral life unsatisfactory due to unemployment. Low birthrate. Group of "Old Catholics" sowing general terror. Premarital relations between the sexes. Abstainers from *Osterkommunion*—2,677 (1930). (NSDAP vote in 1930: 25.5 percent)
Haslach (+4 villages) pop. 3,135	Situation still good. Abstainers from *Osterkommunion*—2,364 (1924). (*NSDAP* vote in 1930—24.4 percent)
Oberkirch (+5 villages) pop. 5,997	Situation satisfactory. The youth need to be brought closer to Catholic youth groups. Only a few individuals apathetic to religion. Communists, *Bibelforscher* ("Jehovah's Witnesses"), and the "Movement for Children's Education" (a movement for reform in Catholic education—O.H.) are the only groups opposing the church. Abstainers from *Osterkommunion*—178 (1932). (*NSDAP* vote in 1932—37.7 percent)
Oppenau pop. 4,011	Certain amount of apathy, otherwise good. A group of "Jehovah's Witnesses" opposes the Church. Many not attending Church. Abstainers from *Osterkommunion*—30 (1929). (*NSDAP* vote in 1930: 32.9 percent)
St. Blasien (+2 villages) pop. 2,538	Situation generally good. Low Church attendance. The number of those receiving the sacrament rose in 1930, the "Year of the Mission," but still room for improvement. Tourists, vacationers, and dam workers in Schluchsee threatening the religious life of the town. Abstainers from *Osterkommunion*—80 (1932). (*NSDAP* vote in 1932: 33 percent)
Schonach (+4 villages) pop. 2,932	Situation satisfactory, danger from the Socialists (1923). Preservation of religious conditions, but moral freedom exists. Criticism of the Church in the factories. Diffusion of modern, immoral ideas. Abstainers from *Osterkommunion*—a lot (1930). (*NSDAP* vote in 1930: 18.3 percent)
Schönau (+9 villages) pop. 4,248	Drop in the number of people going to church and receiving Holy Communion. Good birthrate (1925). Still good, lots of apathy, lack of faith. Group of "Jehovah's Witnesses" sometimes active. Neglect, licentiousness. Need increased circulation of Catholic press. Sharp drop in birthrate. Abstainers from *Osterkommunion*—100 (1932). (*NSDAP* vote in 1932: 36 percent)
Schönwald pop. 1,475	Generally good, congregation faithful and supportive. Abstainers from *Osterkommunion*—10–15 (1923). (*NSDAP* vote in 1930: 27 percent)
Todtnau (+4 villages) pop. 3,452	Situation very good. Brisk activity on part of the "Jehovah's Witnesses." Abstainers from *Osterkommunion*—number not given (1928). (*NSDAP* vote in 1930: 6.5 percent)
Vöhrenbach pop. 2,212	Situation good. Apathy and lack of faith only among men. Abstainers from *Osterkommunion*—120 (1928). (*NSDAP* vote in 1930: 27 percent)
Wolfach (+2 villages) pop. 2,582	Situation still good. Retreat from religious life throughout the entire region. More and more cases of hooliganism and lack of faith. Numerous mixed marriages. Abstainers from *Osterkommunion*—80–100 (1928). (*NSDAP* vote in 1930: 24.2 percent)

Source: As in table 11.

Catholic press. These statistics confirm our theory of numerous workers who opposed, in one way or other, the Catholic Church and its political and social representatives.

Let us turn to the activity of the Catholic *Vereine* in the towns of the Black Forest. In contrast to the Catholic *Vereine* in the villages, a number of towns had class-based Catholic *Vereine* already in the mid-nineteenth century. Thus, for example, there was a *Gesellenverein* in Oberkirch, Neustadt, and Triberg, and toward the end of the nineteenth century and the beginning of the twentieth, in Oppenau, Hausach, Haslach, Schönau, Donaueschingen, and Wolfach. The *KAV,* on the other hand, became active in a few towns only from the final years of the nineteenth century, and especially toward the outbreak of the war. The *Vv* was active in very few towns due, once again, to the harsh geography of the region and the apathy of the local inhabitants. Even though the *Vereine* were closely connected to the Catholic Church and milieu, many were totally secular in nature. A large part of their membership supported liberal or, to a lesser degree, socialist parties. Following the revolution of 1918, many other members began leaning in the direction of socialism, though without renouncing their membership in the Catholic *Vereine.* In Todtnau, the priest ceased his involvement in the *KAV* chapter that he had headed since 1922, where many supported the *SPD,* preferring instead to found a chapter of the *Männerverein* also composed of young workers. The tension that this created between the workers and priest paralyzed the activity of the class-based *Vereine* in town.[33]

Throughout much of Baden, *KAV* activity ground to a halt after 1924. The inflation and salary cuts deeply affected the *Vereine,* for with the loss of contributions came the end of *Verein* activity (see table 15). Moreover, the *Zentrum*'s growing tendency to represent peasant and middle class interests brought down the fury of the workers, who abandoned the *Zentrum* and even the *KAV*. It was for this reason that when hundreds of workers poured into the region of the Schluchsee dam, there was no organized Catholic framework ready to absorb them. According to the priest of St. Blasien, the *KAV* was virtually inactive in the region, so that workers had no choice but to prefer the Protestant *Arbeiterheim,* as we have already seen. As anticlerical propaganda increased among the workers, priests in the region began urging the *KAV* and the trade unions to renew their activities as quickly as possible. The latter justified their inactivity by claiming that most of the workers were socialists or even communists, with little interest in religion. They did not even take part in the election, despite the fact that they were registered voters. The majority were unorganized and did not take part in union meetings. While the *KAV* put the blame on the priests and urged them to greater efforts among the workers, it also alluded to "radical elements [the Nazi Party?] which disrupt our meetings . . ."[34]

Without doubt, the plight of the class-based *Vereine* was due to more than economic problems, for they also had to deal with opposition from the priests at least until 1930. The priests sought to establish religious *Vereine* that would counteract the influence of the class-based *Vereine* and enroll members loyal to the Catholic Church. In Schonach, the collapse of the local *KAV* chapter left workers without any suitable organizational framework, apart from those of the Socialists. There was a perceptible rupture between class-based Catholic *Vereine* in a number of towns, and meetings were sparsely attended. We have already mentioned that in the towns of Wolfach and Furtwangen, leaders of the local councils and bourgeois *Vereine* distanced themselves from the Catholic *Vereine* and took steps to cut off their funds.

With the deterioration of the economic crisis and the subsequent strengthening of political groups to the extreme right and left, the clergy shifted its policy toward the class-based *Vereine*. We have already mentioned that the Church began to favor activity sponsored by the *Vv* and class-based Catholic *Vereine* as a means of dealing with the increased activity of National Socialism. Many priests chose to overlook the secular nature of the class-based Catholic *Vereine*—anything to make sure that these continued to function and to attract new members. With the increased economic pressure, the *KAV* in Neustadt decided that an active member who took sick was entitled to a sum ranging from four to fifteen marks. In contrast, the *Gesellenverein* in Triberg decided for the first time to charge its members for the annual Christmas party. Its straitened finances did not permit it, as in other towns, to maintain a brisk schedule of activity without recouping its expenses. In sum, even the renewal of *Verein* activity was not without problems.

In table 16 we are witness to the decline of the *Vv* in the majority of towns at the beginning of the decade, and to attempts at reestablishing a

TABLE 15.   The *KAV* in Schönau

Year	*Verein* Members	Cath TUs Members	Conferences	Lectures	Circulation of *Verein* Press	*NDSAP* Voters
1924	135	135	12	12	25	—
1926	110	70	8	8	25	—
1928	95	48	8	8	18	8
1930	105	28	7	7	12	48
1932	85	16	5	7	9	314[a]

Source: Pfarrarchive Schönau. Seelsorge, *KAV.*
[a]July 1932.

number of them toward the end, when anticlerical activity resurged in the region. The question mark in table 16 is more than a way of indicating to our readers that we have no details on the subject. It appears in the original as well and was staring up at the leaders of the *Vv* when they tried to make their annual report of *Verein* activity. They themselves testified that there were many chapters in existence, but that these were virtually inoperative due to nonpayment of membership dues. Even local chapters were not always active over the course of the decade. We are witness to a similar trend even among class-based *Vereine* such as the *KAV* and *Gesellenverein.*

In sum, workers and craftsmen, though not them alone, found it difficult to satisfy their social needs in the framework of the professional and occupation-based *Vereine.* The alternative was to join the local *Verein* organized by the local priest—even when relations with the priest were strained,[35] or the *Verein* too clerical for individual taste—or to join the bourgeois *Vereine,* as indeed some did, despite the straitened finances of these *Vereine* from 1930–31 (see chap. 10). Another alternative open to Catholic, but anticlerical workers and craftsmen was to join the Socialist *Vereine.* These, of course, had stepped up their activity since the beginning of the crisis. Their other option was to support and join a social group or party ready to offer them a social life similar to that of the class-based *Vereine,* in addition to a sense of class-consciousness and the promise of a financially improved future.

Before turning to discuss this latter alternative, let us take a look at the problems preventing many people, and not only workers and crafts-

TABLE 16. **Membership in the *Volksverein* in small towns**

Chapter	1924	1930
Furtwangen	—	—
Haslach	—	Inactive following initial establishment in 1926
Oberkirch	—	Chapter founded in 1930
Oppenau	—	Chapter founded in 1929
St. Blasien	?	110
Schönau	?	150
Schönwald	—	—
Schonach	—	—
Todtnau	?	—
Vöhrenbach	—	—
Wolfach	?	250

Source: See tables 11, 12.

Note: (—) No chapter in existence. (?) No details available.

men, from giving their support to the socialist *Vereine*. While there were some who inclined in this direction, the political culture of the region effectively kept many workers from supporting socialist and communist groups. This culture, as we have already mentioned, was characterized until 1914 by the strong antisocialist leanings of liberal-bourgeois groups and parties and, needless to say, of political Catholicism as well. The Catholic milieu in the Black Forest (and not there alone) was characterized by intolerance and even fear and hatred of the socialists long before it began to show hostility toward the extreme right. To be sure, there were many people in the region who tended to support the *SPD* after the war, including the peasants. Many of those who joined the newly formed *BLB* had formerly belonged to the Socialist Party, not because of any love for socialism, but because of hatred for political Catholicism. There were obviously economic aspects to this support. Immediately after the war, the Socialists made impressive electoral gains across Germany, and many people in the region, peasants included, sought to turn a profit by allying themselves with the new and dominant political power (as we saw in chap. 5). During the course of the 1920s, many of these lost the leftist fervor that characterized them following the revolution of 1918. Chief among their reasons was disappointment over the inability of the *SPD* to fulfill their expectations on both the national and local levels of things, and the *SPD*'s relations with the *Zentrum* in the Landtag of Baden. The SPD did not even try to tighten its grip on the Black Forest region. It had few chapters and little activity, so that the link between the party and its sympathizers in the region was extremely weak.[36]

The primary reason behind the reluctance of Black Forest workers to join the *SPD* and socialist *Vereine* en masse is rooted in the antisocialist and anti-Bolshevist climate. This climate, which may in fact be termed near-hysteria, characterized the region from the end of the 1920s and was fed by the news of the atrocities that occurred in Russia following the implementation of Stalin's Five-Year Plan and the harsh measures against the peasants. We have already had occasion to see this hysteria at work in a number of different contexts. In our discussion of the Nazi Party, we showed how the anti-socialist-communist propaganda struck a responsive chord in the general climate of fear in the region. The clerical and bourgeois press reported the atrocities in Russia on almost a daily basis.[37] The Catholic press dwelled on the terror that the communist regime had unleashed against the churches, priests, peasants, and workers, and it warned its readers against a similar disaster in Germany. In the words of the press, the communists were sowing famine and fear.[38] The local press and the Catholic *Vereine* rushed to bring the "horrifying testimonies" of workers who had tried to find work in Russian factories, only to beat a quick retreat to the Black Forest. Socialism and communism were one and the same for the Catholic Church and press, which rallied to the cause by pronouncing the Catholic *Vereine*—the class-based *Vereine* and the *Vv* in particular—a veritable "wall of defense against the danger."[39]

Thus, the antisocialist tendency inherent to the Catholic milieu in the region became even more firmly entrenched with the hysteria over the bad news from Russia. The activity of the Communist Party in Germany in general, and in the Black Forest in particular, also created fear. We have already had more than one occasion to see that activists of the Communist Party were treated differently from those of the Nazi Party. We saw that communism and socialism were regarded as the number one enemy of German Catholicism, and that the *Vv* were mobilized toward the end of the 1920s in order to fight the leftist danger. The traditional aversion to socialism and communism both in and out of the Catholic milieu prevented considerable parts of the workers and craftsmen (though not all of them), and even peasants and members of the middle class, from going over to the social and organizational frameworks of the Socialists, or, subsequently, to those of the Communist Party.

All this left an organizational vacuum in the life of large segments of Catholic workers and craftsmen. As we have already noted in regard to the Catholic *Vereine* in rural regions, the Nazi Party made no attempt to infiltrate or take control of the *Vereine,* even when they were class-based and active in towns. Any priest who stood at the head of the *Verein* or who played a considerable role in determining its course, who was a central figure close to the Church and *Zentrum,* was on guard against undesirable elements. The socio-organizational vacuum stretched through the ranks of anticlerical workers adrift in society; workers who were able to vote but preferred not to do so for long periods of time.[40] (We reviewed this phenomenon in chap. 5, when discussing local voting patterns up until 1928.) Beginning in the mid-1920s, when the first signs of a rift began to appear in the local Catholic milieu, many of the workers decided to leave. Some of them joined other anticlerical social groups (such as the *BLB* or the *CSRP*) unconnected to the Catholic milieu. The Nazi alternative that first presented itself to the peasants in the southern part of the region in 1928, and to the workers in Furtwangen and Triberg from 1929, was not all that appealing at first glance, especially when compared with the organizational frameworks of the Catholic milieu, those the Catholic peasants and workers had left behind. However, this alternative answered a number of the workers' basic demands: first of all, the fight against communism; second, class-based social populism, oriented toward the workers (see chap. 9); third, opposition to political Catholicism that did not ask for a renunciation of faith during the campaigns of 1929 through 1932. Finally, it was a new and youthful alternative, one that was not implicated in the disasters wrought by the Weimar parties; a refuge for the disenchanted Catholic worker.

Here we come full circle, in a process we have sought to chart beginning with our description of local voting patterns in the 1920s. There we
noted the large number of people—mostly former supporters of the *SPD*
and the *Zentrum*—who refrained from casting their vote from 1920, and
especially from 1924. From there we described the propaganda themes
used by the Nazi Party, which was dubbed by both its supporters and
detractors as "right-wing Bolshevism" and a "Workers' Party." And
finally, we described the climate of anti-Catholicism and the socio-organizational vacuum stretching through the ranks of the workers (and obviously the peasants) from the late 1920s on. We reviewed the efforts of the
clergy to rehabilitate this organizational framework and saw that despite
partial success in some towns in the region, the efforts came too little and
too late. In the final account, this step was unable to restore the lost workers to the fold of the Catholic milieu (just as it was unable to restore the
peasants). It was for these reasons that large sections of the population
made easy prey for the Nazi Party, which had only recently taken its first
hesitant steps in the region.

Summary

As in the anticlerical bourgeois camp, so in other strata of society are we
witness already from the mid-1920s to the processes of atomization in different occupational groups. These were social groups that had cut themselves off from the Catholic social life linked to the Church, and from the
socio-organizational frameworks linked to political Catholicism. Among
the workers this trend grew even more pronounced following the harsh
economic crisis that struck local industry. There were other factors as well,
including the hostility of the Church and the organizations of political
Catholicism, the religious "reawakening" that characterized Catholic society under Weimar, and political decisions of the *Zentrum* leaders, mainly
after 1928.

What makes the Black Forest unique was the sociopolitical alternative chosen by the workers of the region. It was not the left that they chose,
and not the traditional right. Following a long period in which many people remained politically inactive, the majority chose to support the Nazi
Party. If in addition to the workers and craftsmen we take into account the
peasants of the southern Black Forest and the bourgeois stratum that
began to defect to the Nazi camp from 1931, then the importance of this
study increases, since it testifies to the overall decline of the Catholic
milieu. This is an unusual phenomenon, to judge by the existing historiography, which emphasizes the resistance of the Catholic milieu to the
National Socialist threat. Unusual, since even in the studies dealing with
the hardships that faced the Catholic milieu (both rural and urban), this

milieu ultimately remained faithful to the Catholic Church and to political Catholicism. The absence of additional studies on regions in which the Nazi Party scored electoral victories, apparently in the wake of the milieu's decline, makes it difficult for us to bolster our claims. One desideratum of future study is to focus on regions that might have served us as a control group, first and foremost, the region of the Allgäu and of southern and lower Silesia (whose voting patterns are briefly discussed in chapter 7). In these regions, where the geographical and socioeconomic conditions resemble those of the Black Forest, we might reasonably expect similar results.[41]

Although we emphasized the social groups that openly challenged the Catholic milieu, we would like to stress that even in 1930 approximately one-half of the region's inhabitants still belonged to the local Catholic milieu and to political Catholicism. In 1932 the number decreased, but we are still talking about a mature and significant social stratum. The economic crisis and the activity of the Nazi Party did little to influence their political and religious behavior. Even more importantly, the reasons that we presented in detail in this chapter for the decline of the Catholic milieu in the Black Forest—such as geographical isolation, the sense of "ghettoization," the anticlerical tradition, the leaning toward national-liberal groups, the lack of organization and decline of *Verein* activity—did little to influence those who supported and remained in the Catholic milieu. We are speaking first and foremost of women, who from 1919 provided the Catholic milieu with its strongest support group. There were also peasants in the region who still supported the *Zentrum* and Church. The socioeconomic backwardness so characteristic of the peasants in the southern Black Forest found less expression in the regions north of it. The extent to which the memory of *Kulturkampf* lingered in the region after the tumultuous years of the 1870s influenced the extent to which the *Zentrum* received support. In the southern Black Forest, where anticlericalism ran high, the memory of *Kulturkampf* received less emphasis. There the national-liberals achieved an early and well-consolidated hegemony, and only the faintest echoes of *Kulturkampf* made their way into the region. In the central parts of the Black Forest the *Zentrum* managed to consolidate its grasp.[42] The stratum of officials, teachers, and white-collar workers also provided the Church and *Zentrum* with an importance source of support. After the shift to the right within political Catholicism, the interests of these groups were represented with greater alacrity. The populist and socialist rhetoric of the Nazi Party still frightened them, despite their anxiety over the Bolshevist menace. In contrast to the workers and craftsmen—who were attracted to the Nazi Party because of its battle against Bolshevism and its position on workers' rights, and who abandoned or were ejected from the Catholic organizational frameworks—the petite bourgeoisie in the region was largely composed of white-collar workers and small-scale merchants. These groups were still organized under the auspices of the Church and the Catholic milieu, and they continued to believe that the *Zentrum* would be able to defend Germany from Bolshevism, effectively oppose Nazism, and look out for their interests during the economic crisis.

This study has sought to examine among other things the Catholic bourgeoisie at the local level during the period of the Weimar Republic, and to clarify the role that the local *Verein* played in this society. We have done so in order to examine the extent to which the "bourgeois infrastructure" was socially unified, and the extent to which it was vulnerable. In doing so, we hope to have contributed to the studies dealing with these problems. From our study it emerges that together with the undeniable differences between the workers and the local bourgeoisie, there is also much that is similar: anticlericalism, a desire to break free of the Church and political Catholicism, the sense of isolation and social remoteness from the large urban centers in Baden, and last of all, the collapsing social frameworks of both of these strata, and the choice of the National Socialist solution. The most significant difference is that for the workers and craftsmen, membership in the bourgeois *Vereine* meant more than a way of seeking new organizational frameworks to satisfy their social life. It also signified the desire to adopt a bourgeois identity. For this reason, the collapse of the bourgeois *Vereine* had a powerful impact on the identity that the workers tried to create for themselves. They had lost their place in the Catholic milieu, suffered losses due to the economic crisis that struck local industry in the mid-1920s, and now, with the destruction of their new socio-organizational frameworks, their world collapsed once again.

Let us return to the question that runs though our study like a scarlet thread. What contributed more to the success of the Nazi Party in the Black Forest, Nazi activity, organization, and propaganda, or the socioeconomic structure of the region and the organization of its inhabitants? We have dealt with both of these questions. We pointed out the organizational failure of the party, its inability to efficiently present its propaganda. During our discussion of the latter question, we noted how important the sociogeographic isolation was, how it loomed to most inhabitants in the region. We tried to prove that in most of the Black Forest, the socio-organizational vacuum that stretched through the ranks of important social groups existed even before the party took its first few steps in the Black Forest. This vacuum encouraged the processes of atomization at work in the anticlerical strata of society. Some of these strata were more backward than others; some (mainly the local bourgeoisie) felt the impact of the sociogeographical isolation to a greater degree. In the wake of the increasingly severe social and political crisis activated by the Great Economic

Crisis, the frustration grew even deeper. Fear of the "Red peril" became stronger, as did the readiness to support the new sociopolitical alternative, despite the less than appealing aspects of Nazi activity and propaganda. It was against this background that the town square became increasingly crowded with dozens of people waiting in the rain for the arrival of a Nazi speaker, while in the church just across, the priest was delivering a Sunday morning sermon that denounced, amongst other things, the National Socialist danger. This picture eloquently captures local life in the region from the 1930s on. Even more distressing is the picture of the now desolate *Stammtisch,* no longer able to handle the droves of new members: bourgeois or worker, all were Catholic, and all were searching for a new alternative to the socio-organizational frameworks in which they had only recently taken part.

Conclusion

This study has sought to examine the social and political behavioral patterns of the Catholic population during the Weimar Republic, and particularly during the critical final years of this period. The region that we chose for this purpose, the southern part of the state of Baden-Württemburg, has not been previously investigated.

The following represents the principal conclusions of our study, and the reasons that have led us to describe the chosen region as the Achilles' heel of German Catholicism in comparison to other Catholic regions. During the period under discussion, this region was geographically and socially isolated, and socioeconomically underdeveloped. The major occupational groups in the area—workers, craftsmen, and peasants—were characterized by strong anticlerical tendencies. There was also an economically affluent bourgeois stratum, which adopted the behavioral patterns of the Protestant bourgeoisie. The sociogeographical isolation and the ghetto mentality characteristic of German Catholicism since the end of the nineteenth century contributed to the powerful desire of the local bourgeoisie to break out of its ghetto confines. This desire found political expression in the vote for anticlerical parties such as the National-Liberals during the Second Reich, the *Badische Landbund* (*BLB*) in the early years of the Weimar Republic, and, finally, the Nazi Party. One of the socio-organizational aspects of this desire of the bourgeoisie to break out of its confinement was the establishment of social clubs modeled on the Protestant bourgeois Vereine, together with their radical anticlerical rhetoric.

The voting patterns in the region show an increasing tendency to support the Nazi Party from 1928 onward. Thus the voting patterns of German Catholics were far from uniform in this period. We discussed other Catholic areas in Germany that showed massive support for the Nazi Party, such as the Allgäu in Bavarian Schwabia, and the Catholic districts in Lower Silesia and in Upper and Middle Franconia. The heterogeneous picture that we discovered of the religious and social base of the Nazi

Party strengthens the oft-repeated claim that this was indeed the first "people's party" (*Volkspartei*) in the history of modern Germany.

We have tried to discover the reason for this profound support for the Nazi Party in South Baden through a study of local Nazi activity and propaganda. Of the various conclusions that we reached, the first is that the social profile of the local party chapters was largely made up of workers, skilled workers, and craftsmen. We examined the instability and fluidity of the social profile of the party chapters and saw, for example, that not every individual described as being a party member did in fact belong to the party. Many sympathizers and activists refused to join the Nazi Party up to and including 1932, despite explicit orders to do so. The voters for the Nazi Party in 1928 came from the local peasantry and, from 1929 onward, they were joined by ex-*SPD* voters. Many of these people had not voted for years. In 1930 the party drew its strength mainly from this pool of new voters. Two years later many members of the bourgeoisie joined the Nazi voting public, though in the same year, many former supporters from the ranks of the peasants and workers ceased their support of the party.

The proletarian character of the party members and voters up to 1931 was also reflected in the propaganda during this stage. We have noted three particularly striking propaganda elements in the period from 1929 onward: the attack on the Weimar system, the anti-Bolshevist-communist rhetoric, and the socialistic features. The last of these undoubtedly demonstrates correct understanding that the local Nazi leaders had of the map of the party's local social base. Even more significantly, it demonstrates the power of the new members to influence the content of the Nazi propaganda. From 1931 onward, bourgeois motifs also crept into party propaganda together with a strongly anti-Bolshevist content aimed at the middle class. Propaganda motifs such as anti-Semitism, Hitler worship, anticlericalism, and local traditions and problems were ignored in the party propaganda of this region.

However, the emphasis on the socialist-tinged propaganda should not be taken as evidence of Nazi competence in matters of organization and activity in South Baden. Analysis of the National Socialist public sphere has shown that it suffered from many shortcomings. The numerous theories about the innovativeness of Nazi organization and propaganda did not find support in south Baden. Because of its geographical isolation, its role as a center of tourism, and its reputation in the Nazi party center in Karlsruhe as a place in which it was not worth investing effort, there was very little Nazi activity in the region until 1932. Prominent Nazi speakers did not reach the area, and few chapters were established before that time. Local notables refrained from joining the party or giving it public support. The party center did not always succeed in enforcing its authority over the local activists, and the fact that the chapters were in serious financial straits meant that local propaganda activities were more often directed at fund-raising than at winning over new voters and supporters. Moreover, we find quarrels and frequent replacements among the chapter leaders, as well as a shortage of propaganda material, desultory SA activity, and many other signs of mismanagement. All this leads us to the conclusion that party activity and propaganda cannot be seen as a main cause of the massive vote for the Nazi Party. This is a paradox that demands explanation, for despite all the evidence of poor performance in South Baden, the Nazi Party met with great success among the local, mostly Catholic population for whom the dominant political culture, at least in part, was that of political Catholicism.

Part 3 of our study examines the collapse of social life in the region and offers a key for understanding the unexpected success of the Nazi Party in the region. We claim that even before the Great Economic Crisis, the organizational frameworks of sociocultural life began to disintegrate. The process was quite visible in the local bourgeois *Vereine* located outside of the Catholic milieu. The *Vereine,* representatives of local social life and supporters of the local sociocultural order, ran into serious financial trouble, and as they cut back on their activities many members withdrew. The *Vereine* served as a means of expression for the local Catholic bourgeoisie, a social stratum that was largely unconnected to the local Catholic milieu. This stratum used its economic control over the *Vereine* and local councils to express its opposition to the Catholic milieu and organizations. By means of the *Vereine* the local bourgeoisie sought to resemble the Protestant bourgeoisie with whom they came into contact, partly because of their prominence in the local tourist industry. The danger of losing their sociocultural hegemony, the atomization that began to characterize local life, and, above all, the Bolshevist fear whipped up by the local press swept the local bourgeoisie into supporting a political and social alternative that would serve their social needs (i.e., Nazism). Many of them perceived the Nazi movement as a *Verein;* a different kind of *Verein*—a different, more political Verein—whose message was similar to that of the bourgeois *Vereine* and, most importantly, of a clearly anti-Bolshevist nature. The resolute anti-Bolshevism of party propaganda proved effective inasmuch as it helped to draw the bourgeoisie closer to the Nazi Party.

The gradual breakdown of organizational frameworks is evident among other groups as well. The workers in the local industrial towns had opposed the Catholic milieu from the beginning of the Weimar decade, while the peasants in the southeastern Black Forest had opposed it as early as the nineteenth century. This opposition was expressed in hostility toward the clergy and the Church rites and decrees, and indeed in the entire moral order of the local communities. The drift toward the right in the *Zentrum* and the antisocialist trend espoused by the Church and local priests pushed the workers into leaving the Catholic milieu and the *Vereine* that were so characteristic of it. These *Vereine*, such as *"Die Katholischen Arbeitervereine," "Der Volksverein für das katholische Deutschland,"* and the *"Gesellenverein"* found themselves in a serious financial plight, partly because of Church opposition to their activity.

A different picture emerges among the peasants of the southeastern Black Forest. In this backward area, the Achilles' heel of German Catholicism, an anticlerical trend was already evident after 1848. During the Weimar period it found expression in massive support for the local protest movement, the *BLB*. With the disintegration of the *BLB* the Nazi movement picked up considerable support among the local peasants and craftsmen. The Nazi combination of socialist and anti-Marxist motifs, the latter mixed with criticism of political Catholicism, met with success in these circles. Such propaganda was well directed at workers and craftsmen in search of a sociopolitical alternative with socialist leanings, but that still was indisputably anticommunist. The feeling of panic created by the local rumor mill over the events in Russia affected these circles as well.

Thus the social vacuum created by the breakdown of local organizational frameworks, the desire to break out of the ghetto of local society, the deepening economic crisis, and the fear of a communist takeover all led to a search for a politically and economically meaningful alternative to political Catholicism and the bourgeois infrastructure. And thus, without any particular effort, and despite mistakes, mismanagement, and poor organization, the Nazi Party—the only political body to offer a nonestablishment, non-Bolshevist alternative—was able to attract a large group of voters, some of them voting for the first time in years. Paradoxically, the ideological confusion, heterogeneity, and socio-organizational atomization so characteristic of this voting public in the Black Forest were mirrored in the Nazi Party itself, which was faced with similar kinds of problems and which aimed to take over and reshape the society in which it worked.

To what extent do our conclusions agree with those of the studies of the Nazi Party and of Weimar Catholic society, and to what extent do they differ? While there are many studies dealing with political Catholicism and the Catholic public sphere in the Second Reich, there are very few dealing with them in the subsequent period, although in recent years an increasing number of scholars have written about them. Our study is among them.

The extensive scholarly literature dealing with the Nazi Party emphasizes the success of the party, its ability to penetrate the heart of the local infrastructure and to win over broad sections of the population by virtue of its efficient organization and propaganda. Many writers emphasize the turning point of 1929, the political, social, and economic earthquake that took place in that year, and the ability of the Nazi Party to strike to reach out to the agricultural-bourgeois liberal Protestant milieu. On the basis of our study, however, it would seem that not only was the turning point not in 1929, but that no earthquake at all shook the area. The deterioration of social life was a long, drawn-out process, and it was one that had begun years before. And, finally, the activity of the Nazi Party was not that dramatic and stormy. It is not the success of the party that emerges in part 2 of our study but its failure—a failure in terms of organization and propaganda. Many scholars tend to see the electoral achievements as the result of organizational efficiency and innovative propaganda techniques. Moreover, the efficiency shown by the Nazi Party after seizing power in 1933 only reinforces the tendency to perceive it as a dynamic and innovative force even before that time. The success of Nazi propaganda from 1933 onward ("energetic, efficient, virtuoso")[1] cast its shadow over the historiography of the period preceding it as well.

That is not to say that previous studies of the subject were entirely mistaken. The Nazi Party undoubtedly demonstrated admirable efficiency in some cases and regions. But we must ask ourselves whether this activity only appears so striking due to the general inactivity in a given area. In most cases, scholars note that the Nazi activity was highly unique when compared with the inactivity of other parties, including those of the Left.[2] However, even in cases where there was indeed a unique element in Nazi activity, it must be pointed out how different the party's social and political profile was in each particular case. The scholarly literature shows that a similar process apparently occurred in other Catholic areas of a similar socioeconomic structure, such as South Bavaria and a number of districts in Lower Silesia. These were also isolated and mountainous border regions, and a comparative in-depth study might well produce results of the greatest significance for the research of both German Catholicism and the Nazi Party. The Nazi electoral successes in these regions strengthen the perception of the Nazi Party as a *"Volkspartei,"* not only with reference to social class but also to that of religion.[3] Our study also shows the Nazi Party in the role of an "Anti-Milieu Partei."[4] It earns this title on account of the support that it received from the groups that had always been outside of the Catholic milieu as well as from those on its outermost fringes or in the process of abandoning it altogether due to the economic crisis.

Our conclusions diminish the the importance of the contribution supposedly made by such prominent Nazi figures as Hitler, Goebbels, and G. Strasser, and of propaganda motifs such as anti-Semitism, the "Führer" cult, the *"Volksgemeinschaft,"* and many others generally perceived in the research as crucial to the Nazi success. We have noted how the Nazi Party adapted itself to its surroundings. German society did not fall under the spell of Nazi propaganda and leaders. On the contrary, in the Black Forest and the Baar region the party chapters and propaganda were forced to adapt to certain necessities: (1) quiet, low-keyed activity due to the region's tourist and health industry, since noisy and provocative activity might threaten the basis of the local economy; (2) the social profile of the party chapters, composed mainly of workers and craftsmen, which caused the socialist element to be emphasized in party propaganda, in contrast to the practice in other rural areas in Germany; and (3) a widespread use of the anticommunist motif (as elsewhere in Germany), so well-suited to the mood of the region. This last point appears to be of crucial importance in understanding the reasons behind the Nazi rise to power. The profound fear of Russian Bolshevism appears to us to be the most important, perhaps most decisive reason for the success of the Nazi Party in the Black Forest region, and possibly in other regions as well.

The interrelationship between the Nazi Party and the surrounding society, the influence of the latter on Nazi activity, and the perception of the Nazi Party in south Baden as a local protest party inclines us to label the National Socialist group in the region as a movement (*Bewegung*) rather than a party. As a social movement, National Socialism in the area linked itself to the idea of social protest, despite the reality that its activity there was of a limited nature and lacked a well-developed formal power base. The members became connected with the Nazis through the support that they lent the party, and it was essentially through the withdrawal of that support that some of them left it. Although the Nazi Party in the region was part of a whole, a component of a larger political unit, relations between the local chapters and various centers were often characterized by tension and lack of cooperation. The motives of the members for joining also justify our labeling the Nazi groups in the Black Forest and the Baar as a "movement." Such motives included feelings of alienation, deprivation, frustration, and impotence in the local social life, and they found expression in the abandonment or dissolution of the *Vereine*.[5]

An important implicit reason for the Nazi Party's success in South Baden was the connection between the local political tradition expressed during the Second Reich by the heavy support given to the anticlerical National-Liberal Party and the Nazi success twenty to thirty years later. Some local Nazis had been members or supporters of the National-Liberals before the war. Did the activities of the NSDAP in any way resemble National-Liberal activities before the war? Were the Nazis imagined by the local society to be the heirs of the National-Liberal tradition? Does its similarity to the bourgeois *Verein,* the cornerstone of the National-Liberal party, give us any hint of the reasons for the Nazi's success? These questions are relevant to other regions as well, in the same way as in south Baden, regions where the National-Liberal party was the dominant one before the war, and the Nazi Party after 1928. The Catholic Allgäu region and many other regions in north and central Germany can serve us as control groups.[6]

Our treatment of the *Vereine* constitutes a contribution to research. The very fact of using an organization of this kind to examine sociopolitical processes in twentieth-century Germany is to some extent new, as only very few scholars have done so till now.[7] As carriers of the local sociocultural infrastructure in rural areas, the *Vereine* provide important evidence of the way in which social systems function, in this case, the local bourgeois society and Catholic milieu. We have focused our study on a social group previously relegated to the margins of research—the Catholic bourgeoisie. The efforts we have made to define this group and to describe its activity may well provide a starting point for a more detailed and in-depth discussion.

When dealing with the social history of German Catholicism, the term *modernization* is frequently employed. Yet how did Catholicism and modern development react to each other? Our portrayal of Catholic society in South Baden makes frequent use of formulas denoting "backwardness." Such terminology is fairly often employed in modernization theory in order to describe the reactionary attitude of the German Catholics during the Second Reich.[8] Our own use of the term is made in the context of the study of Catholic society under Weimar, a period comparatively neglected in the historiography of German Catholicism. The structuralist explanation of the rise of German Fascism, with its emphasis on the processes of industrialization and modernization, is convincing, in our opinion, for dealing with the mass Catholic support for the Nazi Party in the Black Forest. The 1920s found local Catholic society at a critical stage in the transition to industrialization.[9] The economic crisis of the 1920s struck at this process of industrialization, modernization, and adoption of Protestant social values. The disintegration of Catholic frameworks intensified during the economic crisis, accelerating a process that had begun even before World War I. The results were ominous for Catholic society. The main victims were those Catholics ejected from the frameworks of political Catholicism and the Catholic milieu (the workers), and those who had never belonged to the milieu at all (parts of the bourgeoisie, and the sectors of rural society caught in the transition to modernization). The effects of the economic crisis were devastating for all these groups. The frustrations attendant on an isolated existence were now deepened by the frustrations deriving from the socioeconomic breakdown of traditional frameworks, not excluding the non-Catholic ones that had formerly allowed for private enterprise. The atomization of Catholic society initially generated apathy and frustration, but as the crisis gained wider dimensions and the fear of Bolshevism infected the local elite as well, there was an increasing tendency to support the radical political alternative: that of the Nazi Party.

How do our conclusions fit into the mainstream of research on the history of modern Germany and the Weimar period? Can they point the way to new directions of research or advance the development of existing ones? Undoubtedly, it is somewhat risky to integrate the results of a research at the micro-level, especially in an area as remote as south Baden, with general trends whose scope and perspective are broader than ours. But as previously noted, the general trends are themselves made up of numerous processes and occurrences at the micro-level, and they serve both as a mirror and as testing grounds for processes that occurred at the micro-level in different areas.

Thus the conclusions that emerge from our study are not without significance for the study of modern German history. The first of these is the necessity of taking the processes and events that occurred before 1933 from out of the shadow of events that occurred afterward. Nazi Party activity and the behavioral patterns of German society must be examined against the background of the period in which they occurred, and not against the post-1933 reality. It is not our intention to suggest any relativization of Nazism or to view the Nazi rise to power as some kind of accident. But we have sought to understand the degree to which the Nazi Party was or was not unique prior to 1933, and to restore the entire question to the "realm of history," especially at the micro-level, by examining the lower echelons of the Nazi Party in various regions of Germany.[10]

There can be no understanding of German society and the support that it gave the Nazi Party without taking the fear of a communist revolt into account. This fear gripped wide sectors of society and was augmented by the presence of the Communist Party in Germany, which began to gather strength from 1929. Reports of the collectivization program undertaken by Stalin and the ensuing atrocities caused those strata that were anticommunist to begin with to considerably polarize their attitudes. It was not in South Baden alone that this fear played an important role in Nazi success, and its contribution was decisive to the chain of events leading up to Adolf Hitler's appointment to the chancellorship.[11]

Finally, the crisis of modernization, which was so characteristic of German society in the Weimar period, did not leave Catholic society untouched. The crisis was not confined to the years of inflation (1922–23) or to the period of mass unemployment (1930–33). German society as a whole was a society in crisis, and it remained so throughout the years of the Republic. The Great Economic Crisis was preceded by a whole series of crises, less severe, to be sure, than the one that followed 1929, but no less important. Knut Borchardt's theory of the crisis that preceded the crisis, darkening the "golden age" of Weimar Germany (1924–29),[12] finds expression in our own study as well. The economic aspects of the crisis included the collapse of some local industries in the Black Forest and the Baar in 1925 through 1927, the waves of mass dismissals, the inability of local councils to meet their debts, the objections of employers over expenditures for welfare and social security, the loss of the markets in Alsace-Lorraine, and the impact of this on local industries. The social aspects of the crisis included the difficulties of the *Vereine,* the growing alienation of workers and craftsmen from the Catholic milieu, political apathy, and the fear of the bourgeoisie of losing control of local socioeconomic life. For all these reasons, 1929 cannot be said to have constituted a turning point. Whatever earthquake shook the region began many years earlier, and the Great Economic Crisis of 1929 only brought the crisis-ridden Weimar Republic to its tragic end.

The reflection of these crises in *Verein* activity can serve as a seismograph of German social functioning at the local level, and it is this instrument that we have applied to the forgotten Catholic society of Weimar Germany. The presentation of this society as a socioreligious stratum that was less than monolithic in its opposition to Nazism destroys yet another myth related to the painful subject that so occupies the writers of history, namely, the circumstances that permitted the Nazi Party, in the final account, to seize power in Germany.

Notes

Introduction

1. T. Geiger, "Panik im Mittelstand," in *Die Arbeit* 7 (1930): 637–59, was the first scientist to analyze the success of the NSDAP using the terminology and methodology of the social sciences. See also E. Lind, "Die Wähler der NSDAP (Eine statistische Untersuchung der Wahlergebnisse in Hessen)," in *Frankfurter Zeitung,* nos. 895–900 (Dec. 1930).

2. Good surveys of the development of historiography in Germany are Ian Kershaw, *The Nazi Dictatorship: Problems and Perspectives of Interpretation* (London, 1989); and P. Aycoberry, *The Nazi Question—An Essay on the Interpretations of National Socialism (1922–1975)* (New York, 1981).

3. R. J. Evans, "From Hitler to Bismarck: Third Reich and Kaiserreich in Recent Historiography," in R. J. Evans, *Rethinking German History* (London, 1987), 55–92.

4. The best contribution to research about these questions and about the relation between the NSDAP with respect to the National Socialist Regime and the local population is Martin Broszat et al. (eds.), Bayern in der NS-Zeit, vol. I–IV (Munich, 1977–82); see also Horst Moeller et al. (eds.), *Nationalsozialismus in der Region. Beiträge zur regionalen und lokalen Forschung und zum internationalen Vergleich* (Munich, 1995).

5. Chapter 7 deals with the electional behavior in favor of the NSDAP and will give a detailed bibliographical view on the subject of the Nazi support by Catholics. For the time being see R. Hamilton, *Who Voted for Hitler* (Princeton, 1982), 371–73; T. Childers, *The Nazi Voter. The Social Foundations of Fascism in Germany, 1919–1933* (Chapel Hill, 1983), 188–91, 258–61; K. Scholder, *The Churches and the Third Reich, 1918–1934* (London, 1987), chap. 9; K. Rohe, *Wahlen und Wählertraditionen in Deutschland* (Frankfurt, 1992), 156ff.; J. Falter, *Hitlers Wähler* (Munich, 1991), chap. 6.5.

6. For example, the publishing houses Mathias Grünewald and F. Schöningh, which used to publish works about the Catholic resistance against National Socialism in Germany. A research institute which is working in the same direction is the *Kommission für Zeitgeschichte* which is affiliated with the publishing house M. Grünewald. This institute continuously publishes a research series giving evidence for the resistance of the Catholic Church against National Socialism, especially

files of German bishops about the situation of the Church; Klaus Gotto, Konrad Repgen, Rudolf Lill, Rudolf Morsey, and Heinz Hürten are among the prominent historians who have already been dealing with the subject for years.

7. Examples for new research contributions which argue in favor of the Nazi power of innovations are mentioned in chap. 7 below. As examples see H. U. Thamer, *Verführung und Gewalt—Deutschland 1933–1945* (Berlin, 1987); or C. Fischer, *The Rise of the Nazis* (Manchester, 1995). For an exceptional direction concerning the ability of the Nazi Party, see recently in W. Pyta, *Dorfgemeinschaft und Parteipolitik 1918–1933. Die Verschränkung von Milieu und Parteien in den protestantischen Landgebieten Deutschlands in der Weimarer Republik* (Düsseldorf, 1996).

8. Rainer Lepsius, "Parteisystem und Sozialstruktur: Zum Problem der Demokratisierung der deutschen Gesellschaft," in G. A. Ritter (ed.), *Die deutschen Parteien vor 1918* (Cologne, 1973), 69; for the debate around Lepsius's remarks on the Catholics' milieu see Michael Klöcker, "Das katholische Milieu. Grundüberlegungen," in *Zeitschrift für Religions- und Geistesgeschichte 44* (1992), 241–62; Wilfried Loth, "Soziale Bewegungen im Katholizismus des Kaiserreichs," *Geschichte und Gesellschaft* 17 (1991), 279–310; Antonius Liedhegener, "Marktgesellschaft und Milieu. Katholiken und katholische Regionen in der wirtschaftlichen Entwicklung des Deutschen Reiches 1895–1914," in *Historisches Jahrbuch II 113* (1993): 283–354. Arbeitskreis für kirchliche Zeitgeschichte (AKKZG) Münster, "Katholiken zwischen Tradition und Moderne. Das katholische Milieu als Forschungsaufgabe," in *Westfälische Forschungen* 43 (1993): 588–654.

9. On the importance of regional research in principal and above all for modern German history see S. Laessig et al. (eds.), *Modernisierung und Region im wilhelminischen Deutschland: Wahlen, Wahlrecht und politische Kultur* (Bielefeld, 1996); O. Dann, "Die Region als Gegenstand der Geschichtswissenschaft," in *Archiv für Sozialgeschichte* 24 (1983): 661; H. Gollwitzer, *"Die politische Landschaft in der deutschen Geschichte des 19./20. Jahrhunderts." Land und Volk, Herrschaft und Staat* (Munich, 1964), 523–52; E. Hennig, "Regionale Unterschiede bei der Entstehung des deutschen Faschismus," in *Politische Vierteljahresschrift 21* (1980): 152–73; G. Zang et al., *Provinzialisierung einer Region. Regionale Unterentwicklung und liberale Politik in der Stadt und im Kreis Konstanz im 19. Jahrhundert. Untersuchungen zur Entstehung der bürgerlichen Gesellschaft in der Provinz* (Frankfurt, 1978), 15–29, 503—12; W. Zorn, "Territorium und Region in der Sozialgeschichte," in W. Schieder and V. Sellin (eds.), *Sozialgeschichte in Deutschland,* II (Göttingen, 1986), 137–61. A historian who deals with the importance of region and local cultures for political development in Germany since the nineteenth century is Karl Rohe. Among his numerous works see K. Rohe, "Introduction," in idem. (ed.), *Election, Parties and Political Traditions. Social Foundations of German Parties and Party Systems, 1867–1987* (New York, 1991); idem, *Wahlen* (n. 5).

10. J. Sheehan, "What is German History?" in *Journal of Modern History* (*JMH*) 53 (1981): 21–22; see also the "Diskussionsbeitrag" in Moeller, *Nationalsozialismus in der Region* (n. 4), 47–61.

11. Hennig, *Regionale Unterschiede* (n. 9), 166.

12. R. Gill, *Competing Convictions* (London, 1989), 106

Chapter 1

1. *Schwarzwälder Bote* (*Sch B*), 31.8.1930.

2. On different approaches toward a definition of the territorial area of the Black Forest see B. Ottnad, "Zur Territorialgeschichte des Schwarzwaldes," in K. Liehl and W. Sick (eds.), *Der Schwarzwald. Beiträge zur Landeskunde* (Bühl, 1930), 181–204. Different research works dealing with the Black Forest and presenting different territorial borders are G. Möller, *Die Wirtschaft des Schwarzwaldes* (Oberndorf, 1930); E. Gothein, *Wirtschaftsgeschichte des Schwarzwaldes und der angrenzenden Landschaften* (Straßburg, 1892).

3. On the different origins of the name see B. Bosch, "Zu den Ortsnamen," in Liehl and Sick, *Schwarzwald* (n. 2), 247–49.

4. On these processes see L. Gall, "Gründung und politische Entwicklung des Großherzogtums bis 1848," in *Badische Geschichte: Vom Großherzogtum bis zur Gegenwart* (Stuttgart, 1987), 11–36.

5. On the administrative partition of Baden in the nineteenth century and for the local administrative bodies see T. Pfizer and H. Wehling (eds.), *Kommunalpolitik in Baden-Württemberg* (Stuttgart), chap. 2–3.

6. My decision is based on the location of the files in the local archives according to the district levels, mainly in the following archives: Staatsarchiv Freiburg (StaaF); Generallandesarchiv Karlsruhe (GLAK).

Chapter 2

1. Description and data are from *Die Religionszugehörigkeit in Baden,* Badisches Statistisches Landesamt (BSL) 1928. On the *Altkatholiken* in South Baden see Pfarrarchiv (PfA) Furtwangen, Kirchenvisitation 1930; *Die Religionszugehörigkeit,* 69–72; Grober Konrad, "Der Altkatholizismus in Konstanz," *Freiburger Diözesanarchiv,* 39 (1911): 135–98; idem. "Der Altkatholizismus in Messkirch," ibid., 40 (1912): 97–134; Keller Erwin, *Die altkatholische Bewegung in Tiengen/Oberrhein* (Wangen i.Allg.1961); Josef, F. Waldmeier, *Ein Beitrag zur Geschichte des Altkatholizismus in Südbaden. Der altkatholische Klerus von Säckingen, Waldshut und Zell im Wiesental,* ed. Pfarramt Aarau (Frick, 1984); in the Reich, see J. Sperber, *Popular Catholicism in Nineteenth Century Germany* (Princeton, 1984), 233–40; in general O. Blaschke "Der Altkatholizismus 1870 bis 1945. Nationalismus, Antisemitismus und Nationalsozialismus," *Historische Zeitschrift* 261 (1995): 51–99.

2. Data from *Die Religionszugehörigkeit.* On the importance of the local cattle market see *Donaueschinger Tagblatt* (*DT*), 29.12.1931.

3. For an early example of such anticlerical tendencies in the region of Wutach, see C. Rehm, *Die katholische Kirche in der Erzdiözese Freiburg während*

der Revolution 1848/49 (Munich, 1987), 19–20. Part 3 in our book deals with the Catholic milieu in a more detailed way.

Chapter 3

1. *Die Landwirtschaft in Baden im Jahr 1925,* BSL, 1927; K. Müller, "Der Schwarzwald als Agrarlandschaft," in Liehl and Sick, *Der Schwarzwald* (chap. 1, n. 2), 407–26.

2. *Denkschrift über die Verschuldung der badischen Landwirtschaft im Jahre 1928,* in StaaF, Landeskommissär Konstanz (Lkk), 900. A. Buchenberger, "Die Lage der bäuerlichen Bevölkerung im Großherzogtum Baden," in *Berichte veröffentlicht vom Verein für Sozialpolitik, 3, Schriften des Vereins für Socialpolitik* 24 (Leipzig, 1883), 262–73.

3. StaaF, Bezirksamt (BZ) Villingen - 1985/110, P. 1563 - Ortsbereisung Schonwald, 22.12.1930, P. 1671 - Ortsbereisung Schonach, 1930.

4. Staff, BZ Villingen, Ortsbereisung Schonach, ibid.; data from *Die badische Landwirtschaft im Allgemeinen und in einzelnen Gauen,* BSL, 1932–36.

5. On the Home Industry in the nineteenth century see J. Kocka, *Arbeitsverhältnisse und Arbeiterexistenzen* (Bonn, 1990), chap. 4; K. Bittmann, *Hausindustrie und Heimarbeit im Großherzogtum Baden zu Anfang des XX. Jahrhunderts* (Karlsruhe, 1907).

6. Möller, Wirtschaft (chap. 1, n. 2), 45; P. Assion, "Schwarzwälder Haus-, Handwerks- und Handelskunst," in Liehl, Sick, *Der Schwarzwald* (chap. 1, n. 2), 356–59.

7. StaaF, LKK 3979 - 19.5.1931, Die Finanzlage der Stadtgemeinde Vöhrenbach.

8. G. Bender, *Die Uhrenmacher des hohen Schwarzwaldes und ihre Werke,* 2 vols. (Villingen, 1975–78).

9. StaaF, BZ Neustadt - 1974/31, P. 135 - Ortsbereisung Grafenhausen, 13.2.1930; Schwarzwälder Zeitung "Der Grenzer," 19.2.1931, 20.5.1932.

10. W. Bölcke, "Industrialisierung im Kammerbezirk Schwarzwald-Baar-Heuberg vom 17. Jahrhundert bis 1945," in *Zeitschrift für Württembergische Landesgeschichte 42* (1983), 296; idem, *Sozialgeschichte Baden-Württembergs 1800–1989* (Stuttgart, 1989), 358–59; Möller, *Wirtschaft* (chap. 1, n. 2), 40–41; Heimat- und Gewerbeverein Triberg, *100 Jahre Triberger Gewerbeverein 1853–1953* (Triberg, 1954), 56–63; G. Buchmann, "Die Industrie des Oberen Bergtals im 20. Jahrhundert," in *Furtwanger Mitteilungen 8* (1981): 102–225.

11. Möller, Wirtschaft (chap. 1, n. 2), 15; *Freiburger Zeitung (FZ),* 1.6.1931.

12. StaaF, BZ Neustadt - 1980/10/20, P. 141 - Ortsbereisung, Hinterzarten, 1926; *Der Fremdenverkehr in Baden im Jahre 1930,* BSL, 1931.

13. *FZ,* 19.9.1930; *Schwarzwälder Zeitung "Der Grenzer,"* 20.9.1930; StaaF, BZ Neustadt - 1980/10/20, P. 72 - Ortsbereisung Eisenbach - 1930; *FZ,* 27.6. 25.8.1930; *Der Führer,* 20.8.1931 - Schonach.

14. Möller, *Die Wirtschaft* (chap. 1, n. 2), 84–87.

15. StaaF, BZ Neustadt - 108/32 - 2.4.1928; A typical example for such an industrial condition can be found in H. Berghof, "Konsumgüterindustrie im Nationalsozialismus. Marketing im Spannungsfeld von Profit- und Regimeinter-

essen," *Archiv für Sozialgeschichte* 36 (1996): 288–302. There is a vast research literature about these years; the research publications of K. Borchardt should be mentioned as examples of the pioneer works which developed the argument of "the crisis before the crisis" between 1924 and 1928. See for example: idem, *Wachstum, Krisen, Handlungsspielräume der Wirtschaftspolitik* (Göttingen, 1982); I. Kershaw (ed.), *Why Did Weimar Democracy Fail?* (London, 1993).

16. StaaF, BZ Neustadt 108/32 - 2.4.1928; 240 - 15.2.1930; Buchmann, *Die Industrie* (n. 10), 103–7; StaaF, LKK 3564 - 18.7.1932.

17. On unemployment in Gütenbach see StaaF, LKK 3564–18.7.1932; on the economic situation in Gütenbach see ibid., 3657–7.5.1932 Erzbischöfliches Archiv Freiburg (ErzAF) B2–59–18-22.11.1932; and on Vöhrenbach see chapter 3, note 7 above.

Chapter 4

1. A good historiographical survey on the Catholic "backwardness" can be found in M. Baumeister, *Parität und katholische Inferiorität: Untersuchungen zur Stellung des Katholizismus im Deutschen Kaiserreich* (Paderborn, 1987); for critical remarks on this approach, see Th. Mergel, "Ultramontanism, Liberalism, Moderation: Political Mentalities and Political Behavior of the German Catholic Bürgertum, 1848–1914," *Central European History* 29, 2 (1996): 151–75.

2. On the bad hygiene conditions see *FZ,* 19.9.1929; *Echo vom Hochfirst* (*EvH*) 8.11.1930; *Hochschwarzwald* (*Hschw.*) 4.4.1932; StaaF, BZ Neustadt - 1980/10/20, P. 141 - Ortsbereisung Hinterzarten, 1926; StaaF, BZ Neustadt - 1974/31, P. 135 - Ortsbereisung Grafenhausen, 1924; Hochwächter auf dem Schwarzwald (Hoch.Schw.) 10.12.1931 - Reiselfingen. For further characteristics of the technological and agricultural backwardness of the region see *Der Alemanne,* 3.11.1932 - Neustadt; *FZ,* 20.9.1929 - Hotzenwald; Schw. B, 6.9.1930; *FZ,* 2.10.1929.

3. The reports of the Ortsbereisung in the 1920s can be found in the State Archives of Freiburg under the former district of Neustadt marked as: 1980/10/20 - Ortsbereisung: P. 58 - Dittishausen; P. 141 - Hinterzarten; P. 199 - Löffingen; P. 278 - Oberbränd; P. 376 - Seppenhofen; P. 14 - Bachheim; P. 287 - Reiselfingen; 1974/31 - P. 131 - Ewattingen; P. 114 - Bonndorf; P. 168 - Münchingen; P. 135 - Grafenhausen.

4. StaaF (see note 3 above), Ortsbereisung Münchingen, 1930; Ortsbereisung Löffingen, 1927; BZ Offenburg, Nr. 128; P. 5 - Ortsbereisung Bad-Peterstal; 7.12.1928; *DT,* 29.10.1929. On the inheritance law see G. Koch, *Die gesetzlich geschlossenen Hofgüter des badischen Schwarzwaldes* (Tübingen, 1900).

5. *Die Gebrechlichen in Baden im Jahre 1925,* BSL, 1928, 8–9.

6. E. Föhr, *Die sozialen und wirtschaftlichen Verhältnisse der Waldarbeiter im badischen Schwarzwald* (Aachern, 1921); Anzeiger v. Kinzigtal (*AvK*), 22.11.1930; *Schwarzwälder Zeitung "Der Grenzer,"* 19.12.1931; *Kinzigtäler Nachrichten* (*KN*), 26.2.1932 - Bad Rippoldsau.

7. D. Gessner, *Agrarverbände in der Weimarer Republik* (Düsseldorf, 1976), Avk, ibid.; *DT,* 21.10.1931.

8. *FZ,* 15.7.1930.

9. *TB,* 2.11.1931; *FZ,* 2.10.1929; *Schw B,* 6.9.1930.

10. The district inspector reported during his visit to Schonach about tensions between farmers and workers. See StaaF, LKK, 7348 - 10.22.1932. The fear from left-wing parties in rural regions will be discussed in part 3 (chap. 11) where we will study the decline of the social infrastructure in the regions.

11. Bender, *Die Uhrenmacher* (chap. 3, n. 8), vol. II, 114; *FZ*, 2.8.1932.

12. *Schwarzwälder Zeitung "Der Grenzer,"* 19.12.1931, 20.5.1932.

13. *Hschw*, 7.6.1932; *Schwarzwälder Zeitung,* ibid.

14. *TB*, 2.12.1931.

Chapter 5

1. Although there is no major study about the *Kulturkampf* in the Black Forest so far, this conclusion can be reached using the remarks published in several studies about the *Kulturkampf* in Baden. J. Becker, *Liberaler Staat und Kirche in der Ära von Reichsgründung und Kulturkampf* (Mainz, 1973), 306–9, 331–42; H. Lauer, *Geschichte der katholischen Kirche in der Baar* (Donaueschingen, 1921); C. Zangerl, "Courting the Catholic Vote: The Center Party in Baden 1903–1913," in *Central European History* (*CEH*) 3 (1977): 220–40. On the anticlericalism in the region see Zang, *Provinzialisierung einer Region. Regionale Unterentwicklung und liberale Politik in der Stadt und im Kreis Konstanz im 19. Jahrhundert. Untersuchung zur Entstehung der bürgerlichen Gesellschaft in der Provinz* (Frankfurt 1978); I. Götz von Olenhusen, *Abweichendes Verhalten. Zur Sozialgeschichte katholischer Priester im 19. Jahrhundert: Die Erzdiözese Freiburg* (Göttingen, 1995), 194–96, 385–86; O. Heilbronner, "Regionale Aspekte zum katholischen Bürgertum. Oder: Die Besonderheit des katholischen Bürgertums im ländlichen Süddeutschland," in *Blätter für Deutsche Landesgeschichte,* 131, 1995; idem "In Search of the Catholic (Rural) Bourgeoisie: The Peculiarities of the South German Burgertum." *CEH* 29, 2 (1996): 175–201; idem "Popularer Liberalismus im Südbaden 1871–1912: Entwicklungstendenzen der badischen Wahlkultur," *ZGO*, 146, 1998.

2. See the detailed discussion about political Catholicism and the Catholic milieu in the introduction to part 3.

3. H. Kremer (reviser), *Mit Gott für Wahrheit, Freiheit und Recht* (Stuttgart, 1983), 266.

4. In spite of the numerous publications on the *Zentrum* in Germany during the Weimar Republic only a few studies on the *Zentrum* in Baden during this period had been published so far. Among these few, see S. Fritz, "The Center Cannot Hold—Educational Politics and the Collapse of the Democratic Middle in Germany: The School Bill Crisis in Baden, 1927–28," in *History of Education Quarterly* 25 (1985): 413–37; F. Wielandt, *Weimarer Koalition and SPD in Baden* (Frankfurt, 1976); S. Pluck, *Das badische Konkordat vom 12. Oktober 1932* (Mainz, 1984).

5. *TB*, 11., 13., 26.10.1929; *SchwT*, 10.3.1931 - Hüfingen.

6. See the report of the local priest of St. Blasien about the workers in the region in 1929: PfA St. Blasien, Seelsorge, 5.11.1929.

7. On the *BLB* in the Black Forest see E. Bleibtreu, *Die Bauernbewegung im Bezirk Bonndorf 1919–1922* (Karlsruhe, 1923); *Der Landbund: Sein Auftreten und*

sein Wirken im Bezirk Bonndorf 1922–1924 (Karlsruhe, 1925); J. Albicker, "Bilanz der politischen Bauernbewegung in der Baar," in *DT,* 8.11.1930.

8. *Der Landbund* (n. 7), 9, 103–7, 121.

9. I will discuss this issue in chap. 11.

10. O. Heilbronner, "Weimar Society and the Image of Soviet Russia," *Tel Aviver Jahrbuch für Deutsche Geschichte,* 24 (1995): 179–92.

11. *DT,* 10.9.1930; *TB,* 22.10.1929 - Schonach; on the *DDP* in the region see P. Ostermann, *Wilhelm Stahl. Ein badischer Liberaler* (Freiburg, 1993), 33.

12. *SchwT,* 7., 28.5.1931; 6.1.1932; 23.3.1932; *SchwB,* 7.8.1930; *Hschw.* 4.4.1932, *Schwarzwälder Zeitung* (Bonndorf), 9.3.1932; StaaF, BZ Offenburg - Nr. 128, P. 5 - Ortsbereisung Bad-Peterstal, 7.12.1928.

Introduction to Part 2

1. John Grill, *The Nazi Movement in Baden, 1919–1945* (Chapel Hill, 1983); Ernst Bräunsche, "Die Entwicklung der NSDAP in Baden bis 1932/33," in *Zeitschrift für die Geschichte des Oberrheins 125* (1977), 331–75; idem, "Die NSDAP in Baden. 1928–1933—Der Weg zur Macht," in Thomas Schnabel (ed.), *Die Machtergreifung in Südwestdeutschland. Das Ende der Weimarer Republik in Baden und Württemberg* (Stuttgart, 1982), 15–48.

2. A detailed view of the material about the NSDAP in Baden available to the historians is given by Grill, *Nazi Movement* (n. 1), 668–75.

3. Good examples in this context are the different regional reports (*Bezirksberichte*) in Baden which were sent by request to the Ministery of the Interior. They deal with the problem of certain political activities violating the "Law concerning the Protection of the Republic" (*"Gesetz zum Schutze der Republik"*).The reports cover the period from September 1929 until September 1930 and observe that an exceptional and illegal political activity had to be noticed above all in the northern regions of Baden. During the mentioned period no events violating the "Law concerning the Protection of the Republic" took place in the Catholic jurisdictions (*Amtsbezirke*) in South Baden, i.e., Villingen and Donaueschingen, except one speech delivered by Robert Wagner on March 5, 1930 (cf. StaaF, LKK, 1626).

4. Most of the numerous research works dealing with the descriptions of the NSDAP in several areas of Baden between 1930 and 1933 are devoted to the northern region of the country, in particular to the town of Heidelberg. Important summaries of the developments in South Baden are: Ernst Bräunche, Walter Köhler (eds.), *Machtergreifung in Freiburg und Südbaden* (Freiburg, 1983); Arnim Käffer, *Die Nazis erobern das Ried—Faschisierungsprozeß und Machtwandel in den oberrheinischen Riedgemeinden 1928/29–1935,* M.A. thesis, Freiburg, 1986; H. Faisst, "Die 'Marktfrage' als 'Machtfrage'—Kontinuität und Wandel im ländlichen Raum: der Agrarsektor im Bezirk Bühl in den Jahren 1927–1937," in *Die Ortenau* 74 (1994): 549–67. On the NSDAP in North Baden see Anette Hettinger, "Die NSDAP auf dem Land—Aufstieg, Machtergreifung und Gleichschaltung im badischen Amtsbezirk Adelsheim 1928–1935," in *Württembergisch Franken 72* (1988): 91–195; J. Braun, "Die Entwicklung des Nationalsozialismus im badischen Amtsbezirk Tauberbischofsheim 1924–1932," in *Wertheimer Jahrbuch* (1993): 289–316; C. Rauh-Kühne, *Katholisches Milieu und Kleinstadtgesellschaft, Ettlingen*

1918–1939 (Sigmaringen, 1991). More titles can be found in chapter 7, note 39 below. A historiographical survey is given by John Grill, "Local and Regional Studies on National Socialism: A Review," in *Journal of Contemporary History* (*JCH*) 10 (1986): 270–72.

5. StaaF, LKK, 1617.

Chapter 6

1. Der Führer, März 1935. Zehn Jahre Kampf 1925–1935. Sonderbeilage des Führer "Und endlich im Schwarzwald Vorwärts," 5; "Triberg," 21.

2. In 1924, during the time the Nazi Party had been illegal, Nazi agitators were active under assumed names and in coalition with several other groups.

3. Grill, *Nazi Movement* (chap. 5, n. 1), 98.

4. Der Führer, 22.9.1933; Bundesarchiv Koblenz (BAK), Hauptarchiv der NSDAP NS 26/215; Grill, *Nazi Movement* (chap. 5, n. 1), 73.

5. Der Führer, 1./2.3.1931; StaaF, Staatsanwaltschaft Freiburg, 8.-9.11.1923.

6. Grill, *Nazi Movement* (chap. 5, n. 1), 98–99; Bräunche, Entwicklung (chap. 5, n. 1), 334; StaaF, Staatsanwaltschaft Freiburg, 11. and 21.1.1924, 5. and 6.6.1924.

7. Bräunsche, Entwicklung (chap. 5, n. 1), 335; Die Reichstagswahlen am 7. Dezember 1924 in Baden, BSL, Karlsruhe 1925. For the NSFP see Dietrich Orlow, *The History of the Nazi Party 1919–1933* (Pittsburgh, 1969), chap. 3; D. Jablonsky, *The Verbotszeit—A Study of the Nazi Party Leadership in Dissolution, 9. November 1923–16. Februar 1925* (New York, 1991).

8. For the dilemma the party was confronted with during these election campaigns see Grill, *Nazi Movement* (chap. 5, n. 1), 123; Orlow, *History* (n. 7), 60–63.

9. BAK, Sammlung Schuhmacher, 199, 8.7.1927.

10. Albrecht Tyrell (ed.), *Führer befiehl . . . Selbstzeugnisse aus der "Kampfzeit" der NSDAP. Dokumentation und Analyse* (Düsseldorf, 1969), 245–47, 353. For the question of a new foundation of the party and for the foundation process of chapters (*Ortsgruppen*) in Baden and in the Reich see Grill, *Nazi Movement* (chap. 5, n. 1), 135–50; Orlow, *History* (n. 7), chap. 4.

11. Herbert Müller, "Die NSDAP in Lahr/Baden," in *Die Ortenau 7* (1991), 622–37; O. Wiegert (ed.), *NSDAP Ortsgruppe Offenburg—Festbuch zur 10jährigen Gründungsfeifer am 17. und 18. März 1934* (Offenburg, 1934).

12. "Entstehung und Entwicklung des Stützpunktes Fischerbach der NSDAP," Gemeindearchiv (GmdA) Fischerbach X1/3–1217.

13. Hans Harter, "Gottlieb Trautwein (1892–1953)—Ein Schiltacher Liberaler und kämpferischer Demokrat," in Die Ortenau 68 (1988), 306.

14. See his personal file in the Berlin Document Center (BDC).

15. StaaF, LKK, 1928, 1929.

16. For the foundation of a chapter in Löffingen see Der Führer, 7.4.1928; StaaF, BZ Neustadt, 244/183, 14.5.1928; GmdA Löffingen X13/2648 Chronik der Löffingen NSDAP - 8.11.1938; the first leader of this chapter was Ernst Fritsche, who resigned from the executive board of the chapter in 1931 in consequence of a bribe scandal. For Fritsche see his personal file in the BDC and also GmdA

Löffingen iv2/491 - 20.3.1931. For the foundation of fifteen other chapters in the region see Der Führer, 19.5.1928.

17. StaaF, BZ Neustadt, 244/183, 20.5.1928.

18. Grill, *Nazi Movement* (chap. 5, n. 1), 162–65. Some examples of the success of the NSDAP in different villages of the region: Bachheim, 20 percent; Reiselfingen, 25.7 percent; Bonndorf, 14.9 percent; Unadingen, 10.9 percent; Dittishausen, 29.9 percent; Löffingen, 13.6 percent; Seppenhofen, 54.4 percent; Die Reichstagswahl am 20. Mai 1928.

19. For this subject see the detailed historiographical discussion in the following paragraphs and in notes 91–93. For the electoral success of the NSDAP achieved without any intensive election campaign in May 1928 see also Orlow, *History* (n. 7), 129–30. In the previously mentioned context Grill tends in his analysis of the NSDAP in Baden to underestimate the meaning of the initiatives coming from Munich and to emphasize the local NS factors.

20. StaaF, BZ Neustadt, 244/183, 20.5.1928; Grill, *Nazi Movement* (chap. 5, n.1), 170–71.

21. For Merk see his personal file in the BDC and also *Der Landbund: Sein Auftreten und sein Wirken im Bezirk Bonndorf 1914–1922* (Karlsruhe, 1925), 94–95, 101–2, 103–7; Der Führer, 17.11.1928; StaaF, BZ Neustadt, 244/183, 10.12.1928; for the *BLB* see the remarks in chap. 5 above.

22. On meetings of the party in 1928 see StaaF, BZ Neustadt, 244/183, 19.10.1928, 9.11.1928, 10.12.1928, 30.12.1928, 18.2.1929. On fines and arrests as penalties of Nazi agitators in the course of political agitation during meetings in Löffingen see Staatsarchiv München, Polizeidirektion 6759, 16.3.1929.

23. On the foundation of a chapter in Bonndorf see StaaF, BZ Neustadt, 244/183, 30.12.1928; for Steinhof see his personal file in the BDC and also StaaF, 244/183, 10.5.1931.

24. StaaF, BZ Neustadt, 244/183, 8.10.1929, 10.10.1929, 14.10.1929, 16.10.1929; StaaF, LKK, 1617–5.11.1929; on the campaign toward the Landtag Election in Baden see in a more detailed way: Ellsworth Faris, "The Takeoff Point for the National Socialist Party: The Landtag Election in Baden 1929," in *CEH* 8 (1975): 140–71; Grill, *Nazi Movement* (chap. 5, n. 1), 170–74.

25. BAK, NS 22/1044 - 19.7.1930; Otmar Jung, "Plebiszitärer Durchbruch 1929? Zur Bedeutung von Volksbegehren und Volksentscheid gegen den Youngplan für die NSDAP," in *Geschichte und Gesellschaft 15* (1989), 508.

26. GLAK 347, 1943/18–29, 17.10.1929; 23.20.1929.

27. On the central messages of the regional Nazi propaganda see note 26 above and also 25.11.1929. For the problem of the peasants in the region during the time of inflation see Detlef Herbner, *Die Bezirkssparkasse Donaueschingen. Beispiel einer mit Gemeindebürgschaft versehenen Sparkasse in Baden 1839–1966, Zulassungsarbeit* (Freiburg, 1989), 87–97; idem, *Auf der Baar, für die Baar. 150 Sparkasse Donaueschingen* (Stuttgart, 1989); Willi Bölcke, "Industrialisierung im Kammerbezirk Schwarzwald–Baar–Heuberg vom 17. Jahrhundert bis 1945," in *Zeitschrift für Württembergische Landesgeschichte* 42 (1983): 298. On similar problems among the peasants of a Catholic, but economically further developed region see Robert Moeller, *German Peasants and Agrarian Politics 1914–1924. The Rhineland and Westphalia* (Chapel Hill, 1986), chap. 5–6.

28. Grill and Faris express a contrary opinion, though not about the activities in the Black Forest, when they maintain that an extremely active election propaganda campaign used by the National Socialists in certain places had resulted in rising support during the respective elections. See Faris, *Takeoff* (n. 24) and Grill, *Nazi Movement* (chap. 5, n. 1), 165.

29. On the outcome of the parliament elections see Badische Landtagswahl am 26. Oktober, 1929.

30. On Schlageter see Illustrierter Beobachter, 20.5.1933; on the nationalist and National Socialist cult around his tomb see StaaF, LKK, 1617 - 15.1.1928, 15.8.1928; StaaF, BZ Schopfheim, T. 1–507, 21.5.1929; T. 1–505, 10.2.1930.

31. *TB,* 28.10.1929; GLAK; 347, 1943/18 - 19.7.1929, 21.7.1929.

32. *TB,* 11.10.1929, 26.10.1929.

33. *FZ,* 26.10.1929.

34. *FZ,* 25.10.1929 - Haslach; TB, 22.10.1929 - Schonach.

35. See Löffler-Bericht (n. 12); StaaF, Lkk 1617 15.1.1928; 15.8.1928; Faris, *Take off* (n. 24); Grill, *Nazi Movement* (chap. 5, n. 1), 174–77. On the outcome of the elections and patterns voting in Triberg and Furtwangen see chap. 7 below.

36. GLAK (n. 31 above), 25.11.1929. On the NSDAP's participation in the referendum against the Young Plan see Jung, *Durchbruch* (n. 25); and also Thomas Childers, *The Nazi Voter—The Social Foundations of Fascism in Germany 1919–1933* (Chapel Hill, 1983), 129–30; David Hackett, *The Nazi Party in the Reichstag Election of 1930,* diss., University of Wisconsin, 1971, chap. 2; Gerhard Paul, *Aufstand der Bilder. Die NS-Propaganda vor 1933* (Bonn, 1990), 90–94.

Chapter 7

1. In this context Theodor Geiger, *Die soziale Schichtung des deutschen Volkes* (Stuttgart, 1932), and Werner Stephen, "Zur Soziologie der NSDAP," in *Zeitschrift für Politik 20* (1930), 793–800, are to be mentioned.

2. Good summaries of the literature on this topic are given by Peter Manstein, *Die Mitglieder und Wähler der NSDAP* (Bern, 1988); Detlev Mühlberger, *Hitler's Followers: Studies in the Sociology of the Nazi Party* (London, 1990), chap. 1; idem, "Germany," in idem. (ed.), *The Social Basis of European Fascist Movement* (London, 1987), 56–64.

3. Their works are found in a concentrated form in Reinhard Bendix, Seymour Lipset (eds.), *Class, Status and Power: Social Stratification in Comparative Perspective* (London, 1967); Richard Hamilton, *Class and Politics in the United States* (New York, 1972); Jürgen Falter, *Hitlers Wähler. Der Aufstieg der NSDAP im Spiegel der Wahlen* (Opladen, 1991); Karl Rohe, *Wahlen und Wählertraditionen in Deutschland* (Frankfurt, 1992).

4. Michael Kater's first article "Zur Soziologie der frühen NSDAP" was published in *Vierteljahreshefte für Zeitgeschichte* 19 (1971), 124–59; his conclusions are recapitulated in his book *The Nazi Party: A Social Profile of Members and Leaders, 1919–1945* (Oxford, 1983). Recently, see W. Brustein, *The Logic of Evil. The Social Origins of the Nazi Party 1925–1933* (New Haven, 1996). Brustein's argument is that in the depths of the 1929–33 economic depression, the Nazi Party offered some more promising and rational solutions to all German classes. The

"definitive word" on the social profile of the NSDAP is published in a comprehensive article: J. Falter, M. Kater, "Wähler und Mitglieder der NSDAP," in *Geschichte und Gesellschaft* 19.2 (1993), 155–77.

5. On the problematical use of social sciences methodology for the analysis of the NSDAP social basis see Kater, *Nazi Party* (n. 4), 1–16; J. Genuneit, "Methodische Probleme der quantitativen Analyse früher NSDAP-Mitglieder," in Reinhard Mann (ed.), *Die Nationalsozialisten: Analysen faschistischer Bewegungen* (Stuttgart, 1980), 34–66; Detlev Mühlberger, "The Sociology of the NSDAP. The Question of Working Class Membership," in *JCH* 4 (1989): 494–95, and, more recently, Brustein, *The Logic of Evil* (n. 4), 8–13.

6. Numerous similar examples are mentioned in note 22.

7. Sources for the social profile of the Nazi chapters are: Furtwangen - Staaf, BZ Donaueschingen, 1977/52–345, 4.7.1931; Donaueschingen - Stadtarchiv (StA) Donaueschingen, Chroniken, Politik; DT, 8.11.1930; Triberg - *TB*, 2.11.1930, StA Triberg - AST/2–556; Schonach - Adreßbuch Schonach, 1930; PfA Schonach, NSDAP, Mitgliederverzeichnis 1932, 1933; Wahlvorschlaglisten, 16.11.1930; Ortschronik 1922–1946 - 22.5.1945; Löffingen - GmdA Löffingen iv 2/491–2650; Bonndorf - GmdA Bonndorf iv 2/488; Dittishausen - GmdA Dittishausen A-87; Eisenbach - StaaF, BZ Donaueschingen, ibid.; Schönau - StaaF, BZ Schopfheim - T.1–509, 1932 - Ortsgruppe NSDAP; Haslach - StA Haslach, iv2/106; *KN* 5.11.1930; Wolfach - StA Wolfach 02.13/2–1930; Schiltach - StA Schiltach - iv/2–6–1930; xi/3–5, Gewerbe und Handwerker - Mitgliederverzeichnis 1931. Some files of the Berlin Documentation Centre, above all those of the regional *Ortsgruppenleiter,* were extremely helpful. The social profile of NSDAP members in Baden before 1933 was also published in Partei-Statistik, I (ed.) *Der Reichsorganisationsleiter der NSDAP,* 1935, 246. These data are taken from Kater, *Nazi Party* (n. 4), 250.

8. On the difficult situation of the artisans in the region of the Black Forest see chap. 4 above. There we came to the conclusion that many artisans were forced to work as agricultural, forest, or industrial workers. The decision to count them among the working class is a result of the historiographical approach underlying this analysis. See also Wolfram Fischer, "Bergbau, Industrie und Handwerk 1850–1914," in Hans Aubin, Wolfgang Zorn (eds.), *Handbuch der deutschen Wirtschaft und Sozialgeschichte,* 2 (Stuttgart, 1976), 532; Kater, *Nazi Party* (n. 4), 5–7; Friedrich Lenger, *Sozialgeschichte der deutschen Handwerker* (Frankfurt, 1988), 163–86; K. Ditt, " Fabrikarbeiter und Handwerker im 19.Jh in der neueren deutschen Sozialgeschichtsschreibung," *Geschichte und Gesellschaft* 20, 2 (1994): 299–322.

9. See the demands of the artisans in the region of Freiburg: *FZ,* 15.7.1932. The image of the NSDAP as a party with socialist character will be discussed in the context of the Nazi Party propaganda later on. At this point only the *"Donaubote"* should be mentioned which wrote in an article "that a new socialist wave had overflown the middle classes (Bürgertum) in the last years—National Socialism . . ." ("Bürger, sei auf der Hut . . ." 25.7.32).

A quite high concentration of craftsmen in a Nazi chapter had been documented in the village of Schiltach. Sixty percent of the candidates for the election to the city council in 1930 were craftsmen. See StA Schiltach, IV, 2/6 - 1930. A suggestion accounting for the strength of this support of the NSDAP may be found in the fact that only a few of these craftsmen had been organized in the craftsmen association (*Handwerkerverein*); only five out of thirteen craftsmen registered as party members were also members of the craftsmen association. Three of them left the association in 1930/31. It may be assumed that the craftsmen association did not answer the expectations of these members. In their search for a new political identity they discovered the NSDAP which, as already mentioned, showed according to their opinion a socialist character answering the needs and expectations of craftsmen during the time of economic crisis.

10. On the case of Müssle see StaaF, BZ Neustadt - 244/184, 21.2.1932; *Der Alemanne*, 21.2.1932. On the head of the trade association (*Gewerbeverein*) in Zell a.H. see Wolfgang Mössinger, "Zell a.H. Am Ende der Weimarer Republik," in *Die Ortenau* 67–68 (1987–88), 3632–363. As a rare example for a change of workers from one party to the other, including the NSDAP, see the case of Fehrenbach: StaaF, BZ Neustadt, 244/183, 24.11.1930. On Schönwald see *TB*, 10–9.1930. On the workers of the Baar-Region see *Schwärzwalder Tagblatt (Schw T)*, 18.3.1932 - Möhringer. It looks as if one of the main reasons for the workers' difficulties finding a political home meeting their socioeconomic needs was their alienation from the Catholic church and the local Catholic milieu. This problem will be central to our discussion later on.

11. According to *Lahrer Anzeiger*, 8.11.1930. On the bourgeois orientation toward the NSDAP see also the *"Donaubote"* (n. 9). One of the historians dealing with the phenomenon of the erosion of the middle classes toward the political right in general, and toward National Socialism especially, is Hans Mommsen, for example in his articles "Zur Verschränkung traditioneller und faschistischer Führungsgruppen in Deutschland beim Übergang von der Bewegungs- zur Systemphase," in Wolfgang Schieder (ed.), *Faschismus als soziale Bewegung* (Göttingen, 1983), 157–82, and "Die Auflösung des Bürgertums seit dem späten 19. Jahrhundert," in Jürgen Kocka (ed.), *Bürger und Bürgerlichkeit im 19. Jahrhundert* (Göttingen, 1987), 288–315.

12. See the list of Nazi candidates for the local elections in the region of Villingen: StaaF, BZ Villingen - 1979/82–1790; in the region of Neustadt: StaaF, BZ: Neustadt - 1979/85–243; one has to distinguish between candidates of the NSDAP for the community councils (*Gemeinderäte*), in which the party represented its members and activists—in this context artisans and workers had an important function—and the candidates for the influential district councils (*Kreis- und Bezirksräte*), who represented the Ministry of the Interior of Baden in the district. For these corporations people of high economic and social rank were usually chosen by direct personal elections.

13. Some examples: B. Kuner, representative of the party for the District Council (*Bezirksrat*) in the district of Villingen, had been a council member of the Zentrum since 1924 and head of the local ski and sport association between 1920 and 1934. See *TB*, 21.10.1929; Werner Hamm, *Chronik der Gemeinde Schonach im Schwarzwald* (Karlsruhe, 1981), 600, 614. In the village of Lenzkirch the party candidate for the district council of Neustadt was Erwin Weishaar, council member since 1926 of a local bourgeois group and member of the peasant council in the district after 1918. See *Der Alemanne*, 5.10.1932; StaaF, BZ Neustadt 1979/85–243.

Eight of the persons mentioned on the list of NSDAP candidates in Triberg were members in different social associations; three of them were small industrialists. See *TB,* 2.11.1930. A. Glöckler, owner of a printing press and head of the local soccer association from Neustadt is an example for a change from right-bourgeois parties to the NSDAP. During the regional elections of 1930 he had been member of the Economic Union List (*Liste der Wirtschaftsvereinigung*) and changed later on to the NSDAP. See StaaF, BZ Neustadt 246/175 - 4.7.1932, 7.12.1931. See also BZ Neustadt-3212; Alfred Albanus and Hermann Heinz, two of the Nazi council members in the village of Wolfach, had been candidates of a bloc of right-wing parties for regional representation back in 1926; see StA Wolfach, 02.13/1–2. The most well-known Nazi activist in the region was Franz Merk, the leader of the peasant movement. He joined the party in 1928. Merk was member of the community council in Grafenhausen. See *Der Führer,* 17.11.1928 and also his personal file in the BDC. In spite of the given examples local notables did not support the NSDAP until 1933. Among this group were the heads of the associations, the leaders of other political parties and economic pressure groups, the great industrialists, the mayors of the villages and small towns, and others. The phenomenon seen in other, mainly Protestant regions in Germany of local notables joining the NSDAP was limited in the Catholic region of the Black Forest.

14. Also Kater stresses the relatively high age of the Nazi activists. But he talks about the leading activists as the *Ortgruppenleiter* in the region: Kater, *Nazi Party* (n. 4), 177–79. Among the average party members without any official post the representative average age of the majority lay between 18 and 30 (37.6 percent), Kater, *Nazi Party* (n. 4), 61. Sources for these conclusions about the age of the NSDAP members in the Black Forest are the file of party members in the BDC, and the lists of NSDAP members prepared by French troops after the war in some villages. An excellent list can be found in StA Haslach, Politische Ausschreitungen - 1946, GmdA Löffingen - 2650; PfA Schonach - NSDAP, Ortschronik 1922–46, 22.5.1945.

15. On the social profile of the SA members see chap. 8.

16. The fact that the party turned toward the younger age groups only in 1932 in order to get them for National Socialism is without doubt evidence for the lack of success of Nazi propaganda.

17. Female members were only registered in two chapters. In Furtwangen the wife of the local veterinarian was a member of the chapter; in Schonach a woman joined the group in April 1932 (cf. note 7 above). In the village of Haslach 137 women supported the Nazi Party in summer 1930, but no woman was mentioned on the member list.

18. Geoffrey Pridham, *Hitler's Rise to Power—The Nazi Movement in Bavaria 1923–1933* (New York, 1973), 186–88; Zdenek Zofka, *Die Ausbreitung des National-sozialismus auf dem Lande* (Munich, 1979), 64–67; Martin Broszat, "Zur Struktur der NS-Massenbewegung," in *VJFZG* 1 (1983): 69. On the region of the Black Forest see *FZ,* 17.9.1930, "Der Schwarzwald und die Reichstagswahl." On the difficulties of paying the membership subscriptions see the section of this analysis dealing with the financial aspects of the Nazi activity. Kuner, head of the Nazi chapter in Schonach, maintained that his business suffered severely due to his

intensive activity on behalf of the NSDAP: PfA Schonach - NSDAP, Ortschronik 1922–1946, 21.1.1932; Kater, *Nazi Party* (n. 4), 180–81.

19. On this topic see chap. 11 below.

20. This suggests the *BLB*, especially the activity of this peasant movement in the Black Forest and above all in the southern part of the region. The movement confronted the local political and religious establishment and won wide support from the Catholic peasants who sympathized with the anticlerical aims of the movement, but did not join the movement as regular members. For the *BLB* see *Der Landbund: Sein Auftreten* (chap. 5, n. 7), as well as E. Bleibtreu, *Die Bauernbewegung im Bezirk Bonndorf.*

21. On the chapter in Löffingen see GmdA Löffingen - 491 (candidate list of the party for the community council); 2650 (Mitgliederliste); StA Haslach - Politische Ausschreitungen 1946; iv/2–106 (candidate list for the community council). This phenomenon had not been limited to the first phase of Nazi activities in the Black Forest. Even after the Reichstag Election of summer 1932 and after the reorganization of the party's structure by Gregor Strasser, the phenomenon of party activists who were not regular members was extremely common in the region. In a memorandum sent to Kuner by the *Gauleitung* in Karlsruhe, a lot of detailed information about the Nazi chapters in the district of Villingen is given. Several activists had taken upon themselves important key functions although they were not regular party members; see PfA Schonach, 5.8.1932. It is possible that these activists saw in an alike behavior an opportunity to avoid the membership subscription. The party was quite sensitive concerning the membership subscriptions. The payment of the subscription was a basic condition for the official registration as a new member of the party. Overdue payments were a reason for exclusion from the NSDAP. Some cases are mentioned in PfA Schonach - 9.4.1930, 9.9.1931, 28.12.1931. The importance of membership subscription for the financing of party activities will be discussed in chap. 8.

22. On members leaving the chapter in Schonach see two membership lists of 1932 and 1933 (cf. n. 7 above). On the peasants in the region of Schwarzwald-Baar see *Hschw.* - Seppenhofen - 7.2.1932; on the massive abandonment of party membership toward the end of 1932 see *Donaubote*, 7.11.1932. On the project of the dam lake near Schluchsee and the chapter of the NSDAP see PfA St. Blasien-Seelsorge, 5.11.1929; StaaF, BZ Neustadt, 244/183, 9.9.1930; PfA Schluchsee, Kirchenvisitationen - 1931; *Der Alemanne*, 3.12.1932. On the change of 15 NSDAP members to the Communist Party see *Schw T*, 31.7.1931. On the exclusion of party members see the case of Hettich, who had been excluded from the NSDAP, because he did not attend the meetings and could not pay his membership subscription. See PfA Schonach - NSDAP, 9.9.1931.

23. See note 7 above on the party statistics and also Grill, *Nazi Movement* (intro., pt. 2, n. 1), 225–31, and Kater, *Nazi Party* (n. 4), 250.

24. Klaus Tenfelde, "Proletarische Provinz. Radikalisierung und Widerstand in Penzberg/Oberbayern 1900–1945," in Martin Broszat, Elke Fröhlich, Anton Grossman (eds.), *Bayern in der NS-Zeit*, vol. 4 (Munich, 1984), 161; Mühlberger, "Germany" (n. 2), 111–13; idem, *Hitler's Followers;* on Brustein's argument that 40 percent of party members were workers, see his *Logic of Evil* (n. 4); Max Kele, *Nazis and Workers: National Socialist Appeals to German Workers 1919–1933*

(Chapel Hill, 1972), 170, 198–200; Martin Broszat, Elke Fröhlich, "Politische und soziale Macht auf dem Lande: die Durchsetzung der NSDAP im Kreis Memmingen," in *VJFZG* 25 (1977): 548–55; Geoffrey Pridham, *Hitler's Rise* (n. 18), 188; Franz Heyen, *Nationalsozialismus im Alltag—Quellen zur Geschichte des Nationalismus, vornehmlich im Raum Mainz-Koblenz-Trier* (Boppard, 1967), 52–56; Gerhard Paul, *Die NSDAP des Saargebietes 1920–1935* (Saarbrücken, 1987), 176–77; Rauh-Kühne, *Ettlingen,* 281; see also the case of Johann Langenegger from Rosenheim who went through the *SPD, USPD, KPD* to the *NSDAP.* P. Miesbeck, *Bürgertum und Nationalsozialismus in Rosenheim* (Rosenheim, 1995), 206–7.

25. On the phenomenon of nonorganized, though not Catholic workers who sympathized with the NSDAP, see T. Mason, *Sozialpolitik im Dritten Reich. Arbeiterklasse und Volksgemeinschaft* (Opladen, 1977), chap. 2; Childers, *The Nazi Voter* (chap. 6, n. 36), 257; Broszat, "Struktur" (n. 18), 57.

26. Two research works have mainly influenced the research on social groups supporting Hitler; they concentrate on the time before and after 1914: Rolf Dahrendorf, *Society and Democracy in Germany* (Garden City, 1967); and Moore Barrington, *Social Origins of Dictatorship and Democracy* (Boston, 1966). See also Hans-Jürgen Pühle, *Agrarische Interessenpolitik und preußischer Konservatismus im Wilhelminischen Reich 1893–1914* (Hannover, 1967); Shulamit Volkov, *The Rise of Popular Antimodernism in Germany. The Urban Master Artisans* (Princeton, 1978); Heinrich A. Winkler, *Mittelstand, Demokratie und Nationalsozialismus* (Cologne, 1972); idem, "From Social Protectionism to National Socialism—The German Small Business Movement in Comparative Perspective," in *JMH* 48 (1976): 1–18; see recently, K. Rohe, *Wahlen und Wählertraditionen* (n. 3), J. Winkler, *Sozialstruktur, Politische Traditionen und Liberalismus. Eine empirische Längsschnittstudie zur Wahlenentwicklung in Deutschland 1871–1933* (Opladen, 1995).

27. Among the pioneer works causing a lively discussion about the thesis of continuity and showing with great success the particularities of the Second Reich compared with the Weimar Republic with respect to social groups and classes are D. Blackbourn and G. Eley, *The Peculiarities of German History* (Oxford, 1984); David Blackbourn, "The Mittelstand in German Society and Politics 1871–1924," in *Social History* 4 (1977): 409–33.

28. For this context see *Statistik des Deutschen Reiches,* 382, I, Die Wahlen zum Reichstag am 14. September 1930; 434, Die Wahlen zum Reichstag am 31. Juli und 6. November 1932 und am 5. März 1933. The election results in Baden were published by the *Badisches Statistisches Landesamt,* Die Reichstagswahl am 20. Mai 1928, am 14. September 1930, 31. Juli und 6. November 1932, und am 5. März 1933, in Baden; Landtagswahl am 27. Oktober 1929. The results on the village level for the district elections on November 16, 1930, and the results of the presidential elections on February 2, 1932, and April 10, 1932, were only published in the regional newspapers. The results of the presidential election in the Reich and in Baden were only published in the *Statistik des Deutschen Reiches,* 434, 1932.

29. Heinz Haupt, "Mittelstand und Kleinbürgertum in der Weimarer Republik. Zu Problemen und Perspektiven ihrer Erforschung," in *Archiv für Sozialgeschichte* 26 (1986), 217–38; Friedrich Lenger, "Mittelstand und Nationalsozialismus? Zur politischen Orientierung von Handwerkern und Angestellten in der

Endphase der Weimarer Republik," in *Archiv für Sozialgeschichte* 29 (1989), 173–98.

30. See views on the support for the NSDAP by the lower middle classes: Richard Hamilton, *Who Voted for Hitler* (Princeton, 1982), chap. 2; Manstein, *Mitglieder* (n. 2), 46–89, 165–93; Winkler, *Sozialstruktur* (n. 26), 25–45. Historians having dealt with this topic before 1933 were H. Laswell, "The Psychology of Hitlerism," in *Political Quarterly* 4 (1933): 373–84; Theodor Geiger, "Panik im Mittelstand," in *Die Arbeit* 7 (1930): 637–59; Stephen, *Soziologie* (n. 1). See also Lenger's view on the historiography before 1933: Lenger, *Mittelstand* (n. 29), 176–80. During war time: Erich Fromm, *Escape from Freedom* (New York, 1941). Immediately after the war: S. Pratt, *The Social Bases of Nazism and Communism in Urban Germany*, M.A. thesis (Michigan State University, 1948); William Kornhauser, *The Politics Mass Society* (Glencoe, 1959); A. Beegle, C. Loomis, "The Spread of German Nazism in Rural Areas," in *American Sociological Review* 11 (1946): 724–34; Rohe, *Wahlen* (n. 3), chap. 4.3; Phillips Shively, "Party Identification, Party Choice, and Voting Stability: The Weimar Case," in *American Political Science Review* 66 (1972): 1203–25.

31. Rohe, *Wahlen* (n. 3), 160ff.; Hamilton, *Hitler* (n. 30); Childers, *Nazi Voter* (chap. 6, n. 36), 262–69; some examples from Jürgen Falter articles: "Wahlen und Wählerverhalten unter besonderer Berücksichtigung des Aufstiegs der NSDAP nach 1928," in K. D. Bracher et al. (eds.), *Die Weimarer Republik 1918–1933* (Düsseldorf, 1987), 484–504; idem, "Die Wähler der NSDAP 1928–1933: Sozialstruktur und parteipolitische Herkunft," in W. Michalka (ed.), *Die nationalsozialistische Machtergreifung* (Munich, 1984), 47–59. Besides the articles mentioned and many others, Falter summarized the results of his research in his book *Hitlers Wähler* (n. 3), especially in chapter 7.2; see also the review article of J. O'Loughlin et al., "The Geography of the Nazi Vote: Context, Confession and Class in the Reichstag Election of 1930," *Annals of the Association of American Geographers* 84, 3 (1994): 35–80.

32. On the votes cast by new voters for the success of the NSDAP in 1930 see Geiger, *Soziale Schichtung* (n. 1), 112; Maximilian Meyer, "Der Nichtwähler," in *Allgemeines Statistisches Archiv* 21 (1931): 495–525; H. Neisser, "Sozialistische Analyse des Wahlergebnisses," in *Die Arbeit* 7 (1930): 654–59; Hackett, *Nazi Party* (chap. 6, n. 36), 355–57; David Arns, *Grass-Roots Politics in the Weimar Republic: Long Term Structural Change and Electoral Behavior in Hessen-Darmstadt to 1930*, diss. (State University of New York at Buffalo, 1979), 377–79; Jeremy Noakes, *The Nazi Party in Lower Saxony* (Oxford, 1971), 153; Hamilton, *Hitler* (n. 30), 61; O'Loughlin, "Geography " (n. 31). On the difficulty of identifying the Nazi voters in 1930 and 1932 see Jürgen Falter, "The National Socialist Mobilisation of New Voters: 1928–1933," in Thomas Childers (ed.), *The Formation of the Nazi Constituency 1919–1933* (London, 1987), 202–31. Among the historians who deny a casting contribution of new voters to the success of the NSDAP are Reinhard Bendix, Seymour Lipset, "On the Social Structure of Western Societies," in *Berkeley Journal of Sociology* 5 (1959): 12. In this article Bendix follows Lipset, although he had supported the argument of new voters seven years ago in his article, Reinhard

Bendix, "Social Stratification and Political Power," in *American Political Review* 46 (1952): 357–75. See also Childers, *Nazi Voters* (chap. 6, n. 36), 191 and Shively, *Party Identification* (n. 30), 1216.

33. On the age of the voters see Pratt, *Social Bases* (n. 30), 206, 218; Falter, *National Socialist* (n. 32), 227; Childers, *The Nazi Voter* (chap. 6, n. 36), 227–28; on the question of support for the Nazi movement by German women see R. Evans, "German Women and the Triumph of Hitler," in *JMH* 1 (1976) (Demend Publication); H. Boak, "Our Last Hope. Women's Votes for Hitler—A Reappraisal," in *German Studies Review 2* (1989), 289–310; Shively, "Party Identification" (n. 30), 1220; Childers, *The Nazi Voter* (chap. 6, n. 36), 260, 264; M. Kater, "Frauen in der NS-Bewegung," in *VJFZG* 2 (1983), 202–41; J. Stephenson, "National Socialism and Women before 1933," in P. Stachura (ed.), *The Nazi Machtergreifung* (London, 1983), 33–48; on Catholics voting for the NSDAP see O. Heilbronner, D. Mühlberger, "Who Voted for Hitler Reconsidered: The Catholic Voters," *European History Quarterly,* vol. 27, 2 (1997), 217–46; Childers, *The Nazi Voter* (chap. 6, n. 36), 188–91, 258–61; Hamilton, *Hitler* (n. 30), 40–41, 371–73, 382–85; Falter, *Hitlers Wähler* (n. 3), chap. 6; Pridham, *Hitler's Rise* (n. 18), 139–45, 283–84; J. Horstmann, "Katholiken und Reichstagswahlen 1920–1933," in *Jahrbuch für Christliche Sozialwissenschaften* 27 (1986): 63–95; J. Henke, "Die Hochburgen der katholischen Parteien," in J. Dülffer et al. (eds.), *Deutschland in Europa. Kontinuität und Bruch* (Frankfurt, 1990), 354–63; also relevant is Rohe, *Wahlen* (n. 3), chap. 4.3; Winkler, *Sozialstruktur* (n. 26), 334–38.

34. See note 28 above and Hamilton, *Hitler* (n. 30), chap. 4–5.

35. See the bibliographical reference in note 33 above, and also Johannes Schauff, *Das Wahlverhalten der deutschen Katholiken im Kaiserreich und in der Weimarer Republik* (Mainz, 1975); R. Morsey, "Die katholische Volksminderheit und der Aufstieg des Nationalsozialismus," in K. Gotto, K. Repgen (eds.), *Kirche, Katholizismus und Nationalsozialismus* (Stuttgart, 1980); J. Hunt, "Between Ghetto and the Nation. Catholics in the Weimar Republik," in M. Dobkowski, I. Wallimann (eds.), *Towards the Holocaust* (Westport, 1983), 218.

36. Falter, *Hitlers Wähler* (n. 3), chap. 66; Hamilton, *Who Voted for Hitler* (n. 30), 40–41; A. Weber, *Soziale Merkmale der NSDAP-Wähler: Eine Zusammenfassung bisheriger empirischer Untersuchungen und eine Analyse in den Gemeinden der Länder Baden und Hessen,* diss. (Freiburg, 1969), 149; Horstmann, *Reichstagswahlen* (n. 33), 72–73; Hackett, *Nazi Party* (chap. 6, n. 36); T. Schnabel, "Das Wahlverhalten der Katholiken in Württemberg 1928–1933," in *Rottenburger Jahrbuch für Kirchengeschichte* 2 (1983): 103–4; Rohe, *Wahlen* (n. 3), 156.

37. Weber, *Soziale Merkmale* (n. 36), 120–25, 134; Falter, *National Socialist* (n. 32), 211; Arns, *Grass Roots* (n. 32), 354; Rohe, *Wahlen* (n. 3), 157; Hackett, *Nazi Party* (chap. 6, n. 36), 444–45; Paul, *NSDAP* (n. 24), 203–6; Rau-Kühne, *Ettlingen* (intro., pt. 2, n. 4), 280ff.

38. Rohe, *Wahlen* (n. 3); G. Plum, *Gesellschaftsstruktur und politisches Bewußtsein in einer katholischen Region, 1928–1933. Untersuchungen am Beispiel Regierungsbezirk Aachen* (Stuttgart, 1972), 112–14; Pridham, *Hitler's Rise* (n. 18), 142, 282; K. Holmes, *The NSDAP and the Crisis of Agrarian Conservatism in*

Lower Bavaria. National Socialism and the Peasants' Road to Modernity, diss. (Georgetown University, 1982), 230; Moeller, *German Peasants* (chap. 6, n. 27), 157–59; Heyen, *Nationalsozialismus* (n. 24), 24, 27; Zofka, *Ausbreitung* (n. 18), 45–55, 59–61; M. Broszat, E. Fröhlich, *Alltag und Widerstand: Bayern im Nationalsozialismus* (Munich, 1987), 117; Hackett, *Nazi Party* (chap. 6, n. 36), 436–57; Falter, *Hitlers Wähler* (n. 3), chap. 6.5.5, 6.5.6.

39. Grill, *Nazi Movement* (intro., pt. 2, n. 1), 190, 238; Bräunsche, *NSDAP in Baden 1928–1933* (intro., pt. 2, n. 1), 28–29; Braun, *Tauberbischofsheim* (intro., pt. 2, n. 4). This position is empirically backed up by a new research about election tendencies in favor of the NSDAP in Württemberg and Baden: J. Falter, H. Bobermann, "Die unterschiedlichen Wahlerfolge der NSDAP in Baden und Württemberg," in D. Oberndorfer, K. Schmitt (eds.), *Parteien und regionale politische Traditionen in der Bundesrepublik Deutschland* (Berlin, 1991), 283–98; Rohe, *Wahlen* (n. 3), 156; cf. also D. Ohr et al., "Weimarer Wahlen in zwei Dörfern des badischen Grenzlandes," in *Historical Social Research* 17/21 (1992): 4–48; W. Rinderle, B. Norling, *The Nazi Impact on a German Village* (Kentucky, 1993).

40. On the Nazi activity in the region of Koblenz see Heyen, *Nationalsozialismus* (n. 24), 81– 82. Heyen points to a crisis of the chapters in the region in 1931. It is quite possible that this can explain the stagnant development of 1932. On the region of Bamberg and for the Nazi activity in the region see W. Blessing, "Deutschland in Not, wir im Glauben . . . Kirche und Kirchenvolk in einer katholischen Region 1933–1949," in M. Broszat (ed.), *Von Stalingrad zur Währungsreform* (Munich, 1988), 3–20. T. Breuer, *Verordneter Wandel? Der Widerstreit zwischen nationalsozialistischem Herrschaftsanspruch und traditioneller Lebenswelt im Erzbistum Bamberg* (Mainz, 1992). On the support of the NSDAP by Catholic peasants in the Allgäu see Pridham, *Hitler's Rise* (n. 18), 105; D. Thränhardt, *Wahlen und politische Strukturen in Bayern 1848–1953* (Düsseldorf, 1973), 71–78; Winkler, *Sozialstruktur* (n. 26), 337. The present geographical and political situation of Silesia does not favor research about the NSDAP in this region. This obstacle may be removed in the coming years. The few existing works are: R. Bessel, *Political Violence and the Rise of Nazism: The Storm Troopers in Eastern Germany 1925–1934* (New Haven, 1984); H. Neubach, *Politiker und Parteien in Schlesien* (Dortmund, 1987), Rohe, *Wahlen* (n. 3), 156.

41. Thomas Klein, *Die Hessen als Reichstagswähler. Tabellenwerk zur politischen Landesgeschichte 1867–1933. Bd.II–I Regierungs-Bezirk Wiesbaden 1918–1933* (Marburg, 1993); F. Schmidt, "Wahlen und Wählerverhalten in der Weimarer Republik am Beispiel des Kreises Limburg," *Nassauische Annalen* 105 (1994): 195–221; R. Gabriele, *Wer wählte die NSDAP? Eine lokale Fallstudie im Kreis Euskirchen an Hand der Ergebnisse der politischen Wahlen 1920 bis 1933,* Ph.D. diss. (Bonn, 1984); F. Schäfer, *Das Eindringen des Nationalsozialismus in das Alltagsleben einer unterfränkischen Kleinstadt, dargestellt am Beispiel Hammelburgs* (Würzburg, 1994); on the Bavarian tourists see Hamilton, *Hitler* (n. 30), chap. 9; Hackett, *Nazi Party* (chap. 6, n. 36), 455–57; Pridham, *Hitler's Rise* (n. 18), 284–85; W. Schuster, "Die Reichs- und Landtagswahlen im Bezirksamt Traunstein 1920–1933." In *Historischer Verein für den Chiemgau zu Traunstein e.V. Jahrbuch* 6 (1994): 78; for general trends among Catholic voters see Heilbronner, Mühlberger, "Who Voted for Hitler Reconsidered" (n. 33).

Chapter 8

The epigraph by J. Goebbels is cited in J. Fest, *Hitler* (London, 1977), 473.

1. *Public sphere* in our context means the sphere that mediates between society and state in which the public organizes itself as the bearer of public opinion. In this sphere of society social and political life intersect. The fascist public sphere usually has an active, racist character beyond nationalism without class contradictions. On theory and definition of the public sphere see Jürgen Habermas, *Strukturwandel der Öffentlichkeit: Untersuchungen zu einer Kategorie der bürgerlichen Gesellschaft* (Berlin, 1962), chap. 1–2. On the fascist public sphere and the importance of fascist party organization see "Perspectives on the Fascist Public Sphere," a Discussion with Peter Bruckner et al., in *New German Critique* 11.1 (1977): 94–132; S. Payne, "The Concept of Fascism," in S. U. Larsen et al. (eds.), *Who Were the Fascists* (Bergen, 1980), 14–25; J. Linz, "Some Notes Toward a Comparative Study of Fascism in Sociological Historical Perspective," in W. Laqueur (ed.), *Fascism, A Reader's Guide* (Middlesex, 1982), 63; H. Jaschke, *Soziale Basis und soziale Funktion des Nationalsozialismus: Studien zur Bonapartismustheorie* (Opladen, 1982), 162–222; on the importance of the organization of the NSDAP several works have been published among which the most important and most well known should be mentioned here: W. Horn, *Führerideologie und Parteiorganisation in der NSDAP, 1919–1933* (Düsseldorf, 1972), chap. 4; P. Stachura, *Gregor Strasser and the Rise of Nazism* (London, 1983); idem, "The Political Strategy of the Nazi Party 1919–1933," in *German Studies Review* 3 (1980): 279; T. Childers, *The Nazi Voter* (chap. 6, n. 36); A. Tyrell, *Führer befiehl* (chap. 6, n. 10); Hackett, *Nazi Party* (chap. 6, n. 36); Hamilton, *Hitler* (chap. 7, n. 30), chap. 12–13. Other important research works on the topic are: D. Orlow, *History* (chap. 6, n. 7); T. Arafe, *The Development and Character of the Nazi Political Machine, 1928–1930, and the NSDAP Electoral Breakthrough,* Ph.D. thesis (Louisiana State University, 1976); J. Ciolek-Kümper, *Wahlkampf in Lippe* (Munich, 1976); Paul, *Aufstand* (chap. 6, n. 36); D. Ohr, "War die NSDAP-Propaganda nur bei 'nationalistischen' Wählern erfolgreich? Eine Aggregatdatenanalyse zur Wirkung der nationalsozialistischen Versammlungspropaganda," in *Kölner Zeitschrift für Soziologie und Sozialpsychologie* 4 (1994): 646–67; R. Bytwerk, "Die nationalsozialistische Versammlungspraxis. Die Anfänge vor 1933," in G. Diesener, Rainer Gries (eds.), *Propaganda in Deutschland. Zur Geschichte der politischen Massenbeeinflussung im 20. Jh.* (Darmstadt, 1996), 35–50.

2. In the manner of the "label" which was put on the *"Bielefelder Schule"* by James Sheehan in the framework of the research of modern German history, and especially of the Second Reich, see his critical remarks in *JOMH* 48 (1976), 567.

3. See note 13 below.

4. On the foundation, structure, and function of the early chapters in Bavaria see D. Douglas, *The Early Ortsgruppe: The Development of National Socialist Chapters 1919–1923,* Ph.D. thesis (University of Kansas, 1968); Tyrell, *Führer befiehl* (chap. 6, n. 10), 215–16, 230–32; on the part of the chapter see Hackett, *Nazi Party* (chap. 6, n. 36), 124–26; H. A. Turner, *Big Business and the Rise of Hitler* (Oxford, 1986); 117–18; J. Farquharson, *The Plough and the Swastika: The NSDAP and Agriculture in Germany 1928–1945* (London, 1976), 42. Changes in the function of chapters between 1931 and 1932 can be shown systematically in the

orders of the *Reichsleitung* published regularly in the official gazette of the *NSDAP Reichsleitung* (*Verordnungsblatt der Reichsleitung der NSDAP—VOBL*).

5. Orlow, *History* (chap. 6, n. 7), 129–30; 148–51, 207, 221; *VOBL*, 1, 1.6.1931, 1–2; Tyrell, *Führer befiehl* (chap. 6, n. 10), 245–47; P. Stachura, "Der kritische Wendepunkt? Die NSDAP und die Reichstagswahlen vom 20. Mai 1928," in *VJFZG* 26 (1978): 66–99; idem, *Gregor Strasser* (n. 1), 67–72; Arafe, *Development* (n. 1), chap. 4; Hackett, *Nazi Party* (chap. 6, n. 36), 118–26. On the regional aspect see J. Noakes, *Lower Saxony* (chap. 7, n. 32), 108–55; Examples for a power limitation of chapters in Baden see in: BAK, Sammlung Schuhmacher, 199, Rundschreiben Nr. 1, 15.12.1930. For a critical approach toward the argument of a "turn toward the rural regions in 1928" see J. Grill, "The Nazi Party's Rural Propaganda Before 1928," in *CEH* 2 (1982), 149–85.

6. Paul, *Aufstand* (chap. 6, n. 36), 95–103; Orlow, *History* (chap. 6, n. 7), 257–60; Stachura, *Gregor Strasser* (n. 1), 86–89; Grill, *Nazi Movement* (intro., pt. 2, n. 1), 231–34. On the election campaign 1932 see Childers, *Nazi Voter* (chap. 6, n. 36), chap. 4.

7. As a contemporary witness for the development of the NSDAP organization see C. Mierendorff, "Gesicht und Charakter der nationalsozialistischen Bewegung," in *Die Gesellschaft* 7, part 1 (1930): 493. Reports of the Prussian police and the German Ministry of the Interior, which showed them deeply impressed by the organizational ability of the NSDAP, may be found in BAK, NS 20/61 - Ausbreitung über die politische Entwicklung der NSDAP; BAK, R134/58 - Über die Entwicklung der Nationalsozialistischen Deutschen Arbeiterpartei seit Anfang 1929; R134/90 - Das hochverräterische Unternehmen der NSDAP. The press in the Black Forest which stood in opposition to the NSDAP realized the party's talent for organization and activity already in 1929. See *TB*, 28.10.1929, and the reports about political parties in Baden: StaaF, Lkk, 1617 - 19.8.1930; GLAK - 233/28388. "Die politische Lage in Baden," 5. October 1931.

8. Above all the British historians D. Blackbourn, G. Eley, and R. Evans. Among their numerous publications one should mention: Blackbourn, Eley, *The Peculiarities* (chap. 7, n. 27); G. Eley, *From Unification to Nazism* (London, 1986); R. Evans (ed.), *Society and Politics in Wilhelmine Germany* (London, 1986).

9. W. S. Allen, *The Nazi Seizure of Power. The Experience of a Single German Town 1922–1945* (New York, 1965). The following arguments are based on the newly revised edition from 1984, 295. In his critical remarks on the publication of the new edition Robert Moeller agrees that one should pay more attention to the problematic connection between the party's *Reichsleitung* in Munich and the chapters. See *JMH* 58 (1986): 369.

10. Hamilton, *Hitler* (chap. 7, n. 30), chap. 12–13; idem, "Reply to Commentators," in *CEH 1* (1984), 72–85, Zofka, *Ausbreitung* (chap. 7, n. 18); D. Mühlberger, "Central Control versus Regional Autonomy: A Case Study of Nazi Propaganda in Westphalia 1925–1932," in Childers, *The Formation* (chap. 7, n. 32), 64–103.

11. R. Bessel, "The Rise of the NSDAP and the Myth of Nazi Propaganda," in *The Wiener Library Bulletin* 51–52 (1980): 20–29. An indirect verification for Bessel's argument about the independence of the chapters can be found in Turner, *Big Business* (n. 4). See similar approaches toward the independence of chapters in this period or another in the history of the Nazi Party in H. Behrend, *Die Beziehun-*

gen zwischen der NSDAP-Zentrale und dem Gauverband Süd-Hannover-Braunschweig 1921–1933 (Frankfurt, 1981). Even though Grill does not deal with this specific question, one may understand his explanations in the way that the *Gau* of Baden several times took independent initiatives. On Baden see Grill, *Nazi Movement* (intro., pt. 2, n. 1); Jung, Durchburch (chap. 6, n. 25), 508.

12. Childers, *Nazi Voter* (chap. 6, n. 36); idem, "The Limits of National Socialist Mobilisation: The Elections of 6 November 1932 and the Fragmentation of the Nazi Constituency," 232–59; M. Richter, "Resource Mobilisation and Legal Revolution: National Socialist Tactics in Frankonia," 104–30; both in Childers (ed.), *Formation* (chap. 7, n. 32); I. Kershaw, "Ideology, Propaganda and the Rise of the Nazi Party," in P. Stachura (ed.), *The Nazi Machtergreifung* (London, 1983), 162–81. A new research work which continues the traditional centralistic methodology typical of historians in the sixties and seventies and does not use the new methodology typical of this school is: H. U. Thamer, *Verführung und Gewalt: Deutschland 1933–1945* (Berlin, 1987), 131–147; more recently, see Ohr, *Propaganda* (n. 1).

13. S. Barnowski, "Convergence on the Right. Agrarian Elite Radicalism and Nazi Populism in Pomerania 1928–1933," in L. E. Jones, J. Retallack (eds.), *Between Reform, Reaction and Resistance. Studies in the History of German Conservatism from 1789 to 1945* (Providence, 1993), 407–32; O. Heilbronner, "The Failure that Succeeded. The Nazi Party Activity in a Catholic Region in Germany 1929–1932," in *Journal of Contemporary History* 3 (1992): 544; idem, "Die NSDAP: Ein bürgerlicher Verein?" *Tel Aviver Jahrbuch für Deutsche Geschichte XXIV*, (1995): 65–78; M. Kieserling, *Faschisierung und gesellschaftlicher Wandel, Wiesbaden* 1991; Zofka, *Ausbreitung* (chap. 7, n. 18); idem, "Between Bauernbund and National Socialism: The Political Reorientation of the Peasants in the Final Phase of the Weimar Republic," in Childers, *Formation* (chap. 7, n. 32), 37–63; Mommsen, *Verschränkung* (chap. 7, n. 11), 166; W. S. Allen, "The Nazi Rise to Power: A Comprehensible Catastrophe," in C. Maier (ed.), *The Rise of the Nazi Regime* (Boulder, 1986), 16; idem, "Farewell to Class Analysis in the Rise of Nazism: Comment," in *CEH* 1 (1984): 54–62. Rudi Koshar used this argument for some years in a convincing way. See R. Koshar, *Social Life, Local Politics and Nazism—Marburg 1880–1935,* (Chapel Hill, 1987); idem, "Contentious Citadel: Bourgeois Crisis and Nazism in Marburg/ Lahn, 1880–1933," in Childers, *Formation* (chap. 7, n. 32), 11–36 (especially 30–32); idem, "From Stammtisch to Party— Nazi Joiners and the Contradiction of Grass Roots Fascism in Weimar Germany," in *JMH 1* (1987): 1–24; idem, "Two 'Nazisms'—The Social Context of Nazi Mobilization in Marburg and Tübingen," in *Social History* 1 (1982): 27–42. See also Linz, *Some Notes* (n. 1), 64; H. Mommsen, "National Socialism: Continuity and Change," in Laqueur, *Fascism* (n. 1), 185–86; Broszat, *Struktur* (chap. 7, n. 18), 65–66.

14. Tyrell, *Führer befiehl* (chap. 6, n. 10).

15. R. Wagner, *Propaganda und Organisation im Gau Baden der NSDAP* (Karlsruhe, 1931), 28.

16. PfA Schonach - NSDAP, 9.4.1930; *Der Alemanne,* 9.3.1932 - Menzenschwand.

17. StaaF, BZ Neustadt, 244/183 - 24.11.1930. A policeman reported about the

existence of a chapter in Hammereisenbach, although the party itself just reported about two members in this village: A. Zähringer was representative in the assembly of district representatives (*Bezirksverordnetenversammlung*), see *DT,* 17.11.30; F. Krammer joined the party only in 1931; see his personal file in the BDC. Cf. also StaaF, egd., 245/184 - 7.3.1932. Another example: StaaF, ibid., 244/183 -31.8.1930. The police reported about the existence of a chapter in Lenzkirch, which had organized a meeting in the village of Kappel. A week later (9.9.1930) the local policeman reported a meeting in the village which, as he said, had been organized on the initiative of the chapter in Grafenhausen. In early 1932 there was no chapter in Lenzkirch. See StaaF, ibid., 245/184 - 4.3.1932.

18. Der Führer, 28.2.1931 - Hüfingen; *Donaubote,* 8.1.1932 - Hüfingen; StaaF, BZ Neustadt, ibid., 11.5.1931 - Hinterzarten. Some months later only fourteen people appeared at a meeting in the village who came mainly from the surrounding area. The meeting had been organized on the initiative of the chapter in Grafenhausen. See StaaF, ibid., 31.8.1931 - Titisee; StaaF, Plakatsammlung, 1, 30.8.1931.

19. *DT,* 25.6.1930, Löffingen.

20. BAK, NS 22/1044 - Richtlinien für die Bildung von Ortsgruppen, Stützpunkten, Zellen; Wagner, *Propaganda* (n. 15).

21. Beside the examples at the beginning of part 2, which deals with the period until 1929, some more examples from the region may be mentioned: on the eve of the presidential elections in March–April 1932 the party organized meetings only in the villages of the Wutach region and did that in an irregular way. The first meeting for years was organized in the village of Göschweiler during this period. Here Hitler's party got 45.4 percent of the voters in March 1932. A meeting was held in Dittishausen on the eve of the second ballot of the presidential elections. Outcome: first ballot: Hitler, 47.1 percent; second ballot: Hitler, 47.5 percent. See StaaF, BZ Neustadt, 245/184 - 13.3. 1932; StaaF, BZ Neustadt, 246/185 - 4.4. 1932; *Hschw.,* 11.4.1932.

22. In 1930 the party got 18.5 percent of the total votes in Hüfingen, although the chapter was only founded in 1932. In Eisenbach the foundation of a chapter took place in 1931. A year before the party had got 26.1 percent of the votes. See StaaF, BZ Neustadt; 244/183 - 1.9.1931.

23. On the foundation of a Nazi chapter in Donaueschingen see StA Donaueschingen - Chroniken der Stadt *Donaueschingen* - Politik - 27.4.1930; V. Huth, *Donaueschingen, Stadt am Ursprung der Donau,* Sigmaringen 1989, 192–93. The party got 11.2 percent of the votes in this town in September 1930. On the foundation of a chapter in Neustadt see the reminiscences of F. Sattler in BAK, NS 26/132 19.11.1937 under the title *Die Entwicklung der NSDAP in Neustadt, Schwarzwald;* on the foundation of a chapter in Oberkirch see Renchtäler, 2.8.1930.

24. For Triberg see chapter 6, note 31, above. The *Bezirksleiter* in Furtwangen lived in the region of Donaueschingen and coordinated the party's activity from there. On intensive activities beyond propaganda meetings organized on initiative of the chapter, see GLAK, 347, 1943/18–29, 17.3.1930, 10.6.1930.

25. See note 19 above, and also the discussion concerning the supporters of the NSDAP who were not regular members of the party in chap. 7.

26. StaaF, BZ Neustadt, 244/183 - 28.7.1930 - Bonndorf; *SchwT,* 8.4.1932 - Seppenhofen; *Der Führer* 23.5.1931 - Hinterzarten.

27. PfA Schonach, ibid., 26.1.1931.

28. *Der Alemanne,* 16.8.1932.

29. *FZ,* 1.6.1931.

30. Wagner, *Propaganda* (n. 97), 6–9: see also Bytwerk, *Die nationalsozialistische Versammlungspraxis* (n. 83).

31. GLAK, 233/27915 - "Der agrarpolitische Apparat der bad. Nationalsozialisten," 7.

32. Party member Becker rented a room in the local inn of Furtwangen under a false name so that he could not be identified as a Nazi. See *Donaubote,* 21.3.1931.

33. For example, the inn "Lafette" in Titisee, the inn "Zum Ochsen" in St. Blasien, the assembly room "Gebert" in Löffingen, the inn "Zum Engel" in Neustadt. In Lenzkirch the NSDAP always used the "Hotel Adler" which belonged to Erwin Weishaar. In Grafenhausen party meetings were held in Franz Merk's inn "Zur Krone."

34. For a description of intensive Nazi activity beyond the election campaigns see Noakes, *Lower Saxony* (chap. 7, n. 32), 142; Orlow, *History* (chap. 6, n. 7), 161. On the Black Forest as a region "difficult to conquer" see chapter 6, note 1, above. On the infrastructual problems making political activity in the region difficult see ErzAF - B2- 55-146 Katholischer Volksverein - Tätigkeitsbericht - 1920/1921. On the problems arising for the organization of Nazi meetings because of the large distance to the central cities, see for example: StaaF, BZ Neustadt, 245/184, 25.1.1932 - Holzlebruck; the speaker Köbele delivered his speech in haste and without concentration, because he was afraid to miss the last train, so that he had to stay in the village overnight. Therefore, the meeting was unsuccessful, and the NSDAP left a bad impression behind.

35. On the propaganda concentration see Tyrell, *Führer befiehl* (chap. 6, n. 10), 256; Arafe, *Development* (n. 1), 100–101. An example for such an unusual event in the Black Forest region of Furtwangen in early 1930 is: GLAK, 347 - 1943/18 - 29., 17.3.1930.

36. Hitler only visited the larger towns at the bottom of the Black Forest: Offenburg - November 1930; Schweningen - April 1932; Freiburg - July 1932. Göring, Goebbels, Strasser, and Himmler did not visit the region at least until 1932. Even popular speakers like Münchmeyer, Crown Prince August Wilhelm, and others did not come to the Black Forest. Speakers of the party's head office in Baden, like Wagner and Roth, appeared very rarely in the region.

37. StaaF, BZ Neustadt, 244/183 - 24.8.1930 - Hinterzarten; *TB,* 12.8.1930, Schonwald.

38. See note 34 above.

39. StaaF, ibid., 245/184, 4.3.1932 - Lenzkirch; 6.3.1932 - Neustadt; ibid., 246/185 - 5.4.1932 - Neustadt; PfA Schonach, ibid., 9.11.1930, 1.3.1932. G. Huber, *Die Amtszeit von Bürgermeister Josef Huber in Todtnau von 1923–1933* (Bonn, 1993), 48.

40. Some examples for meetings canceled due to bad weather conditions and snow: ibid., 245/184, 11.3.1932, 10.3.1932; examples for lacking coordination and doubling of invitations: ibid., 246/185 - 31.7.1931.

41. Ibid., 244/183 - 30.8.1931, Kappel; 246/185, 27.7.1932 - Kappel; on success-ful meetings in 1932 after years of disappointment and low attendance see ibid., 244/183 - 25.1.1932 - Joostal; 245/184 - 1.2.1932 - St. Blasien; StaaF, BZ Schopfheim, T. 1 - 511 - 30.5.1932, 26.5.1932 - Schönau.

42. *Der Alemanne,* 9.3.1932 - Menzenschwand; *Donaubote,* 8.1.1932 - Hüfingen; StaaF, ibid., 246/185 - 27.7.1932 - Kappel.

43. *SchwB,* 3.4.1930 - Gutach; StaaF, ibid., 244/183 - 21.9.1931, Grafenhausen.

44. See note 34 on the meeting in Holzlebruck. On the carousals joined after the meetings see StaaF, ibid., 15.3.1931 - St. Blasien.

45. The research literature describes the Ortsgruppenleiter in general as a fight-ing leader personality. A condition for the foundation of a chapter, according to the common opinion, was the fact that there had been a person around matching the characteristics for an *Ortsgruppenleiter.* The *Reichsleitung* in Munich did not in general intervene with the nomination of an *Ortsgruppenleiter,* because it was thought that the fittest would win the struggle for that post in any case. See Hamil-ton, *Hitler* (chap. 7, n. 30), 323–24; Noakes, *Lower Saxony* (chap. 7, n. 32), 36, 96–97; Allen, *Seizure* (n. 9), 32–33.

46. On Erwin Weishaar see StaaF, BZ Neustadt, 1980/10/20, P. 176 Orts-bereisung; Lenzkirch - 1924; 1930; *Der Alemanne* - 5.10.1932. The NSDAP got 10 percent of the votes in this town in September 1930; on Dr. Rohde from Vöhren-bach see *DT,* 18.8.1930; *EvH,* 4.11.1930; on Altenstein, the pastor in Todtmoos, see *Der Alemanne,* 24.4.1932; StaaF, BZ Schopfheim, T.1 -510. There were 1,552 inhabitants in Todtmoos, 90 percent of them Catholic. In September 1930 the NSDAP got 22 percent of the votes, and already in summer 1932, 38.2 percent.

47. On Kuner see his personal file in the BDC. Extensive material about him can be found in PfA Schonach - NSDAP. For his nomination as *Ortsgruppenleiter* see 20.11.1931; on his change to the NSDAP: *TB,* 13.10.1929; on his popularity in the village see StaaF, LKK 7348, 11/1932.

48. *Der Alemanne,* 27.11.1932; StaaF, BZ Neustadt, 245/184, 26.2.1932, 29.2.1932.

49. StaaF, ibid., 244/183, 28.7.1930; Hschw., 18.1.1932 - Bonndorf.

50. E. Föhr, *Die sozialen und wirtschaftlichen Verhältnisse der Waldarbeiter im badischen Schwarzwald,* Achern i.B. 1921. On Serrer in the village of Oberharm-ersbach see K. Lehmann, "Die Zeit der Weimarer Republik und des National-sozialismus in Oberharmersbach," in *Die Ortenau* 67 (1987), 413. The NSDAP got 31.5 percent of the votes in the village in September 1930. On *Ortsgruppenleiter* Diehr in the town of Furtwangen see GLAK, 347 - 1943/18–29, 1.9.1930. More examples: F. Sattler, first *Ortsgruppenleiter* in Neustadt, was a traveling trader (see note 23 above). In Löffingen the mechanic Leopold Berger had been *Ortsgruppen-leiter* since 1931. In the village of Schönwald the carter Leopold Joos had been *Ortsgruppenleiter* since 1930.

51. See note 47 above.

52. Steinhof in Bonndorf was replaced by Hugo Weishaar, who had been leader of the party's faction in the community council since 1930. See his personal file in the BDC. Fritzsche in Löffingen was followed by Leopold Berger, who was also the district candidate of the NSDAP in the district council. In Schonach Kuner signed all the correspondence with the Party Head Office, although Hans Seitz was

the official *Ortsgruppenleiter*. Karl Hertrich was the following candidate for this post. Finally Kuner was nominated *Ortsgruppenleiter;* see PfA Schonach - NSDAP, 20.11.1931.

53. On police activity against Gemmecker, teacher, and *Ortsgruppenleiter* in Schönau, see StaaF, BZ Schopfheim, T.1–509, 28.3.1932. On police searches in the houses of the *Ortsgruppenleiter* in the administrative district of Donaueschingen see StaaF, BZ Donaueschingen, 1977/52–345, 29.7.1931. Sattler reported in 1937 on social and economic boycott of the inhabitants of Neustadt (see note 23 above). The same is true for Löffler, who reported about the NSDAP activity in the region of Haslach-Fischerbach. See chap. 6, note 12, above.

54. In 1931 altogether 21 propaganda events, meeting of members, German Evenings and Christmas celebrations were organized in the administrative district of Neustadt. Between July and September 1930, however, twice the number of events took place. See remarks on the issue of the linkage between election results and the frequency of propaganda events in Ohr, *Propaganda* (n. 1).

55. In these towns the support of the population for the NSDAP in September 1930 was largely above the average of the *Reich*. In summer 1932 this support clearly dropped below the average of the *Reich*.

56. Orlow, *History* (chap. 6, n. 7), 207, 221; *VOBL*, 1.6.1931; BAK, Sammlung Schumacher, 199, 20.12.1930, Rundschreiben Nr. 1.

57. For example Kuner in Schonach, who was a leading expert in municipal politics besides his position as *Ortsgruppenleiter*. On the activity of the *Ortsgruppenleiter* in municipal tasks see Grill, *Nazi Movement* (intro., pt. 2, n. 1), 194–205.

58. On the intensive propaganda activity in Germany in 1932 see Childers, *The Nazi Voter* (chap. 6, n. 36), chap. 4; in Baden: Grill, *Nazi Movement* (intro., pt. 2, n. 1), 235–39; in the Black Forest: GLAK, 347–1943/18 - 34, 2.3.-3.3.1932; StaaF, BZ Schopfheim, T.1-510. The previously mentioned characteristics were listed in the police reports, in lists about the frequency of meeting, about dates, subjects, and the names of speakers and heads of meetings.

59. See the list of titles in chapter 8, notes 1, 4, 5, 9–12, above.

60. Pridham, *Hitler's Rise* (chap. 7, n. 18), chap. 4 and 6; E. Fröhlich, "Die Partei auf lokaler Ebene: Zwischen gesellschaftlicher Assimilation und Veränderungsdynamik," in G. Hirschfeld, L. Kettenacker (ed.), *Der Führerstaat— Mythos und Realität: Studien zur Struktur und Politik des Dritten Reiches* (Stuttgart, 1981), 257–63; J. Kuropka, "Auf dem Weg in die Diktatur: Zu Politik und Gesellschaft in der Provinzialhauptstadt Münster 1929–1934," in *Westfälische Zeitschrift* 134 (1984): 157–99; Schäfer, *Eindringen* (chap. 7, n. 40), 73–90; Heyen, *Nationalsozialismus* (chap. 7, n. 24), 50, 57, 333–51; Braun, *Tauberbischofsheim* (intro., pt. 2, n. 4), 314–15; see also Faisst, "Marktfrage" als "Machtfrage" (intro., pt. 2, n. 4), 560–67.

61. The "seduction" by the NSDAP expressed in the descriptions of Nazi propaganda and activity is also reflected in title and results of the research of Thamer, *Verführung und Gewalt* (n. 12). See also Allen, *Seizure* (n. 9), 32, 85–86; in the Catholic region see, for example, Schäfer, *Eindringen* (chap. 7, n. 40), 67–93.

62. Zofka, *Ausbreitung* (chap. 7, n. 18); idem, *Bauernbund* (n. 13); Koshar, *Stammtisch* (n. 13), 23; W. Pyta, *Dorfgemeinschaft und Parteipolitik 1918–1933. Die Verschränkung von Milieu und Parteien in den protestantischen Landgebieten*

Deutschlands in der Weimarer Republik (Düsseldorf, 1996); S. Baranowski, *The Sanctity of Rural Life. Protestantism, Agrarian Politics and Nazism in Pomerania* (Oxford, 1996).

63. Hamilton, *Reply* (n. 10), 80–82; I think the British researcher D. Mühlberger is the only one who has paid attention to the problem. See his "Central Control versus Regional Autonomy: A Case Study of Nazi Propaganda in Westphalia 1925–1932," Childers, *The Formation* (chap. 7, n. 32), 64–103. See also H. Behrend, *Die Beziehungen zwischen der NSDAP Zentrale und dem Gauverband Süd-Hannover-Braunschweig 1921–1933* (Frankfurt a.M., 1981).

64. BAK, NS 22/1044, 25.11.1930, 1.12.1930 - Überlingen; 28.5.1931 - Heidelberg; 19.9.1929 - Offenburg; PfA Schonach - NSDAP - 13.4.1930.

65. See, for example, BAK, ibid., 18.12.1930, on the attempt of the *Gauleitung* to enlarge control over the *Ortsgruppenleiter* in Baden-Baden and on the intimidation to dismiss him in case of irregularities in his work.

66. In a letter of Wagner to Munich of July 19, 1930.

67. GLAK, 347 - 1943/18–29, 17.3.1930.

68. PfA Schonach - NSDAP - 19.1.1931; BAK, Sammlung Schumacher -199, Rundschreiben Nr. 1, 13.12.1930. The Nazi press from the *Kampfzeit* stressed this image again and again. Still, at the end of 1931 *Der Alemanne* wrote that the inhabitants of the Black Forest "woke up" at last (regarding the Nazi activity). *Der Führer,* however, wrote that no meeting of the party had taken place in the region until the end of 1931. See *Der Alemanne* 13.12.1931; *Der Führer,* 26.9.1931.

69. StaaF, LKK, 1648 - 14.11.1934.

70. See note 68 above and also BAK, Sammlung Schuhmacher - 199, Organisation der Gauleitung Baden, 31.1.1931; Grill, *Nazi Movement* (intro., pt. 2, n. 1), 231–34.

71. See note chapter 6, note 12, above, and also BAK, NS 26/132 - Die Entwicklung.

72. On the nomination of an *Ortsgruppenleiter* in Bonndorf see StaaF, BZ Neustadt, 244/183 - 28.7.1930 - Bonndorf. On the way Kuner had been nominated *Ortsgruppenleiter* in Schonach see PfA Schonach - NSDAP - 28.11.1931. On the instruction of the *Reichsleitung* in Munich, that the *Ortsgruppenleiter* had to be nominated only by the *Gauleiter,* see *VOBL,* 1.6.1931.

73. On the complaint of the *Ortsgruppenleiter,* his chapter would not get enough support from the *Gauleitung* in Karlsruhe, because it only had sent them inadequate speakers, see BAK, NS 22/1044, 1.12.1930, Überlingen, PfA Schonach - NSDAP - 9.11.1930; 19.1.1932, 1.3.1932.

74. See note 64 above.

75. BAK, NS 22/1044 - 26.6.1929, 18.11.1930.

76. Ian Kershaw, *The Hitler Myth, Image and Reality in the Third Reich* (Oxford, 1989), 26.

77. See the documents in Tyrell, *Führer befiehl* (chap. 6, n. 10). Evidence for an irregular use of the *Hitler-Gruß* can be found even in the *Reichsleitung* in Munich during the years 1932–33. On this topic see BAK, NS 22/1, 26.11.1932, 5.1.1933.

78. BAK, NS 22/1044, 19.9. 1929 - Offenburg.

79. On the correspondence with party institutions see PfA Schonach - NSDAP,

4.8.1931; on the correspondence with the community councils see GmdA Löffingen, iv2/491 - 29.10.1930, 20.3.1931.

80. PfA Schonach - NSDAP - 5.8.1932.

81. StaaF, Plakatsammlung, Teil 1, NSDAP. The conclusion is based on the study of 50 propaganda pamphlets of the NSDAP between April 1931 until April 1932.

82. StaaF, ibid., Plakat 19, 16.5.1931.

83. BAK, NS 26/132, ibid.; StaaF, BZ Neustadt, 245/184, 17.1.1932, Neustadt; StaaF, ibid., 244/183, 27.11.1932.

84. Wagner, *Propaganda* (n. 15), 6–9. On the other hand there were many meetings in the Black Forest which were not attended by enough adherents in order to sing the *"Horst-Wessel-Lied."* In these cases the meeting was closed without a musical ending; on some occasions the gramophone was put into action: StaaF, BZ Neustadt, 246/185, 29.5.1932 - Neustadt. On communists participating in the Nazi meetings, see *Der Führer,* 13.8.1931, Triberg; StaaF, BZ Neustadt, 245/184 - 7.3.1932; ibid., 246/185, 4.7.1932 - Rudenberg. During a meeting in Rudenberg several non-party members participated in the discussion. Party members who were not heads of a meeting or official speakers joined the discussion after the speech: StaaF, BZ Neustadt, 244/183, 1.9.1931, Eisenbach, 27.10.1931 - Urach.

85. GLAK, 233/27916, Der "Agrarpolitische Apparat." On the structure of the SA in the NSDAP in the region see the arguments below. On the relations between the associations (Vereine) and the NSDAP see chapter 10 below.

86. On the party speakers see BAK, Sammlung Schumacher, ibid., Rundschreiben Nr. 1, 15.12.1930, 20.12.1930; Arafe, *Development* (n. 1), chap. 5. On the growing share of local agitators in the propaganda activity see StaaF, BZ Schopfheim, T. 1-510; GLAK, 347 - 1943/18-34, 2.3., 3.3.1932.

87. The instructions of the *Gauleitung* in Karlsruhe were regularly published in the column *"Auf Schwarzem Brett"* ("On Black Board"). On activities and circulation of the Nazi press see chap. 8, under "The Press."

88. PfA Schonach, NSDAP, 20.11.1931, 4.8.1931, 18.5.1931.

89. Childers, *The Nazi Voter* (chap. 6, n. 36), 138, 151, 194, 198, 200–202; Childers, *Limits* (n. 12); Hamilton, *Hitler* (chap. 7, n. 30), 324.

90. Allen, *Seizure* (n. 9), 295. See also Behrend, *Die Beziehungen zwischen der NSDAP-Zentrale* (n. 63).

91. Zofka, *Ausbreitung* (chap. 7, n. 18), 64–72; Pridham, *Hitler's Rise* (chap. 7, n. 18), 98, 104.

92. *Der Führer,* March 1935. (See chapter 6, note 1, above.)

93. See the summary in I. Kershaw, *The Nazi Dictatorship: Problems and Perspectives of Interpretation* (London, 1989), chap. 3. The most well known discussion took place between David Abraham and Henry Turner. It is documented in numerous articles. See for example: "Debate," in CEH 2–3 (1984): 159–93; D. Abraham, *The Collapse of the Weimar Republic,* New Edition (New York, 1986); Turner, *Big Business* (n. 4). On the less vehement discussion between Turner and the German historian Dirk Stegmann see D. Stegmann, "Zum Verhältnis von Großindustrie und Nationalsozialismus 1930–1933," in *Historische Zeitschrift* 221 (1975), 18–68.

94. Turner, *Big Business* (n. 4); Hamilton, *Hitler* (chap. 7, n. 30), chap. 13; Hackett, *Nazi Party* (chap. 6, n. 36), 149–76.

95. Statements of the archives of the Rheingau treasurer can be found in H. Matzerath, H. Turner, "Die Selbstfinanzierung der NSDAP 1930–1932," in *Geschichte und Gesellschaft* 3 (1977): 59–92.

96. Turner, *Big Business* (n. 4), 115–23; Hackett, *Nazi Party* (chap. 6, n. 36), 149–76.

97. BAK, NS 22/1044, Richtlinien für die Bildung von Ortsgruppen; Wagner, *Propaganda* (n. 15), 8, 30–32.

98. Turner, *Big Business* (n. 4), 119–20; Hackett, *Nazi Party* (chap. 6, n. 36), 156–57; *VOBL,* 1, 1.6.1931, 2, 27.6.1931, 5, 19.8.1931.

99. The payment of membership subscriptions was one of the conditions for the existence of a chapter in Schonach. See PfA Schonach - NSDAP, 9.4.1930. In spite of his high rank in the village of Rohrhardsberg party member Primus Hettich was to be excluded from the party, because he did not pay his subscription. See PfA Schonach, 9.9.1931. The chapter of Löffingen was dissolved due to financial irregularities. See *DT,* 25.6.1930 - Löffingen. *Ortsgruppenleiter* Ernst Fritzsche was excluded from the NSDAP due to suspicions of corruption connected with his name. See GmdA Löffingen, iv2/491 - 20.3.1931. On sanctions against dilatory chapters see BAK, Sammlung Schumacher, 199, Rundschreiben Nr. 1, 20.12.1930; Turner, *Big Business* (n. 4), 119–20.

100. BAK, NS 22/1044 - 28.5.1931.

101. Orlow, *History* (chap. 6, n. 7), 148; Wagner, *Propaganda* (n. 15), 30–32; *Schw T,* 23.1.1932; Der Führer, 28.2.1931 - Haslach; PfA Schonach, NSDAP, 17.9.1930.

102. PfA Schonach, NSDAP, 26.1.1931, 28.12.1931.

103. Prices for January 1929 from: *Statistisches Jahrbuch für das Land Baden,* BSL, 1930, 184–86.

104. PfA Schonach, NSDAP, 26.1.1931, 1.3.1932.

105. On the importance of the local inn for the local social life see chap. 10 of this analysis which deals with the middle-class infrastructure and its decline.

106. On the events of the *Deutscher Abend* as means for financial readjustment see PfA Schonach, NSDAP, 26.1.1931.

107. On the financial expenses connected with the organization of an intensive election campaign, for example toward the presidential elections, see PfA Schonach, NSDAP, 29.2.1932.

108. PfA Schonach, NSDAP, 9.11.1930; 1.3.1932.

109. See the case reported by the anti-Nazi newspaper "Lahrer Anzeiger": speaker Huber from Ibach worked for the NSDAP because he had been in need of money. According to the newspaper report Huber had explained that he could deliver a political speech for every party, if it would offer him a well-paid position. On the speaker profession as an income source see StaaF, LKK, 1617 - 20.2.1930; BAK, NS 22/1044 - 19.7.1930.

110. On Friedrich Sattler's recollection of his activity in the region see Neustadt BAK, NS 26/132.

111. Paul, *Aufstand* (chap. 6, n. 36), 256; PfA Schonach, NSDAP, 20.2.1932, 27.2.1932.

112. On pamphlets of the *Reichsleitung* and the *Gauleitung* in Munich and Karlsruhe and the local print products see StaaF, Plakatsammlung, Teil 1.

113. Bessel, "Rise of the NSDAP" (n. 11). The critical remarks are published in Kershaw, "Ideology" (n. 12), 171–73.

114. Heyen, *Nationalsozialismus* (chap. 7, n. 24), 50; L. Haupts "Nationalsozialismus in Aachen," *Z. des Aachener Geschichtsvereins, II,* 1992/93, 612–13. For East Bavaria see W. Stäbler, *Weltwirtschaftskrise und Provinz: Studien zum wirtschaftlichen, sozialen und politischen Wandel im Osten Altbayerns 1928 bis 1933* (Kallmuenz, 1992), 314–15; for Hammelburg see Schäfer, *Eindringen des Nationalsozialismus* (chap. 7, n. 40), 92.

115. Allen, *Seizure* (n. 9), 79–82; Hamilton, *Hitler* (chap. 7, n. 13), 320; Matzerath-Turner, *Selbstfinanzierung* (n. 95).

116. K. D. Bracher, *Die Auflösung der Weimarer Republik* (Villingen, 1964), 648–54; Allen, *Seizure* (n. 9), 84; Kershaw, *Ideology* (n. 12), 172; Mommsen, *Verschränkung* (chap. 7, n. 11), 166; B. Peterson, "Regional Elites and the Rise of National Socialism, 1920–1933," in M. Dobkowski, I. Wallimann (eds.), *Radical Perspectives of the Rise of Fascism in Germany, 1919–1945* (New York, 1989), 172–93; Baranowski, "Convergence on the Right" (n. 13).

117. Max Weber, *Wirtschaft und Gesellschaft* (Tübingen, 1976), 170; for a modern definition see for example Richard Trainor, *Black Country Elites: The Exercise of Authority in an Industrialised Area 1830–1900* (Oxford, 1994), 18 ("those individuals, from whatever class or stratum, who held leadership posts in the major institutions of the district or one of its towns").

118. G. Wurzbacher, *Das Dorf im Spannungsfeld industrieller Entwicklung* (Stuttgart, 1954), 33–39. On the local notables in rural areas of the Weimar Republic see also W. Kaschuba, C. Lipp, *Dörfliches Überleben* (Tübingen, 1982), 572–98; Koshar, *Social Life* (n. 13), 14; Z. Zofka, "Dorfeliten und NSDAP. Fallbeispiele der Gleichschaltung aus dem Kreis Günzburg," in M. Broszat (ed.), *Bayern in der NS-Zeit,* 4 (Munich, 1981), 384–434, and only recently, Pyta, *Dorfgemeinschaft und Parteipolitik 1918–1933* (n. 62), 433–38, whose main concern is local Protestant notables.

119. Blackbourn, Eley, *Peculiarities* (chap. 7, n. 27), 251–60; D. Blackbourn, *Populists and Patricians. Essays in Modern German History* (London, 1987), 123–35; Hamilton, *Hitler* (chap. 7, n. 13), 437–53, 631, Peterson, *Elites* (n. 116); Pyta, *Dorfgemeinschaft und Parteipolitik 1918–1933* (n. 62), 457–71.

120. The position of the priest at the end of a list of local notables is above all the result of the fact that Wurzbacher's research mainly dealt with Protestant villages after 1945. Ample evidence of the struggle of Catholic priests against the NSDAP is given in ErzAF, BN/NS2; an exceptional case can be found in the village of Legau/Allgäu. There the local Catholic priest M. Goett supported the Nazi Party while most of the inhabitants rejected the party. See P. Hoser, "Hitler und die katholische Kirche," in *VJZG,* 3 (1994), 473–84.

121. During a police search of houses of Nazi activists *Gerichtsrat* Dr. Schmoll was exposed as a sympathizer with the NSDAP. See StA Donaueschingen, Chroniken der Stadtverwaltung, Donaueschingen, 19.8.1931, StaaF, BZ Donaueschingen, 1977/52 - 345, 3.8. 31. During a police search in the region of Triberg

connections between *Regierungsrat* Alfred Scherer and the SA were exposed: StaaF, BZ Villingen, 1979/82 - 1244, 18.4.1931.

122. See the case of Müssle in Neustadt mentioned in note 148 above. Friedrich Sattler from Neustadt had an important post in the municipality after World War I. According to his evidence his joining the NSDAP was vehemently criticized in the town. See BAK, NS 26/132.

123. BAK, ibid.; ErzAF B2/NS 2, 13.7.1932, 24.5.1931 - Zell. a.H.

124. Merk's inn in Grafenhausen; *Nationalsozialistisches Jahrbuch,* 1932; *Der Alemanne,* 24.4.1932, Todtmoos.

125. StaaF, BZ Neustadt 246/185 - Rudenberg - 4.7.1932. Ludwig Winterhalder, an important personality from Neustadt, and Alfred Schworer, the treasurer of the village of Friedenweiler, justified the ideology of the NSDAP during a meeting in the village. The chapter in Löffingen invited the local notabes to a closed meeting of the NSDAP. They agreed to visit the meeting. See GmdA Löffingen X13/2648.

126. Grill, *Nazi Movement* (intro., pt. 2, n. 1), 203–5.

127. On Kuner see note 47 above.

128. On the notables from Furtwangen, see StaaF, BZ Donaueschingen 1977/52–345, Juli 1931. On the Protestant pastor of Todtmoos see *Der Alemanne,* 24.4.1932. On the postman and village mayor from Breitnau see Detlef Herbner, *40 Jahre CDU Breitnau* (Titisee - Neustadt 1986), 3–4. On the pharmacist of Vöhrenbach see *DT* 18.8.1930 - Vöhrenbach; EvH, 4.11.1930. On the dentists from the region of Donaueschingen see *SchwT,* 2.4.1932; ErzAF - B2/NS 1, 18.10. 1930 - Furtwangen.

129. ErzAF - B2/NS 1, 18.10.1930 - Furtwangen.

130. On Emil Wehrle see M. Kimmig, *Die Chronik von Rohrbach im Schwarzwald* (Furtwangen 1981), 222. On the circulation of the *Völkische Beobachter* in Dr. Ruch's consultation room see BAK, NS 26/132. On Dr. Gemmecker from Schönau see the BDC; on Stengele from St. Blasien see *Der Alemanne,* 4.2.1932; on Hermann Leitz, publisher and editor of the *Schwarzwälder Tagblatt,* see *DT,* 20.1.1932 - Furtwangen.

131. Lists of the local officeholders in small towns and villages were published in the records of the *Ortsbereisungen* which were conducted by the district inspectors in the villages of the region every four or five years; they were also published in the different address booklets of the bigger towns of the region. With the exception of Weishaar and Merk there were no holders of high or important offices among the NSDAP members. The lists of peasants' representatives and of the heads of the agricultural chambers can be found in StaaF, BZ Neustadt, 1986/68–623, Landwirtschaftlicher Bezirksverein; StaaF, BZ Neustadt, P. 93/199 - Bezirksbauernrat; StaaF, BZ Neustadt, Kart. 93/201 - Landwirtschaftskammer - Wahlen, 1925. With the exception of Huber, Dorer, Primus, and Weishaar nobody was a member of or sympathizer with the NSDAP later on. Huber and Primus appeared as representatives of the peasant association and the agricultural association; a list of all commercial enterprises in towns and villages of the administrative district of Neustadt can be found in Bad. Gewerbeaufsichtsamt Verzeichnis der Betriebe der Amtsbezirke Neustadt vom 2.8.1926; StaaF BZ Neustadt Kart. 28/67.

132. Adrian Kopf and Alfred Wildmann, artisans and the heads of the local trade association in Zell a.H., were also Nazi activists. See Mössinger, *Zell* (chap.

7, n. 10), 358, 362–63; the situation in Schiltach was similar, see StA Schiltach IV/2–6 - 1930, XL/3–5, Gewerbe und Handwerker - Mitgliederverzeichnis 1931.

133. Until 1925 Dr. Vogel from Grafenhausen had been a member of the SPD, which got at this time two to five percent of the votes. Primus and Dorer had previously been members of the peasant parties, but had not succeeded in strengthening the position of these parties in the region of Furtwangen. The *BLB* was extremely weak in the region. Many representatives of the *BLB* had joined the Wirtschaftspartei or the DNVP, which were relatively weak in the southern part of the region, before they finally joined the NSDAP. Leitz, publisher and editor of the largest newspaper in Furtwangen, had been a member of the DVP, which could not get more than five percent of the votes in the town.

134. Primus Hettich was a council member in Rohrhardsberg, but had lost his interest in the NSDAP since summer 1931. Also Alfred Scherer from Triberg left the party after its success in summer 1932. See PfA Schonach, NSDAP, 9.9.1931, 8.8.1932.

135. On the *BLB* see chapter 7, note 20, above. On the management of the *BLB* after it had left the peasant's movement see the article by Josef Albicker, one of its representatives. On the *BLB* in the Baar region, see *DT,* 8.11.1930.

136. Albicker, who had changed from the *BLB* to the NSDAP, was considered a local poet (*Heimatdichter*) in the region of Donaueschingen and a popular partner for discussions. See *SchwT,* 8.3.1932. More examples were Josef Berger from Löffingen, an excellent athlete, and Rudolf Schyle from Schonach, a popular jazz musician. See Hamm, *Chronik* (chap. 7, n. 13), 168.

137. Take for example a high rank officer, who visited Hinterzarten and replaced the otherwise prevented speaker during a Nazi meeting in the village: StaaF, BZ Neustadt, 244/183, 24.8.1930 - Hinterzarten.

138. On Goett see Hoser, *Hitler* (n. 120); on Senn see Rau-Kühne, *Ettlingen* (intro., pt. 2, n. 4), 265ff; for Liebel see Pridham, *Hitler's Rise* (chap. 7, n. 18), 108–13, especially n. 111.

139. Mommsen, *Verschränkung* (chap. 7, n. 11), 166; Hamilton, *Hitler* (chap. 7, n. 30), 371–73, 382–85; Pyta, *Dorfgemeinschaft* (n. 118).

140. On notables in Catholic regions see also E. Peterson, *The Limits of Hitler's Power* (Princeton, 1969), 411; Kaschuba, *Dörfliches Überleben* (n. 118); E. Kleinöder, "Verfolgung und Widerstand der katholischen Jugendvereine. Eine Fallstudie Eichstatt," in Broszat, *Bayern in der NS Zeit,* II (chap. 7, n. 24), 186–91.

141. E. Fröhlich, *Partei auf lokaler Ebene* (n. 60), 262; Zofka, *Ausbreitung* (chap. 7, n. 18), 100–104; idem, "Bauernbund" (n. 13), 49–50.

142. O. Hale, *The Captive Press in the Third Reich* (Princeton, 1964), 1–75; H. Wilcox, "The Nazi Press before the Third Reich: Völkische Presse, Kampfblätter, Gauzeitungen," in F. Homer, L. Wilcox (ed.), *Germany and Europe in the Era of the Two World Wars* (University of Virginia Press, 1986), 106–7.

143. P. Stein, *Die NS-Gaupresse 1925–1933* (Munich, 1987), 175; Paul, *Aufstand* (chap. 6, n. 36), 185.

144. Hamilton, *Hitler* (chap. 7, n. 30); idem, *Reply* (n. 10).

145. Grill, *Nazi Movement* (intro., pt. 2, n. 1), 207–8; BAK, NS 26/1014 - *Der Führer.*

146. *EvH,* 4.10.1930 - Furtwangen; *DT,* 17.12.1931, 24.6.1931 - Furtwangen.

147. BAK, NS 26/132; StaaF, BZ Neustadt, 253/192 - Zeitungen, *Feldberg Rundschau;* BAK, NS 26/1008 - Feldberg Rundschau, 7.11.1931.
148. StaaF, ibid., 11.12.1931, 27.11.1931; BAK, ibid.
149. BAK, ibid.; ErzAF, B2/NS2 - 11.11.1930 - Schenkenzell.
150. *Der Alemanne,* Mittelstand; Sondernummer zur Reichspräsidentenwahl, 2.3.1932; "Der Bolschewismus vor den Toren," *Der Alemanne,* Sondernummer zur Reichspräsidentenwahl, 6.3.1932.
151. Beside the evidence for an irregular distribution of the newspaper we have information about the circulation of the *Schwarzwälder Tagblatt* and its regional editions. In summer 1932 the newspaper (including the regional editions) was distributed in 6,500 copies. Six thousand had been copies of the main newspaper (*Kopfzeitung*) so that only several hundred copies of the regional editions were distributed. There is no way of discovering to whom these editions were distributed. How many readers actually read these papers? How many copies returned from the shops to the distributors, because nobody wanted to buy them? The large circulation of the *Schwarzwälder Tagblatt* was not new. Years before, the newspaper had already been the paper with the largest circulation in Furtwangen and the surrounding villages. See Sperlings Zeitschriften - Adreßbuch, 1930–33, Furtwangen; Stein, Gaupresse (n. 143), 273. See also StaaF, BZ Neustadt, 253/192, 27.11.1931.
152. BAK, NS 26/132.
153. *Der Alemanne,* 27.9.1932.
154. StaaF, BZ Neustadt, 244/183 - 27.19.1931, Urach; in Haslach, where the *Anzeiger* was published, 457 inhabitants supported the party in 1930; in July 1932 only 455 supporters were left.
155. Grill based his work on the paper *Der Führer* as a main primary source about the NSDAP in Baden before 1933.
156. On the report about the foundation of a chapter in Hüfingen at least one year before its actual foundation see note 22 above. According to a police report less than 200 persons had joined a Nazi meeting in Grafenhausen, while the report in the newspaper *Der Führer* reported at least 400 participants. See StaaF, BZ Neustadt, 244/183 - 21.9.1931; *Der Führer,* 26.9.1931. *Der Führer* also reported that party member Dreher had spoken at the meeting, while the police reported that Dreher did not appear at the meeting due to a nervous breakdown.
157. Advertisements of Robert Schechter from Villingen and the department store Knopf in Freiburg: *SchwT,* 9.10.1931, 16.10.1931.
158. Renchtäler, 30.9.1931, 23.4.1931; ("Die Zeitung wird gegen die nationalsozialistische Partei in ihrem Kampf gegen der regionale katholische Presse keine feindliche Position beziehen"); *DT,* 7.11.1930; ("Hitler muß Kanzler werden") *Hoch.Schw.,* 4.8.1932; *AvK,* 12.9.1930. On the *Anzeiger* see also M. Hildenbrand, "Die nationalsozialistische Machtergreifung in einer Kleinstadt - Haslach i.K. im Jahre 1933," in *Die Ortenau* 63 (1983), 3–4; *EvW,* 30.7.1932 - Schonach. ("Nazis should not be blamed for throwing stones through the windows of the Church as long as there is no clear evidence for that.")
159. A description of the bourgeois-liberal press, including the press of the *BLB,* can be found in chap. 5 above.
160. On the economic difficulties of the Catholic newspaper readers see *TB,*

12.10.1931; on the crisis of the Catholic newspapers see PfA Schonach - ibid., 20.12, 1931. See also i 17.12, 1931 - Furtwangen.

161. *KN,* 11.2.1932 - Schutterwald: *Donaubote,* 27.11.1931; *TB,* 13.1.1932, 20.2.1932. These are only some examples. A more detailed discussion of the anti-communist position of the Catholic press can be found in chapter 11 about the decline of the Catholic infrastructure in the region.

162. See note 145 above.

163. Pridham, *Hitler's Rise* (chap. 7, n. 18), 244–53; Norbert Frei, *National-sozialistische Eroberung der Provinzpresse* (Stuttgart, 1980), 86–112; Rau-Kühne, *Ettlingen* (intro., pt. 2, n. 4), 271; another bourgeois *Wegbereiter* for the Nazi Party was the *Rosenheimer Anzeiger.* See Miesbeck, *Bürgertum* (chap. 7, n. 25), 337.

164. Details from Stein, *Gaupresse* (n. 143), 191–222.

165. P. Merkel, *The Making of a Stormtrooper* (Princeton, 1980); C. Fischer, *Stormtroopers: A Social, Economic and Ideological Analysis, 1929–1935* (London, 1983); C. Bloch, *Die SA und die Krise des NS-Regimes 1934* (Frankfurt, 1970); H. Bennecke, *Hitler und die SA* (Munich, 1962); J. Nyomarkay, *Charisma and Factionalism in the Nazi Party* (Minneapolis, 1967); P. Longerich, *Die braunen Bataillone—Geschichte SA* (Munich, 1989); E. Reiche, *The Development of the SA in Nürnberg 1922–1934* (Cambridge, 1986); D. R. Wernette, *Political Violence and German Elections, 1930 and July 1933,* diss. (University of Michigan, 1974).

166. On the "martyrs of the Party" from the lines of the SA see J. Baird, "Goebbels, Horst Wessel and the Myth of Resurrection and Return," in *JOCH* 4 (1982): 633–49. On the SA as a financial source see Hackett, *Nazi Party* (chap. 6, n. 36), 167–73. On the revolutionary and fighting character of the SA see R. Bessel, *Political Violence and the Rise of Nazism. The Storm Troopers in Eastern Germany 1925–1934* (New Haven, 1984); Reiche, Development (n. 165); Fischer, *Stormtroopers* (n. 165).

167. Bessel, Fischer, and Reiche reached equivalent conclusions in their works on the social structure of the SA. See also M. Jamin, *Zwischen den Klassen: Zur Sozialstruktur der SA-Führerschaft* (Wuppertal, 1984). Jamin tries to show the the social structure of the SA was broader than usually thought and included numerous members of the middle classes in responsible positions. On the connection between SA members and the Communist Party and the fluctuation between these two groups see C. Fischer, "Class Enemies or Class Brothers? Communist-Nazi Relations in Germany 1929–1933," in *European History Quarterly* 3 (1985): 259–80.

168. GLAK, 347 - 1943/18–29 - 10.6.1930 - Triberg - Furtwangen; StaaF, BZ Villingen 1979/82 - 1243, 10.6.1930.

169. On the opening of the *Gausturmvorschule* of the SA in 1931 see StaaF, BZ Villingen, 1979/82 - 1245, 15.4.1932, 16.4.1932. On the SA in Eisenbach see *Donaubote,* 2.10.1931.

170. See Dr. Vogel's call on the youth in the Black Forest to join the SA: StaaF, BZ Neustadt 244/183, 1.6.1931 - Eisenbach. On the SA units in the adminstrative district of Donaueschingen see StaaF, BZ Donaueschingen, 1977/52 - 345, 29.7.1931, 4.7.1931. On the SA members in the administrative district of Villingen in 1932 see StaaF, Bz Villingen, ibid., 18.4.1932; PfA Schonach, NSDAP, 19.1.1931. The following supplemental data should be mentioned: there were 14

SA members in Triberg; in Schonach there were nine; a year before, seven members were counted.

171. GLAK, 233/17916, a - 4.12.1932. Organisation der S.A.

172. *Donaubote,* 2.10.1931 - Eisenbach; StaaF, BZ Neustadt, 246/185 - 23.7.1932 - Grafenhausen. Although there is no detailed information about the exercises of the SA in Eisenbach, one can come to the conclusion—according to the average age of the SA members (all above 30 years were accepted)—that these exercises in no way demanded excellent physical conditions or extreme sportsmanship of the participants.

173. On the event in Hornberg see the memories of 1935 which had been published in *Der Führer* (cf. chap. 6, n. 1 above).

174. See note 29 above.

175. StaaF, BZ Donaueschingen, 1977/52 - 345, 29.7.1931. On the event in St. Georgen see *Donaubote,* 25.7.1931, "Mobilmachung"; StaaF LKK, 1615 - 6.9.1931.

176. ErzAF, B2/NS2 - 7.7.1932 - Waldkirch, 12.7.1932 - Löffingen; StaaF, BZ Neustadt, 245/186, 12.7.1932.

177. *Der Alemanne,* 3.11.1932 - Bonndorf.

178. Fischer, *Stormtrooper* (n. 165), 53–54, 183.

179. Pridham, *Hitler's Rise* (chap. 7, n. 18), 165–65; Heyen, *Nationalsozialismus* (chap. 7, n. 24), 33–34.

Chapter 9

1. A. Hitler, *Mein Kampf,* 2 (Munich, 1940), chap. 6; J. Goebbels, *Vom Kaiserhof zur Reichskanzlei* (Berlin, 1934).

2. Z. Zeman, *Nazi Propaganda* (Oxford, 1973), chap. 1; E. Bramsted, *Goebbels and National Socialist Propaganda 1925–1945* (London, 1965); M. Broszat, *German National Socialism* (Santa Barbara, 1966), 193; Tyrell, *Führer befiehl* (chap. 6, n. 10), chap. 6; Horn, *Führerideologie* (chap. 8, n. 1), chap. 5; Marxian historiographers, who stress the importance of Nazi propaganda, are: W. Rüge, *Deutschland von 1917 bis 1933* (Berlin [Ost], 1967), 354; W. Münzenberg, T. Schulz (eds.), *Propaganda als Waffe: Ausgewählte Schriften 1919–1940* (Frankfurt, 1977).

3. See notes 10, 11, and 12 in chap. 8; Gerhard Paul's work was recently published. It is the first systematic attempt to analyze the propaganda system of the NSDAP during the *Kampfzeit.* See Paul, *Aufstand* (chap. 6, n. 36); for shorter analysis see Bytwerk, "Die nationalsozialistische Versammlungspraxis" (chap. 8, n. 1).

4. Broszat, *Struktur* (chap. 7, n. 18), 66; Kershaw, *Ideology* (chap. 8, n. 12), 163–67.

5. Childers, *The Nazi Voter* (chap. 6, n. 36); M. Broszat, *Hitler and the Collapse of Weimar Germany* (London, 1988), 79; Kershaw, *Ideology* (chap. 8, n. 12). A useful survey can be found in C. Fischer, *The Rise of the Nazis* (Manchester, 1995).

6. Ciolek-Kümper, *Wahlkampf in Lippe* (chap. 8, n. 1), 155; Allen, *Seizure* (chap. 8, n. 9), 87; H. Mommsen, "The Breakthrough of the National Socialists as

a Mass Movement," in M. Laffan (ed.), *The Burden of German History* (London, 1989), 108; Noakes, *Lower Saxony* (chap. 7, n. 32), 219–20.

7. O. Heilbronner, "The Role of Nazi Antisemitism in the Nazi Party's Activity and Propaganda—A Regional Historiographical Study," in *Leo Baeck Institute Year Book 35* (1990), 397–439.

8. Kershaw, *Hitler Myth* (chap. 8, n. 76).

9. Bessel, *Rise* (chap. 8, n. 11); Mommsen, *Breakthrough* (n. 6); and especially Paul, *Aufstand* (chap. 6, n. 36), 255ff.

10. Paul, *Aufstand* (chap. 6, n. 36), 64–69; Childers, *The Nazi Voter* (chap. 6, n. 36), 122–29, 194; Mühlberger, "Central Control" (chap. 8, n. 10), 72–73; Orlow, *History* (chap. 6, n. 7), chap. 5.

11. Arafe, *Development* (chap. 8, n. 1), chap. 4; Hackett, *Nazi Party* (chap. 6, n. 36), chap. 3.

12. Paul, *Aufstand* (chap. 6, n. 36), 70–82; Childers, *The Nazi Voter* (chap. 6, n. 36), 137–40; U. Kissenkoeter, *Gregor Strasser und die NSDAP* (Stuttgart, 1978), 55–60; Hackett, *Nazi Party* (chap. 6, n. 36), chap. 5; Arafe, *Development* (chap. 8, n. 1), 112–15.

13. Paul, *Aufstand* (chap. 6, n. 36), 95–97; Bytwerk, *Die nationalsozialistische Versammlungspraxis* (chap. 8, n. 1); Kissenkoeter, *Gregor Strasser* (n. 12); Childers, *The Nazi Voter* (chap. 6, n. 36), 194–95; idem, *Limits* (chap. 8, n. 12), 234–35; Orlow, *History* (chap. 6, n. 7), 204–6.

14. On the defeat of the party during the elections and its reasons see Childers, *Limits* (chap. 8, n. 12), 232–59; Paul, *Aufstand* (chap. 6, n. 36), 108–9.

15. Ciolek-Kümper, *Wahlkampf in Lippe* (chap. 8, n. 1).

16. Grill, *Nazi Movement* (intro, pt. 2, n. 1), 206–7; BAK, Sammlung Schumacher, 199, Rundschreiben NR. 1, 15.12.1930, 20.12.1930.

17. Grill, *Nazi Movement* (intro., pt. 2, n. 1), 232–33, BAK, ibid., 13.1.1931.

18. Hauptstaatsarchiv Stuttgart, E151a, Bü 879, 26. February, 15. September 1930; *DT,* 6.2.1930, 9.10.1930; *Donaubote,* 14.1.1930; *FZ,* 17.9.1930; *TB,* 10.10.1930 (Schonach, Schönwald), 4.9.1930- St. Georgen; on the situation of the craftsmen: *FZ,* 19.7.1930; Bonndorf; on the successful harvest: *FZ,* 6.10.1930; SchwB, 24.9.1930 - Gutach 6.9.1930; *EvH,* 10.10.1930 - Grafenhausen; on the successful tourist season: *Schw B,* 24.9.1930 - Tennenbronn; Der Fremdenverkehr in Baden - 1930, BSL; on the industrial crisis and the temporary recovery of the clock industry see *FZ,* 6.10.1930; *DT,* 15.5.1930; the clock factory J. Bürger and Söhne announced the dismissal of 100 workers due to the heavy order recession since December; see StaaF, LKK, 7349 - 15.12.1930 - Schonach.

19. BAK, NS 22/1044 - 19.7.1930.

20. On the organizational activity in the region see chap. 8 about the organization of the Nazi chapters in the Black Forest. On the local police reports about political silence in the region between autumn 1929 and September 1930 see StaaF, LKK, 1626.

21. StaaF, BZ Neustadt 244/183, 16.8.1930 - St. Blasien.

22. Hackett, *Nazi Party* (chap. 6, n. 36), 265–66.

23. Some examples: 120 vacationers attended a meeting in St. Blasien; 100 in a meeting in Bonndorf. 40 vacationers came in the village of Kappel, 200 in

Neustadt, 150 in Hinterzarten. In most of the mentioned villages there did not yet exist a chapter of the NSDAP at that time.

24. StaaF, BZ Neustadt, 244/183 - 25.8.1930 - Lenzkirch, 24.8.1930 - Bonndorf.

25. *DT,* 16.8.1930; *FZ,* 17.9.1930 - "Der Schwarzwald und die Reichstagswahl."

26. Hackett, *Nazi Party* (chap. 6, n. 36), 229–30, 271–74; Childers, *The Nazi Voter* (chap. 6, n. 36), 138–39.

27. Hackett, *Nazi Party* (chap. 6, n. 36), 284–91; Turner, *Big Business* (chap. 8, n. 4), 113–14.

28. Childers, *The Nazi Voter* (chap. 6, n. 36), 151; Hamilton, *Hitler* (chap. 7, n. 13), 422.

29. That was also the position of the *Freiburger Zeitung* which analyzed the election campaign before the presidential elections and came to the conclusion that propaganda and activities of the NSDAP corresponded with the middle-class parties. See *FZ,* 17.9.1930.

30. *DT,* 12.8.1930 - Donaueschingen; *EvH,* 6.9.1930 (article of Professor Spiegelhalder), 28.8.1930, 11.9.1930.

31. The *Freiburger Zeitung* pointed out this aspect in its analysis of the Reichstags elections. According to the newspaper's opinion, the local population's main reason for supporting the NSDAP was not sympathy with the National Socialists or Hitler, but the vacuum created by the internal conflicts and partitions and by the middle classes' inability to act. See *FZ,* 17.9.1930.

32. Childers, *The Nazi Voter* (chap. 6, n. 36), 200–201.

33. PfA Schonach - NSDAP, 29.2.1932; An sämtliche Amtswalter des Gaues Baden der NSDAP, 21.2.1932, 7.3.1932.

34. Paul, *Aufstand* (chap. 6, n. 36), 95–99; Childers, *The Nazi Voter* (chap. 6, n. 36), 198; PfA Schonach, ibid., Sonderrundschreiben zur Reichspräsidentenwahl am 13.März 1932.

35. In the district of Schopfheim the Communist Party organized thirteen meetings in January (NSDAP - 9), six in February (NSDAP - five). In the election month of March the Communists organized twenty-three meetings, the NSDAP, however, forty-six. See StaaF, BZ Schopfheim, T.1 - 510; GLAK, 347 - 1943/18–34 - 2.3.1932, 7.3.1932; *Schw T,* 27.3.1932.

36. On meetings cancelled due to bad weather conditions see chapter 8, note 40, above. On the lack of contact between the *GPL* and the chapters see PfA Schonach, NSDAP, 1.3.1932.

37. Only two speakers from outside the region appeared at seventeen meetings organized in the district of Donaueschingen on March 2 and 3. The other fifteen speakers were local residents. For the eleven meetings in the villages of Schonau, Todtnau, and Berenau in the district of Schopfheim, three speakers from outside the region participated and the others were locals.

38. StaaF, BZ Schopfheim, T.1–512 "Wehrataler."

39. StaaF, BZ Neustadt, 253/192 "Hitler wird Reichspräsident. Wahlzeitung Nr. 2."

40. Ibid., "Deutsche Volksgenossen Nr. 28."

41. A meeting in Unterbalding is an example of one attended by the local inn owner as central speaker who referred especially to the problems of the local farm-

ers. Josef Albicker also delivered a speech at that meeting. See GLAK, 347 - 1943/18–34, 11.1.1932. His subject was "National Socialism and the Peasants." On a similar subject he delivered a speech in Dittishausen. There he called for Hitler's election in order to help the peasants. See StaaF, BZ Neustadt, 246/185, 4.4.1932. An example for stressing the Catholic issue was the distribution of the pamphlet "Catholicism and National Socialism!" in which words of the priest Senn about the German Catholics were mentioned; Senn had joined the NSDAP. On the exposure of resistance from the *Zentrum* against Hindenburg in 1925 and his support by the *Zentrum* in 1932 see StaaF, BZ Schopfheim, T.1–512 - *"Wie sie lügen!"*

42. Heyen, *Nationalsozialismus* (chap. 7, n. 24), 33–37, 52–54.

43. Pridham, *Hitler's Rise* (chap. 7, n. 18), 137–38.

44. Zofka, *Ausbreitung* (chap. 7, n. 18), 77–78, 116, 122–25; idem, "Bauern-bund" (chap. 8, n. 13), 44, 51–56.

45. M. Broszat et al. (eds.), *Bayern in der NS-Zeit, 1, Soziale Lage und politisches Verhalten im Spiegel vertraulicher Berichte* (Munich, 1977), 40–48; Schäfer, *Eindringen des Nationalsozialismus* (chap. 7, n. 4), 78–80; Miesbeck, *Bürgertum* (chap. 7, n. 25), 197.

46. Nyomarkay, *Charisma* (chap. 8, n. 165); Horn, *Führerideologie* (chap. 8, n. 1); Tyrell, *Führer befiehl* (chap. 6, n. 10); Orlow, *History* (chap. 6, n. 7), M. Broszat, "Soziale Motivation und Führerbindung des Nationalsozialismus," in *VJFZ 18* (1970), 392–409; Kershaw, *Hitler Myth* (chap. 8, n. 76).

47. On the central position of Hitler in the discussion between historians of the "functional" and "intentional" schools see Kershaw, *Nazi Dictatorship* (chap. 8, n. 93), chap. 4.

48. Hamilton, *Hitler* (chap. 7, n. 30), 359; Allen, *Rise to Power* (chap. 8, n. 13), 12, 15; Koshar, *Contentious Citadel* (chap. 8, n. 13), 29; Farquharson, *Plough and Swastika* (chap. 8, n. 4), 42.

49. Kershaw, *Hitler Myth* (chap. 8, n. 76), 34–36; Pridham, *Hitler's Rise* (chap. 7, n. 18), 180–81.

50. *AvK*, 30.11.1930.

51. On Hitler as a source of inspiration and belief for local agitators see *Entstehung und Entwicklung des Stützpunktes Fischerbach der NSDAP* (chap. 6, n. 12, above). Sattler in his memoirs, on the other hand, did not refer to Hitler in the context of propaganda and local agitation in the district of Neustadt. See chapter 8, note 23, above.

52. *Der Führer*, 31.12.1931; *Schw T*, 31.12.1932.

53. *Donaubote*, 15.4.1931, Dittishausen; *Der Alemanne*, 27.11.1932 - Neustadt.

54. Ninety-one people were brought from Schonach in three mail trucks to the Hitler meeting in Schwenningen. See PfA Schonach, NSDAP, Hitler Versammlung in Schwenningen am 9. April 1932; *Schw T*, 10.4.1932.

55. In 1928 Gauleiter Wagner proclaimed that "Hitler is the Führer of Germany according to God's will." See StaaF, BZ Neustadt, 244/183, 29.10.1928 - Löffingen. In 1931 Dr. Vogel (NS-propaganda leader in the region) mentioned that Hitler is the Führer of the National Socialist movement, who wanted to be Reichskanzler. See StaaF, BZ Neustadt 244/183, 1.6.1931 - Schollach; and the speech of the local party member Huber in which he called Hitler an important politician; see StaaF, ibid., 31.8.1931 - Hinterzarten. On a first mention of the mag-

ical powers of Hitler and his personality as the Führer of the nation by a local party agitator see StaaF, BZ Neustadt 245/184, 18.1.1932 - Kappel; on calling Hitler a god who will save Germany, see GLAK 347, 1943/198–34, 11.1.1932 - Unterbaldingen.

56. On the exclusion of party members from the chapter in Schopfheim we find a report in *Der Führer* on 13.10.1931; an example for the deletion of Hitler's name on a propaganda pamphlet can be found in StaaF, BZ Schopfheim T.1–511, 9.4.1932. On peasants leaving the party in 1932, see *Donaubote*, 7.11.1932.

57. *Schw T,* 10.2.1932 - Löffingen.

58. On the priest in Zell a.H. see ErzAF - B2/NS 2 - 24.5.1932. On the opinion of the population in Bräunlingen see *Schw T,* 22.3.1932.

59. *Lahrer Anzeiger,* 28.8.1930; *DT,* 17.2.1932 ("Bürgertum, NSDAP und Eiserne Front"); *Hochschw,* 4.8.1932.

60. ErzAF B2/NS 1. 11.11.1930 - Schenkenzell.

61. Zofka, "Bauernbund" (chap. 8, n. 13), 44; idem, *Ausbreitung* (chap. 7, n. 18), 83–84; Miesbeck, *Bürgertum* (chap. 7, n. 25), 217–18.

62. See the detailed discussion in my articles "Where Did Nazi Anti-Semitism Disappear to? A Historiographical Study," in *Yad Vashem Studies 21* (1991), 263–68, and "To the Anti-Semitic Character of the Nazi Party before 1933," in O. Heilbronner (ed.), *The Jews in the Weimar Republic* (Hebr.) (Jerusalem, 1994).

63. Heilbronner, *Role of Nazi Anti-Semitism* (n. 7).

64. Heilbronner, *Role of Nazi Anti-Semitism* (n. 7), 413–15.

65. StaaF, Plakatsammlung, Teil 1 - NSDAP; examples for the pamphlets printed in Karlsruhe on which the prohibition *"Juden haben keinen Zutritt"* ("No entrance for Jews") had been deleted as soon as they were distributed in the Black Forest are the pamphlets no. 19, 244, 246, 273, 275, and others. Pamphlets printed in the Black Forest without the prohibition are no. 21, 243, 245, 285, 287, and others.

66. *Der Alemanne,* 9.12.1932 - Neustadt.

67. StaaF, BZ Neustadt, 244/ 183 - 20.5.1928, 29.10.1928, 9.11.1928, 10.12.1928, 11.5.1931.

68. StaaF, BZ Staufen 312, 12.2.1932.

69. On Merk's positions toward different religious beliefs see *Landbund* (chap. 6, n. 21), 123–27. On his declaration at his joining the NSDAP see *Der Führer,* 17.11.1928. On his political credo, see *Feldberg Rundschau,* 7.11.1931. On his remarks about Jews, see GLAK, 237, 1943/ 18–29, 17.10.1929.

70. On Sattler's position toward Jews as expressed in his memoirs, see BAK, NS 26/ 132. An anti-Semitic article in the Nazi regional paper was published on April 13, 1932, in the *Schwarzwälder Tagblatt* ("Mussolini . . ."). On anti-Semitic remarks of Dr. Vogel see StaaF, BZ Neustadt 245/ 184 - 17.1.1932 - Neustadt, 246/ 185 - 8.4.1932 - Häusern.

71. *Donaubote,* 4.2.1932 - Riedböhringen, 9.3.1932; *Lahrer Anzeiger,* 28.8.1930. On the Catholic resistance against anti-Semitism in the time of the Weimar Republic see also W. Hannot, *Die Judenfrage in der katholischen Tagespresse Deutschlands und Österreichs 1923–1933* (Mainz, 1990); U. Mazura, *Zentrumpartei und Judenfrage 1871–1933* (Mainz, 1993), 53–72.

72. Miesbeck, *Bürgertum* (chap. 7, n. 25), 201; Rau-Kühne, *Ettlingen* (intro.,

pt. 2, n. 4), 263; for general discussion see Paul, *Aufstand* (chap. 6, n. 36), 236–39; Kershaw, *Ideology* (chap. 8, n. 12), 167; see also the regional survey in Heilbronner, *Role of Nazi Anti-Semitism* (n. 7).

73. Childers, *The Nazi Voter* (chap. 6, n. 36), 258.

74. Scholder, *The Churches and the Third Reich,* vol. 1, 1918–34 (London, 1987), 74–98; J. Conway, "National Socialism and the Christian Churches during the Weimar Republic," in P. Stachura (ed.), *The Nazi Machtergreifung* (London, 1983), 124–45.

75. Childers, *The Nazi Voter* (chap. 6, n. 36), 258–60; Pridham, *Hitler's Rise* (chap. 7, n. 18), 179–83.

76. *Der Alemanne,* 23.12.1931, 30.1.1932 - Schönau; *KN,* 13.5.1932.

77. *Schw T,* 16.3.1932; StaaF, BZ Neustadt, 246/ 185 - 4.7.1932 - Bärental, 244/ 183 - 1.6.1931 - Schollach.

78. *Schw T,* 27.7.1932 - Gütenbach; StaaF, BZ Neustadt 244/ 183, 12.10.1931 - Seppenhofen, 27.10.1932 - Urach; GLAK, 347, 1943/ 18–29 - 17.10.1929, Bräunlingen; *Hschw.* - 29.2.1932 - Hinterzarten; this was the argument of the pro-Nazi Catholic priest Goett in the Allgäu. See Hoser, "Hitler" (chap. 8, n. 120).

79. *ErzAF* - B2/ NS2 - 24.5.1932, Zell a.H., 7.7.1932, 12.7.1932; 14.7.1932 - Grafenhausen, 20.10.1931. On the corruption among the bishops see *ErzAF,* ibid., 10.10.1931 - Furtwangen.

80. *Schw T,* 16.3.1932, 28.5.1931 ("Das positive Christentum der NSDAP").

81. W. Senn, *Halt! Katholizismus und Nationalsozialismus* (Augsburg, 1931).

82. ErzAf - B2/ NS2 - 24.5.1932, Zell a.H.; B2/ NS1 - 11.11.1930, 7.3., 8.4.1931 - Schenkenzell.

83. Pridham, *Hitler's Rise* (chap. 7, n. 18), 146–83; Hoser, *Hitler* (chap. 8, n. 120).

84. Holmes, *NSDAP* (chap. 7, n. 38), 287; Zofka, *Ausbreitung* (chap. 7, n. 18), 73–75, 173; Stäbler, *Weltwirtschaftskrise,* (chap. 8, n. 114) 324–34; for Upper-Lower Franconia see Broszat, *Bayern in der NS-Zeit* (chap. 7, n. 24), I, 45; Breuer, *Verordneter Wandel* (chap. 7, n. 40); Schäfer, *Eindringen des Nationalsozialismus* (chap. 7, n. 40), 155ff.

85. Paul, *NSDAP* (chap. 7, n. 24), 162.

86. Doris Kaufmann, *Katholisches Milieu in Münster 1928–1933. Politische Aktionsformen und geschlechtsspezifische Verhaltensräume* (Düsseldorf, 1984); L. Grevelhörster, "Anfänge und Entwicklung der NSDAP in Münster bis zur Machtergreifung," in H. Lahrkamp (ed.), *Beiträge zur Stadtgeschichte* (Münster, 1984), 155–95; Rau-Kühne, *Ettlingen* (intro., pt. 2, n. 4), 256ff.

87. H. Matzerath, *Nationalsozialismus und kommunale Selbstverwaltung* (Stuttgart, 1970), 38–52; R. Hourand, *Die Gleichschaltung der badischen Gemeinden 1933/ 34,* diss. (Freiburg, 1985), 43–50.

88. *TB,* 13.10.1930 - Schonach.

89. Grill, *Nazi Movement* (intro., pt. 2, n. 1), 194–96.

90. *EvH,* 30.8.1930; *Schwarzwälder Zeitung* (Bonndorf), 4.11.1930.

91. Some examples: in Vöhrenbach a joint list of NSDAP and WP stood for the community elections; see *EvH,* 6.10.1930. In Grafenhausen the NSDAP stood for the elections in a list together with the *Zentrum;* see *EvH,* 11.11.1930 - Grafenhausen. In Schönwald the NSDAP renounced its own list; its representative Gop-

pert stood for election in favor of the *Freie Bürgervereinigung* and won the elections; see *TB,* 17.11.1930.

92. GmdA Haslach, iv/ 2 - 10b.

93. *TB,* 16.10.1930; *Echo vom Wald,* 7.11.1930 - Schonach.

94. GmdA Haslach - iv/ 2–13 - February 1932; GmdA Einbach, XIII/ 188 - Niederschrift über die Verhandlungen der Kreisversammlung des Kreises Offenburg - 9.6.1931; GmdA Löffingen Bürgerausschuß Protokollbuch 220, 16.1.1931, 19.11.1931; GmdaA Bonndorf - iv2/ 493 - 9.12.1930; *Schw T,* 24.5.1931 - Furtwangen; *Der Führer,* 9.12.1931 - Wolfach; *Schw T,* 13.4.1932 - Furtwangen; PfA Schonach - NSDAP, 17.5.1931 - Kuner, *Tätigkeitsbericht.*

95. Zofka, *Bauernbund* (chap. 8, n. 13), 51–52; Holmes, *NSDAP;* Stäbler, *Weltwirtschaftskrise* (chap. 8, n. 114), 322–24.

96. A detailed view on the historians who consider the anti-Bolshevist element as central in the Nazi propaganda can be found in two articles by Heilbronner, *Nazi Antisemitism* (n. 62) and *Role of Nazi Antisemitism* (n. 7). Beyond that, a historian who deals with Nazi propaganda on a regional level and stresses the anti-Marxist element, not the anti-Jewish, as a central element of the party's propaganda is C. Striefler, *Kampf um die Macht. Kommunisten und Nationalsozialisten am Ende der Weimarer Republik* (Berlin, 1993).

97. Material on the Bolshevist danger believed to be threatening the population of the region can be found in *ErzAf,* B2 - 55 - 146, Katholischer Volksverein, Tätigkeitsbericht - 1930, "Zentrale gegen den Bolschewismus," and daily in the Catholic regional papers (see chap. 11).

98. *Der Führer,* 13.8.1931 - Triberg, 30.9.1931 - Oberkirch; *Schw T,* 29.11.1930, 3.1.1932, 5.1.1932, 23.1.1932, 24.1.1932. In a series of articles about the sad experience of workers of the clock industry in Russia the Nazi local paper described the misery of peasants and workers in Russia: *Schw T,* 28.3.1931, 31.3.1931, 3.4.1931.

99. See the description of a communist meeting in Triberg given by the local policeman. The policeman recorded that the local inhabitants ridiculed the communists using abusive words. During a Nazi meeting, on the contrary, people left a good impression behind; see GLAK, 347 - 1943/ 18–29 - 10.6.1930 - Triberg.

100. *FZ,* 26.10.1929.

101. Examples for the fact that the NSDAP was believed to be close to the middle classes can be found in *DT,* 17.2.1932 - "Bürgertum, NSDAP und Eiserne Front." On NS propaganda aiming toward the middle classes, but hiding its true intentions, see *Donaubote,* 26.7.1932, "Bürger! Sei auf der Hut!"

102. StaaF, BZ Donaueschingen, 1977/ 52 - 345, 35.7.1931.

103. O. Heilbronner, "Weimar Society: The Image of Soviet Russia," *Tel Aviver Jahrbuch für Deutsche Geschichte,* 24 (1995): 179–92; Holmes, *NSDAP* (chap. 7, n. 38), 210–11; Paul, *NSDAP* (chap. 7, n. 24), 158–60; Pridham, *Hitler's Rise* (chap. 7, n. 18), 177; Breuer, *Verordneter Wandel* (chap. 7, n. 40), 68–69; Zofka, *Bauernbund* (chap. 8, n. 13), 54–56; Rau-Kühne, *Ettlingen* (intro., pt. 2, n. 4), 266.

104. Heilbronner, *Role of Nazi Antisemitism* (n. 7).

105. StaaF, BZ Neustadt 246/ 185 - 24.7.1932 - Oberfischerbach, 25.7.1932 - Löffingen.

106. Thomas Childers, "The Social Language of Politics in Germany: The Soci-

ology of Political Discourse in the Weimar Republic," in *American Historical Review* 2 (1990), 331–59; idem, *The Nazi Voter* (chap. 6, n. 36), 9–11.

107. See chapter 7, note 21, above.

108. Childers, *The Nazi Voter* (chap. 6, n. 36), 151, 215–19; Farquharson, *Plough and Swastika* (chap. 8, n. 4), chap. 2; Pyta (chap. 8, n. 118), *Dorfgemeinschaft und Parteipolitik 1918–1933*, 325–35.

109. Grill, *Nazi Movement* (intro., pt. 2, n. 1), 225–30; Bräunsche, *NSDAP in Baden 1928–1930* (intro., pt. 2, n. 1), 35–37; GLAK 233/ 27916, "Der agrarpolitische Apparat der badischen Nationalsozialisten."

110. In Schönwald and in Schonach the list of the National Socialists stood against the list of the "Unified Farmers."

111. GLAK 233/ 27916, "Der agrarpolitische Apparat der badischen Nationalsozialisten"; Pridham, *Hitler's Rise* (chap. 7, n. 18), 229–30.

112. Examples for such meetings are: StaaF, BZ Neustadt, 244/ 183 - 16.10.1929 - Grafenhausen, 31.8.1930 - Kappel, 26.1.1931 - Rotenbach.

113. The adviser for agricultural questions, who resigned from his post, was Primus Dold; see StaaF, BZ Donaueschingen, 1977/ 52 - 345, 29.7.1931. On examples for meetings at which the anti-Bolshevist element had been stressed, see *Der Alemanne*, 1.11.1931; StaaF, BZ Neustadt, 244/ 183 - 26.1.1931 - Rotenbach; *Der Alemanne*, Bauern-Sondernummer, 8.3.1932.

114. StaaF, Plakatsammlung Teil 1 - NSDAP, Nr. 246 - Bonndorf, Nr. 273 - Hinterzarten, Nr. 254 - Löffingen. During the election campaign for the Reichstag Election in July 1932 the NSDAP organized ten meetings in the peasant villages, including the district of Neustadt. During the election campaign for the Reichstag Election in summer 1930 it had only organized one meeting in one village; see StaaF, BZ Neustadt, 244/183, 246/ 185; *Der Alemanne*, 7.2.1932 - Oberkirch, 24.2.1932 - St. Peter.

115. R. Allgeier, "Grenzland in der Krise. Die badische Wirtschaft 1928–1933," in T. Schnabel (ed.), *Machtergreifung in Südwestdeutschland* (intro., pt. 2, n. 1), 159; R. Holzgreve, *NS-Agrarpolitik in Baden 1933–1936*, M.A. thesis (Freiburg, 1980), 21; *Der Führer*, 4.5.1931 - Villingen; *Der Alemanne*, 21.1.1932, 10.8.1932.

116. GLAK, 347, 1943/ 18–34 - 11.1.1932 - Unterbaldingen.

117. For East Bavaria see Holmes, *NSDAP* (chap. 7, n. 38), 139–42; Schuster, *Traunstein* (chap. 7, n. 40). Schuster stresses the inability of the Nazi Party to combat the *BBB;* for the same conclusion see also T. Siegert "Braune Spurensuche. Die Anfänge der NSDAP in der Nordoberpfalz. 2 Teil," *Heimat-Landkreis Tirschenreuth* 1 (1989): 93–148. For more on the *BBB* in Bavaria see H. Bergmann, *Der Bayerische Bauernbund und der Bayerische Christliche Bauernverein 1919–1928* (Munich, 1986); W. Stäbler, " 'Die neue Bauernbewegung'. Oberbayerischer Bauernprotest in der Endphase der Weimarer Republik," in *Zeitschrift für Bayerische Landesgeschichte* 81 (1988), 901–15; for Günzburg see Zofka, "Bauernbund" (chap. 8, n. 13), 51–52; idem, *Ausbreitung* (chap. 7, n. 18), 84–85, 124–25; for the Allgäu see Pridham, *Hitler's Rise* (chap. 7, n. 18), 224–36; Broszat, *Bayern in der NS-Zeit* I (chap. 7, n. 24), 39–63.

118. Winkler, *Mittelstand* (chap. 7, n. 26); Haupt, *Mittelstand und Kleinbürgertum* (chap. 7, n. 29); Lenger, *Sozialgeschichte* (chap. 7, n. 8), 163–86. Other works

about the old middle classes during the Weimar time are mentioned at the beginning of chap. 7.

119. Childers, *The Nazi Voter* (chap. 6, n. 36), 213–14.

120. StaaF, *BZ Neustadt,* 244/183 - 24.11.1930 - Schollach.

121. Erz Af, B2/NS 1 - Flugblatt Nr. 3 der NSDAP - O.G. Lahr - "Höre! Deutscher Geschäftsmann, Höre! Deutscher Gewerbetreibender."

122. StaaF, BZ Neustadt, 255/183 - 1.6.1931 - Eisenbach; GLAK 233/17915 - 9.2.1930 - Furtwangen, 20.12.1930 - Wolfach.

123. See the remarks about the party propaganda during district and regional elections in chap. 2.

124. GLAK, 347 - 1943/18–29 - 1.9.1930 - Furtwangen.

125. Merk was the owner of the inn in Grafenhausen. Erwin Weishaar from Lenzkirch and August Heil from Kappel were hotel owners.

126. Zofka, *Ausbreitung* (chap. 7, n. 18), 146–52.

127. Childers, *The Nazi Voter* (chap. 6, n. 36), 228–32.

128. *Schw T,* 23.5.1931 - Furtwangen; *Der Führer,* 19.2.1931 - Wolfach; *DT,* 16.9.1930, *Schw T,* 28.2.1932 - Riedöschingen; *TB,* 10.9.1930 - Schönwald.

129. *Der Alemanne,* 22.10.1932 - Neustadt.

130. Orlow, *History* (chap. 6, n. 7), chap. 5, belongs to a small group of historians who postulate a turning point in the party propaganda. Among the group of historians stressing the central positon of the socialist propaganda are Detlef Mühlberger, *Germany* (chap. 7, n. 2); Childers, *The Nazi Voter* (chap. 6, n. 36), 24; and lately also Paul, *Aufstand* (chap. 6, n. 36), 242–47.

131. Paul, *Aufstand* (chap. 6, n. 36); Childers, *The Nazi Voter* (chap. 6, n. 36), 245–49; idem, "Social Language" (n. 106), 350.

132. *DT,* 12.8.1930, 28.8.1930, 11.9.1930; *FZ,* 26.10.1929. See also chapter 8, notes 1 and 6, above.

133. *Schw T,* 24.5.1931, 8.4.1932, 13.4.1932, *Feldberg Rundschau,* 7.11.1931. On the eve of the second ballot of the presidential elections the *Schwarzwälder Tagblatt* dedicated its entire second part to the question of Hitler and the workers. See *Schw T,* 9.4.1932.

134. StaaF, BZ Neustadt, 244(183) - 11.5.1931, 245/184 - 13.3.1932, 5.4.1932. On a meeting where the speaker addressed the peasants see StaaF, BZ Neustadt, 245(184), 20.3.1932.

135. At a meeting in the village of Eisenbach, in which the majority of workers were employed in the clock industry, Captain Werber from Freiburg spoke about his adventures at sea! See StaaF, BZ Neustadt, 246/185 - 7.4.1932 - Eisenbach.

136. PfA Schonach, NSDAP, 29.2.1932; *Schw T,* 18.3.1932 - Möhringen, 24.5.1931, 1.4.1932, 13.4.1932 - Furtwangen.

137. StaaF, BZ Neustadt, 253/192 - "Hitler Reichspräsident," Wahlzeitung NR. 2; "Was bedeutet der 5-Jahresplan für den deutschen Arbeiter?"; StaaF, BZ Schopfheim T. 1. - 512; "Wehrataler" *Echo der Zeit,* 5.11.1932.

138. *DT,* 31.3.1931 - Vöhrenbach.

139. StaaF, BZ Neustadt, 1974/31 - P. 135, Ortsbereisung, Grafenhausen, 1930.

140. ErzAF, B2 - 59 -18, 22.11.1932 "Bericht über die Notlage in der Gemeinde Gütenbach." In the village the NSDAP got 18.1 percent of the votes in summer 1932, while the KPD got 21.1 percent of the votes.

141. For example in Halach and Wolfach.

142. Pridham, *Hitler's Rise* (chap. 7, n. 18), 188; Zofka, "Bauernbund" (chap. 8, n. 13), 47–48; Paul, *NSDAP* (chap. 7, n. 24), 160.

143. On the definition of this term see chapter 8, note 1, above.

144. On the term of "negative participation" see J. Bergmann, K. Megerle, "Gesellschaftliche Mobilisierung und negative Partizipation: Zur Analyse der politischen Orientierungen und Aktivitäten von Arbeitern, Bauern und gewerblichem Mittelstand in der Weimarer Republik," in P. Steinbach (ed.), *Probleme politischer Partizipation im Modernisierungsprozeß* (Stuttgart, 1982), 376–438.

145. In this context I object to the differentiation made by Rohe according to which the NSDAP had been a *Volkspartei* in social and cultural aspects, but from the political aspect belonged to the national camp. In the Black Forest such a differentiation was hardly in evidence. Voters of the NSDAP and sympathizers came from all segments of society and did not support the NSDAP only for political reasons. For the same results see W. Pyta, "Politische Kultur und Wahlen in der Weimarer Republik," G. A. Ritter (ed.), *Wahlen und Wahlkämpfe in Deutschland* (Düsseldorf, 1997), 197–240, esp.114; for Rohe's argument see his *Wahlen* (chap.7, n. 3), 161–62.

146. See the discussion about the term *local public sphere* in H. Dunckelmann, *Lokale Öffentlichkeit: Eine gemeindesoziologische Untersuchung* (Stuttgart, 1975).

147. See the discussion in Jaschke, *Soziale Basis* (chap. 8, n. 1), 164–70, 223–25.

Introduction to Part 3

1. T. Nipperdey, *Religion im Umbruch. Deutschland 1870–1918* (Munich, 1988), 24–31; K. Rohe, *Wahlen und Wählertraditionen in Deutschland* (Frankfurt, 1992), 73–83; Rainer Lepsius, "Parteisystem und Sozialstruktur: Zum Problem der Demokratisierung der deutschen Gesellschaft," in G. A. Ritter (ed.), *Die deutschen Parteien vor 1918* (Köln, 1973), 69; M. Klöcker, "Das katholische Milieu. Grundüberlegungen," in *Zeitschrift für Religions- und Geistesgeschichte* 44 (1992): 241–62; W. Loth, "Soziale Bewegungen im Katholizismus des Kaiserreichs," in *Geschichte und Gesellschaft* 17 (1991): 279–310; A. Liedhegener, "Marktgesellschaft und Milieu. Katholiken und katholische Regionen in der wirtschaftlichen Entwicklung des Deutschen Reiches 1895–1914," in *Historisches Jahrbuch II* 113 (1993): 283–354. Arbeitskreis für kirchliche Zeitgeschichte (AKKZG) Münster, "Katholiken zwischen Tradition und Moderne. Das katholische Milieu als Forschungsaufgabe," in *Westfälische Forschungen* 43 (1993): 588–654; J. Mooser, "Das katholische Milieu in der bürgerlichen Gesellschaft," O. Blaschke and F.-M. Kuhlemann (eds.), *Religion im Kaiserreich. Milieus-Mentalitäten-Krisen* (Gütersloh, 1996), 59–92.

2. Rohe, Wahlen (n. 1), 14–30; Liedhegener, Marktgesellschaft (n. 1), 348–54.

3. The definition of "cultural hegemony" is given according Gramsci in his book *Selection from the Prison Notebooks* (selection and translation by Q. Haurse and G. N. Smith) (New York, 1971), 123. See the discussion on the topic and on the problem of definition in T. J. Jackson Leans, "The Concept of Cultural Hegemony: Problems and Possibilities," in *American Historical Review* 3 (1985): 567–92, esp. 568–70.

Chapter 10

1. D. Langewiesche, *Liberalismus in Deutschland* (Frankfurt, 1988), 240–51; L. E. Jones, *German Liberalism and the Dissolution of the Weimar Party System 1918–1935* (Chapel Hill, 1988); H. Mommsen, "Die Auflösung des Bürgertums seit dem späten 19. Jahrhundert," in J. Kocka (ed.), *Bürger und Bürgerlichkeit im 19. Jahrhundert* (Göttingen, 1987), 288–315.

2. Mommsen, "Auflösung" (n. 1), 304; see also idem, "Zur Verschränkung traditioneller und faschistischer Führungsgruppen in Deutschland beim Übergang von der Bewegungs- zur Systemphase," in Wolfgang Schieder (ed.), *Faschismus als soziale Bewegung* (Göttingen, 1983), 166; Rudy Koshar, "From Stammtisch to Party: Nazi Joiners and the Contradictions of Grass Root Fascism in Weimar Germany," in *Journal of Modern History* 1 (1987): 1–25; Jermey Noakes, *The Nazi Party in Lower Saxony* (Oxford, 1970), 130ff.

3. W. Struve, *Elites against Democracy: Leadership Ideals in Bourgeois Political Thought in Germany 1890–1933* (Princeton, 1973); Mommsen, "Auflösung" (n. 1), 302–3.

4. D. Abraham, *The Collapse of the Weimar Republic: Political Economy and Crisis* (Princeton, 1981); R. Neebe, *Großindustrie, Staat und NSDAP 1930–1933. Paul Silverberg und der Reichsverband der deutschen Industrie in der Krise der Weimarer Republik* (Göttingen, 1981); a different opinion is expressed by H. A. Turner, *German Big Business and the Rise of Hitler* (Oxford, 1984); from regional aspect see N. Ferguson, *Paper and Iron. Hamburg Business and German Politics in the Era of Inflation 1897–1927* (Cambridge, 1995), 463ff.

5. D. Gessner, *Agrarverbände in der Weimarer Republik: Wirtschaftliche und soziale Voraussetzungen agrarkonservativer Politik vor 1933* (Düsseldorf, 1976); H. Gies, "NSDAP und landwirtschaftliche Organisationen in der Endphase der Weimarer Republik," in *VJfZG* 15 (1967): 341–76; Mommsen, "Auflösung" (n. 1), 294–96. The opposite opinion, that the bourgeois side was unified and not divided, can be found in Peter Fritzsche, *Rehearsal for Fascism. Populism and Political Mobilization in Weimar Germany* (Oxford, 1990); H. J. Bieber, *Bürgertum in der Revolution* (Hamburg, 1992); a good recent summary of these topics can be found in Bernd Weisbrod, "The Crisis of Bourgeois Society in Interwar Germany," R. Bessel (ed.), *Fascist Italy and Nazi Germany, Comparison and Contrasts* (Cambridge, 1996), 23–39, and H. Möller, "Bürgertum und bürgerlich-liberale Bewegung nach 1918," L. Gall (ed.), *Bürgertum und bürgerlich-liberale Bewegung in Mitteleuropa seit dem 18-Jahrhundert,* (Munich 1997), 298–342.

6. T. Nipperdey, "Verein als soziale Struktur in Deutschland im späten 18. und frühen 19. Jahrhundert," in idem, *Gesellschaft, Kultur, Theorie* (Göttingen, 1976), 174–205; D. Blackbourn, J. Eley, *The Peculiarities of German History, Bourgeois Society and Politics in Nineteenth-Century Germany* (Oxford, 1984), 195–98; Mommsen, "Auflösung" (n. 1), 291; Koshar, Stammtisch (n. 2), 2–3; O. Dann, "Vorwort," in idem. (ed.), *Vereinswesen und bürgerliche Gesellschaft in Deutschland,* in *Historische Zeitschrift,* Beiheft 9 (Munich 1984), 5–9; idem, "Vereine und Verbände in der modernen Gesellschaft," in H. Best (ed.), *Vereine in Deutschland* (Bonn, 1993), 119–42; K. Tenfelde, "Die Entfaltung des Vereinswesens während der industriellen Revolution in Deutschland (1850–1873)," in Dann, ibid., 76;

George Mosse, *The Nationalization of the Masses* (New York, 1975), chap. 6; R. Hopwood, "Paladins of the Bürgertum: Cultural Clubs and Politics in Small German Towns 1918–1925," in *Historical Papers (Canadian Historical Association* 1974), 213–36.

7. *Handausgabe des Bürgerlichen Gesetzbuches für das Deutsche Reich von Dr. Hugo Neumann,* vol. 1 (Berlin, 1990), 44.

8. Nipperdey, *Verein als soziale Struktur* (n. 6); Blackbourn, *Peculiarities* (n. 6); Rudy Koshar, *Social Life, Local Politics and Nazism. Marburg 1880–1935* (Chapel Hill, 1986), 289.

9. J. H. Siewert, "Vereinswesen in der deutschen Soziologie," in Dann, *Vereinswesen* (n. 6), 152; Hezinger, Ch. Köhle, "Gemeinde und Verein," in *Rheinisches Jahrbuch für Volkskunde* 22 (1978): 181–202; Jörg H. Siewert, "Der Verein," in H. G. Wehling (ed.), *Dorfpolitik* (Opladen, 1977); Dieter Jauch, "Die Wandlung des Vereinslebens in ländlichen Gemeinden Südwestdeutschlands," in *Zeitschrift für Agrargeschichte und Agrarsoziologie* 1 (1980): 48; R. Pflaum, "Die Vereine als Produkt und Gegengewicht sozialer Differenzierung," in G. Wurzbacher (ed.), *Das Dorf im Spannungsfeld industrieller Entwicklung* (Stuttgart, 1954), 151–82; W. Gordon, N. Babchuk, "A Typology of Voluntary Vereins," in *American Sociological Review* 1 (1959): 22–29.

10. Pflaum, *Vereine als Produkt* (n. 9), 151; Jauch, *Wandlung* (n. 9), 59; Siewert, *Verein* (n. 9), 81; H. Schmitt, *Das Vereinsleben der Stadt Weinheim* (Weinheim, 1963); Hopwood, Paladins (n. 6); C. Eisenberg, "Arbeiter, Bürger und der bürgerliche Verein 1820–1870," in J. Kocka (ed.), *Bürgertum im 19. Jahrhundert,* vol. 2 (Munich, 1988), 190.

11. Hopwood, Paladins (n. 6), 232; see also Lothar Gall, *Bürgertum in Deutschland* (Berlin, 1989), 196–97, 213.

12. Nipperdey, *Verein als soziale Struktur* (n. 6), 177–83; Koshar, *Social Life* (n. 8), 92–95; D. Hein, "Soziale Konstituierungsfaktoren des Bürgertums," in Lothar Gall (ed.), *Staat und Bürgertum im Übergang von traditioneller zu moderner Gesellschaft* (Munich, 1993), 151–82; T. Mäntel, "Reputation und Einfluß der gesellschaftlichen Führungsgruppen," in Gall, *Staat und Bürgertum* (n. 12), 295–314; critical remarks on the argument about the importance of the Vereine for the rise of the German Bürgertum can be found in Gall, *Stadt und Bürgertum,* 238–39 and Paul Nolte, *Gemeindebürgertum und Liberalismus in Baden 1800–1850* (Göttingen, 1994), 161.

13. Koshar, *Social Life* (n. 8), 96–106; Mommsen, "Auflösung" (n. 1), 292–97; Vernon Lidke, "Burghers, Workers and Problems of Class Relationships 1870–1914," in J. Kocka (ed.), *Arbeiter und Bürger im 19. Jahrhundert* (Munich, 1986), 42–43; and also V. Lidke, "Die kulturelle Bedeutung der Arbeitervereine," in G. Wiegelmann (ed.), *Kultureller Wandel im 19. Jahrhundert* (Göttingen, 1973), 146–56. See the following chapter about the Catholic *Vereine.*

14. Siewert, *Vereinswesen* (n. 9), 157; idem, Verein (n. 9), 69; E. Wallner, "Die Rezeption stadtbürgerlichen Vereinswesens durch die Bevölkerung auf dem Lande," in Wiegelmann, *Kultureller Wandel* (n. 13), 160–71; H. Binder, "Ein dörflicher Verein als Spiegelbild gesellschaftlicher Entwicklungen," in *Beiträge zur Volkskunde in Baden-Württemberg* 1 (1985): 103–13.

15. Hezinger, *Gemeinde und Verein* (n. 9), 190–93; Pflaum, *Vereine als Produkt*

(n. 9), 171, 179; Jauch, *Wandlung* (n. 9), 49–50; Siewert, *Verein* (n. 9), 68; Schmitt, *Vereinsleben* (n. 10), 180; Tenfelde, *Entfaltung* (n. 6), 111–14; Wolfgang Kaschuba, Carola Lipp, *Dörfliches Überleben—zur Geschichte materieller und sozialer Reproduktion ländlicher Gesellschaft im 19. und frühen 20. Jahrhundert* (Tübingen, 1982), 594–96.

16. Tenfelde, *Entfaltung* (n. 6); Kaschuba, *Dörfliches Überleben* (n. 15), 595; Siewert, *Verein* (n. 9), 75–79; Hopwood, "Paladins" (n. 6), 220–21; Walker M., *German Home Towns. Community, State and General Estate 1648–1871* (Ithaca, 1971), 423–26.

17. Tenfelde, *Entfaltung* (n. 6), 112; Schmitt, *Vereinsleben* (n. 10), 97.

18. Siewert, *Vereinswesen* (n. 9), Pflaum, *Verein als Produkt* (n. 9); Hopwood, *Paladins* (n. 6); Jauch, *Wandlung* (n. 9), 59; Kaschuba, *Dörfliches Überleben* (n. 15), 594; Koshar, *Social Life* (n. 8), 106; Mosse, *Nationalization* (n. 6); Gall, *Bürgertum* (n. 11), 498–501; Dieter Düding, *Organisierung gesellschaftlichen Nationalismus (1809–1847). Bedeutung und Funktion der Turner- und Sängervereine für die deutsche Nationalbewegung* (Munich, 1984); D. Klenke "Nationalkriegerisches Gemeinschaftsideal als politische Religion. Zum Vereinsnationalismus der Sänger, Schützen und Turner am Vorabend der Einigungskriege," in *Historische Zeitschrift* 2, 260 (1995): 395–448.

19. Mommsen, "Auflösung" (n. 1), 292–97; Hopwood, *Paladins* (n. 6), 220–21; Kaschuba, *Dörfliches Überleben* (n. 15), 596; Koshar, *Social Life* (n. 8), 143; Gall, *Bürgertum* (n. 11), 498–501; D. Klenke, "Bürgerlicher Männergesang und Politik in Deutschland," in *Geschichte in Wissenschaft und Unterricht* 2.9 (1989): 458–85; Peter Fritzsche, *Rehearsal* (n. 5), 75–82; R. Hopwood, "Mobilization of a Nationalist Community," *German History* 2 (1992): 149–76.

20. Koshar, *Social Life* (n. 8), 127–67; Hopwood, ibid.

21. Koshar, *Social Life* (n. 8). Schmitt, *Vereinsleben* (n. 10), 13; Hopwood, *Paladins* (n. 6), 220–30; idem, *Mobilization* (n. 19); C. Rauh-Kühne, *Katholisches Milieu und Kleinstadtgesellschaft. Ettlingen 1918–1939* (Sigmaringen, 1991), 185–95; Peter Miesbeck, *Bürgertum und Nationalsozialismus in Rosenheim* (Rosenheim, 1994), 331–36.

22. Fritzsche, Mommsen, Hopwood, and Bieber are according to my knowledge the only historians who try, briefly, to deal with these questions.

23. Koshar, *Social Life* (n. 8), 130–38.

24. B. Hagtevet, "The Theory of Mass Society and the Collapse of the Weimar Republic," in U. Larsen, B. Hagtevet (eds.), *Who Were the Fascists: Social Roots of European Fascism* (Oslo, 1980), 66–117; Fritzsche, *Rehearsal* (n. 5), 14, 233; W. S. Allen, *The Nazi Seizure to Power* (New York, 1984), 17–20; H. G. Haupt, "Mittelstand und Kleinbürgertum in der Weimarer Republik. Zu Problem und Perspektive ihrer Erforschung," in *Archiv für Sozialgeschichte* 26 (1986), 236; B. Burckhardt, *Eine Stadt wird braun. Die nationalsozialistische Machtergreifung in der Provinz. Eine Fallstudie* (Hamburg, 1980), 15–20; Z. Zofka, *Die Ausbreitung des Nationalsozialismus auf dem Lande* (Munich, 1979), 37, 81, 167–68; Miesbeck, *Rosenheim* (n. 21), 334–35; T. Siegert, "Braune Spurensuche. Die Anfänge der NSDAP in der Nordoberpfalz. 2 Teil," in *Heimat—Landkreis Tirscheureuth* (1990), Bd. 2, 134; A. Oberschall, *Social Conflict and Social Movement* (Englewood Cliffs, 1973), 108–13; Koshar, *Social Life* (n. 8), chap. 5; H. Mommsen, "National

Socialism: Continuity and Change," in Walter Laqueur (ed.), *Fascism: A Reader's Guide* (London, 1979), 160–61; J. Linz, "Some Notes Toward a Comparative Study of Fascism in Sociological Historical Perspective," in ibid., 64. On the "Mass Society Theory" itself see H. Arendt, *The Origins of Totalitarianism* (London, 1986), 311–12, 317; W. Kornhauser, *The Politics of Mass Society* (Glencoe, 1959).

25. Several short remarks about the difficulties of the *Vereine* in the early thirties can be found: F. Zunkel, "Die westdeutschen Bürgergesellschaften zwischen Kaiserreich und Nationalsozialismus," in J. Heideking et al. (eds.), *Wege in die Zeitgeschichte* (Berlin, 1989), 36; see also R. Koshar, "'Cult of *Vereins*'. The Lower Middle Class in Weimar Germany," in idem. (ed.), *Splintered Classes: Politics and the Lower Middle Classes in Interwar Europe* (New York, 1990), 44. According to a different opinion the difficulties in the *Verein*'s activities were not a result of the economic situation, but of changes in the way leisure time was spent; see on this topic K. Düssel and M. Frese, "Von traditioneller Vereinskultur zu moderner Massenkultur? Vereins- und Freizeitangebote in einer südwestdeutschen Kleinstadt 1920–1960," in *Archiv für Sozialgeschichte* 33 (1993): 59–105.

26. Things have started to change recently. See T. Mergel, *Zwischen Klasse und Konfession. Katholisches Bürgertum im Rheinland 1794–1914* (Göttingen, 1994); idem, "Ultramontanism, Liberalism, Moderation: Political Mentalities and Political Behavior of the German Catholic Bürgertum, 1848–1914," *CEH* 29, 2 (1996): 151–75; O. Heilbronner, "Wohin verschwand das katholische Bürgertum?—oder: Der Ort des katholischen Bürgertums in der neueren deutschen Historiographie," in *Zeitschrift für Religions- und Geistesgeschichte* 47, 4 (1995): 320–37; idem, "Regionale Aspekte zum katholischen Bürgertum. Oder: Die Besonderheit des katholischen Bürgertums im ländlichen Süddeutschland," in *Blätter für Deutsche Landesgeschichte* 131 (1995), 223–59; idem, "In Search of the Catholic (rural) Bourgeoisie: The Peculiarities of the South German Bürgertum," *CEH* 29, 2 (1996): 175–201.

27. C. Bauer, "Der deutsche Katholizismus und die bürgerliche Gesellschaft," in idem, *Deutscher Katholizismus. Entwicklungslinien und Profile* (Frankfurt, 1964), 28–53; D. Blackbourn, Introduction, in idem, R. Evans (eds.), *The German Bourgeoisie* (London, 1991), 9–10; M. Klöcker, "Katholizismus und Bildungsbürgertum. Hinweise zur Erforschung vernachlassigter Bereiche der deutschen Bildungsgeschichte im 19. Jahrhundert," in R. Kosseleck (ed.), *Bildungsbürgertum im 19. Jahrhundert, Part II: Bildungsgüter und Bildungswissen* (Stuttgart, 1990), 117–38; W. Loth (ed.), *Deutscher Katholizismus im Umbruch zur Moderne* (Stuttgart, 1991); Mergel, *Zwischen Klasse* (n. 26), 5–14; Heilbronner, *Wohin verschwand* (n. 26), 320–25.

28. Cf. Jürgen Kocka, "Bürgertum und Bürgerlichkeit als Probleme deutscher Geschichte vom späten 18. bis zum frühen 20. Jahrhundert," in idem, *Bürger und Bürgerlichkeit* (n. 1), 34.

29. On the small number of *Vereine* in the regions see StaaF, BZ Neustadt - 1980/10–1980/20, P. 287 - Reiselfingen, Ortsbereisung - 5.8.1929; P. 14 - Bachheim - 1930; 1974/31, P. 168 - Münchingen - 1930. An extraordinary phenomenon in the region was the fact that peasants were not ready to join sport, music, or cultural

Vereine or societies with economic aims. See Binder's remark on the peasant's reason for not joining the *Verein:* Binder, *Dörflicher Verein* (n. 14), 110–13.

30. Some examples for the foundation of Vereine can be found in StaaF, BZ Villingen, 1985/110 - 2025, Vereine in Triberg; 1635–1636, Vereine in Schönwald.

31. W. Blessing, "Umwelt und Mentalität im ländlichen Bayern. Eine Skizze zum Alltagswandel im 19. Jahrhundert," in *Archiv für Sozialgeschichte* 19 (1979), 38.

32. StA Furtwangen 233/ 12a/ 1574, 27.6.1923, Gesangverein "Arion" und Oskar Ketterer; GmdA Eisenbach, XI, 3/ 3 - Firma Morat; Todtnau - 100 Jahre Turnverein Todtnau, 53.

33. H. J. Kremer, "Die Krieger- und Militärvereine in der Innenpolitik des Großherzogtums Baden (1870–1914)," in *Zeitschrift für die Geschichte des Oberrheins* 133 (1985), 326; PfA Bonndorf - 252, 20.6.1928; StA Wolfach 055–00/1 - Turnverein Wolfach - 1866, 11.2.1932; ErzAF B2–55–135, 8.10.1930 - Löffingen.

34. O. Heilbronner, "The Impact and Consequences of the First World War in a Catholic Rural Area," in *German History* 1 (1993), 1–16; *Statistisches Jahrbuch für das Land Baden,* BSL 1925 - Sportvereine, 162; StA Lenzkirch 332 - Fußballklub, 329 - Schützengesellschaft; StaaF, BZ Offenburg - 128, P. 5 - Ortsbereisung Bad Peterstal, 7.12.1928; the local music Verein had been founded in 1927; StA Haslach, XI, 3/ 5.23.10.31, *Turnverein;* on the *sportvereine* in Weimar Republic see C. Eisenberg, "Massensport in der Weimarer Republic: Ein statistischer Überblick," in *Archiv für Sozialgeschichte* 33 (1993): 137–77; Eisenberg has argued that the *Sportvereine* had bourgeois character, while workers, women, and young people joined mainly the *Turnvereine,* which were committed to a particular political and religious worldview.

35. On the "golden years" of the Weimar Republic see H. James, *The German Slump: Politics and Economics 1924–1936* (Oxford, 1987); G. Feldman, *The Great Disorder. Politics, Economics and Society in the German Inflation 1914–1924* (Oxford, 1993), 837–54; Ferguson, *Paper and Iron* (n. 4); In the Black Forest - StA Furtwangen, Gesangsverein "Orion" 322/ 12a-1574, 112/ 311–1037, 21.99.1927, 1.5.1929, GmdA Breitnau, 368 - Musikverein - 2.6.1927; GmdA Bonndorf, 1789 - Männergesangsverein - 22.8.1929; GmdA Eisenbach, XI, 3/ 2 - 21.7.1928, XI, 3/ 4 - 31.5.1928.

36. GmdA Breitnau, 368, 2.6.1927; GmdA Eisenbach, XI, 3/4 - 21.7.1928.

37. *TB,* 4.2.1932, Schönwald - Turnverein. See also note 55 below: StaaF, BZ Neustadt - 1980/ 10, P.287 - Ortsbereisung Reiselfingen, 5.8.1929; 1974/ 31, P. 168 - Ortsbereisung Münchingen, 21.7.1930.

38. StA Schönau, XI/ 3 - 15.6.1928 - Turnverein.

39. *SchwB* - Lautenbach, 14.2.1930; *DT,* 31.1.1930; StA Schiltach, Lehengericht, XI, 3/ 2 - 16.4.1930 - Musikverein.

40. *Hoch Schw* - Löffingen, 4.9.1929; *TB,* 27.12.1929 - Schonach; *SchwT,* 23.2.1932 - Riedböhringen; *TB,* 10.12.1931 - Schonach. "Kreuz und Sowjetstern" (*Cross and Soviet Star*) was such an anti-Bolshevist film which described the terror in Russia; more details can be found in O. Heilbronner, "Weimar Society: The Image of Soviet Russia," in *Tel Aviver Jahrbuch für Deutsche Geschichte* 24 (1995): 179–92.

41. Fritzsche, Rehearsal (n. 5), 6–13; C. Maier, *Recasting Bourgeois Europe*

(Princeton, 1988), 36–37; H. U. Wehler, "Wie bürgerlich war das deutsche Kaiserreich?" in Kocka, *Bürger und Bürgerlichkeit* (n. 1), 273; Kocka, *Bürgertum und Bürgerlichkeit als Probleme* (n. 28), 33; Mommsen, "Auflösung" (n. 1), 289; G. Eley, "Conservatives and Radical Nationalists in Germany: The Production of Fascist Potentials 1912–1928," in M. Blinkhorn (ed.), *Fascists and Conservatives* (London, 1990), 51.

42. *FZ*, 7.9.1929 - Furtwangen.

43. G. Wilke, "The Sins of the Fathers: Village Society and Social Control in the Weimar Republic," in R. Evans, W. Lee (ed.), *The German Peasantry* (London, 1986), 174–204; W. Kaschuba, "Peasants and Others: The Historical Contours of Village Class Society," also in Evans, *German Peasantry,* 259–61; Kaschuba, *Dörfliches Überleben* (n. 15), 177–204, 265–66.

44. *Schwarzwälder Zeitung* (Bonndorf), 4.11.1930; Kaschuba, *Dörfliches Überleben* (n. 15), 595–96; T. Pfizer, H. Wehling (eds.), *Kommunalpolitik in Baden-Württemberg* (Stuttgart, 1985), 35–40. Some examples: Haslach - *Fortschrittliche Wahlgemeinschaft;* Lenzkirch - *Parteilose Wirtschaftsvereinigung;* Furtwangen - *Bürgerliche Vereinigung;* Wolfach - *Gemeindeinteressen Vertretung.*

45. StaaF, BZ Villingen - 1979/82, 1584 - 29.6.1929; KN 25.1.1930 - Haslach. Until 1929 more than half of the members of the *Krieg- und Militärverein* in Eisenbach left. See GmdA Eisenbach Bücher, XII/4 - KuMV - 1917–1929; *HochSchw,* 24.2.1932 - Altglashütten; *Schw T,* 4.3.1932 - Furtwangen. On the desire of the Black Forest's inhabitants for political peace, in order to protect the name of the region as a holiday resort, see StaaF, BZ Villingen, ibid.; *FZ,* 1.6.1931; BZ Schopfheim, T.1 - 505, 10.2.1930 - Bernau.

46. *Hschw,* 29.3.1932 - Neustadt; *TB;* 4.2.1932 - Schönwald; *Hoch Schw.* - Neustadt, 2.3.1932; *FZ,* 6.6.1932; StA Wolfach, 032/Bd.2 - Männergesangsverein - 3.9.1930, 5.3.1931.

47. On the decline of the *Verein's* activities see table 10. On the importance of the *Verein* as a financial source see *Hschw,* 12.5.1932 - Waldau. On the decline of the activities of the *Vereine,* the cancellation of Christmas celebrations and of the activities outside the communities, see *TB,* 16.12.1930 - Schonach, 3.11.1932 - Schönwald; *FZ,* 7.8.1932 - Neustadt; 100 Jahre Musikverein Schenkenzell, 1975, 33; *SchwT,* 14.7.1931 - Furtwangen; HochSchw, 15.12.1931 - Lenzkirch; *TB,* 21.12.1931 - Triberg; StA Wolfach 032/Bd. 2 - 9.12.1930. On the decline of invitations by hotels and tourist organizations see StA Neustadt, 3182 - 14.7.1932. On the cutback of financial support by the community councils see StA Neustadt, 3208 - Gemeinderatssitzung, Ratsprotokoll 39/25 - 23.4.1931; GmdA Grafenhausen 322 - 19.12.1931; H. Cottel, *Chronik der Stadtmusik Neustadt;* Donaubote, 17.2.1932.

48. *Hschw,* 19.1.1932 - Lenzkirch; *FZ,* 18.9.1930; *Hschw,* 30.4.1932 - Seppenhofen; *SchwT,* 4.3.1931 - Furtwangen; *Hschw,* 8.6.1932, 12.1.1932 - Lenzkirch; K. Maier, *Die Geschichte einer Schwarzwaldgemeinde: Oberwolfach* (Oberwolfach, 1958), 172.

49. GmdA Bonndorf - 1798 - 22.8.1929 - Männergesangsverein.

50. *Donaubote,* 26.7.1932; *FZ,* 6.6.1932; StaaF, LKK, 3657 - 2.8.1932 Gütenbach.

51. Benedikt Kuner from Schonach had been head of the *Turnverein* between

1920 and 1922. Eight years later he joined the NSDAP and became Ortsgruppen-leiter. See W. Hamm, *Chronik der Gemeinde Schonach* (Karlsruhe, 1981), 614; PfA Schonach, NSDAP - Ortgruppe Schonach, 28.11.1931. Robert Köhler from Eisen-bach was member of the *Krieg- und Militärverein* between 1919 and 1929. In 1930 he joined the NSDAP. See GmdA Eisenbach, XII/4; StaaF, BZ Donaueschingen - 1977/52 - 345, Eisenbach, 4.7.1931. Valentin Schneider, head of the local fire brigade in Schonach in 1927, joined the NSDAP in 1931. See Hamm, ibid., 534; PfA Schonach, ibid., Mitgliederverzeichnis, 1932.

52. GLAK, 233/27915 - 1932 - Der agrarpolitische Apparat der bad. National-sozialisten, 7; for an expression of different opinions, see Zofka, *Ausbreitung* (n. 24), 37, 81; Kaschuba, *Dörfliches Überleben* (n. 15), 267; R. Koshar, *Social Life, Local Politics and Nazism. Marburg/Lahn, 1880–1955* (Chapel Hill, 1987), chap. 5.

53. O. Heilbronner, "Die nationalsozialistische Partei—ein bürgerlicher Verein?" in *Tel Aviver Jahrbuch für deutsche Geschichte* 24 (1994): 61–79; R. Chickering, "Political Mobilization and Vereinal Life: Some Thoughts on the National Socialist German Workers Club (e.V.)," in L. E. Jones, J. Retallock (eds.), *Elections, Mass Politics and Social Change in Modern Germany* (Cam-bridge, 1992), 307–28. - *Donaubote,* 26.7.1932, 17.2.1932 ("Brief aus dem mit-tleren Schwarzwald"); M. Hildenbrand, "Die nationalsozialistische Machtergrei-fung in einer Kleinstadt - Haslach i. Kinzigtal im Jahre 1933," in *Die Ortenau* 63 (1983): 27–29.

54. During a discussion about the problem of wearing uniforms in the church, the local priest in Lahr/Schw. compared the local Turnverein with the NSDAP, and not only because of his refusal to let both of them enter the church, but because of their anticlerical stances. See ErzAF B2/NS1. Other Catholic regions where the Nazi Party's activity resembled the bourgeois Vereine can be found in Rauh-Kühne, *Ettlingen* (n. 21), 271; Friedrich Schäfer, *Das Eindringen des Nation-alsozialismus in das Alltagsleben einer unterfränkischen Kleinstadt dargestellt am Beispiel Hammelsburg* (Würzburg, 1994), 65; Siegert, "Braune Spürensuche," Teil II (n. 24), 134.

55. StA Wolfach, 055–00/ 1 - 21.1.1932; *KN,* 19.3.1932, Haslach, Wan-derverein.

56. A general discussion about the modern and antimodern characteristics of the NSDAP can be found in I. Kershaw, *The Nazi Dictatorship. Problems and Per-spectives of Interpretation* (London, 1989), chap. 7. Michael Prinz, Rainer Zitel-mann (eds.), *Nationalsozialismus und Modernisierung* (Darmstadt, 1991), 1–20.

57. Mommsen, "Verschränkung" (n. 2); R. Hamilton, *Who Voted for Hitler* (Princeton, 1982), chap. 12, 13; Allen, *Seizure* (n. 24), 144; Noakes, *Lower Saxony* (n. 2), 211; G. Pridham, *Hitler's Rise to Power: The Nazi Movement in Bavaria 1923–1933* (New York, 1973), 110–11; I. Kershaw, *The 'Hitler Myth'* (Oxford, 1987), 37–47; H. U. Thamer, *Verführung und Gewalt—Deutschland 1933–1945* (Berlin, 1987), 148–59; W. Horn, *Führerideologie und Parteiorganisation in der NSDAP 1919–1933* (Düsseldorf, 1972), chap. 5. See the discussion on these topics in chap. 8 above.

58. See the conclusions in Kocka, *Bürgertum und Bürgerlichkeit* (n. 1). Recently, a turning point was evident with everything concerning the post-1918 German bourgeoisie. See Mommsen, "Auflösung" (n. 1); Fritzsche, *Rehearsal*

(n. 5); Koshar, *Social Life* (n. 8); Hopwood, "Paladins" (n. 6); idem, "Mobilization of a National Community," (n. 19); Bieber, *Bürgertum* (n. 4); Ferguson, *Paper and Iron* (n. 4); O. Heilbronner, "Der verlassene Stammtisch. Vom Verfall der bürgerlichen Infrastruktur und dem Aufstieg der NSDAP am Beispiel der Region Schwarzwald," in *Geschichte und Gesellschaft* 19, 3 (1993): 178–201; K. Tenfelde and H. U. Wehler (eds.), *Wege zur Geschichte des Bürgertums* (Gottingen, 1994); H. Siegrist, "Ende der Bürgerlichkeit? Die Kategorien 'Bürgertum' und 'Bürgerlichkeit' in der westdeutschen Gesellschaft und Geschichtswissenschaft der Nachkriegsperiode," in *Geschichte und Gesellschaft* 21, 4 (1995): 549–80; on the German bourgeoisie and the Nazi Party see H. Matthiesen, "Das Gothaer Bürgertum und der Nationalsozialismus 1918–1930," in Detlev, Heiden, Günther Mai (eds.), *Nationalsozialismus in Thüringen* (Weimar, 1995), 97–118; idem, *Bürgertum und Nationalsozialismus. Das bürgerliche Gotha von 1918 bis 1933* (Jena, 1995); C. C. Szejnmann, *The Rise of the Nazi Party in Saxony between 1921 and 1933,* Ph.D. thesis (University of London, 1995), 222–73; Weisbrod, "The Crisis of Bourgeois Society" (n. 5); Miesbeck, *Rosenheim* (n. 21). Still, these studies (except Heilbronner) do not concentrate on the bourgeois *Vereine*. Here we need more studies that will help us to compare our results from the Black Forest with other regions in Germany. A historiographical survey of the whole bourgeois history during the Weimar period can be found in Möller, "Bürgertum und bürgerlich-liberale Bewegung" (n.s.).

59. Noteworthy are Rau-Kühne, *Ettlingen* (n. 21); G. Plum, *Gesellschaftsstruktur und politisches Bewußtsein in einer katholischen Region 1928–1933. Untersuchungen am Beispiel des Regierungsbezirks Aachen* (Stuttgart, 1973), and Robert Moeller, *German Peasants and Agrarian Politics 1914–1924. The Rhineland and Westphalia* (Chapel Hill, 1986). See also the regional studies mentioned in chapter 11, note 6.

60. *Donaubote,* 26.7.1932 ("Bürger, sei auf der Hut").

61. StaaF, BZ Neustadt - 245/184, 25.1.1932 Joostal - Titisee.

Chapter 11

1. The articles in Blaschke, Kuhlemann, *Religion im Kaiserreich* (intro., pt. 3, n. 1) reveal the nature of the different Catholic milieus. See also the titles in n. 1, introduction to part 3.

2. T. Nipperdey, *Religion im Umbruch* (intro., pt. 3, n. 1), 24; H. Jedin (ed.), *Handbuch der Kirchengeschichte,* VI/2 (Freiburg, 1973), 220; Klöcker, *Katholisches Milieu* (intro., pt. 3, n. 1), 260–62; Mooser, "Das katholische Milieu," Blaschke and Kuhlemann, *Religion im Kaiserreich* (intro., pt. 3, n. 1), 59–92.

3. On the Center Party see D. Blackbourn, *Populists and Patricians: Class, Religion and Local Politics in Wilhelmine Germany* (New Haven, 1980). On the the aclerical character of the Center Party see M. L. Anderson, "The Zentrumsstreit and Catholicism in Germany," in *CEH* 4 (1988): 350–78; W. Loth, *Katholiken im Kaiserreich* (Düsseldorf, 1984).

4. On the Volksverein in general see E. Ritter, *Die katholisch-soziale Bewegung in Deutschland im 19. Jahrhundert und der Volksverein* (Cologne, 1954); H. Heitzer, *Der Volksverein für das katholische Deutschland im Kaiserreich 1890–1918* (Mainz,

1979); on the Volksverein in Baden, which is the focus of our discussion, see H. J. Kremer, "Der Volksverein für das katholische Deutschland in Baden 1890–1933," in *Freiburger Diözesanarchiv* 104 (1984): 208–80; idem, *Mit Gott für Wahrheit, Freiheit und Recht. Quellen zur Organisation und Politik der Zentrumspartei und des politischen Katholizismus in Baden 1888–1914* (Stuttgart, 1983), 219–25.

5. R. Brack, *Deutsches Episkopat und Gewerkschaftsstreit 1900–1914* (Cologne, 1976); H. Heitzer, *Kardinal Georg Kopp und der Gewerkschaftsstreit 1900–1914* (Cologne, 1983); Anderson, *Zentrumsstreit* (n. 3).

6. On the Center Party during the Weimar Republic see above all H. Hürten, *Deutsche Katholiken 1918–1945* (Paderborn, 1992), 49–177; K. Ruppert, *Im Dienst am Staat von Weimar. Das Zentrum als regierende Partei in der Weimarer Demokratie* (Düsseldorf, 1992); R. Morsey, *Die deutsche Zentrumspartei 1917–1923* (Düsseldorf, 1966); idem, *Der Untergang des politischen Katholizismus—Die Zentrumspartei zwischen christlichem Selbstverständnis und "Nationaler Erhebung" 1932/ 33* (Stuttgart, 1977). On the *BVP* see K. Schönhoven, *Die Bayerische Volkspartei 1924–1932* (Düsseldorf, 1972). On the relations with the *DNVP* and the difficulties of the Catholic milieu in the Rhineland see Moeller, *German Peasants* (chap. 10, n. 59). On the Catholic milieu in Westphalia during the Weimar Republic see H. Smula, *Milieus und Parteien: Eine regionale Analyse der Interdependenz von politisch-sozialen Milieus, Parteiensystem und Wahlverhalten am Beispiel des Landkreises Lüdinghausen 1919–1933* (Münster, 1993); Doris Kaufmann, *Katholisches Milieu in Münster 1928–1933. Politische Aktionsformen und geschlechtsspezifische Verhaltensräume* (Münster, 1984); Stefan Rüping, *Parteiensystem und Sozialstruktur in zwei dominant katholischen und überwiegend ländlichen Regionen 1912–1972* (Münster, 1990); C. Kösters, *Katholische Verbände und moderne Gesellschaft. Organisationsgeschichte und Vereinskultur im Bistum Münster 1918–1945* (Paderborn, 1995).

7. Hürten, *Deutsche Katholiken* (n. 6), 119–33; on the *Vv* see D. H. Müller, *Arbeiter, Katholizismus, Staat. Der Volksverein für das katholische Deutschlands in der Weimarer Republik* (Bonn, 1995); on the *KAV* see J. Aretz, *Katholische Arbeiterbewegung und Nationalismus—Der Verband katholischer Arbeiter und Knappenvereine Westdeutschlands 1923–1945* (Mainz, 1978); Plum, *Gesellschaftsstruktur* (chap. 10, n. 59), 66–95. On the *CSRP* see D. Fricke et al. (eds.), *Lexikon zur Parteiengeschichte—Die bürgerlichen und kleinbürgerlichen Parteien und Verbände in Deutschland 1789–1945,* 1 (Leipzig, 1983), 455–63; on the local level see Plum, *Gesellschaftsstruktur* (chap. 10, n. 59); Rauh-Kühne, *Ettlingen* (chap. 10, n. 21), 141–56.

8. Hürten, *Deutsche Katholiken* (n. 6), 162ff.; K. Scholder, *The Church and the Third Reich,* vol. 1, 1918–1934 (London, 1987), chap. 9–10.

9. On this case see ErzAF, B2/NS1–11.11.1930, 7.3.1931, 8.4.1931. This and similar cases have already been discussed in the analysis of the Nazi propaganda and the party's position toward Church and Center Party (chap. 9).

10. See the publications in ErzAF, B1-B2/NS1-NS2. A general description on Baden can be found in J. Köhler, "Die katholische Kirche in Baden und Württemberg in der Endphase der Weimarer Republik," in T. Schnabel (ed.), *Die Machtergreifung in Südwestdeutschland—Das Ende der Weimarer Republik in Baden und Württemberg* (Stuttgart, 1983), 257–94; similar cases in Bavaria are described by

Thomas Breuer, *Verordneter Wandel? Der Widerstreit zwischen nationalsozialistischem Herrschaftsanspruch und traditionaler Lebenswelt im Erzbistum Bamberg* (Mainz, 1992), chap. 3.; Schäfer, *Das Eindringen des Nationalsozialismus* (chap. 10, n. 54) 93–105; in Baden see Rau-Kühne, *Ettlingen* (chap. 10, n. 21), 270–79; on Münster see D. Kaufmann, *Katholisches Milieu in Münster* (n. 6), 160–67.

11. ErzAF, B2–55–135 (Sportvereine), 8.10.1930, 23.11.1930 - Löffingen; the analysis below is based on my article "Catholic Plight in a Rural Area of Germany and the Rise of the Nazi Party," *Social History* 20, 2 (1995): 219–34.

12. ErzAF, B2–55–146, Katholischer Volksverein, Tätigkeitsbericht, 1920/ 21; PfA Bonndorf, 254 - 6.12.1924; Kremer, *Volksverein* (n. 4), 267–73; Kremer, *Wahrheit* (n. 4), 291–311.

13. The different *Vereine* are localized by Kremer, *Wahrheit* (n. 4), 291–311; PfA Bonndorf, 254, *Volksverein.* On the activities of the *Vereine* before 1914 see the reports (*Kirchenvisitationen*) which were presented in Freiburg by the clerical inspectors after the visits in the parishes. These *Kirchenvisitationen* (*Kv*) about visits before 1914 are stored in the parish archives of the villages and towns and also in the ErzAF.

14. H. Lauer, *Geschichte der katholischen Kirche in der Baar* (Donaueschingen, 1921 [1928]), 364–65; *Der Landbund: Sein Auftreten und sein Wirken im Bezirk Bonndorf 1922–1924,* (Karlsruhe, 1925), 9–62; E. Bleibtreu, *Die Bauernbewegung im Bezirk Bonndorf—1919–1922* (Karlsruhe, 1923); ErzAF, B3 403 - Dekanat Kinzigtal, 17.4.1930, Schenkenzell; B3 - 765 - Dekanat Neustadt, 5.9.1932 - Altglashütten; Personalia, Göschweiler, Pfarrer A. Brugger, 20.2.1932.

15. PfA Rohrbach, Seelsorge, 24.11.1929; PfA Löffingen, Seelsorge, 28.8.1930; *KN,* 25.11.1930, Wolfach; StaaF, BZ Neustadt, 1974/ 31 - P. 135, Ortsbereisung Grafenhausen, 1924. Extensive material on the living conditions of the priests can be found in the reports of *Kirchenvisitationen;* see PfA Schluchsee, Kv - 1924; PfA Bonndorf, Kv. 1925. On the cutback in the priests' salary see *TB,* 14.11.1931.

16. *TB,* 14.8.1930 - Schonach; PfA Schönau, Seelsorge, 1930–1931; StaaF BZ Neustadt - 1980/ 10/ 20, P. 278 - Ortsbereisung Oberbränd, 20.11.1930; PfA Oberwolfach, Kv 1928.

17. *EvH,* 13.9.1930 - Eisenbach; PfA Gütenbach, Seelsorge, 31.8., 5.9.1931.

18. *DT,* 17.2.1931 - Furtwangen.

19. During a year of Mission (*Missionsjahr*) Catholic personalities from outside used to visit the village. The activities of Catholic *Vereine* were strengthened, and divine services with the Holy Communion for all inhabitants and prayer meetings for the masses took place. See "Mission," *Lexikon für Theologie und Kirche* (Freiburg, 1962). On the mission in Schenkenzell see PfA Schenkenzell, Kv. 1928.

20. On the question of Catholic morality in general see T. Zeldin, *France 1848–1945* (Oxford, 1979), chap. 11; idem, "The Conflict of Moralities. Confession, Sin and Pleasure in the Nineteenth Century," in idem, *Conflicts in French Society* (London, 1970), 13–50. On the situation in the Black Forest see O. Heilbronner, *The Achilles' Heel of German Catholicism. The Weimar Society between Crisis and Nazism,* Ph.D. thesis (Hebrew University of Jerusalem, 1992), chap. 13.

21. *Der Alemanne,* 3.12.1932 - Lenzkirch.

22. ErzAF, B2–55–146 - Katholischer Volksverein - 1930, Personalia, Bonndorf, F. Huber Jahresbericht 1929, 1930.

23. *Hschw,* 7.3.1932 - Löffingen; ErzAF, B2–55–82, 14.1, 4.4.1923 - Hüfingen.
24. ErzAF, B2-55-146 - Katholischer Volksverein, Tätigkeitsbericht 1921, 1924.
25. PfA Hinterzarten, Kv- 1928; PfA St. Blasien, Kv - 1932.
26. See notes 23 and 11 and also *EvH,* 25.10.1930 - Hammereisenbach; *Der Alemanne,* 3.12.1931 - Oppenau; PfA Reiselfingen, Seelsorge, 1.9.1931.
27. ErzAF, Personalia, A. Mayer, Schluchsee Jahresbericht, 1930; B3 - Dekanat Donaueschingen, 27.10.1930; Dekanat Neustadt, 22.10.1930; Dekanat Kinzigtal, 22.10.1930; Dekanat Villingen, 23.10.1929, 27.10.1930.
28. ErzAf, B2-55-84 - Christlicher Metallarbeiter-Verband Deutschland. Geschäftsstelle Villingen - 4.10.1928. A detailed analysis can be found in my article "The Disintegration of the Workers' Catholic Milieu and the Rise of the Nazi Party," in C. Fischer (ed.), *Weimar, Workers and National Socialism* (Oxford, Providence, 1996), 217–35.
29. PfA St. Blasien, Seelsorge - 6.4.1929, 26.6.1929, 5.9.1929, 10.10.1929, 5.11.1929.
30. *FZ,* 1.8.1932 - Schonach; *TB,* 14.8.1930, 14.11.1930 - Schonach; *Echo vom Wald,* 7.11.1930, 30.7.1932 - Schonach; W. Hamm, *Chronik der Gemeinde Schonach,* Karlsruhe, 1981, 260–261; ErzAF, Dekanat Villingen, B3-1090, 1930.
31. ErzAF, Personalia, Wilhelm Fichter, Schonach Jahresbericht 1907, 1908. Hamm, Chronik (n. 30), 353–54, 565; PfA Schonach, Kv - 1923, 1930; *TB,* 18.10.1929, 27.8.1930, 3.9.1930 - Schonach. In Gütenbach the relationship between workers and priest was extremely tense, due to the priest's decision to exclude workers who did not fulfill their religious obligations from opportunities to work: PfA Gütenbach, Seelsorge - 31.8., 5.9.1931; ErzAF - B2–55–18, 22.11. 1932 - Gütenbach; PfA Furtwangen, Kv - 1930.
32. See note 20 above.
33. PfA Todtnau Seelsorge - 10.2.1922, Kath. Männerverein.
34. See note 29 above.
35. ErzAF, B2-55-146, Tätigkeitsbericht, 1928, 1929, 1931; ErzAF, B2-55-18, Gütenbach, 22.11.1932.
36. "Lokalorganisationen der SPD in Baden, Stand 31.12.1929," in J. Schadt (ed.), *Im Dienst an der Republik: Die Tätigkeitsberichte des Landesvorstandes der SPD Badens 1914–1932* (Stuttgart, 1977), 105–7, 157–59.
37. H. Heitzer, "Deutscher Katholizismus und 'Bolschewismusgefahr' bis 1933," in *Historisches Jahrbuch II* 113 (1993): 355–87; H. Smolinsky, "Das katholische Russlandbild in Deutschland nach dem Ersten Weltkrieg und im 'Dritten Reich,' " in H.-E. Volkmann (ed.), *Das Russlandbild im Dritten Reich* (Köln, 1994), 323–56; propaganda pamphlets of the Center Party which described the terror of Bolshevism can be found in GLAK, 347 - 1943/18–34. On the bourgeois press see the discussion about the relation between this press and the NSDAP in chap. 8 above. The central argument about the influence of information about the communist terror in Russia on the German population has been developed by E. Nolte, *Der europäische Bürgerkrieg, 1917–1945* (Berlin, 1987). See also C. Striefler, *Kampf um die Macht. Kommunisten und Nationalsozialisten am Ende der Weimarer Republik* (Berlin, 1993); O. Heilbronner, "Weimar Society: The Image of Soviet Russia," *Tel Aviver Jahrbuch für Deutsche Geschichte* 24 (1995): 179–92.
38. On the fate of women in Russia see *Donaubote,* 10.10.1931. On the persecu-

tions of religious believers in Russia, see *Schw B*, 31.3.1930, "Hirtenbrief"; *Hschw*, 26.4.1932. On the terror against peasants, see *TB*, 20.2.1932.

39. *Bonndorfer Volksblatt*, 9.3.1931.

40. For example, according to remarks of the head of the Catholic trade union, the workers of the dam at Schluchsee had not been interested in voting in the Landtag Election in Baden in 1929. PfA St. Blasien, Seelsorge, 5.11.1929.

41. The similarities between the Allgäu and East Baden (Baar Region and Black Forest) were already recognized by Jonathan Sperber in the context of his research on anticlerical movements inside the Catholic milieu in the middle of the nineteenth century; see J. Sperber, *Popular Catholicism in Nineteenth Century Germany* (Princeton, 1984), 291; see also Heilbronner, "Regionale Aspekte zum katholischen Bürgertum" (chap. 10, n. 26); idem, "In Search of the Catholic (rural) Bourgeoisie" (chap. 10, n. 26); Rohe, *Wahlen* (intro., pt. 3, n. 1), 76–77, 156.

42. Although research contributions about the *Kulturkampf* in the south and east of Baden are not available, the argument about the affinity between the intensity of the *Kulturkampf* and the strengthening of political Catholicism and the piety among the population in Baden (and elsewhere) can be found in numerous publications. See, for example, L. Gall, "Die partei- und sozialgeschichtliche Problematik des badischen Kulturkampfes," in *Zeitschrift für die Geschichte des Oberrheins* 113 (1965): 151–96; M. L. Anderson, "The Kulturkampf and the Course of German History," in *CEH* 1 (1986): 82–115; Sperber, *Popular Catholicism* (n. 41), chap. 5; Rohe, *Wahlen* (intro., pt. 3, n. 1), 73–83; C. Weber, *"Eine starke enggeschlossene Phalanx," Der politische Katholizismus und die erste deutsche Reichstagswahl* (Essen, 1992); G. Kroff, "Kulturkampf und Volkfrömmigkeit," in W. Schieder (ed.), *Volksreligiosität in der modernen Sozialgeschichte* (Gottingen, 1986), 137–51; D. Blackbourn, *The Marpingen Visions. Rationalism, Religion and the Rise of Modern Germany* (London, 1995); I. Götz v. Olenhusen, *Klerus und abweichendes Verhalten. Zur Sozialgeschichte katholischer Priester im 19.Jahrhundert. Die Erzdiözese Freiburg* (Göttingen, 1994).

Conclusion

1. J. Noakes, *The Nazi Party in Lower Saxony* (Oxford, 1971), 211.

2. R. Hamilton, *Who Voted for Hitler?* (Princeton, 1982), 367.

3. T. Childers, *The Nazi Voter. The Social Foundations of Fascism in Germany, 1919–1933* (Chapel Hill 1983), 265; see recently, O. Heilbronner and D. Mühlberger, "Who Voted for Hitler Reconsidered: The Catholic Voters" *European History Quarterly*, vol. 27, 2 (1997): 217–46.

4. K. Rohe, *Wahlen und Wählertraditionen in Deutschland* (Frankfurt, 1992), 161–62.

5. L. M. Killian, "Social Movements," in *Encyclopedia Britannica*, vol. 16, 974–80. See also H. G. Jascke, *Soziale Basis und soziale Funktion des Nationalsozialismus* (Opladen, 1982), 141–42; P. Burke, *History and Social Theory* (Oxford, 1992), 88–91.

6. See my forthcoming articles, "Popularer Liberalismus im Allgäu 1871–1932: Ein abweichender Fall?" in *Zeitschrift für Bayerische Landesgeschichte*, 901 (1998), 297–315; "Popularer Liberalismus in Südbaden 1871–1912:

Entwicklungstendenzen der badischen Wahlkultur," in *Zeitschrift für die Geschichte des Oberrheins* 146 (1998).

7. The only historians who present something comparable are Rudy Koshar in his *Social Life, Local Politics and Nazism. Marburg/Lahn, 1880–1955* (Chapel Hill, 1987); idem, "'Cult of Vereins'. The Lower Middle Class in Weimar Germany," in idem. (ed.), *Splintered Classes: Politics and the Lower Middle Classes in Interwar Europe* (New York, 1990), and Robert Hopwood in his "Mobilization of a Nationalist Community," *German History,* 2 (1992): 149–76; See also O. Heilbronner, "Die NSDAP. Ein bürgerlicher Verein?" in *Tel Aviver Jahrbuch für Deutsche Geschichte* 23 (1994): 62–79.

8. See the historiographical survey in chap. 4.

9. See a general discussion about this problematic topic of the society of the Weimar Republic: D. Peukert, *The Weimar Republic* (London, 1992), chap. 1; G. Feldman, "The Weimar Republic: A Problem of Modernization?" in *Archiv für Sozialgeschichte* 26 (1986): 1–26.

10. A similar tendency dominates the series about Bavarian society (after 1933) published by Martin Broszat. See M. Broszat et al. (eds.), *Bayern in der NS Zeit, Munich 1977–1981;* idem, "Plädoyer für eine Historisierung des Nationalsozialismus," in *Merkur* 39 (1985): 373–85.

11. Hamilton, *Hitler* (n. 2), 329ff., 416–19; E. Nolte, *Der europäische Bürgerkrieg 1917–1945. Nationalsozialismus und Bolschewismus* (Berlin, 1987), chap. 9. H. Heitzer, "Deutscher Katholizismus und Bolschewismusgefahr bis 1933," in *Historisches Jahrbuch II* 113 (1993): 355–87; C. Striefler, *Kampf um die Macht. Kommunisten und Nationalsozialisten am Ende der Weimarer Republik* (Berlin, 1993). Some examples of the fear of bourgeois society can be found in the diary of Frau Solmitz, quoted in W. Jochmann, *Nationalsozialismus und Revolution. Ursprung und Geschichte der NSDAP in Hamburg 1922–1933* (Frankfurt, 1963), 400–32; Oded Heilbronner "Weimar Society: The Image of Soviet Russia," in *Tel Aviver Jahrbuch für Deutsche Geschichte* 24 (1995): 179–92; and, recently, H. Berghof, "Konsumgüterindustrie im Nationalsozialismus.Marketing im Spannungsfeld von Profit- und Regimeinteressen," in *Archiv für Sozialgeschichte* 36, (1996): 302.

12. K. Borchardt, *Wachstum, Krisen, Handlungsspielräume der Wirtschaftspolitik* (Göttingen, 1982). The discussion about Borchardt's argument is documented in I. Kershaw (ed.), *Weimar: Why did German Democracy Fail?* (London, 1990). See lately also G. Feldman, *The Great Disorder. Politics, Economics and Society in the German Inflation, 1914–1924* (Oxford, 1993), 837–54.

Bibliography

Archives

Bundesarchiv Koblenz (BAK)
NS 22: Reichsorganisationsleitung der NSDAP
NS 20: Kleine Erwerbungen
NS 26: Hauptarchiv der NSDAP
R 134: Reichskommissar für Überwachung der öffentlichen Ordnung

Berlin Document Center (BDC)
Personalakten der badischen Parteimitglieder und -führer. Zentral- und Gaumitgliederkartei

Staatsarchiv München
Polizeidirektion

Generallandesarchiv Karlsruhe (GLAK)
233: Staatsministerium
347: Bezirksamt Donaueschingen

Hauptstaatsarchiv Stuttgart
E 151a - Bü: Landesarbeitsamt Südwestdeutschland

Erzbischöfliches Archiv Freiburg (ErzAF)
B2/ NS 1–NS 4: NSDAP
B2/ 55 - 1: Vereine
B2/ 55 - 14: Katholischer Arbeiterverein
B2/ 55 - 18: Wohlfahrtspflege
B2/ 55 - 82–83: Gesellenvereine
B2/ 55 - 84: Gewerkschaftsvereine
B2/ 55 - 97: Katholische Aktion
B2/ 55 - 135: Sportverein
B2/ 55 - 146: Katholischer Volksverein
B3/: Dekanat - Kapitalkonferenzen: 132 - Donaueschingen; 403 - Kinzigtal;
    765 - Neustadt; 1090 - Villingen
Personalakten

Staatsarchiv Freiburg (StaaF): Old Signatures
Landeskommissär Konstanz (LKK)
Bezirksämter (BZ): Donaueschingen, 1977/ 52; Neustadt, 26, 28, 93, 108, 201, 209,
    228, 240, 244–246, 253, 1974/ 31, 1979/ 85, 1980/ 10–1980/ 20, 1986/ 68; Offen-
    burg - Nr. 128, 1601, 1740; Schopfheim - T. 1; Staufen - 318; Villingen - 1973/
    39, 1979/ 82, 1985/ 110.
Staatsanwaltschaft Freiburg
Plakatsammlung NSDAP: Teil 1

Stadtarchive (StA), Gemeindearchive (GmdA)
    Altglashütten, Bonndorf, Breitenau, Dittishausen, Donaueschingen, Ein-
    bach, Eisenbach, Furtwangen, Fischerbach, Grafenhausen, Haslach, Hin-
    terzarten, Lehengericht, Lenzkirch, Löffingen, Neustadt, Schiltach, Schönau,
    Seppenhofen, Schonach, Triberg, Wolfach.

Pfarrarchive (PfA; in the Erzbischöfliches Archiv in Freiburg)
    Bachheim, Ewattingen, Fischerbach, Furtwangen, Grafenhausen, Güten-
    bach, Haslach, Hinterzarten, Oberkirch, Oberwolfach, Oppenau, Reisel-
    fingen, Rohrbach, St. Blasien, Schenkenzell, Schluchsee, Schönwald, Todt-
    nau, Todtmoos, Vöhrenbach, Wolfach.

Pfarrarchive (in the community)
    Bonndorf, Löffingen, Schönau, Schonach.

Newspapers

Der Alemanne 1931
Anzeiger vom Kinzigtal 1930–32 (*AvK*)
Die Arbeit 1931–32
Bonndorfer Volksblatt 1930–32
Donaubote 1931–32
Donaueschinger Tagblatt 1929–32 (*DT*)
Echo vom Hochfirst 1930–31 (*EvH*), from 1931 under the name *Hochschwarzwald*
    1931–32 (*Hschw*)
Echo vom Wald 1930–32
Feldberg Rundschau 1931
Freiburger Zeitung 1929–32 (*FZ*)
Der Führer 1928–31
Führer Korrespondenz. Zeitschrift für das soziale Vereinswesen, Dr. August Piper
    (ed.), 1928–32
Hochwächter auf dem Schwarzwald 1930–32 (*HochSchw*)
Kinzigtäler Nachrichten 1930–32 (*KN*)
Lahrer Anzeiger 1930–32
Renchtäler 1930
Schopfheimer Zeitung 1930
Schriften des Vereins für Sozialpolitik, Leipzig 1883, 1889
Schwarzwälder Bote 1930 (*SchwB*)

Schwarzwälder Post 1928
Das Schwarzwälder Tagblatt (Villingen) 1930
Schwarzwälder Tagblatt (Furtwangen-Ausgabe für die Baar) 1931–32 (*SchwT*)
Schwarzwälder Zeitung (Bonndorf) 1930–32
Schwarzwälder Zeitung. "Der Grenzer" (Freudenstadt) 1930–32
Triberger Bote 1930–32 (*TB*)

Official Publications and Statistical Data

Publication of the Badisches Statistisches Landesamt Karlsruhe (*BSL*)
　　Badische Gemeindestatistik - 1927
　　Die badische Landwirtschaft im Allgemeinen und in einzelnen Gauen 1932, 1936
　　Die Ergebnisse der Volkszählung vom 16.6.1933 in Baden, 1933
　　Der Fremdenverkehr in Baden, 1925
　　Die Gebrechlichen in Baden, 1925
　　Handel und Verkehr in Baden, 1925
　　Die Industrie in Baden, 1925
　　Die Landwirtschaft in Baden, 1927
　　Reichspräsidentenwahl 1925 in Baden (Erster und zweiter Wahlgang), 1926
　　Die Religionszugehörigkeit der Bevölkerung in Baden in den letzten 100 Jahren,
　　　　1928
　　Statistisches Jahrbuch für das Land Baden, 1925, 1930, 1938
　　Die Wahlen in Baden zur deutschen Nationalversammlung im Jahr 1919
　　Die Wahlen zum Badischen Landtag am 30.10.1921, 25.10.1925, 27.10.1929
　　Die Wahlen zum Reichstag am 6.6.1920, 4.5.1924, 7.12.1924, 20.5.1928,
　　　　14.9.1930, 31.7.1932, 6.11.1932, 5.3.1933 in Baden
　　Die Wohnbevölkerung in Baden und ihre Religionszugehörigkeit, 1934
　　Wohnungszählung und Wohnungsbau in Baden, 1928
　　Denkschrift über die Verschuldung der Badischen Landwirtschaft im Jahre
　　　　1928. Der Minister des Inneren, Karlsruhe, 1928

Statistische Mitteilungen über das Großherzogtum Baden
　　Die Ergebnisse der Reichstagswahlen, Bd. XX 1903 (Sondernummer),
　　　　Bd.XXIV, 1907 (Sondernummer), Neue Folge V, 1912

Publication of the Statistik des deutschen Reiches - *Berlin*
　　Vol. 332 - *Volksbegehren und Volksentscheid* "Enteignung der Fürstenvermö-
　　　　gen"
　　Vol. 382 - *Die Wahlen zum Reichstag am 14.9.1930*
　　Vol. 417, 11b - *Volks-, Berufs- und Betriebszählung vom 16.6.1925.*
　　　　Gewerbliche Betriebszählung - Südwestdeutschland
　　Vol. 427 - *Die Wahlen des Reichspräsidenten am 13.3.1932 und 10.4.1932*
　　Vol. 434 - *Die Wahlen zum Reichstag am 31.7.1932, 6.11.1932, 5.3.1933*
　　Vol. 451 - *Volkszählung. Die Bevölkerung des Deutschen Reiches nach den*
　　　　Ergebnissen der Volkszählung 1933

Vol. 456 - *Berufszählung 1933. Die berufliche und soziale Gliederung der Bevölkerung in den Ländern und Landesteilen Südwestdeutschlands und Hessens*
Vol. 465, 11 - *Gewerbliche Betriebszählung 1933. Die gewerblichen Niederlassungen in den Ländern Württemberg, Baden*

Other Primary Sources

Adreßbuch für die Städte Furtwangen und Triberg 1922. Munich, 1922.
Adreßbuch für Stadt und Amtsbezirk Neustadt im Schwarzwald 1928/1929. Neustadt i. Schwarzwald, 1929.
Adreßbuch des Amtsbezirks Villingen 1930/ 31. Villingen, 1931.
Adreß- und Geschäftshandbuch der Stadtgemeinde Furtwangen 1928. Furtwangen, 1928.
Brot ist Freiheit, Freiheit ist Brot. Dokumente zur Geschichte der Arbeiterbewegung in Südbaden 1832–1952. Heilbronn, 1991.
Die Gemeinden der Amtsbezirke Donaueschingen und Neustadt in historischer Darstellung. Versammelt und bearbeitet von Ludwig Heizmann. Munich, 1933.
Historischer Atlas von Baden-Württemberg. Stuttgart, 1972.
H. J. Kremer, rev. *Mit Gott für Wahrheit, Freiheit und Recht. Quellen zur Organisation und Politik der Zentrumspartei und des politischen Katholizismus 1888–1914.* Stuttgart, 1983.
F. Lautenschlager, ed. *Bibliographie der Badischen Geschichte* (9 vol.). Stuttgart, 1961–81.
Lexikon für Theologie und Kirche. Freiburg i. B., 1957–67.
R. Morsey, ed. *Katholizismus, Verfassungsstaat und Demokratie. Vom Vormärz bis 1933.* Paderborn, 1988.
B. Ottnad, ed. *Badische Biographien.* Stuttgart, 1982–91.
A. Rapp. *Die badischen Landtagsabgeordneten 1905–1929.* Karlsruhe, 1929.
A. Rapp (rev.), *Die Parteibewegung in Baden 1905/1928. Tabellen und Text.* Karlsruhe, 1929.
J. Schadt, ed. *Im Dienst an der Republik. Die Tätigkeitsberichte des Landesverbandes der SPD Badens 1914–1932.* Stuttgart, 1977.
Sperlings Zeitschriften—Adreßbuch. Handbuch der deutschen Presse. Leipzig, 1928, 1920, 1931, 1933.
Staatslexikon, Im Auftrag der Görres Gesellschaft. Freiburg i. B., 1926–32, 1983, 1987.
A. Tyrell, ed. *"Führer befiehl . . . "—Selbstzeugnisse aus der "Kampfzeit" der NSDAP. Dokumentation und Analyse.* Düsseldorf, 1969.

Selected Literature

Abeler, P. *Die Arbeitsmarktverhältnisse der Schwarzwälder Uhrenindustrie in der Nachkriegszeit.* Ph.D. thesis. Münster, 1928.
Allen, W. S. "Farewell to Class Analysis in the Rise of Nazism: Comment." *Central European History 1* (1984): 54–62.

———. "The Nazi Rise to Power: A Comprehensible Catastrophe." In C. Maier et al. (eds.), *The Rise of the Nazi Regime: Historical Reassessments,* 9–19. Boulder, 1986.

———. *The Nazi Seizure of Power: The Experience of A Single German Town.* Revised edition. New York, 1984.

Allgeier, R. "Grenzland in der Krise. Die badische Wirtschaft 1928–1933." In T. Schnabel (ed.), *Die Machtergreifung in Südwestdeutschland,* 150–83. Stuttgart, 1982.

Anderson, M. L. "The Zentrumsstreit and the Dilemma of Catholicism in Wilhelmine Germany." *Central European History* 4 (1988): 350–78.

Anschütz, K. *Protestantismus und Arbeiterschaft. Von der Bewältigung des Alltags in St. Georgen im Schwarzwald in den Jahren 1914–23.* Stuttgart, 1992.

Arafe, T. *The Development and Character of the Nazi Political Machine 1928–1930 and the NSDAP Electoral Breakthrough.* Ph.D. thesis. Louisiana State University, 1976.

Arendt, H. *The Origins of Totalitarianism.* London, 1986.

Aretz, J. *Katholische Arbeiterbewegung und Nationalsozialismus: Der Verband katholischer Arbeiter- und Knappenvereine Westdeutschlands 1923–1945.* Mainz, 1978.

Arns, D. *Grass Roots Politics in the Weimar Republic: Long Term Structural Change and Electoral Behavior in Hessen-Darmstadt to 1930.* Ph.D. thesis. State University of New York at Buffalo, 1979.

Badische Geschichte: Vom Großherzogtum bis zur Gegenwart. Stuttgart, 1979.

Baranowski, S. *The Sanctity of Rural Life. Protestantism, Agrarian Politics and Nazism in Pomerania.* Oxford, 1996.

Barrington, M. I. *Social Origins of Dictatorship and Democracy. Lord and Peasant in the Making of the Modern World.* Boston, 1966.

Bauer, C. *Deutscher Katholizismus—Entwicklungslinien und Profile.* Frankfurt, 1964.

Baumeister, M. *Parität und katholische Inferiorität: Untersuchungen zur Stellung des Katholizismus im Deutschen Kaiserreich.* Paderborn, 1987.

Behrend, H. *Die Beziehungen zwischen der NSDAP-Zentrale und dem Gauverband Süd-Hannover-Braunschweig 1921–1933.* Frankfurt, 1981.

Bendix, R., and S. Lipset. *Class, Status and Power: Social Stratification in Comparative Perspective.* London, 1968.

Bessel, R. "The Rise of the NSDAP and the Myth of Nazi Propaganda." *The Wiener Library Bulletin 51–52* (1980): 20–29.

Best, H., ed. *Vereine in Deutschland.* Bonn, 1994.

Bieber, H. *Bürgertum in der Revolution.* Hamburg, 1993.

Blackbourn, D. *Class, Religion and Local Politics in Wilhelmine Germany: The Catholic Centre Party in Württemberg before 1914.* New Haven, 1980.

Blackbourn, D., and R. J. Evans, eds. *The German Bourgeoisie: Essays on the Social History of the German Middle Class from the Late Eighteenth to the Early Twentieth Century.* London, 1991.

———. *Marpingen. Apparition of the Virgin Mary in Bismarckian Germany.* Oxford, 1993.

Blackbourn, D., and G. Eley. *The Peculiarities of German History, Bourgeois Society and Politics in Nineteenth-Century Germany.* Oxford, 1984.

Blaschke, Olaf. "Der Altkatholizismus 1879 bis 1945. Nationalismus, Antisemitismus und Nationalsozialismus." *Historische Zeitschrift,* 261 (1995): 51–99.

Bleibtreu, E. *Die Bauernbewegung im Bezirk Bonndorf—1919–1922.* Karlsruhe, 1923.

Blessing, B. "Diskussionsbeitrag: Nationalsozialismus unter 'regionalem Blick.'" In H. Moeller et al. (eds.), *Nationalsozialismus in der Region,* 47–56.

Borchardt, K. *Wachstum, Krisen, Handlungsspielräume der Wirtschaftspolitik.* Göttingen, 1982.

Bracher, K. D. *The German Dictatorship.* Middlesex, 1980.

Bracher, K. D., et al., eds. *Die Weimarer Republik 1918–1933.* Düsseldorf, 1987.

Braun, Joachim. "Die Entwicklung des Nationalsozialismus im badischen Amtsbezirk Tauberbischofsheim 1924–1932." *Wertheimer Jb.* 33 (1993): 289–316.

Braunsche, E. "Die Entwicklung der NSDAP in Baden bis 1932/ 33." *Zeitschrift für die Geschichte des Oberrheins* 125 (1977): 331–75.

Breuer, T. *Verordneter Wandel? Der Widerstreit zwischen nationalsozialistischem Herrschaftsanspruch und traditioneller Lebenswelt im Erzbistum Bamberg.* Mainz, 1992.

Broszat, M. *Hitler and the Collapse of Weimar Germany.* London, 1988.

———. "Plädoyer für eine Historisierung des Nationalsozialismus." *Merkur* 39 (1985): 373–85.

———. "Soziale Motivation und Führerbindung des Nationalsozialismus." *VJfZG* 18 (1970): 392–409.

———. "Zur Struktur der NS-Massenbewegung." *VJfZG* 1 (1983): 52–76.

Broszat, M., and Elke Fröhlich. *Alltag und Widerstand: Bayern im Nationalsozialismus.* Munich, 1987.

———. *Bayern in der NS-Zeit, vol. I, II, IV,* Munich, 1977–81.

———. "Politische und soziale Macht auf dem Lande. Die Durchsetzung der NSDAP im Kreis Memmingen." *VJfZG* 25 (1977): 546–72.

Brustein, W. *The Logic of Evil: The Social Origins of the Nazi Party 1925–1933.* New Haven, London, 1996.

Burke, P. "Religion and Secularisation." In P. Burke (ed.), *The New Cambridge Modern History, XIII,* Companion Volume, Cambridge (1979), 293–317.

———. *History and Social Theory.* Oxford, 1992.

Bytwerk, R. "Die nationalsozialistische Versammlungspraxis. Die Anfänge vor 1933." In G. Diesener and Rainer Gries (eds.), *Propaganda in Deutschland: Zur Geschichte der politischen Massenbeeinflussung im 20. Jh.,* 35–50. Darmstadt, 1996.

Childers, T., ed. *The Formation of the Nazi Constituency 1919–1933.* London, 1986.

———. *The Nazi Voter: The Social Foundations of Fascism in Germany 1919–1933.* Chapel Hill, 1983.

———. "The Social Language of Politics in Germany: The Sociology of Political Discourse in the Weimar Republic." *American Historical Review* 2 (1990): 258–332.

————. "Who, Indeed, Did Vote For Hitler?" *Central European History* 1 (1984): 45–53.

Ciolek-Kümper, J. *Wahlkampf in Lippe.* Munich, 1976.

Dann, O., ed. *Vereinswesen und bürgerliche Gesellschaft in Deutschland.* Beiheft 9, *Historische Zeitschrift.* Munich, 1984.

Dobkowski, M., and I. Wallimann, eds. *Radical Perspectives on the Rise of Fascism in Germany 1919–1945.* New York, 1989.

Dussel, K., and M. Frese. "Von traditioneller Vereinskultur zu moderner Massenkultur? Vereins- und Freizeitangebote in einer südwestdeutschen Kleinstadt 1920–1960." *Archiv für Sozialgeschichte* 33 (1993): 59–105.

Evans, R. J. "Religion and Society in Modern Germany." *European Studies Review* 3 (1982): 249– 88.

Evans, R. J., and W. R. Lee, eds. *The German Peasantry.* London, 1986.

Falter, J. *Hitlers Wähler. Der Austieg der NSDAP im Spiegel der Wahlen.* Munich, 1991.

————. "The National Socialist Mobilization of New Voters 1928–1933." In T. Childers (ed.), *The Formation of the Nazi Constituency 1919–1933,* 202–31. London, 1986.

————. "Wahlen und Wahlverhalten unter besonderer Berücksichtigung des Aufstiegs der NSDAP nach 1928." In K. D. Bracher et al. (eds.), *Die Weimarer Republik 1918–1933.* Düsseldorf, 1987.

Falter, J., and M. Kater. "Wähler und Mitglieder der NSDAP." *Geschichte und Gesellschaft* 19.2 (1993): 155–77.

Faris, E. "Takeoff Point for the National Socialist Party: The Landtag Election in Baden 1929." *Central European History* 8 (1975): 140–71.

Farquharson, J. *The Plough and the Swastika. NSDAP and Agriculture in Germany 1924–1945.* London, 1976.

Feldman, G. "The Weimar Republic: A Problem of Modernization?" *Archiv für Sozialgeschichte* 26 (1986): 1–26.

————. *The Great Disorder. Politics, Economics and Society in the German Inflation 1914–1924.* Oxford, 1993.

Fischer, C. *Stormtroopers: A Social, Economic and Ideological Analysis 1929–1935.* London, 1983.

Fischer, W. *Wirtschaft und Gesellschaft im Zeitalter der Industrialisierung.* Göttingen, 1972.

Föhr, E. *Die sozialen und wirtschaftlichen Verhältnisse der Waldarbeiter im badischen Schwarzwald.* Achern i. B., 1921.

Fröhlich, Elke. "Die Partei auf lokaler Ebene: Zwischen gesellschaftlicher Assimilation und Veränderungsdynamik." In G. Hirschfeld and L. Kettenacker (eds.), *Der 'Führerstaat': Mythos und Realität,* 255–68. Stuttgart, 1981.

Gall, L. *Der Liberalismus als regierende Partei: Das Großherzogtum Baden zwischen Restauration und Reichsgründung.* Wiesbaden, 1968.

Genuneit, J. "Methodische Probleme der quantitativen Analyse früher NSDAP-Mitglieder." In R. Mann (ed.), *Die Nationalsozialisten. Analysen faschistischer Bewegungen,* 34–66. Stuttgart, 1980.

Gothein, E. *Wirtschaftsgeschichte des Schwarzwaldes und der angrenzenden Landschaften.* Straßburg, 1892.

Gotto, K., and K. Repgen, eds. *Kirche, Katholizismus und Nationalsozialismus.* Stuttgart, 1980.

Götz v. Olenhusen, I. *Klerus und abweichendes Verhalten. Zur Sozialgeschichte katholischer Priester im 19.Jahrhundert.* Göttingen, 1994.

Grill, J. *The Nazi Movement in Baden 1920–1945.* Chapel Hill, 1983.

———. "Local and Regional Studies on National Socialism." *Journal of Contemporary History* 2 (1986): 253–94.

Hackett, D. *The Nazi Party in the Reichstag Election of 1930.* Ph.D. thesis. University of Wisconsin, 1971.

Hagtvet, B. "The Theory of Mass Society and the Collapse of Weimar Republic: A Re-Examination." In S. Larsen and B. Hagtvet et al. (eds.), *Who were the Fascists? Social Roots of European Fascism,* 66–117. Bergen, 1980.

Hamilton, R. "Reply to Commentators." *Central European History* 1 (1984): 72–85.

———. *Who Voted for Hitler?* Princeton, 1982.

Handbuch der Baden-Württembergischen Geschichte, Bd3. Vom Ende des Alten Reiches bis zum Ende der Monarchien. Stuttgart, 1992.

Heberle, R. *From Democracy to Nazism. A Regional Case Study on Political Parties in Germany.* New York, 1970.

Heilbronner, O. "The Role of Nazi Antisemitism Propaganda in the Party's Activity and Propaganda: A Regional Historiographical Study." *Leo Baeck Institute Year Book 35* (1990): 397–439.

———. "The Failure that Succeeded: The Nazi Party Activity in a Catholic Region in Germany 1929–1932." *Journal of Contemporary History* 3 (1992): 531–49.

———. "The Impact and Consequences of the First World War in a Catholic Rural Area." *German History* 1 (1993): 1–16.

———. "Der verlassene Stammtisch. Vom Verfall der bürgerlichen Infrastruktur und dem Aufstieg der NSDAP am Beispiel der Region Schwarzwald." *Geschichte und Gesellschaft 2* (1993): 178–200.

———. "Die Leute auf dem Wald. Wirtschaft, Gesellschaft und Politik im Schwarzwald vom Ende des 19. Jahrhunderts bis 1932." *Zeitschrift für Agrargeschichte und Agrarsoziologie* 1 (1995): 206–35.

———. "Die nationalsozialistische Partei: ein bürgerlicher Verein?" *Tel Aviver Jahrbuch ür Deutsche Geschichte* 23 (1994): 63–79

———. "Catholic Plight in a Rural Area of Germany and the Rise of the Nazi Party." *Social History* 21, 2 (1995): 219–34.

———. "Weimar Society and the Image of Soviet Russia." *Tel Aviver Jahrbuch 24* (1995): 3–16.

———. "Wohin verschwand der nationalsozialistische Antisemitismus." *Menora* 5 (1995): 15–44.

———. "The Disintegration of the Workers' Catholic Milieu and Rise of the Nazi Party." In C. Fischer (ed.), *The Rise of National Socialism and the Working Class in Weimar Germany,* 217–35. Oxford, Providence, 1996.

———. "Regionale Aspekte zum katholischen Bürgertum. Oder: Die Besonderheit des katholischen Bürgertums im ländlichen Süddeutschland." *Blätter für Deutsche Landesgeschichte* 131 (1995): 223–59.

————. "In Search of the Catholic (rural) Bourgeoisie: The Peculiarities of the South German Burgertum." *Central European History,* vol. 29 (1996): 175–201.

Heilbronner, O., and D. Mühlberger. "Who Voted for Hitler Reconsidered: The Catholic Voters." *European History Quarterly,* vol. 27, 1 (1997).

Heitzer, H. *Der Volksverein für das katholische Deutschland im Kaiserreich 1890–1918.* Mainz, 1973.

————. "Deutscher Katholizismus und 'Bolschewismusgefahr' bis 1933." *Historisches Jahrbuch* 113.2 (1993): 355–87.

Hennig, E. "Regionale Unterschiede bei der Entstehung des deutschen Faschismus." *Politische Vierteljahresschrift* 21 (1980): 152–73.

Herbner, D. *Titisee-Neustadt. Stadt im Schwarzwald.* Freiburg, 1996.

Hessische Vereinigung für Volkskunde (ed.). *Vereinsforschung,* vol. 16. Gießen, 1984.

Heyen, F. J. *Nationalsozialismus im Alltag: Quellen zur Geschichte des Nationalsozialismus vornehmlich im Raum Mainz-Koblenz-Trier.* Boppard, 1967.

Hoggenmüller, K., and W. Hug. *Die Leute auf dem Wald: Alltagsgeschichte des Schwarzwaldes zwischen bäuerlicher Tradition und industrieller Entwicklung.* Stuttgart, 1987.

Holmes, K. *The NSDAP and the Crisis of Agrarian Conservatism in Lower Bavaria: National Socialism and the Peasants Road to Modernity.* Ph.D. thesis. Georgetown University, 1982.

Hopwood, R. "Paladins of the Bürgertum: Cultural Clubs and Politics in Small German Towns 1918–1925." In *Historical Papers* (Canadian Historical Association) (1974), 213–35.

————. "Mobilization of a Nationalist Community." *German History* 2 (1992): 149–76.

Horn. W. *Führerideologie und Parteiorganisation in der NSDAP 1919–1933.* Düsseldorf, 1972.

Hoser, P. "Hitler und die Kirche. Zwei Briefe aus dem Jahre 1927." *VJZG* 3 (1994): 473–84.

Hürten, H. *Kurze Geschichte des deutschen Katholizismus 1800–1960.* Mainz, 1986.

————. *Deutsche Katholiken 1918–1945.* Paderborn, 1992.

Jaschke, H. G. *Soziale Basis und soziale Funktion des Nationalsozialismus.* Opladen, 1982.

Jerome, J. K. *Three Men on the Bummel.* London, 1900.

Jung, O. "Plebiszitärer Durchbruch 1929? Zur Bedeutung von Volksbegehren und Volksentscheid gegen den Youngplan für die NSDAP." *Geschichte und Gesellschaft* 5 (1989): 489–510.

Kaschuba, W. *Lebenswelt und Kultur der unterbürgerlichen Schichten im 19. und 20. Jahrhundert.* Munich, 1990.

Kaschuba, W., and Carola Lipp. *Dörfliches Überleben: Zur Geschichte materieller und sozialer Reproduktion ländlicher Gesellschaft im 19. und frühen 20. Jahrhundert.* Tübingen, 1982.

Kater, M. *The Nazi Party: A Social Profile of Members and Leaders, 1919–1945.* Oxford, 1983.

Kaufmann, Doris. *Katholisches Milieu in Münster 1928–1933.* Düsseldorf, 1984.

Keitz, C. "Die Anfänge des modernen Massentourismus in der Weimarer Republik." *Archiv für Sozialgeschichte* 33 (1993): 171–207.

Kershaw, I. *The "Hitler Myth."* Oxford, 1987.

———. "Ideology, Propaganda and the Rise of the Nazi Party." In P. Stachura (ed.), *The Nazi Machtergreifung,* 162–181. London, 1986.

———. *The Nazi Dictatorship. Problems and Perspectives of Interpretation.* London, 1989.

———. *Popular Opinion and Political Dissent in the Third Reich. Bavaria 1933–1945.* Oxford, 1983.

———, ed. *Weimar: Why Did German Democracy Fail?* London, 1990.

Kieserling, J., ed. *Faschisierung und gesellschaftlicher Wandel.* Wiesbaden, 1991.

Klöcker, M. "Das katholische Milieu. Grundüberlegungen." *Zeitschrift für Religions- und Geistesgeschichte* 44 (1992): 241–62.

Kocka, J., ed. *Bürger und Bürgerlichkeit im 19. Jahrhundert.* Göttingen, 1987.

———. *Bürgertum im 19. Jahrhundert: Deutschland im europäischen Vergleich.* Munich, 1988.

Köhler, J. "Die katholische Kirche in Baden und Württemberg in der Endphase des Weimarer Republik und zu Beginn des Dritten Reiches." In T. Schnabel (ed.), *Die Machtergreifung in Südwestdeutschland,* 257–94. Stuttgart, 1982.

Koshar, R. "Contentious Citadel: Bourgeois Crisis and Nazism in Marburg/ Lahn, 1880–1930." In T. Childers (ed.), *The Formation of the Nazi Constituency 1919–1933,* 11–36. London, 1986.

———. "Cult of Associations? The Lower Middle Classes in Weimar Germany." In R. Koshar (ed.), *Splintered Classes: Politics and the Lower Middle Classes in Interwar Europe,* 31–54. New York, 1990.

———. *Social Life, Local Politics and Nazism. Marburg/Lahn, 1880–1935.* Chapel Hill, 1987.

———. "From Stammtisch to Party: Nazi Joiners and the Contradictions of Grass Root Fascism in Weimar Germany." *Journal of Modern History* 1 (1987): 1–24.

Koziol, K. *Badener und Württemberger: Zwei ungleiche Brüder.* Stuttgart, 1987.

Kremer, H. J. "Der Volksverein für das katholische Deutschland in Baden 1890–1933. Ein Beitrag zur Organisations- und Wirkungsgeschichte des politischen sozialen Verbandskatholizismus." *Freiburger Diözesanarchiv 104* (1984): 208–80.

———, rev. *Mit Gott für Wahrheit, Freiheit und Recht. Quellen zur Organisation und Politik der Zentrumspartei und des politischen Katholizismus in Baden 1888–1914.* Stuttgart, 1983.

Laessig, S., et al., eds. *Modernisierung und Region im wilhelminischen Deutschland: Wahlen, Wahlrecht und politische Kultur.* Bielefeld, 1996.

Laffan, M., ed. *The Burden of German History 1919–1945.* London, 1988.

Der Landbund: Sein Auftreten und sein Wirken im Bezirk Bonndorf 1922–1924. Karlsruhe, 1925.

Laqueur, W. *Fascism: A Reader's Guide.* London, 1976.

Larsen, S., et al., eds. *Who Were the Fascists? Social Roots of European Fascism.* Bergen, 1980.

Lenger, F. "Mittelstand und Nationalsozialismus? Zur politischen Orientierung von Handwerkern und Angestellten in der Endphase der Weimarer Republik." *Archiv für Sozialgeschichte* 29 (1989): 173–98.

Lepsius, R. *Extremer Nationalismus: Strukturbedingungen vor der nationalsozialistischen Machtergreifung.* Stuttgart, 1966.

———. "Parteiensystem und Sozialstruktur: Zum Problem der Demokratisierung der deutschen Gesellschaft." In G. A. Ritter (ed.), *Die deutschen Parteien vor 1918,* 56–80. Cologne, 1973.

Liedhegener, A. "Marktgesellschaft und Milieu. Katholiken und katholische Regionen in der wirtschaftlichen Entwicklung des Deutschen Reiches 1895–1914." *Historisches Jahrbuch* 113 (1993): 283–354.

Liehl, E., and W. Sick, eds. *Der Schwarzwald: Beiträge zur Landeskunde.* Bühl, 1980.

Lill, R. "Der deutsche Katholizismus in der neueren historischen Forschung." In U. Hehl and K. Repgen (eds.), *Der deutsche Katholizismus in der zeitgeschichtlichen Forschung,* 41–64. Mainz, 1988.

Linz, J. "Some Notes Toward a Comparative Study of Fascism in Sociological Historical Perspective." In W. Laqueur (ed.), *Fascism: A Reader's Guide,* 13–78. Middlesex, 1982.

Lonne, K. E. *Politischer Katholizismus im 19. und 20. Jahrhundert.* Frankfort, 1986.

Loomis, C., and I. Beegle. "The Spread of German Nazism in Rural Areas." *American Sociological Review* 11 (1946): 724–34.

Loth, W. "Soziale Bewegungen im Katholizismus des Kaiserreichs." *Geschichte und Gesellschaft* 3 (1991): 279–310.

———, ed. *Deutscher Katholizismus im Umbruch zur Moderne.* Stuttgart, 1992.

Maier, C. S., et al., eds. *The Rise of the Nazi Regime: Historical Reassessments.* Boulder, 1986.

Maier, H. "Zur Soziologie des deutschen Katholizismus 1803–1950." In D. Albrecht (ed.), *Politik und Konfession: Festschrift für Konrad Repgen,* 159–72. Berlin, 1983.

Manstein, P. *Die Mitglieder und Wähler der NSDAP.* Frankfurt, Bern, 1988.

Mason, T. "National Socialism and the Working Class 1925–May 1933." *New German Critique* 11 (1977): 49–93.

———. "Open Questions on Nazism." In R. Samuel (ed.), *People's History and Socialist Theory,* 205–10. London, 1981.

———. *Sozialpolitik im Dritten Reich. Arbeiterklasse und Volksgemeinschaft.* Opladen, 1977.

Matthiesen, H. *Bürgertum und Nationalsozialismus in Thüringen. Das bürgerliche Gotha von 1918 bis 1930.* Jena, 1995.

Mergel, T. *Zwischen Klasse und Konfession. Katholisches Bürgertum im Rheinland, 1794–1914.* Göttingen, 1994.

———. "Ultramontanism, Liberalism, Moderation: Political Mentalities and Political Behavior of the German Catholic Burgertum, 1848–1914." *Central European History* 29,2 (1996): 151–75.

Merkel, P. *Political Violence under the Swastika.* Princeton, 1975.

Meyer, M. "Die Nichtwähler." *Allgemeines Statistisches Archiv* 21 (1931): 495–525.

Miesbeck, P. *Bürgertum und Nationalsozialismus in Rosenheim.* Rosenheim, 1995.

Moeller, H., et al., eds. *Nationalsozialismus in der Region. Beiträge zur regionalen und lokalen Forschung und zum internationalen Vergleich.* Munich, 1995.

Möller, G. E. *Die Wirtschaft des Schwarzwaldes, ihre wirtschaftsgeographischen Grundlagen und ihre heutigen Probleme.* Oberndorf, 1930.

Mommsen, H. "Die Auflösung des Bürgertums seit dem späten 19. Jahrhundert." In J. Kocka (ed.), *Bürger und Bürgerlichkeit im 19. Jahrhunderts,* 288–315. Göttingen, 1987.

———. "The Breakthrough of the National Socialists as a Mass Movement in the Late Weimar Republic." In M. Laffan (ed.), *The Burden of German History 1919–1945,* 103–15. London, 1988.

———. "National Socialism: Continuity and Change." In W. Laqueur (ed.), *Fascism: A Reader's Guide,* 151–92. Middlesex, 1976.

———. "Zur Verschränkung traditioneller und faschistischer Führungsgruppen in Deutschland beim Übergang von der Bewegungs - zur Systemphase." In W. Schieder (ed.), *Faschismus als soziale Bewegung,* 157–82. Göttingen, 1983.

———. *From Weimar to Auschwitz.* Princeton, 1992.

———. *The Rise and Fall of Weimar Germany.* Chapel Hill, 1996.

Morsey, R. *Die katholische Volksminderheit und der Aufstieg des Nationalsozialismus.* Stuttgart, 1980.

Mosse, G. *The Nationalization of the Masses.* New York, 1975.

Mühlberger, D. "Central Control versus Regional Autonomy: A Case Study of Nazi Propaganda in Westphalia 1925–1932." In T. Childers (ed.), *The Formation of the Nazi Constituency,* 64–103. London, 1986.

———. "Germany." In D. Mühlberger (ed.), *The Social Basis of European Fascist Movements,* 57–165. London, 1987.

———. *Hitler's Followers. Studies in the Sociology of the Nazi Movement.* London, 1991.

———. "The Sociology of the NSDAP: The Question of Working Class Membership." *Journal of Contemporary History* 15 (1980): 494–511.

Nipperdey, T. *Religion im Umbruch. Deutschland 1870–1918.* Munich, 1988.

———. "Verein als soziale Struktur im späten 18. und frühen 19. Jahrhundert." In T. Nipperdey, *Gesellschaft Kultur Theorie,* 174–205. Göttingen, 1976.

Noakes, J. *The Nazi Party in Lower Saxony.* Oxford, 1971.

Nyomarkay, J. *Charisma and Factionalism in the Nazi Party.* Minneapolis, 1967.

Ohr, D. "War die NSDAP- Propaganda nur bei 'nationalistische' Wähler erfolgreich." *Zeitschrift f. Soziologie und Sozialpsychologie* 4 (1994): 646–68.

Ohr, D., et al."Weimarer Wahlen in zwei Dörfern des badischen Grenzlands." *Historical Social Research* 17/2 (1992): 4–48.

O'Loughlin, J., et al. "The Geography of the Nazi Vote: Context, Confession, and Class in the Reichstag Election of 1930." *Annals of the Association of American Geographers* 3 (1994): 351–80.

Orlow, D. *The History of the Nazi Party 1919–1933.* Pittsburgh, 1969.

Ostermann, P. *Wilhelm Stahl. Ein badischer Liberaler.* Konstanz, 1993.

Ott, H. "Der Schwarzwald: Die wirtschaftliche Entwicklung seit dem ausgehenden 18. Jahrhundert." In E. Liehl and W. Sick (eds.), *Der Schwarzwald*, 390–406. Bühl, 1980.

Paul, G. *Aufstand der Bilder: Die NS-Propaganda vor 1933*. Bonn, 1990.

———. *Die NSDAP des Saargebietes*. Saarbrücken, 1987.

Peterson, B. "Regional Elites and the Rise of National Socialism, 1920–1933." In M. Dobkowski and I. Wallimann (eds.), *Radical Perspectives on the Rise of Fascism in Germany, 1919–1945*. New York, 1987.

Peukert, D. *The Weimar Republic*. London, 1992.

Pflaum, Renate. "Die Vereine als Produkt und Gegengewicht sozialer Differenzierung." In G. Wurzbacher (ed.), *Das Dorf im Spannungsfeld industrieller Entwicklung*, 151–82. Stuttgart, 1954.

Plum, G. *Gesellschaftsstruktur und politisches Bewußtsein in einer katholischen Region 1928–1933. Untersuchungen am Beispiel des Regierungsbezirks Aachen*. Stuttgart, 1972.

Pridham, G. *Hitler's Rise to Power: The Nazi Movement in Bavaria 1923–1933*. New York, 1973.

Pyta, W. *Dorfgemeinschaft und Parteipolitik 1918–1933. Die Verschränkung von Milieu und Parteien in den protestantischen Landgebieten Deutschlands in der Weimarer Republik*. Düsseldorf, 1996.

Raem, H. A. *Katholischer Gesellenverein und deutsche Kolpingsfamilie in der Ära des Nationalsozialismus*. Mainz, 1982.

Rau-Kühne, C. *Katholisches Milieu und Kleinstadtgesellschaft. Ettlingen, 1918–1939*. Sigmaringen, 1991.

Rauscher, A., ed. *Der soziale und politische Katholizismus. Entwicklungslinien in Deutschland 1803–1963*. 2 vols. Munich, Wien, 1981.

Repgen, K., and U. Hehl, eds. *Der deutsche Katholizismus in der zeitgeschichtlichen Forschung*. Mainz, 1989.

Richter, M. W. "Resource Mobilisation and Legal Revolution: National Socialist Tactics in Franconia." In T. Childers (ed.), *The Formation of the Nazi Constituency 1919–1933*, 104–30. London, 1986.

Rittberger, V., ed. *1933—Wie die Republik der Diktatur erlag*. Stuttgart, 1983.

Rohe, K. "German Elections and Party Systems in Historical and Regional Perspective: An Introduction." In K. Rohe (ed.), *Elections, Parties and Political Traditions*, 1–24. New York, Oxford, Munich, 1991.

———. *Wahlen und Wählertraditionen in Deutschland*. Frankfurt, 1992.

Schaefer, F. *Das Eindringen des Nationalsozialismus in das Alltagsleben einer unterfränkischen Kleinstadt. Dargestellt am Beispiel Hammelburg 1922–1935*. Würzburg, 1994.

Schauff, J. *Die deutschen Katholiken und die Zentrumspartei: Eine politisch-statistische Untersuchung der Reichstagswahlen seit 1871*. Cologne, 1983.

Schieder, W., ed. *Faschismus als soziale Bewegung*. Göttingen, 1983.

———. "Religion in der Sozialgeschichte." In W. Schieder and V. Sellin (eds.), *Sozialgeschichte in Deutschland*, vol. 3, 9–31. Göttingen, 1987.

———, ed. *Religion und Gesellschaft im 19. Jahrhundert*. Stuttgart, 1993.

Schmidt, F. "Wahlen und Wählerverhalten in der Weimarer Republik am Beispiel des Kreises Limburg." *Nassauische Annalen* 105 (1994): 195–221.

Schnabel, T., ed. *Die Machtergreifung in Südwestdeutschland: Das Ende der Weimarer Republik in Baden und Württemberg.* Stuttgart, 1983.

Scholder, K. *The Churches and the Third Reich,* vol. 1 (1918–1934). London, 1987.

Schonekas, K. "'Christenkreuz über Hakenkreuz und Sowjetstern'—Die NSDAP im Raum Fulda." In E. Hennig (ed.), *Hessen unterm Hakenkreuz,* 127–79. Frankfurt, 1983.

Schreiber, G. *Hitler. Interpretationen. 1923–1983.* Darmstadt, 1984.

Schubnell, H. *Der Kinderreichtum bei Bauern und Arbeitern. Untersuchungen aus Schwarzwald und Rheinebene.* Ph.D. thesis. Freiburg, 1941.

Sedatis, Helmut. *Liberalismus und Handwerk in Südwestdeutschland.* Stuttgart, 1979.

Siegert, Toni. "Braune Spurensuche: Die Anfänge der NSDAP in der Nordoberpfalz." *Heimat Landkreis Tirschenreuth,* Bd. 1, 1989, 94–115, Bd. 2, 1990, 93–148.

Siewert, J. H. "Der Verein: Zur lokalpolitischen und sozialen Funktion der Vereine in der Gemeinde." In H. Wehling (ed.), *Dorfpolitik,* 65–83. Opladen, 1978.

Smith, W. H. "Religion and Conflict: Protestants, Catholics, and Anti-Semitism in the State of Baden in the Era of Wilhelm II." *Central European History* 3 (1994): 283–314.

———. *German Nationalism and Religious Conflict. Culture, Ideology, Politics, 1870–1914.* Princeton, 1995.

Sperber, J. *Popular Catholicism in Nineteenth-Century Germany.* Princeton, 1984.

Stachura, P., ed. *The Nazi Machtergreifung.* London, 1983.

———. "The Political Strategy of the Nazi Party 1919–1933." *German Studies Review* 3 (1980): 261–88.

Stefan S. "Aktivitäten antisemitischer Parteien im Grossherzogtum Baden zwischen 1890 und 1914." *ZGO* 141 (1993): 305–35.

Stein, P. *Die NS-Gaupresse 1925–1933.* Munich, 1987.

Striefler, C. *Kampf um die Macht. Kommunisten und Nationalsozialisten am Ende der Weimarer Republik.* Berlin, 1993.

Szejnmann, C.-C. *The Rise of the Nazi Party in Saxony 1921–1933.* Dissertation. University of London, 1995.

Tenfelde, K. *Proletarische Provinz: Radikalisierung und Widerstand in Penzberg/Oberbayern 1900–1945.* Munich, 1984.

———. "Die Entfaltung des Vereinswesens während der industriellen Revolution in Deutschland (1850–1873)." In O. Dann (ed.), *Vereinswesen und bürgerliche Gesellschaft in Deutschland,* Historische Zeitschrift Beiheft 9 (1984): 55–114.

Tilton, A. T. *Nazism, Neo-Nazism and the Peasantry.* Bloomington, London, 1975.

Turner, H. A. *German Big Business and the Rise of Hitler.* New York, 1985.

Turner, H. A., and H. Matzerathh. "Die Selbstfinanzierung der NSDAP 1930–1932." *Geschichte und Gesellschaft* 3 (1977): 59–92.

Tyrell, A. "Der Aufstieg der NSDAP zur Macht." In K. D. Bracher et al. (eds.), *Die Weimarer Republik 1918–1933,* 467–83. Munich, 1987.

———. *"Führer befiehl . . ."—Selbstzeugnisse aus der 'Kampfzeit' der NSDAP. Dokumentation und Analyse.* Düsseldorf, 1969.

———. "Die NSDAP als Partei und Bewegung: Strategie und Taktik der Machtergreifung." In V. Rittberger (ed.), *1933—Wie die Republik der Diktatur erlag,* 98–122. Stuttgart, 1983.

Wallner, Ernst. *Die Reichstags- und Bundestagswahlen im Landkreis Freiburg seit der Jahrhundertwende.* Bühl, 1965.

Wiegelmann, G., ed. *Kultureller Wandel im 19. Jahrhundert.* Göttingen, 1973.

Winkler, H. A. *Mittelstand, Demokratie und Nationalsozialismus. Die politische Entwicklung von Handwerk und Kleinhandel in der Weimarer Republik.* Cologne, 1972.

Winkler, J. *Sozialstruktur, Politische Traditionen und Liberalismus. Eine empirische Längsschnittstudie in Deutschland 1871–1933.* Opladen, 1995.

Wippermann, W., ed. *Kontroversen um Hitler.* Frankfurt, 1986.

Zangerl, C. "Courting the Catholic Vote: The Center Party in Baden 1903–1913." *Central European History* 3 (1977): 220–40.

Zofka, Z. *Die Ausbreitung des Nationalsozialismus auf dem Lande. Eine regionale Fallstudie zur politischen Einstellung der Landbevölkerung in der Zeit des Aufstiegs und der Machtergreifung der NSDAP 1928–1936.* Munich, 1979.

———. "Between Bauernbund and National Socialism: The Political Reorientation of the Peasants in the Final Phase of the Weimar Republic." In T. Childers (ed.), *The Formation of the Nazi Constituency 1919–1933,* 37–63. London, 1986.

Zunkel, F. "Die westdeutschen Bürgergesellschaften zwischen Kaiserreich und Nationalsozialismus." In J. Heideking et al. (eds.), *Wege in die Zeitgeschichte,* 30–42. Berlin, 1989.

Index